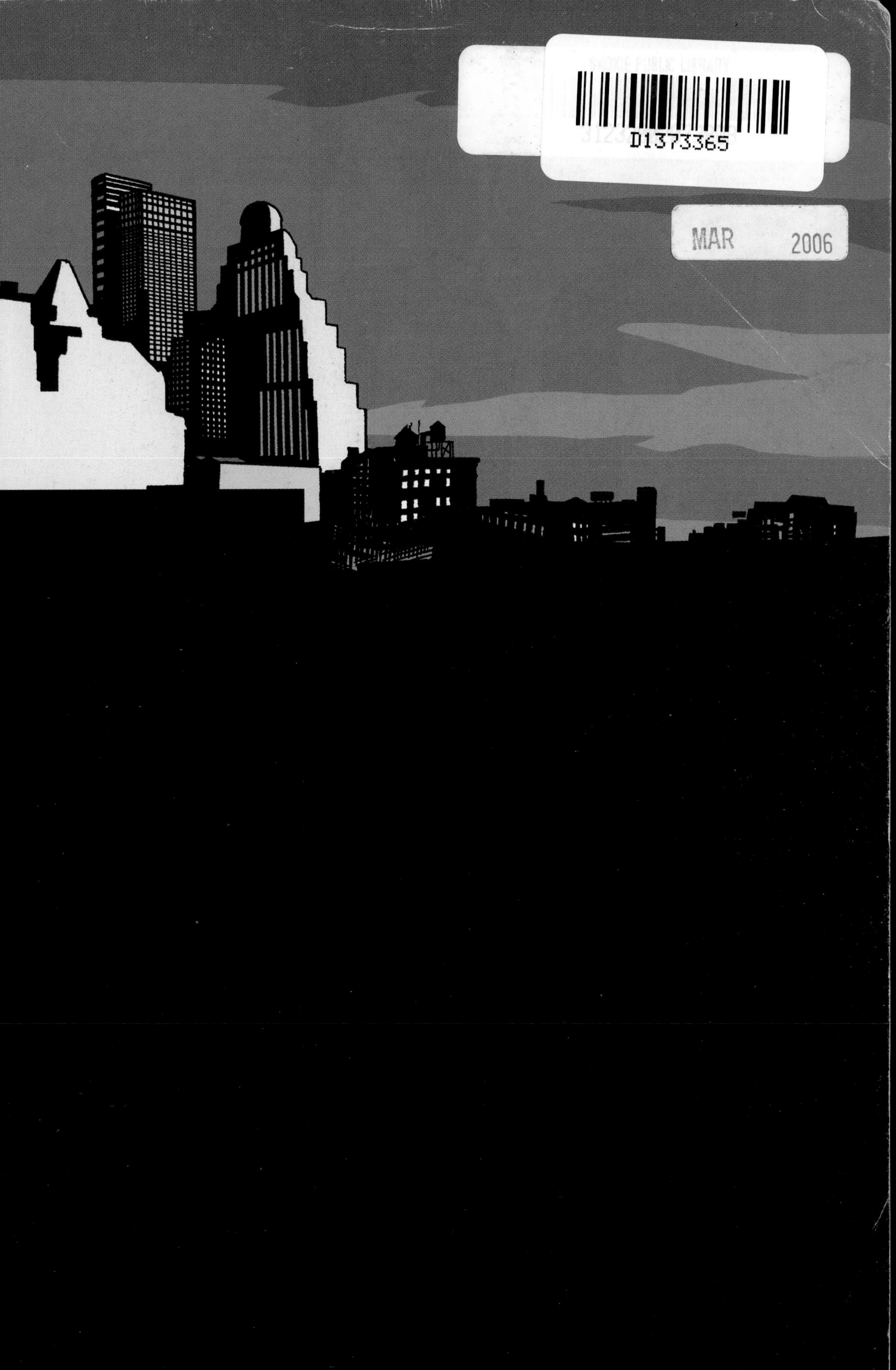

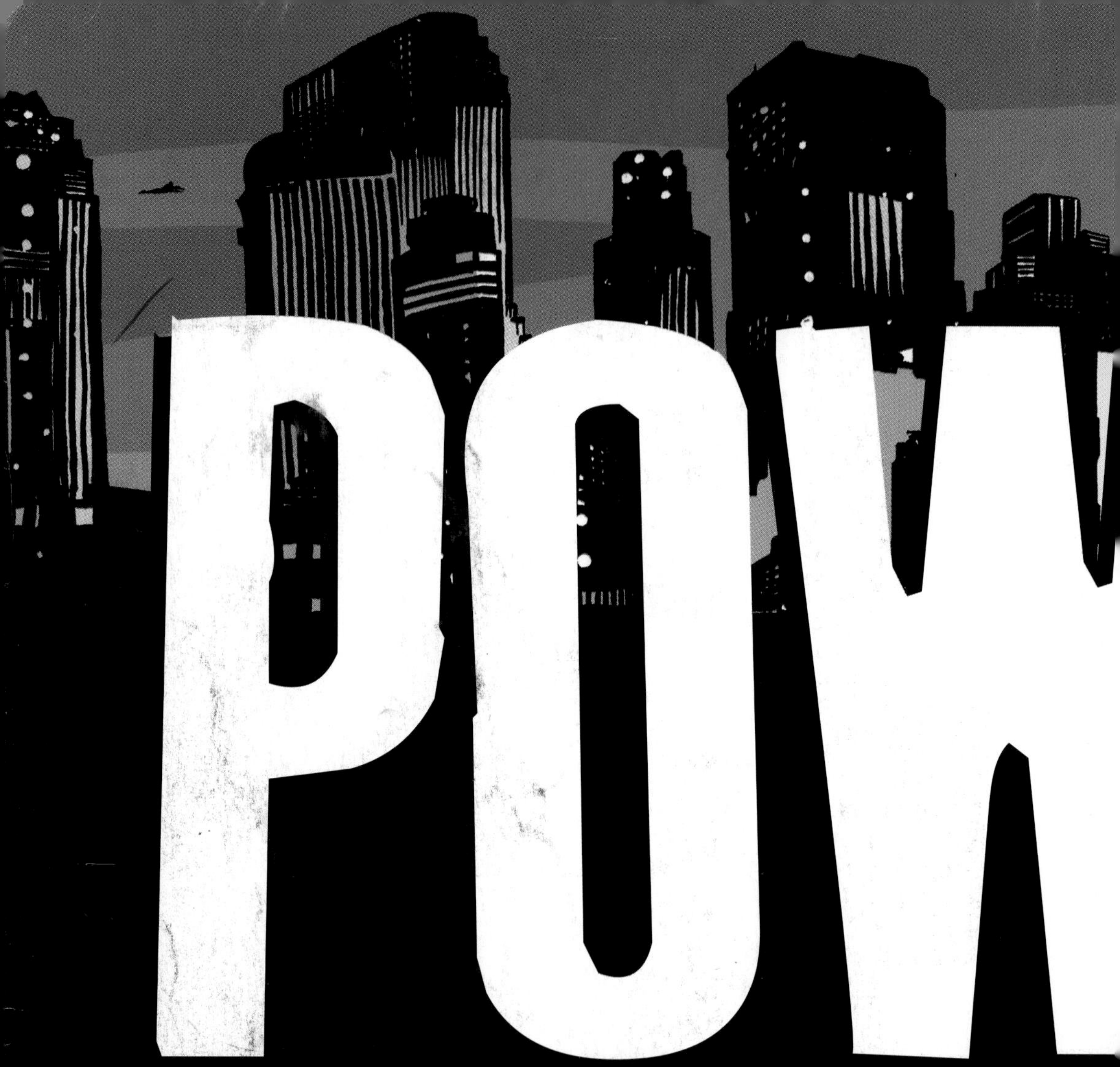

POW

CREATED AND PRODUCED
BY
BRIAN MICHAEL BENDIS
AND
MIKE AVON OEMING

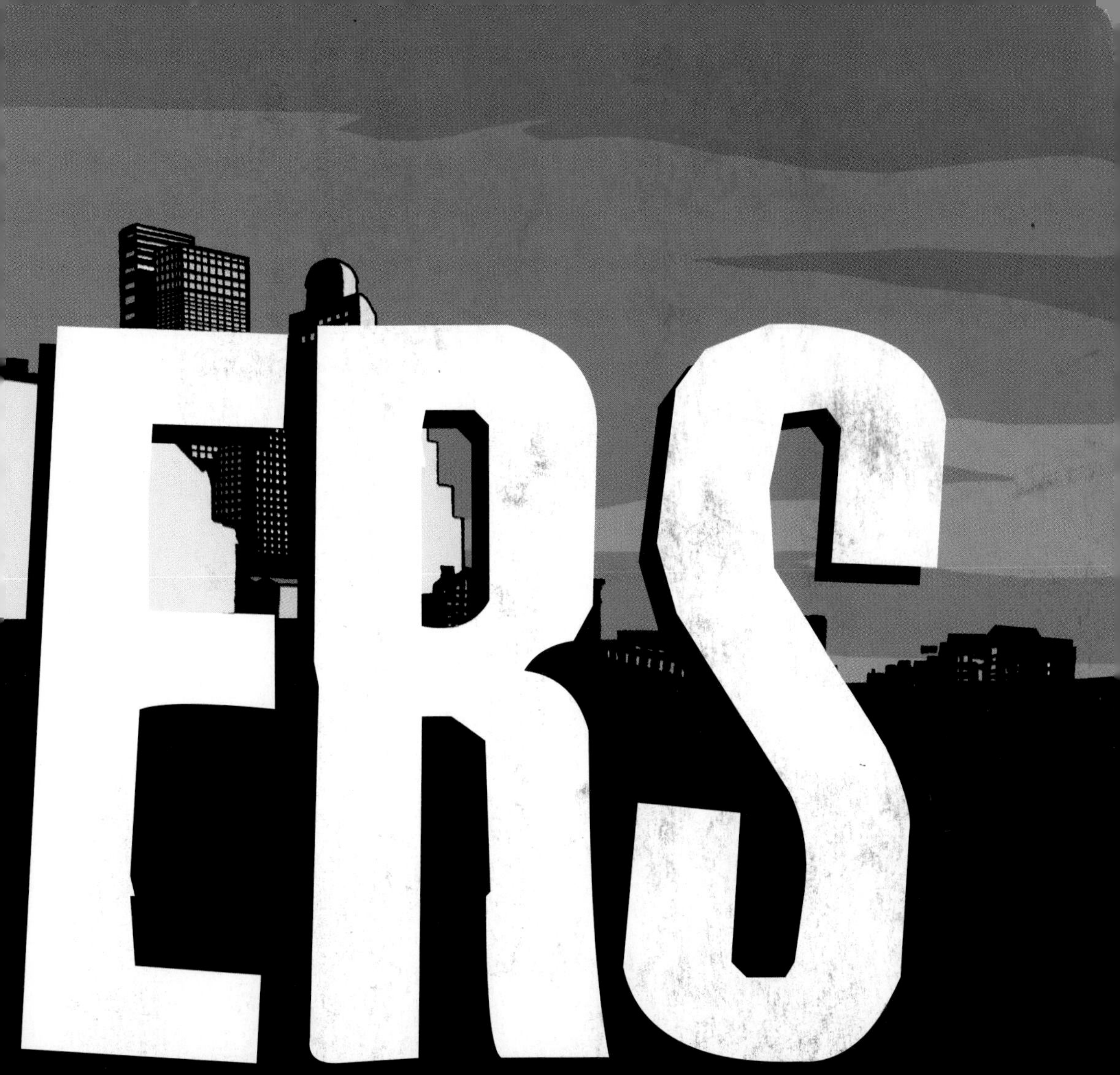
ERS

COLOR ART
PETER PANTAZIS

TYPOGRAPHY
KEN BRUZENAK

EDITORS
KC MCCRORY AND JAMIE S. RICH

BUSINESS AFFAIRS
ALISA BENDIS

DESIGN ASSISTANCE
KEITH WOOD

Previously in Powers

Homicide Detectives Christian Walker and
Deena Pilgrim investigate murders specific
to superhero cases... powers.

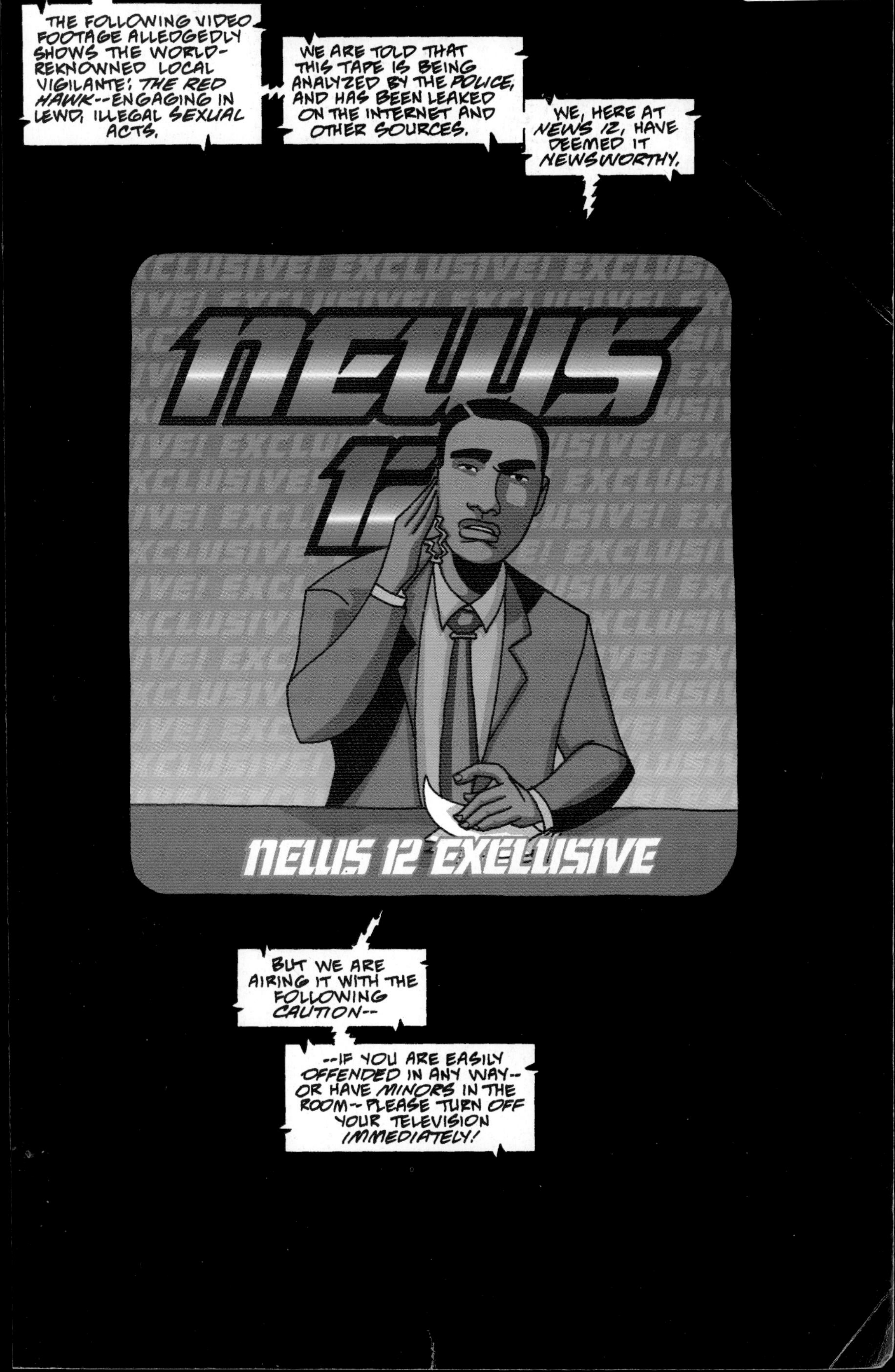
WHAT YOU ARE ABOUT TO SEE WILL SHOCK YOU.
THE FOLLOWING VIDEO FOOTAGE ALLEDGEDLY SHOWS THE WORLD-REKNOWNED LOCAL VIGILANTE: THE RED HAWK--ENGAGING IN LEWD, ILLEGAL SEXUAL ACTS.
WE ARE TOLD THAT THIS TAPE IS BEING ANALYZED BY THE POLICE, AND HAS BEEN LEAKED ON THE INTERNET AND OTHER SOURCES.
WE, HERE AT NEWS 12, HAVE DEEMED IT NEWSWORTHY.
EXCLUSIVE! EXCLUSIVE! EXCLUSIVE!
NEWS 12
NEWS 12 EXCLUSIVE
BUT WE ARE AIRING IT WITH THE FOLLOWING CAUTION--
--IF YOU ARE EASILY OFFENDED IN ANY WAY--OR HAVE MINORS IN THE ROOM--PLEASE TURN OFF YOUR TELEVISION IMMEDIATELY!

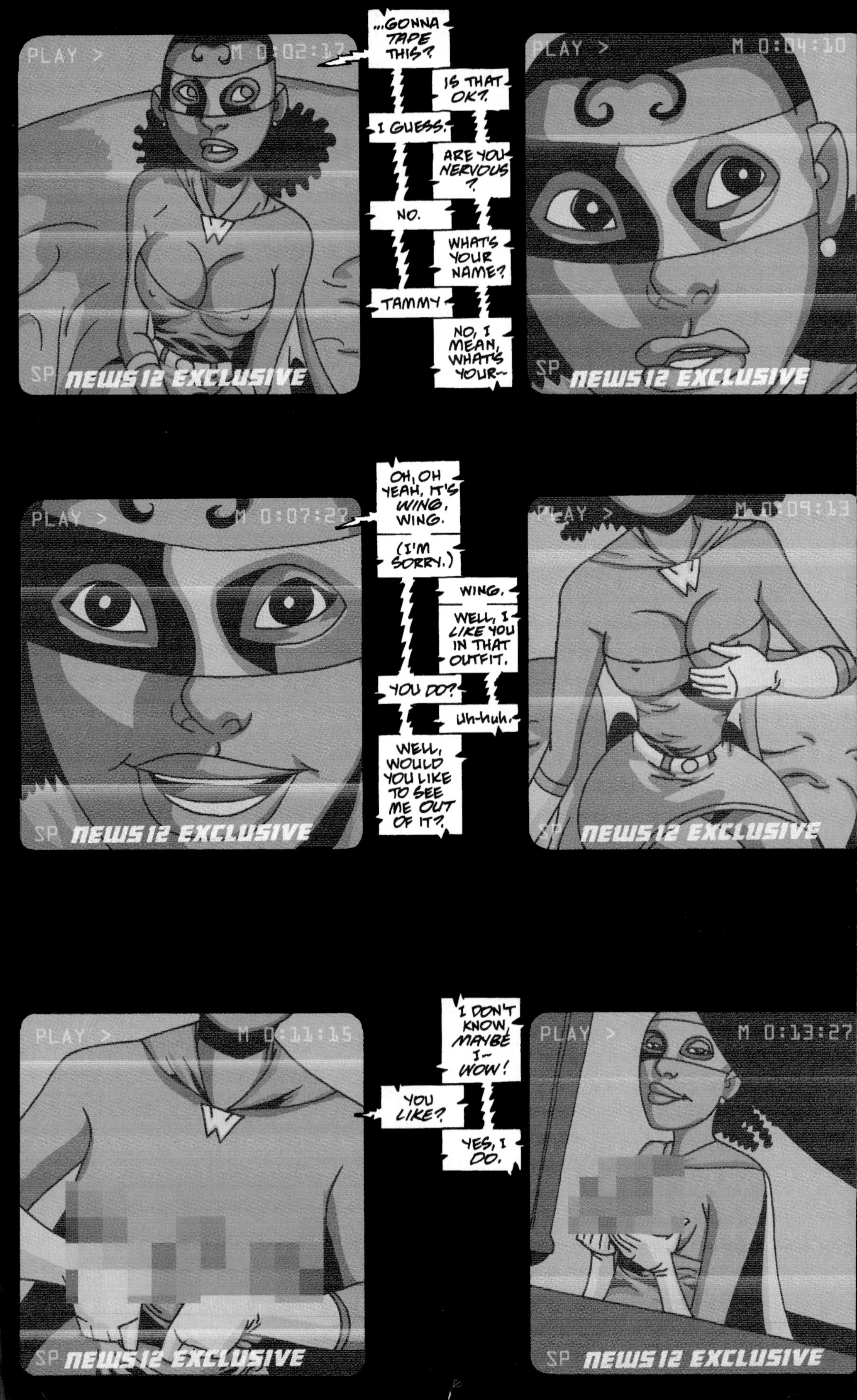
PLAY >
SP NEWS 12 EXCLUSIVE
...GONNA TAPE THIS?
IS THAT OK?
I GUESS.
ARE YOU NERVOUS?
NO.
WHAT'S YOUR NAME?
TAMMY
NO, I MEAN, WHAT'S YOUR--
PLAY >
M 0:04:10
SP NEWS 12 EXCLUSIVE
PLAY >
SP NEWS 12 EXCLUSIVE
OH, OH YEAH, IT'S WING, WING.
(I'M SORRY.)
WING.
WELL, I LIKE YOU IN THAT OUTFIT.
YOU DO?
Uh-huh.
WELL, WOULD YOU LIKE TO SEE ME OUT OF IT?
NEWS 12 EXCLUSIVE
PLAY >
M 0:11:15
SP NEWS 12 EXCLUSIVE
I DON'T KNOW, MAYBE I-- WOW!
YOU LIKE?
YES, I DO.
PLAY >
M 0:13:27
SP NEWS 12 EXCLUSIVE

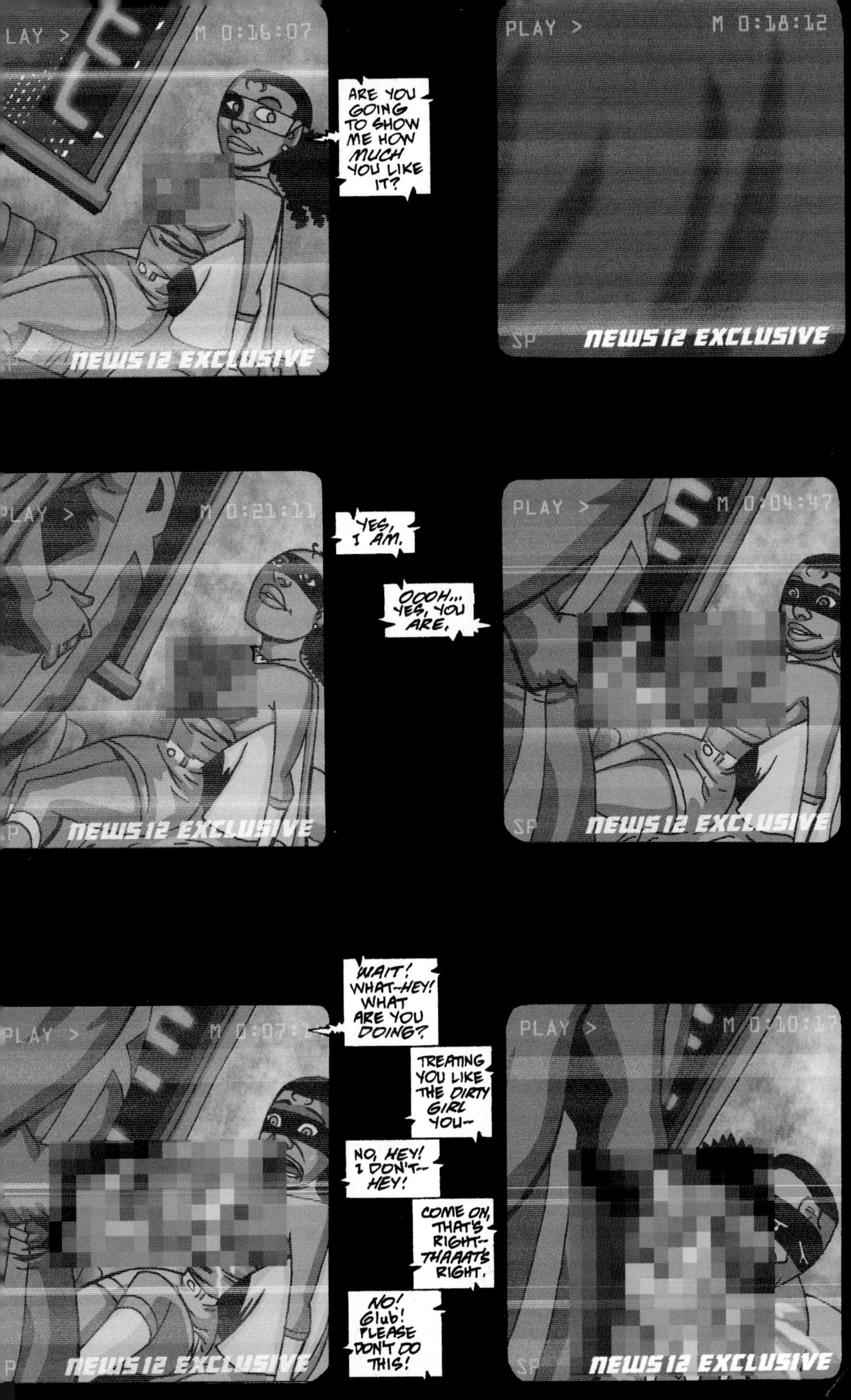
PLAY > M 0:16:07
ARE YOU GOING TO SHOW ME HOW MUCH YOU LIKE IT?
NEWS 12 EXCLUSIVE
PLAY > M 0:18:12
SP
NEWS 12 EXCLUSIVE
PLAY > M 0:21:11
YES, I AM.
NEWS 12 EXCLUSIVE
OOOH... YES, YOU ARE.
PLAY > M 0:04:47
SP
NEWS 12 EXCLUSIVE
PLAY >
WAIT! WHAT--HEY! WHAT ARE YOU DOING?
TREATING YOU LIKE THE DIRTY GIRL YOU--
NO, HEY! I DON'T-- HEY!
COME ON, THAT'S RIGHT-- THAAAT'S RIGHT.
NO! Glub! PLEASE DON'T DO THIS!
NEWS 12 EXCLUSIVE
PLAY >
SP
NEWS 12 EXCLUSIVE

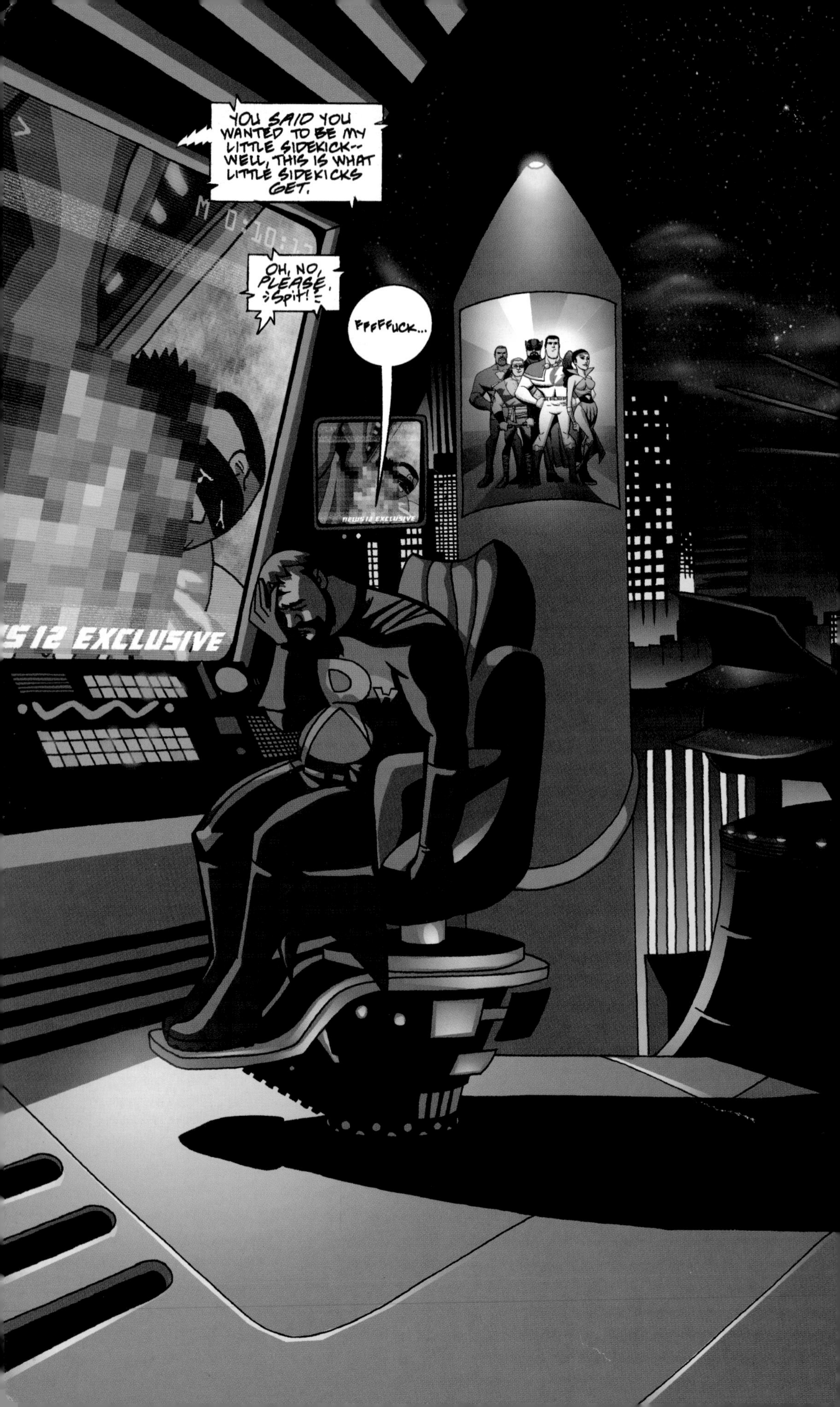
YOU SAID YOU WANTED TO BE MY LITTLE SIDEKICK--WELL, THIS IS WHAT LITTLE SIDEKICKS GET.
OH, NO, PLEASE. SPIT!
FFFFFUCK...
NEWS 12 EXCLUSIVE
S 12 EXCLUSIVE

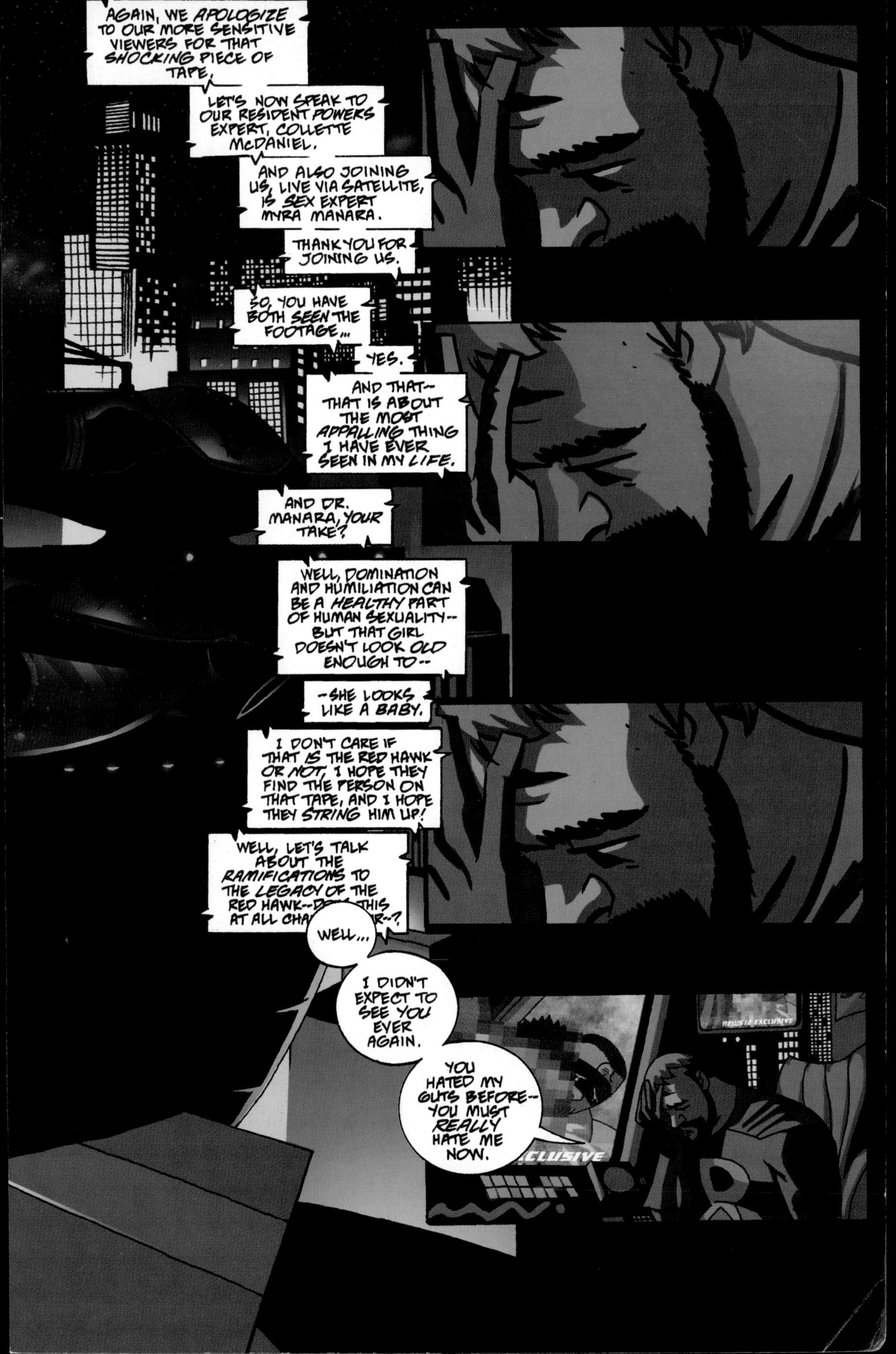
AGAIN, WE APOLOGIZE TO OUR MORE SENSITIVE VIEWERS FOR THAT SHOCKING PIECE OF TAPE.
LET'S NOW SPEAK TO OUR RESIDENT POWERS EXPERT, COLLETTE McDANIEL.
AND ALSO JOINING US, LIVE VIA SATELLITE, IS SEX EXPERT MYRA MANARA.
THANK YOU FOR JOINING US.
SO, YOU HAVE BOTH SEEN THE FOOTAGE...
YES.
AND THAT--THAT IS ABOUT THE MOST APPALLING THING I HAVE EVER SEEN IN MY LIFE.
AND DR. MANARA, YOUR TAKE?
WELL, DOMINATION AND HUMILIATION CAN BE A HEALTHY PART OF HUMAN SEXUALITY--BUT THAT GIRL DOESN'T LOOK OLD ENOUGH TO--
--SHE LOOKS LIKE A BABY.
I DON'T CARE IF THAT IS THE RED HAWK OR NOT, I HOPE THEY FIND THE PERSON ON THAT TAPE, AND I HOPE THEY STRING HIM UP!
WELL, LET'S TALK ABOUT THE RAMIFICATIONS TO THE LEGACY OF THE RED HAWK--
WELL...
I DIDN'T EXPECT TO SEE YOU EVER AGAIN.
YOU HATED MY GUTS BEFORE--YOU MUST REALLY HATE ME NOW.
NEWS12 EXCLUSIVE

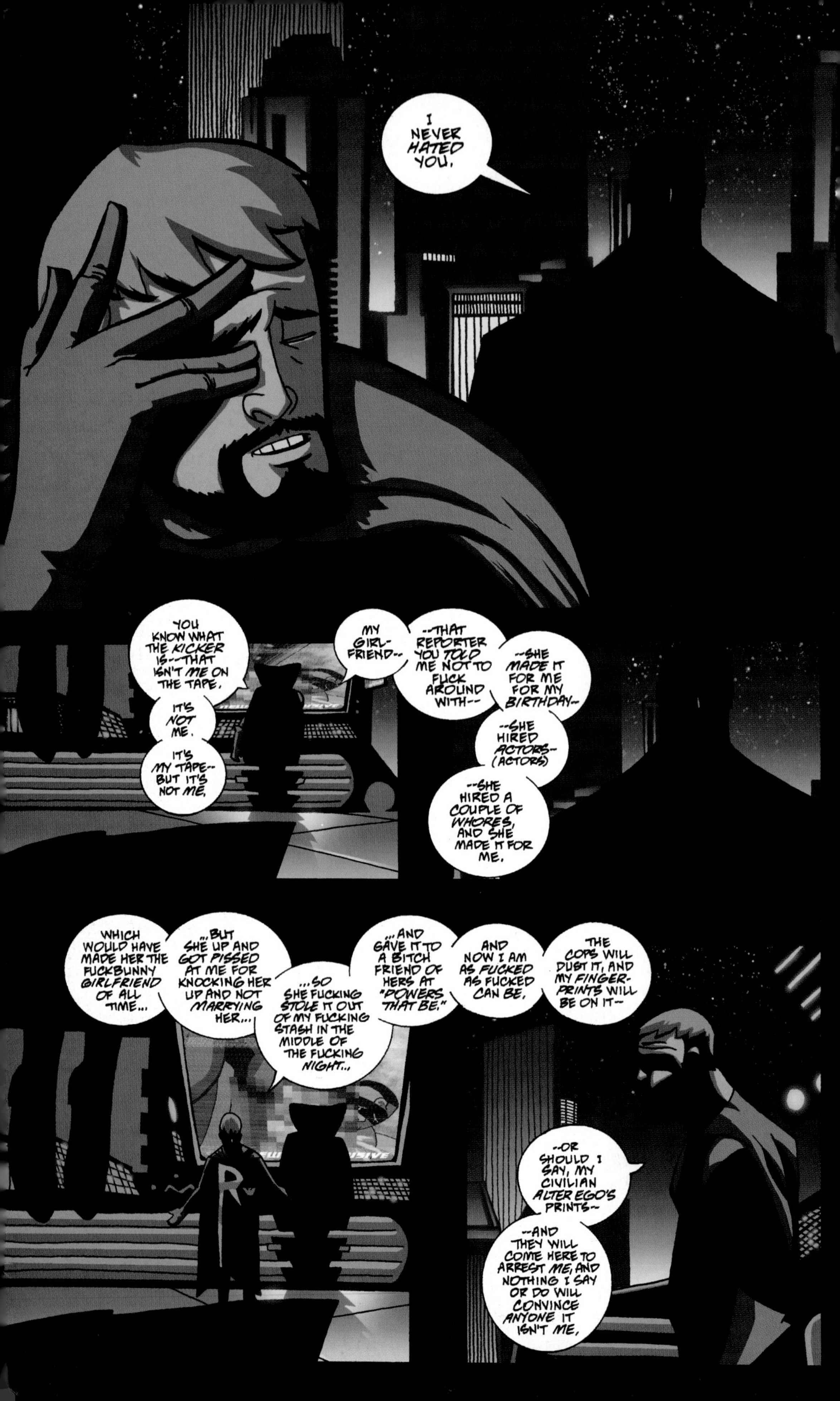
I NEVER HATED YOU.
YOU KNOW WHAT THE KICKER IS--THAT ISN'T ME ON THE TAPE.
IT'S NOT ME.
IT'S MY TAPE--BUT IT'S NOT ME.
MY GIRL-FRIEND--
--THAT REPORTER YOU TOLD ME NOT TO FUCK AROUND WITH--
--SHE MADE IT FOR ME FOR MY BIRTHDAY--
--SHE HIRED ACTORS--(ACTORS)
--SHE HIRED A COUPLE OF WHORES, AND SHE MADE IT FOR ME.
WHICH WOULD HAVE MADE HER THE FUCKBUNNY GIRLFRIEND OF ALL TIME...
...BUT SHE UP AND GOT PISSED AT ME FOR KNOCKING HER UP AND NOT MARRYING HER...
...SO SHE FUCKING STOLE IT OUT OF MY FUCKING STASH IN THE MIDDLE OF THE FUCKING NIGHT...
...AND GAVE IT TO A BITCH FRIEND OF HERS AT "POWERS THAT BE."
AND NOW I AM AS FUCKED AS FUCKED CAN BE.
THE COPS WILL DUST IT, AND MY FINGER-PRINTS WILL BE ON IT--
--OR SHOULD I SAY, MY CIVILIAN ALTER EGO'S PRINTS--
--AND THEY WILL COME HERE TO ARREST ME, AND NOTHING I SAY OR DO WILL CONVINCE ANYONE IT ISN'T ME.

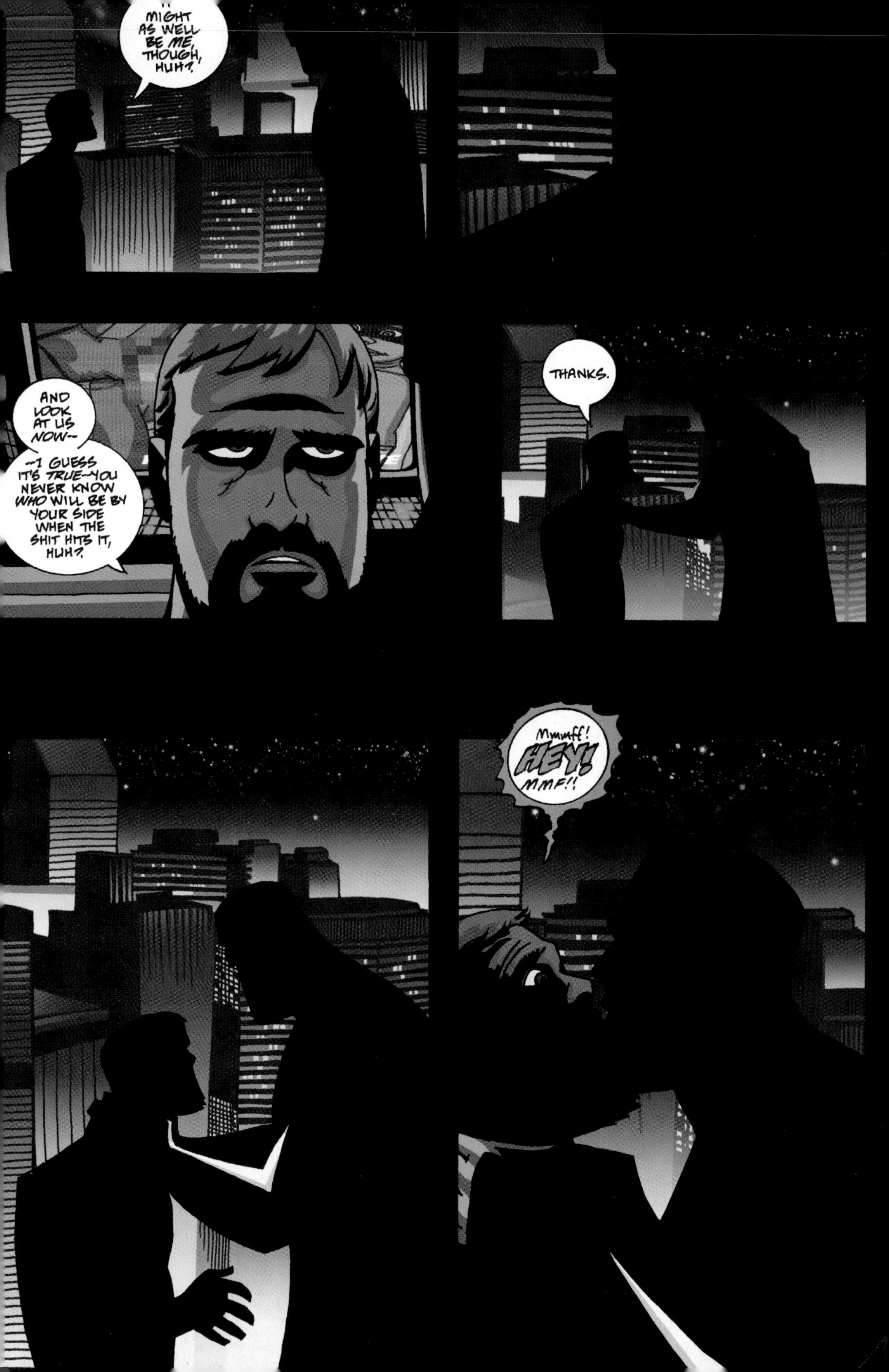

IT MIGHT AS WELL BE ME, THOUGH, HUH?
AND LOOK AT US NOW--
--I GUESS IT'S TRUE--YOU NEVER KNOW WHO WILL BE BY YOUR SIDE WHEN THE SHIT HITS IT, HUH?
THANKS.
Mmmff! HEY! MMF!!

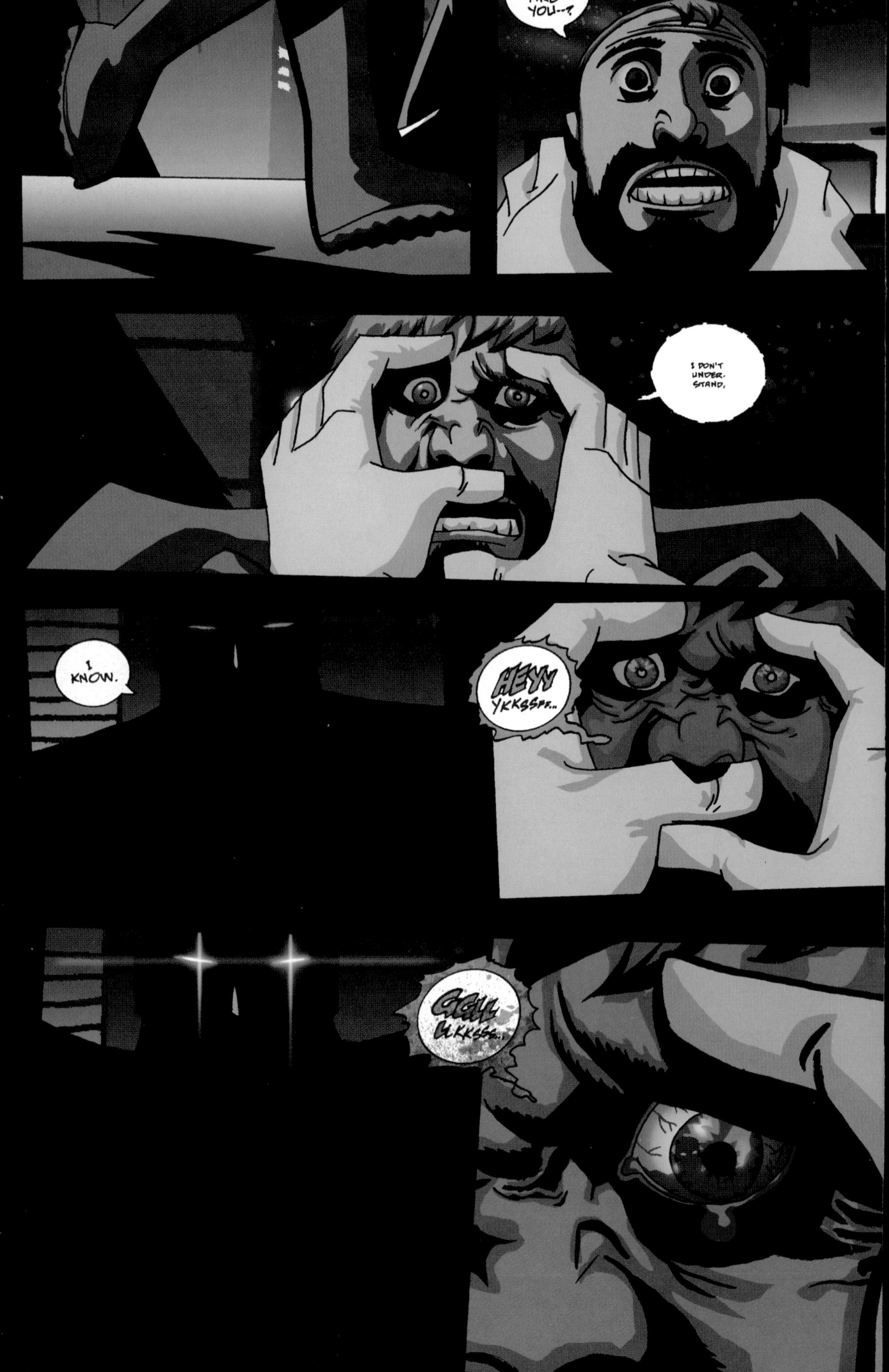
YOU--?
I DON'T UNDER-STAND,
I KNOW.
HEYN YKKSSFF...
GGLL LKKSSS..

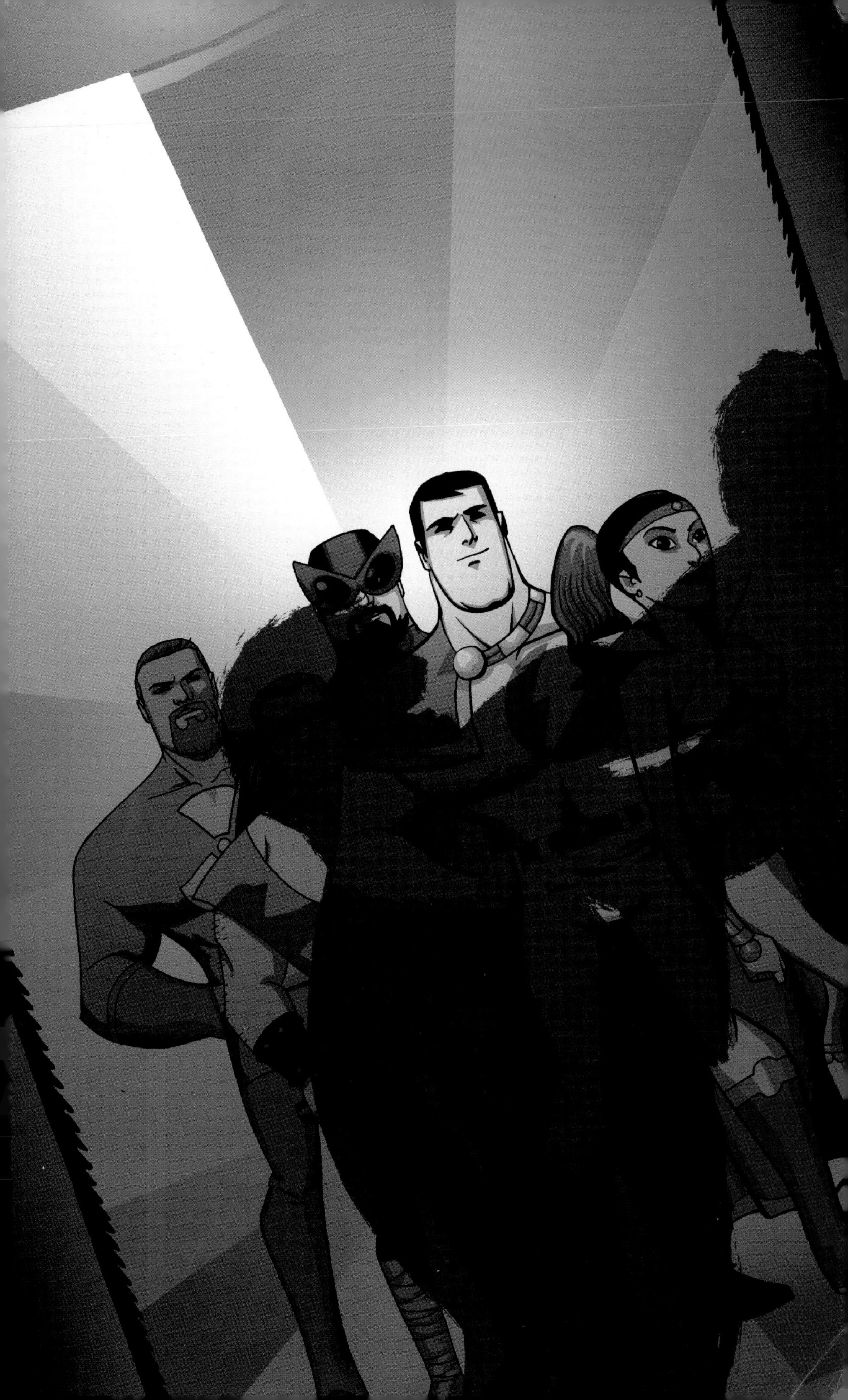

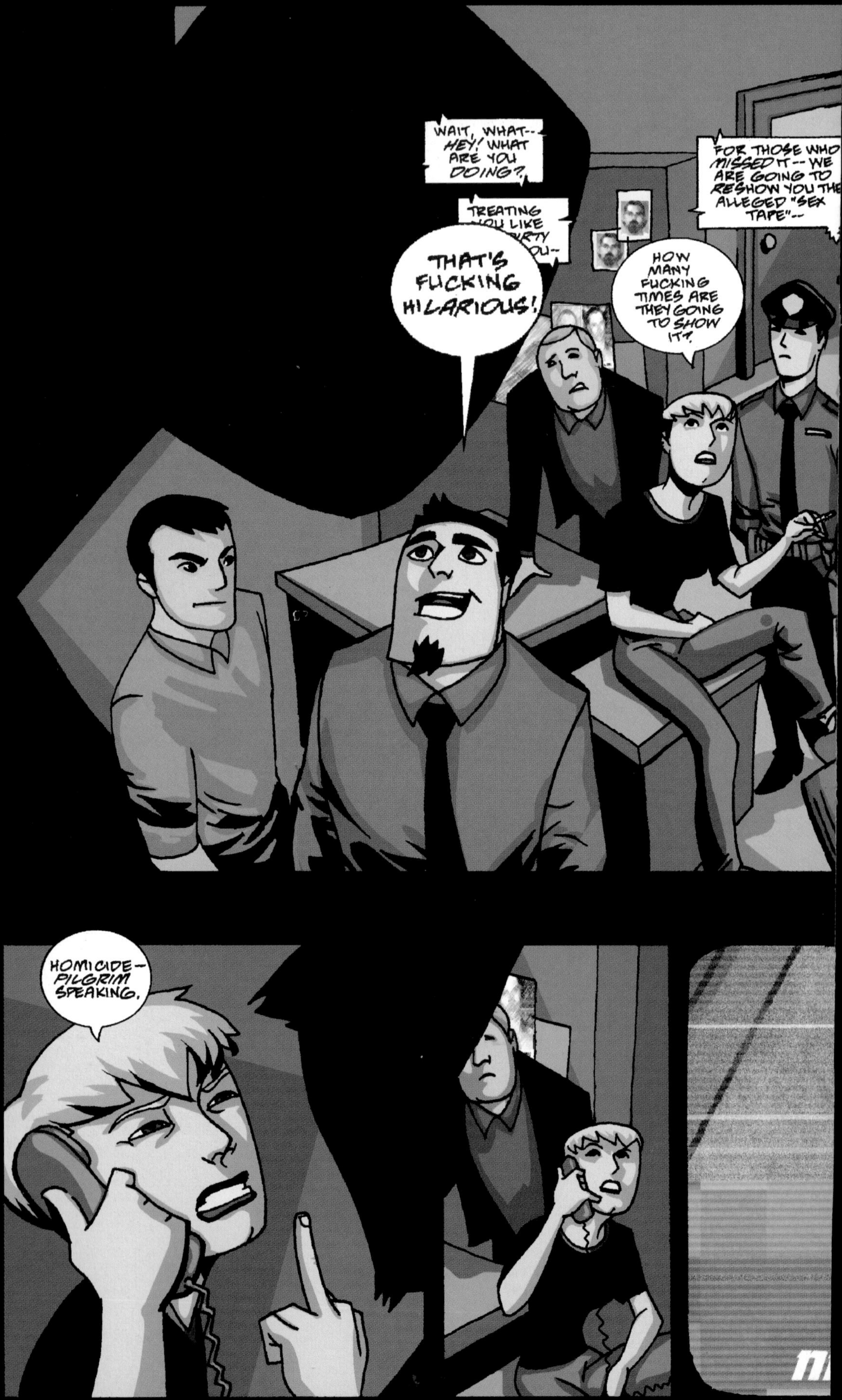
WAIT, WHAT-- HEY! WHAT ARE YOU DOING?
TREATING YOU LIKE
THAT'S FUCKING HILARIOUS!
FOR THOSE WHO MISSED IT -- WE ARE GOING TO RESHOW YOU THE ALLEGED "SEX TAPE"--
HOW MANY FUCKING TIMES ARE THEY GOING TO SHOW IT?
HOMICIDE-PILGRIM SPEAKING.

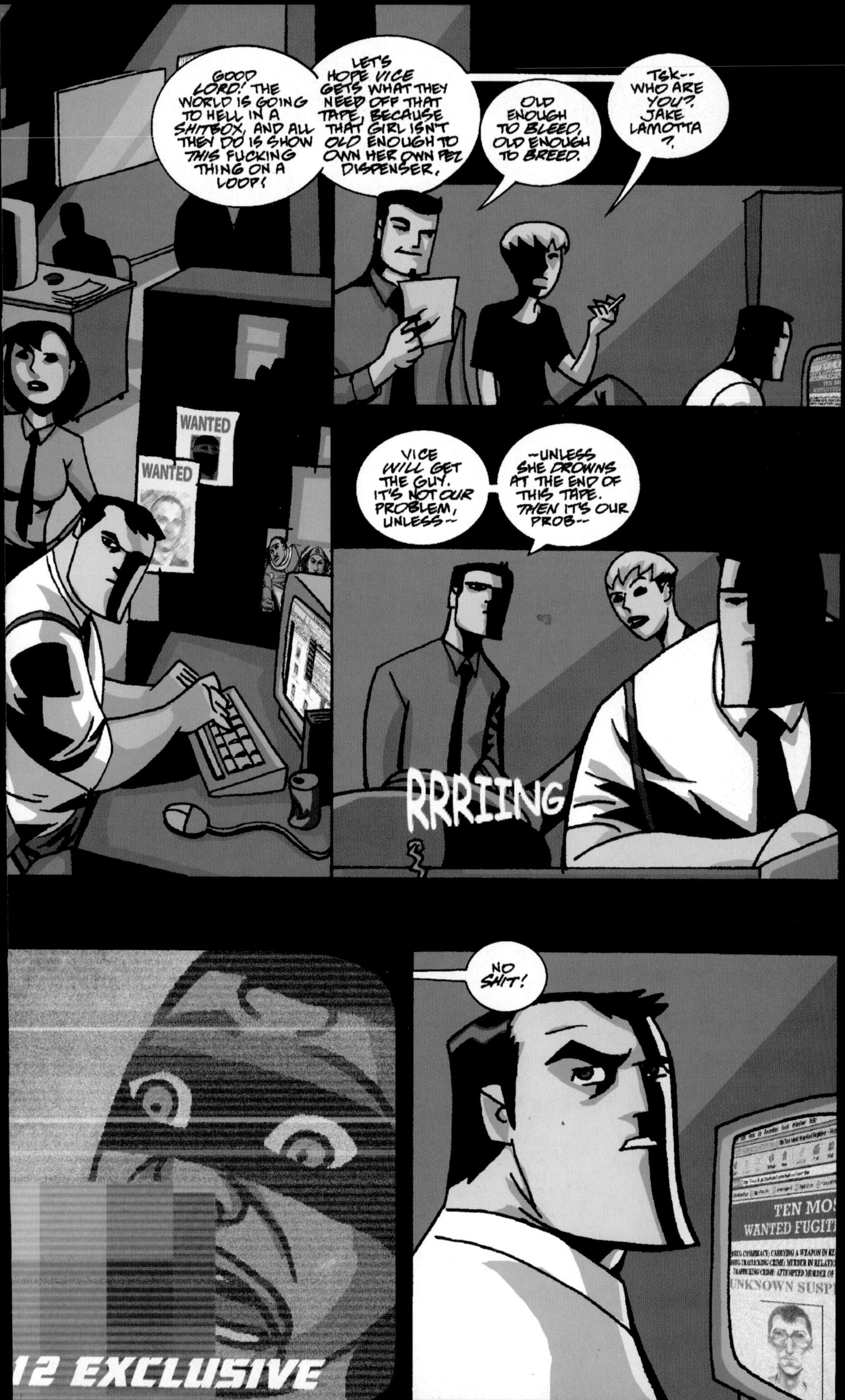
GOOD LORD! THE WORLD IS GOING TO HELL IN A SHITBOX, AND ALL THEY DO IS SHOW THIS FUCKING THING ON A LOOP!
LET'S HOPE VICE GETS WHAT THEY NEED OFF THAT TAPE, BECAUSE THAT GIRL ISN'T OLD ENOUGH TO OWN HER OWN PEZ DISPENSER.
OLD ENOUGH TO BLEED, OLD ENOUGH TO BREED.
TSK-- WHO ARE YOU? JAKE LAMOTTA ?
WANTED
WANTED
VICE WILL GET THE GUY. IT'S NOT OUR PROBLEM, UNLESS--
--UNLESS SHE DROWNS AT THE END OF THIS TAPE. THEN IT'S OUR PROB--
RRRIING
12 EXCLUSIVE
NO SHIT!
TEN MOS
WANTED FUGIT
UNKNOWN SUSP

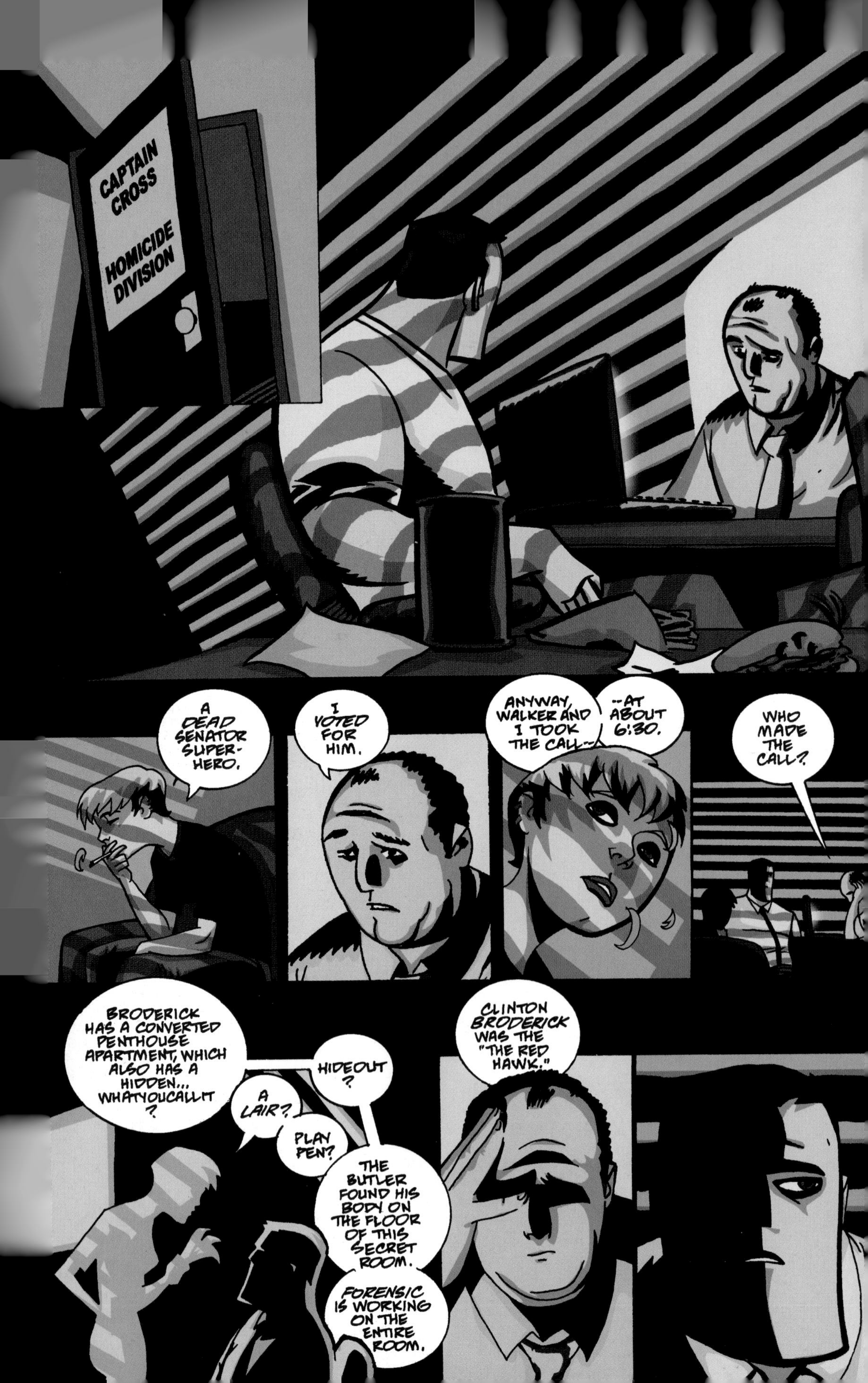
CAPTAIN CROSS
HOMICIDE DIVISION
A DEAD SENATOR SUPER-HERO.
I VOTED FOR HIM.
ANYWAY, WALKER AND I TOOK THE CALL--
--AT ABOUT 6:30.
WHO MADE THE CALL?
BRODERICK HAS A CONVERTED PENTHOUSE APARTMENT, WHICH ALSO HAS A HIDDEN... WHATYOUCALLIT?
HIDEOUT?
A LAIR?
PLAY PEN?
THE BUTLER FOUND HIS BODY ON THE FLOOR OF THIS SECRET ROOM.
FORENSIC IS WORKING ON THE ENTIRE ROOM.
CLINTON BRODERICK WAS THE "THE RED HAWK."

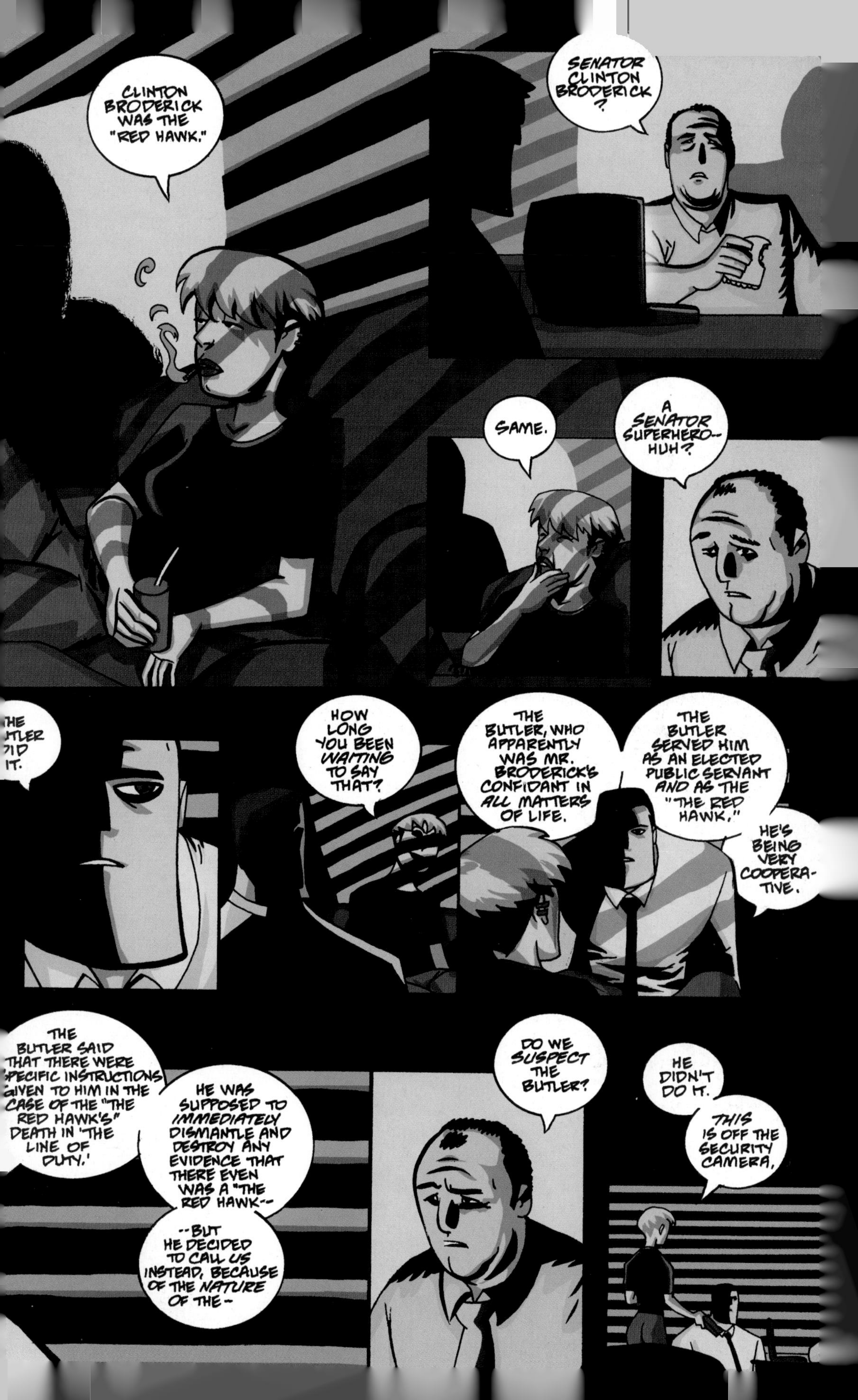
CLINTON BRODERICK WAS THE "RED HAWK."
SENATOR CLINTON BRODERICK?
SAME.
A SENATOR SUPERHERO-- HUH?
THE BUTLER DID IT.
HOW LONG YOU BEEN WAITING TO SAY THAT?
THE BUTLER, WHO APPARENTLY WAS MR. BRODERICK'S CONFIDANT IN ALL MATTERS OF LIFE.
"THE BUTLER SERVED HIM AS AN ELECTED PUBLIC SERVANT AND AS THE "THE RED HAWK."
HE'S BEING VERY COOPERATIVE.
THE BUTLER SAID THAT THERE WERE SPECIFIC INSTRUCTIONS GIVEN TO HIM IN THE CASE OF THE "THE RED HAWK'S" DEATH IN 'THE LINE OF DUTY.'
HE WAS SUPPOSED TO IMMEDIATELY DISMANTLE AND DESTROY ANY EVIDENCE THAT THERE EVEN WAS A "THE RED HAWK--
--BUT HE DECIDED TO CALL US INSTEAD, BECAUSE OF THE NATURE OF THE--
DO WE SUSPECT THE BUTLER?
HE DIDN'T DO IT.
THIS IS OFF THE SECURITY CAMERA,

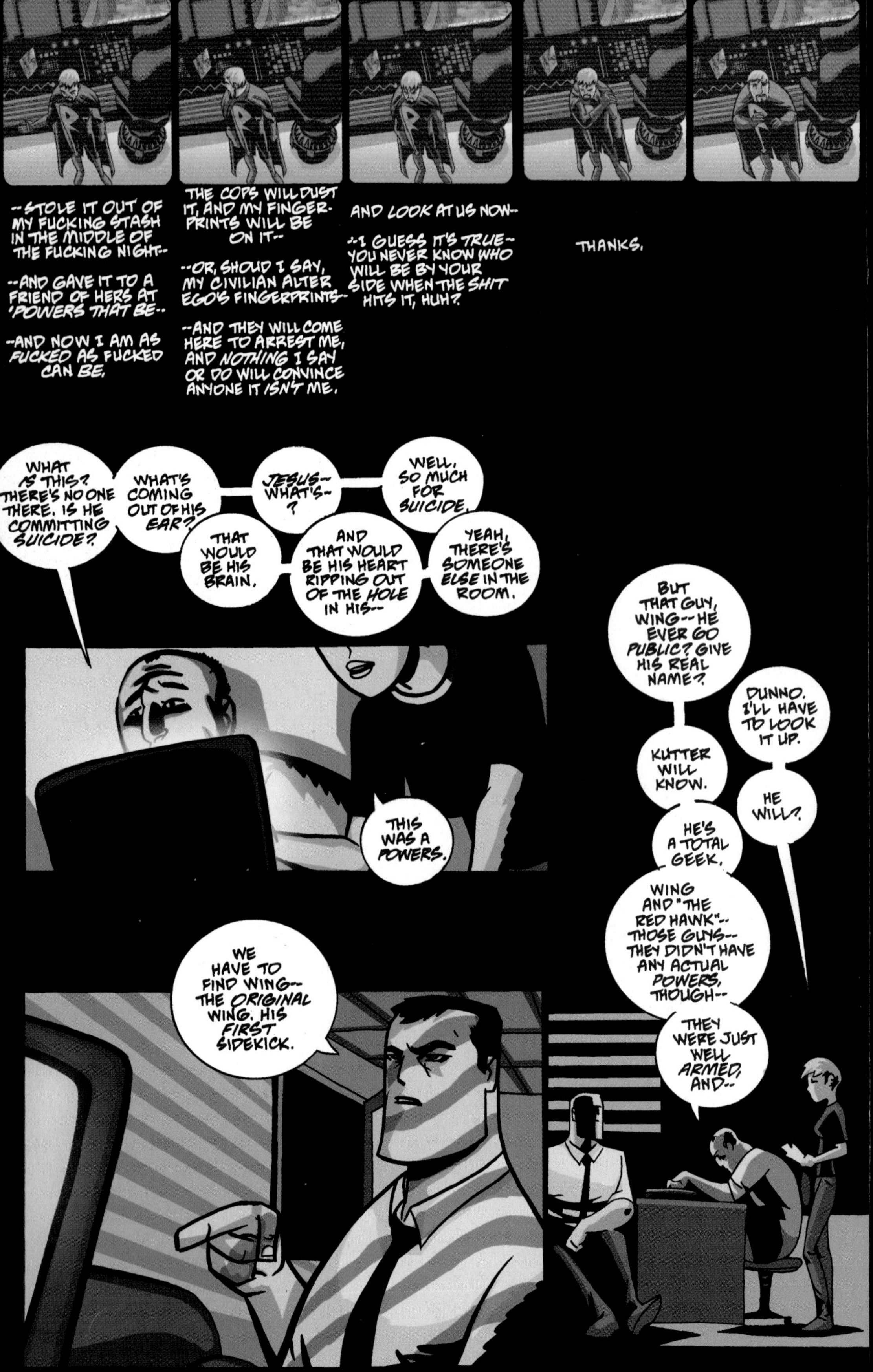
--STOLE IT OUT OF MY FUCKING STASH IN THE MIDDLE OF THE FUCKING NIGHT--
--AND GAVE IT TO A FRIEND OF HERS AT 'POWERS THAT BE--
--AND NOW I AM AS FUCKED AS FUCKED CAN BE.
THE COPS WILL DUST IT, AND MY FINGER-PRINTS WILL BE ON IT--
--OR, SHOUD I SAY, MY CIVILIAN ALTER EGO'S FINGERPRINTS--
--AND THEY WILL COME HERE TO ARREST ME, AND NOTHING I SAY OR DO WILL CONVINCE ANYONE IT ISN'T ME.
AND LOOK AT US NOW--
--I GUESS IT'S TRUE-- YOU NEVER KNOW WHO WILL BE BY YOUR SIDE WHEN THE SHIT HITS IT, HUH?
THANKS.
WHAT IS THIS? THERE'S NO ONE THERE. IS HE COMMITTING SUICIDE?
WHAT'S COMING OUT OF HIS EAR?
THAT WOULD BE HIS BRAIN.
JESUS-- WHAT'S--?
AND THAT WOULD BE HIS HEART RIPPING OUT OF THE HOLE IN HIS--
WELL, SO MUCH FOR SUICIDE.
YEAH, THERE'S SOMEONE ELSE IN THE ROOM.
THIS WAS A POWERS.
WE HAVE TO FIND WING-- THE ORIGINAL WING. HIS FIRST SIDEKICK.
BUT THAT GUY, WING-- HE EVER GO PUBLIC? GIVE HIS REAL NAME?
DUNNO. I'LL HAVE TO LOOK IT UP.
KUTTER WILL KNOW.
HE WILL?
HE'S A TOTAL GEEK.
WING AND "THE RED HAWK"-- THOSE GUYS-- THEY DIDN'T HAVE ANY ACTUAL POWERS, THOUGH--
THEY WERE JUST WELL ARMED, AND--

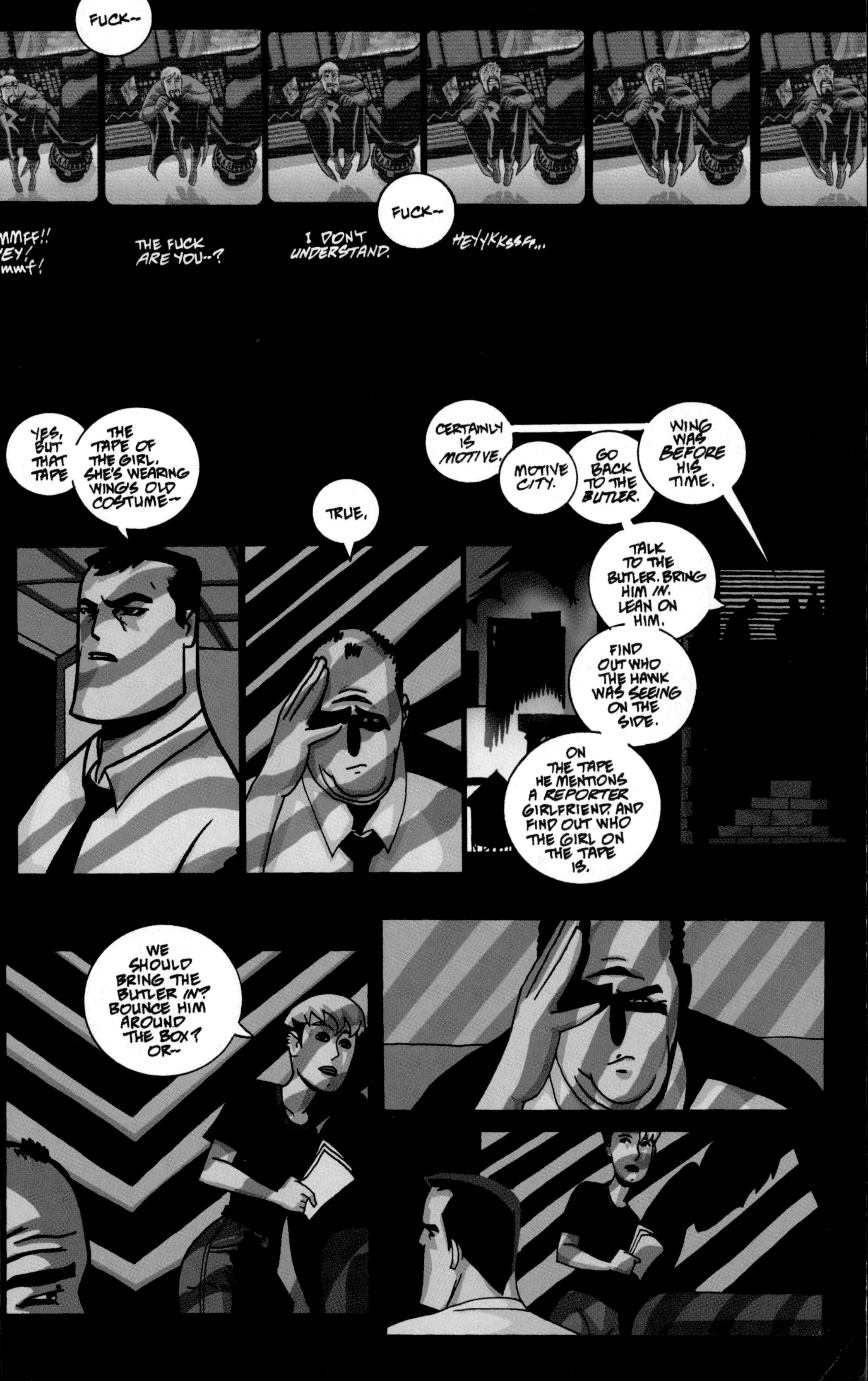
FUCK--
MMFF!!
EY!
mmf!
THE FUCK ARE YOU--?
I DON'T UNDERSTAND.
FUCK--
HEYYKKSSFF...
YES, BUT THAT TAPE
THE TAPE OF THE GIRL, SHE'S WEARING WING'S OLD COSTUME--
TRUE,
CERTAINLY IS MOTIVE.
MOTIVE CITY.
GO BACK TO THE BUTLER.
WING WAS BEFORE HIS TIME.
TALK TO THE BUTLER. BRING HIM IN. LEAN ON HIM.
FIND OUT WHO THE HAWK WAS SEEING ON THE SIDE.
ON THE TAPE HE MENTIONS A REPORTER GIRLFRIEND, AND FIND OUT WHO THE GIRL ON THE TAPE IS.
WE SHOULD BRING THE BUTLER IN? BOUNCE HIM AROUND THE BOX? OR--

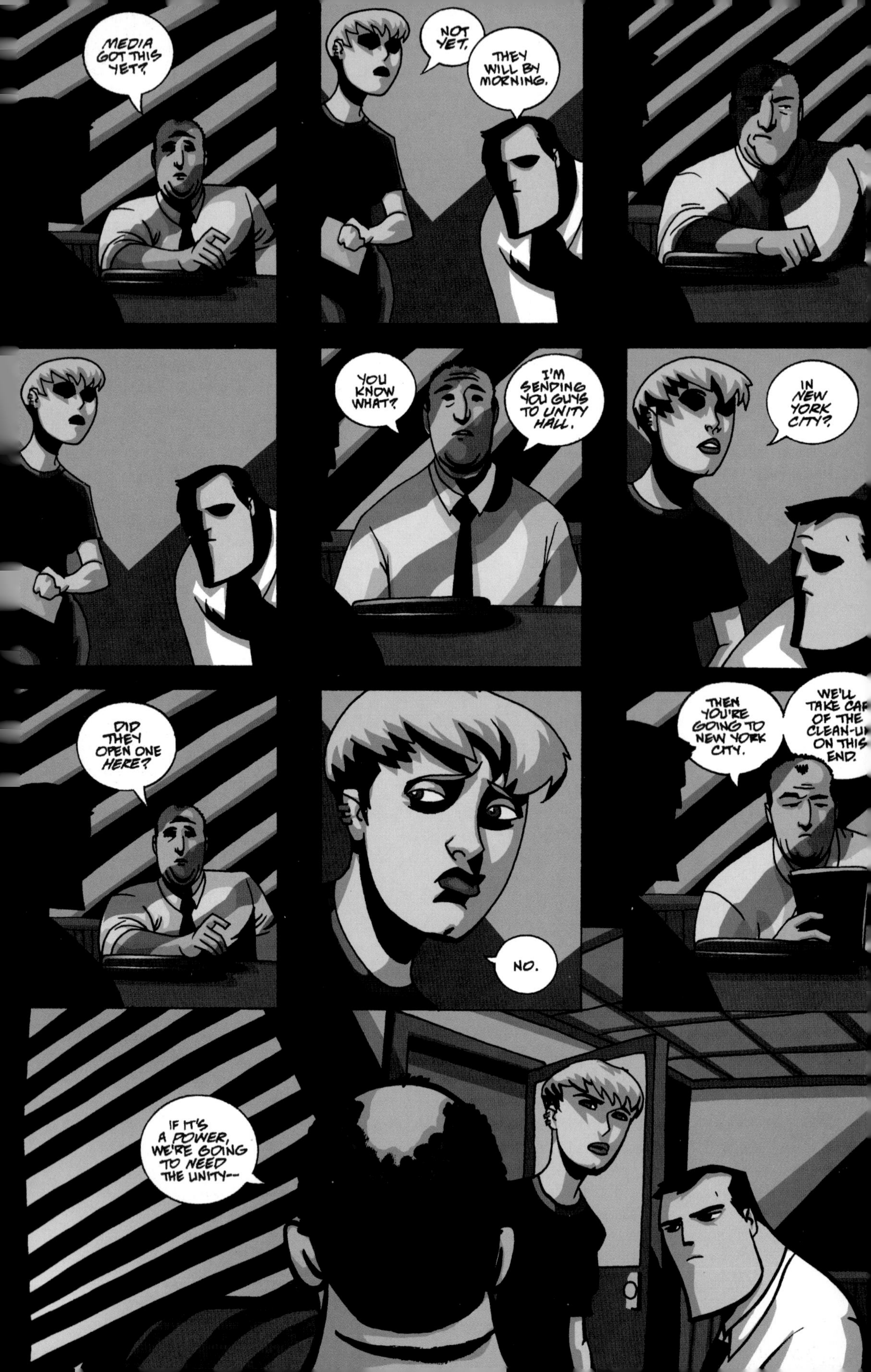
MEDIA GOT THIS YET?
NOT YET.
THEY WILL BY MORNING.
YOU KNOW WHAT?
I'M SENDING YOU GUYS TO UNITY HALL.
IN NEW YORK CITY?
DID THEY OPEN ONE HERE?
NO.
THEN YOU'RE GOING TO NEW YORK CITY.
IF IT'S A POWER, WE'RE GOING TO NEED THE UNITY--

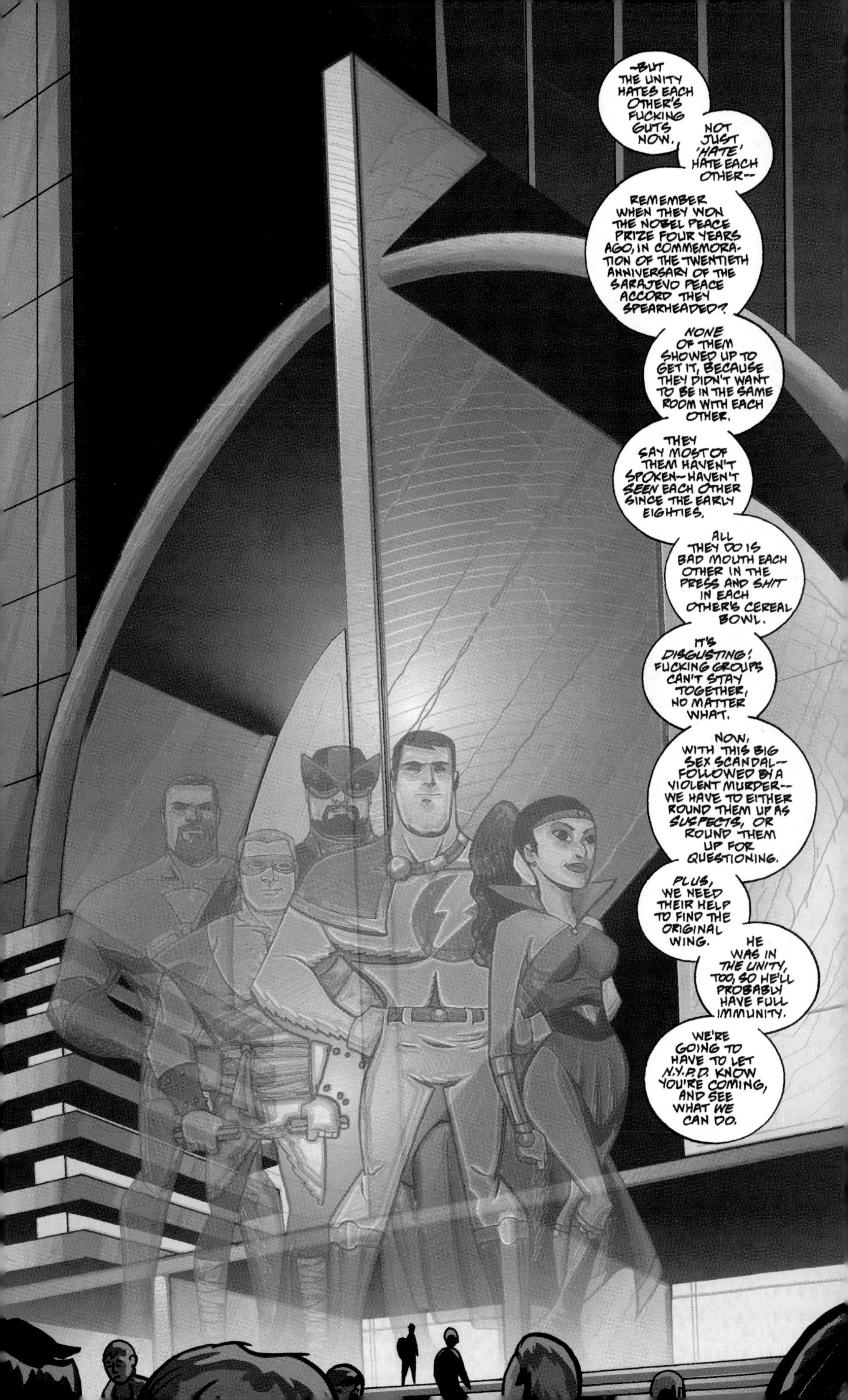
--BUT THE UNITY HATES EACH OTHER'S FUCKING GUTS NOW.
NOT JUST, 'HATE' HATE EACH OTHER--
REMEMBER WHEN THEY WON THE NOBEL PEACE PRIZE FOUR YEARS AGO, IN COMMEMORATION OF THE TWENTIETH ANNIVERSARY OF THE SARAJEVO PEACE ACCORD THEY SPEARHEADED?
NONE OF THEM SHOWED UP TO GET IT, BECAUSE THEY DIDN'T WANT TO BE IN THE SAME ROOM WITH EACH OTHER.
THEY SAY MOST OF THEM HAVEN'T SPOKEN--HAVEN'T SEEN EACH OTHER SINCE THE EARLY EIGHTIES.
ALL THEY DO IS BAD MOUTH EACH OTHER IN THE PRESS AND SHIT IN EACH OTHER'S CEREAL BOWL.
IT'S DISGUSTING! FUCKING GROUPS CAN'T STAY TOGETHER, NO MATTER WHAT.
NOW, WITH THIS BIG SEX SCANDAL-- FOLLOWED BY A VIOLENT MURDER-- WE HAVE TO EITHER ROUND THEM UP AS SUSPECTS, OR ROUND THEM UP FOR QUESTIONING.
PLUS, WE NEED THEIR HELP TO FIND THE ORIGINAL WING.
HE WAS IN THE UNITY, TOO, SO HE'LL PROBABLY HAVE FULL IMMUNITY.
WE'RE GOING TO HAVE TO LET N.Y.P.D. KNOW YOU'RE COMING, AND SEE WHAT WE CAN DO.

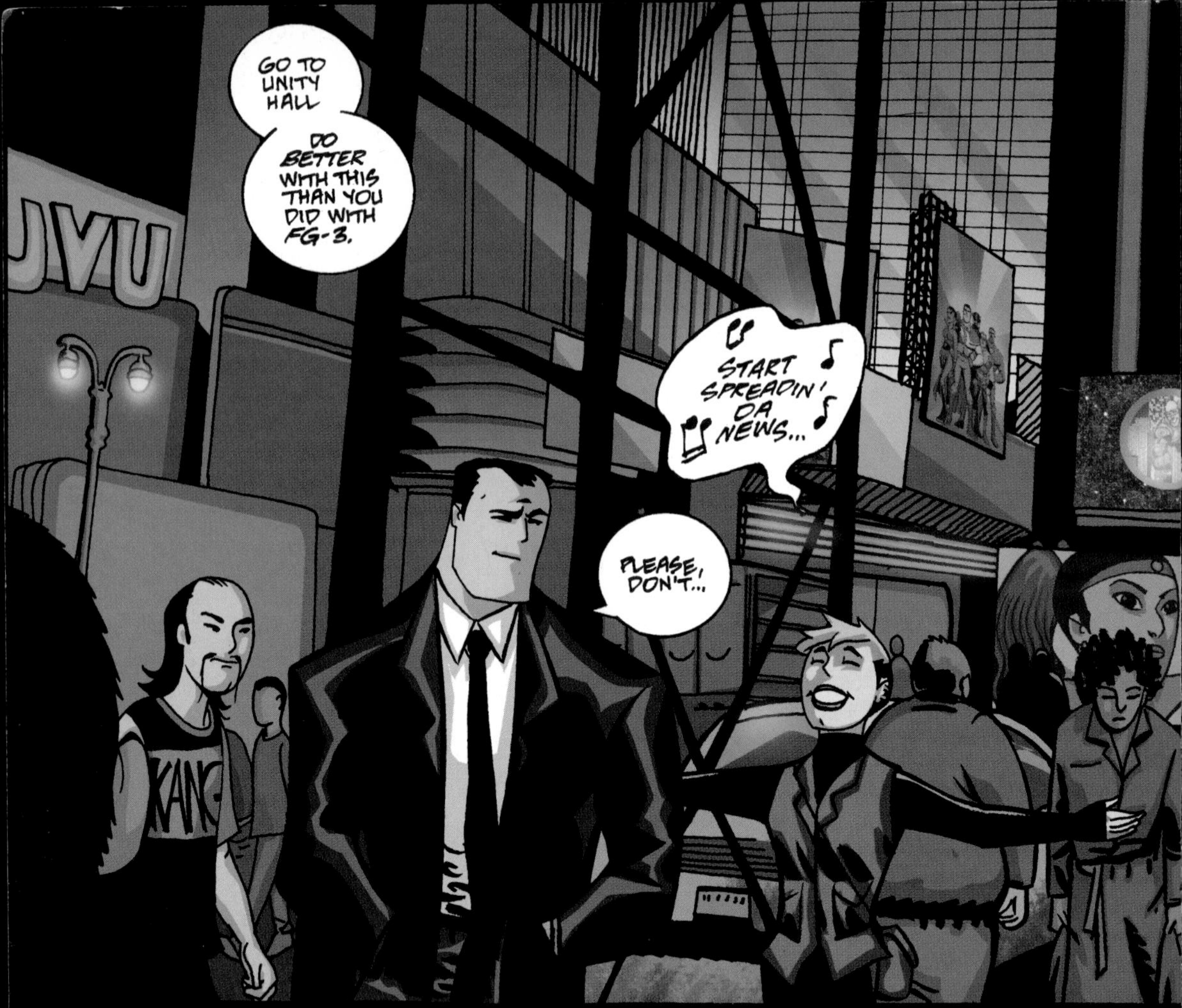
GO TO UNITY HALL
DO BETTER WITH THIS THAN YOU DID WITH FG-3.
START SPREADIN' DA NEWS...
PLEASE, DON'T...

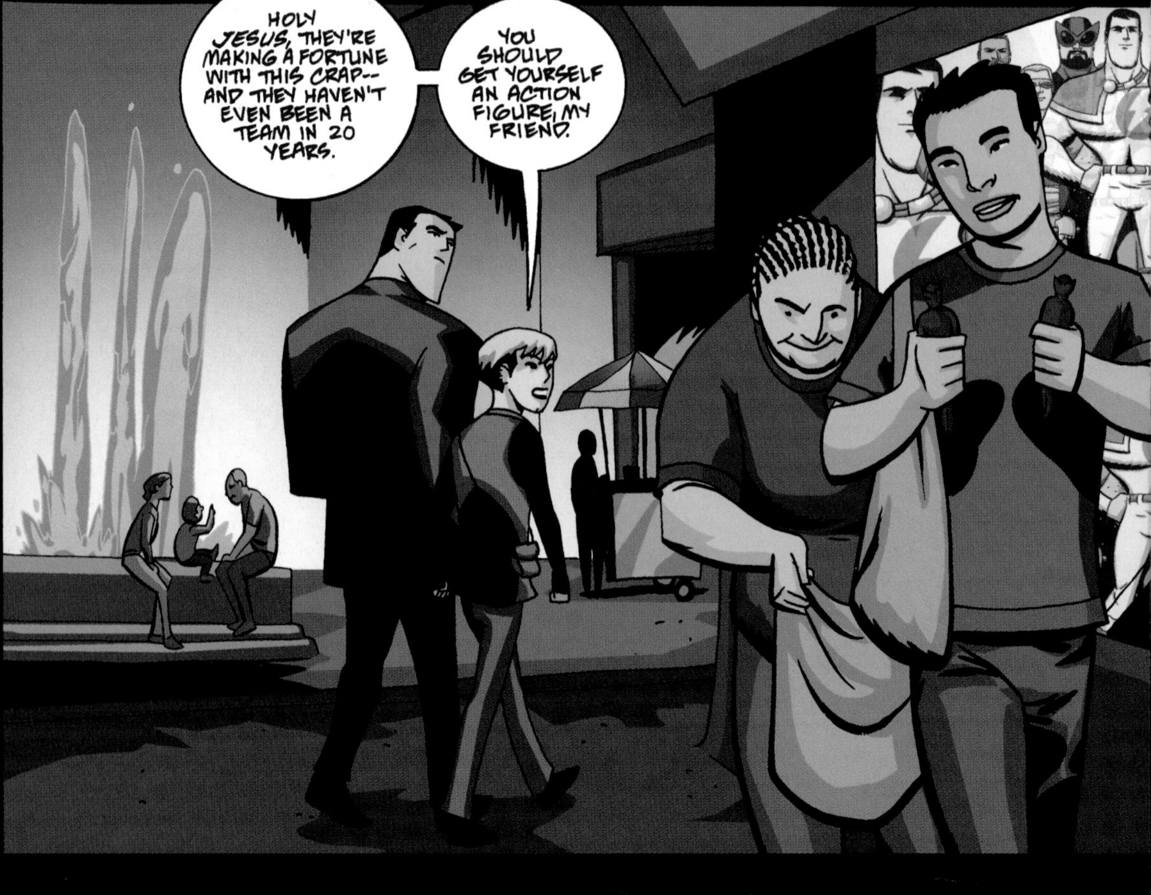
HOLY JESUS, THEY'RE MAKING A FORTUNE WITH THIS CRAP-- AND THEY HAVEN'T EVEN BEEN A TEAM IN 20 YEARS.
YOU SHOULD GET YOURSELF AN ACTION FIGURE, MY FRIEND.

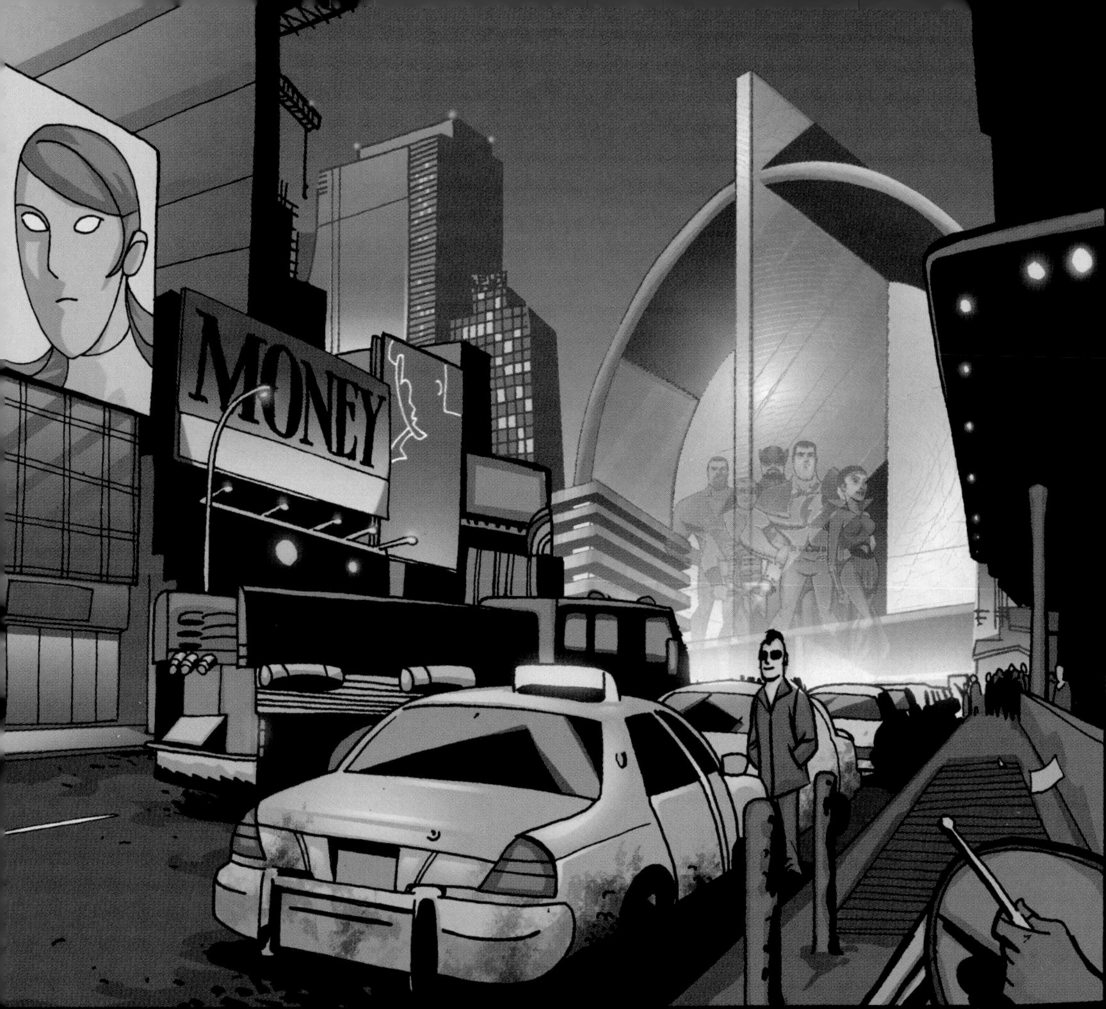
MONEY

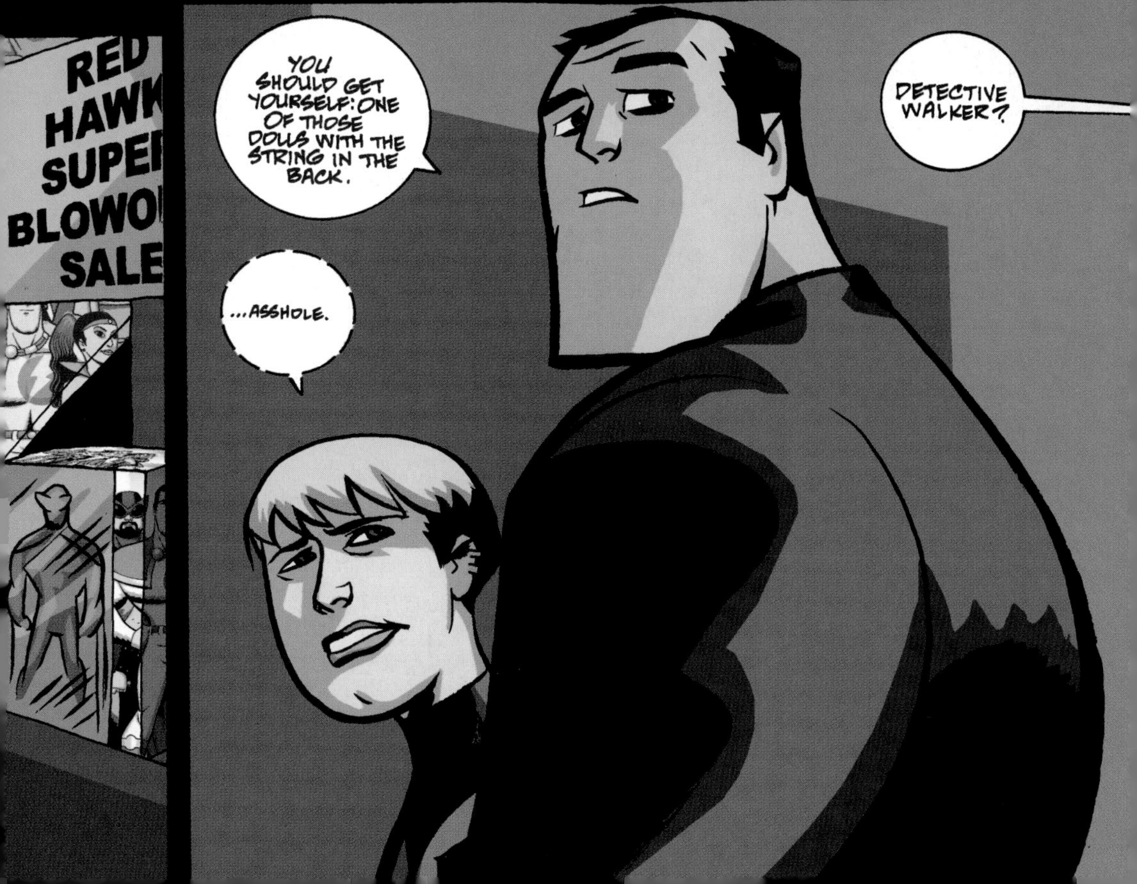
RED HAWK SUPER BLOWO SALE
YOU SHOULD GET YOURSELF ONE OF THOSE DOLLS WITH THE STRING IN THE BACK.
...ASSHOLE.
DETECTIVE WALKER?

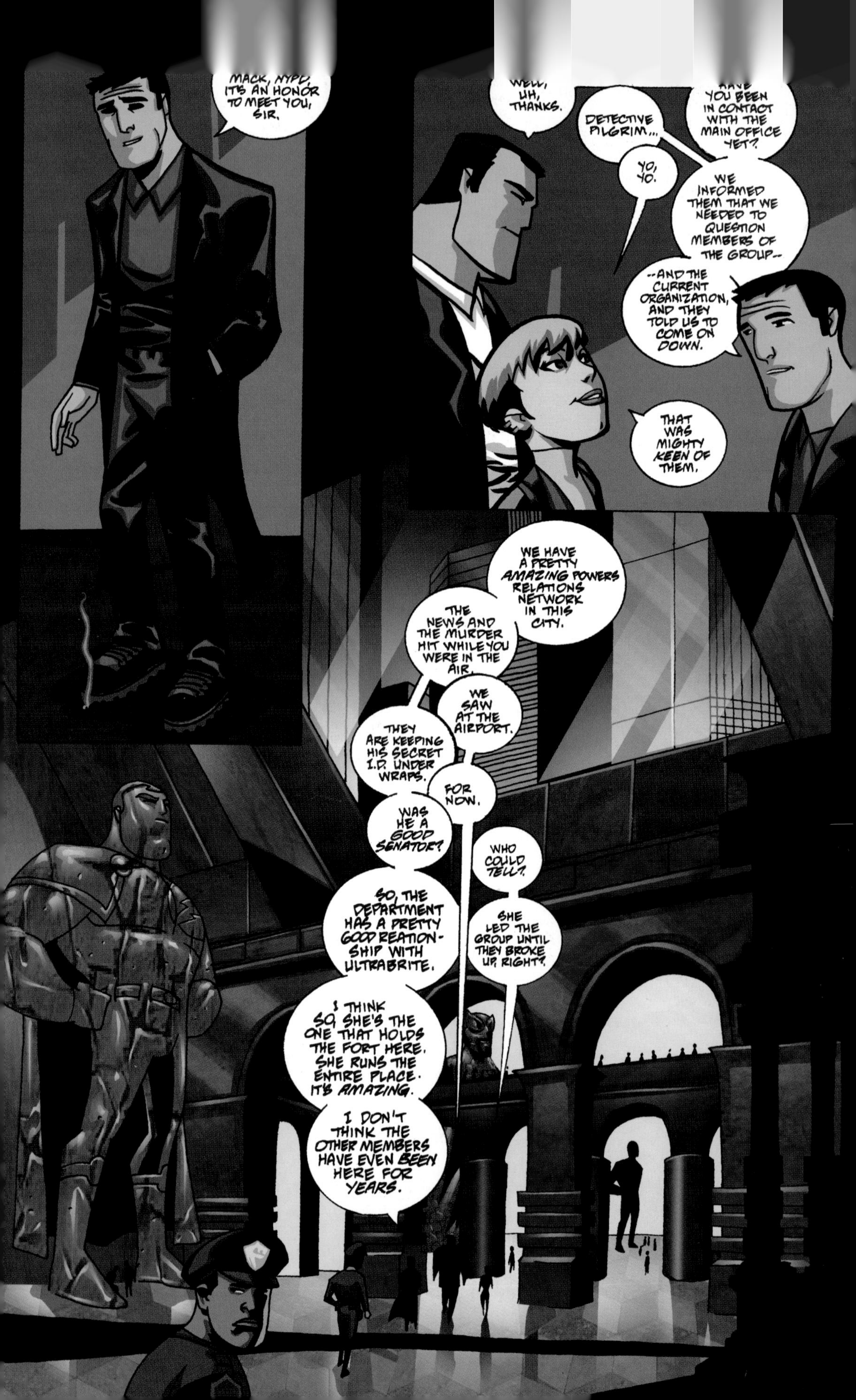
MACK, NYPD, IT'S AN HONOR TO MEET YOU, SIR.
WELL, UH, THANKS.
DETECTIVE PILGRIM...
HAVE YOU BEEN IN CONTACT WITH THE MAIN OFFICE YET?
YO, YO.
WE INFORMED THEM THAT WE NEEDED TO QUESTION MEMBERS OF THE GROUP--
--AND THE CURRENT ORGANIZATION, AND THEY TOLD US TO COME ON DOWN.
THAT WAS MIGHTY KEEN OF THEM.
WE HAVE A PRETTY AMAZING POWERS RELATIONS NETWORK IN THIS CITY.
THE NEWS AND THE MURDER HIT WHILE YOU WERE IN THE AIR.
WE SAW AT THE AIRPORT.
THEY ARE KEEPING HIS SECRET I.D. UNDER WRAPS.
FOR NOW.
WAS HE A GOOD SENATOR?
WHO COULD TELL?
SO, THE DEPARTMENT HAS A PRETTY GOOD REATIONSHIP WITH ULTRABRITE.
SHE LED THE GROUP UNTIL THEY BROKE UP, RIGHT?
I THINK SO. SHE'S THE ONE THAT HOLDS THE FORT HERE. SHE RUNS THE ENTIRE PLACE. IT'S AMAZING.
I DON'T THINK THE OTHER MEMBERS HAVE EVEN BEEN HERE FOR YEARS.

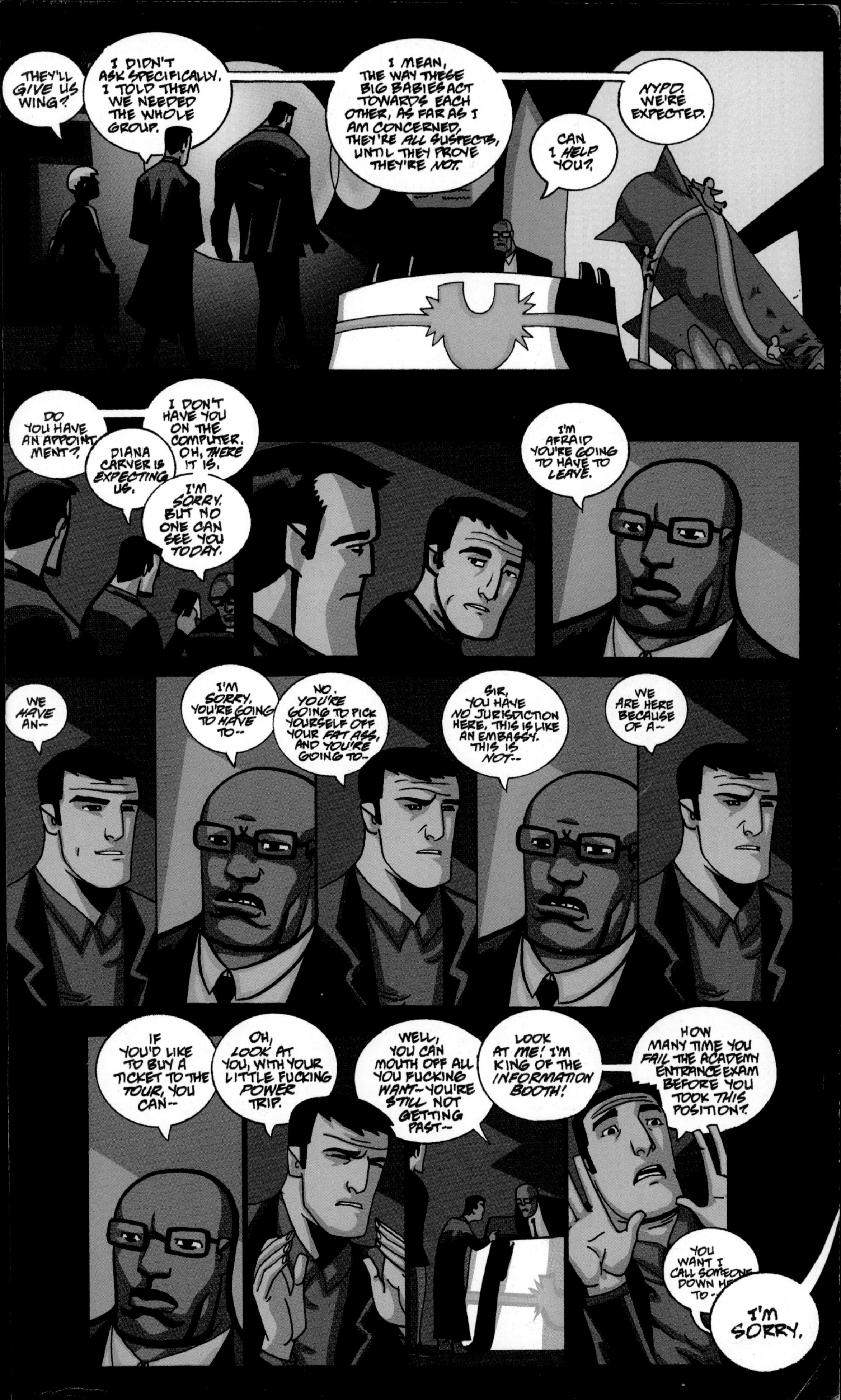

THEY'LL GIVE US WING?
I DIDN'T ASK SPECIFICALLY. I TOLD THEM WE NEEDED THE WHOLE GROUP.
I MEAN, THE WAY THESE BIG BABIES ACT TOWARDS EACH OTHER, AS FAR AS I AM CONCERNED, THEY'RE ALL SUSPECTS, UNTIL THEY PROVE THEY'RE NOT.
CAN I HELP YOU?
NYPD. WE'RE EXPECTED.
DO YOU HAVE AN APPOINTMENT?
DIANA CARVER IS EXPECTING US.
I DON'T HAVE YOU ON THE COMPUTER. OH, THERE IT IS.
I'M SORRY. BUT NO ONE CAN SEE YOU TODAY.
I'M AFRAID YOU'RE GOING TO HAVE TO LEAVE.
WE HAVE AN--
I'M SORRY. YOU'RE GOING TO HAVE TO--
NO. YOU'RE GOING TO PICK YOURSELF OFF YOUR FAT ASS, AND YOU'RE GOING TO--
SIR, YOU HAVE NO JURISDICTION HERE. THIS IS LIKE AN EMBASSY. THIS IS NOT--
WE ARE HERE BECAUSE OF A--
IF YOU'D LIKE TO BUY A TICKET TO THE TOUR, YOU CAN--
OH, LOOK AT YOU, WITH YOUR LITTLE FUCKING POWER TRIP.
WELL, YOU CAN MOUTH OFF ALL YOU FUCKING WANT--YOU'RE STILL NOT GETTING PAST--
LOOK AT ME! I'M KING OF THE INFORMATION BOOTH!
HOW MANY TIME YOU FAIL THE ACADEMY ENTRANCE EXAM BEFORE YOU TOOK THIS POSITION?
I'M SORRY.

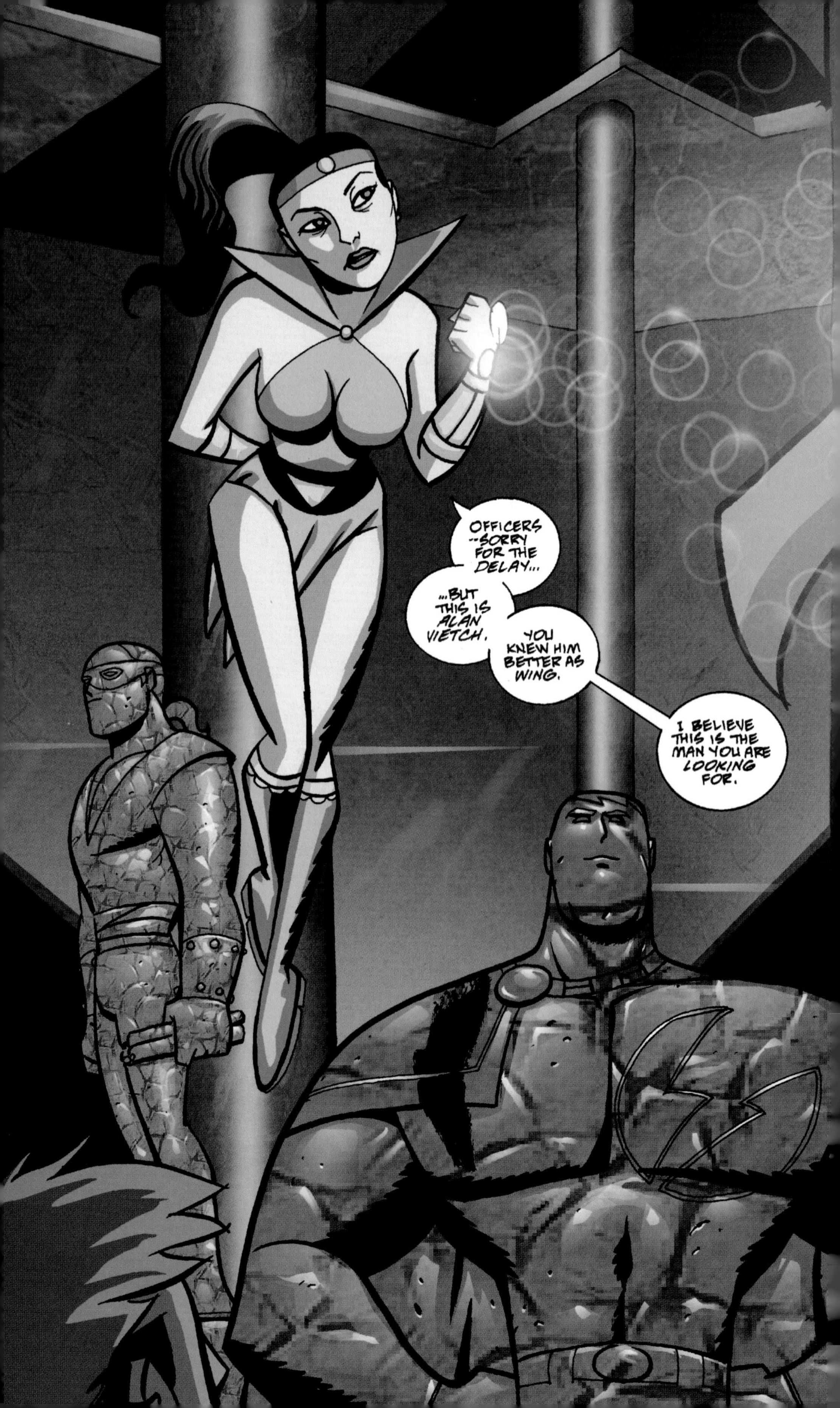
OFFICERS --SORRY FOR THE DELAY...
...BUT THIS IS ALAN VIETCH.
YOU KNEW HIM BETTER AS WING.
I BELIEVE THIS IS THE MAN YOU ARE LOOKING FOR.

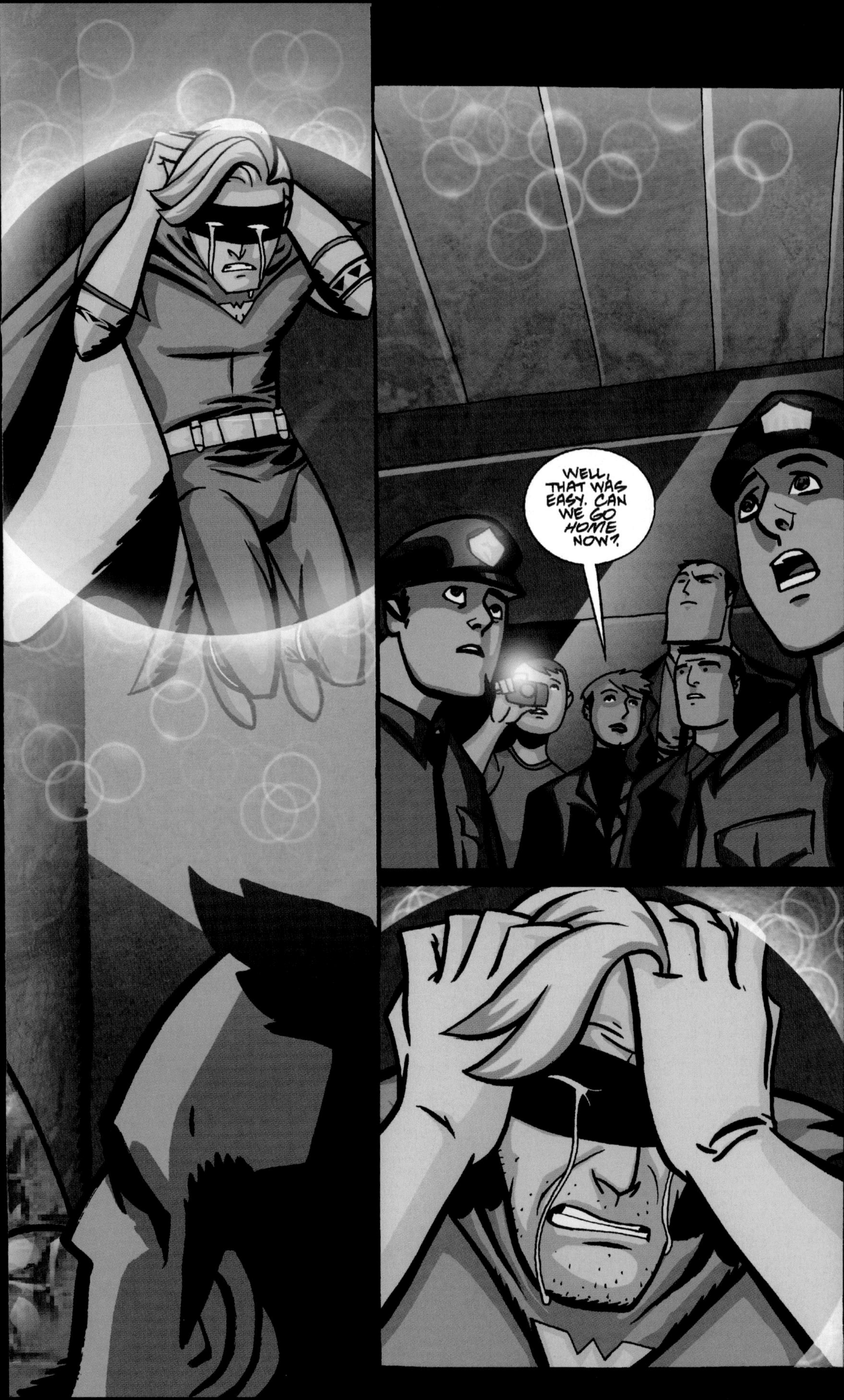
WELL, THAT WAS EASY. CAN WE GO HOME NOW?

P online!

Dateline: NYC

Get Our Free Newsletter > search go

▪HOME ▪NEWS ▪GOSSIP ▪REVIEWS ▪CELEBS ▪CHAT

GOSSIP
ONTENTS

Jnder The Cape
Costume Closet
Ask Alisa
Two Mikes Talkin'

OWERS NEWS

RST LOOK: Men Briefs on Parade

emembering FG-3: e Good Old Days

omino Mask Do's d Don't's

hich Twin Has the OWERS"?

RESH FACES

ew Book Reviews: odpiece: *Costume ordinating with lors, undercover th unity*

eoples' Choice
u Pick the Winners d Losers, Clips, cs, Behind the owl, aftershow party

emories:
owers That Be etrospective, with deo flashbacks om the first contact

d's Couch Trip:
Close & Personal th Forever Man, on persex, superdrugs d superpowers

HE HIT LIST

day's Best Bets:
CAPES On Patrol
Powers *'Trippin'*
Musclebound Freak
ours 17 cities

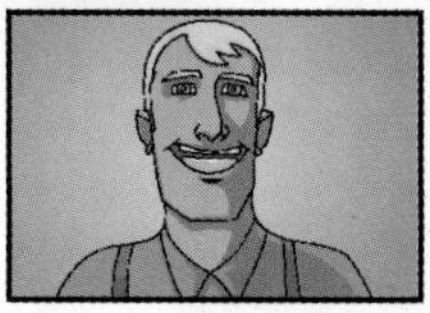

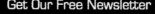

Ted Robinson's Under The Cape

This is where the Dirty Dish gets dumped

Catch Ted Robinson on *P! News Live*
Tuesdays at 4:30 p.m. PT and
Sundays at 2:30 a.m and 7 p.m. PT

Kitchen Is Closed

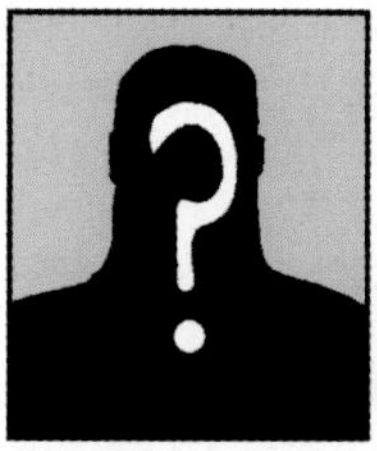

Guess which major-league super person found himself in the local emergency room last week? And it wasn't some hair-raising derring-do that brought our hero of the sky into the hands of medical specialists. Oh--no. It was a kinky act under the sheets.

It seems a certain towering titan and his recent (some say) super slutty partner, were "experimenting" in the boudoir when his most intimate of intimates were scorched with some scalding hot oatmeal.

Oh, yes, you heard me: oatmeal.

Word is that he will heal just fine in time, but for now doctor's orders are, "All food goes into mouth only."

And they say getting egg on your face is embarassing.

Buttering Your Role Models

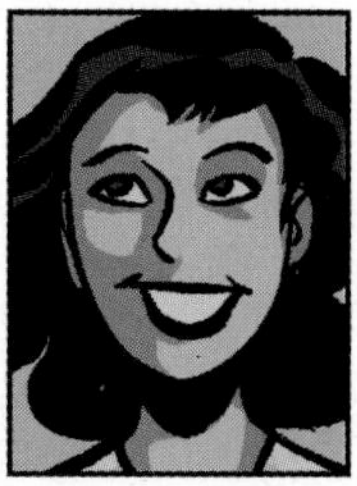

Dear Ted:
I hope when I receive my degree in journalism, that I can be as important and influential as you. You perform a vital public service, keeping us aware that too many Powers are just puffed-up egomaniacs with padded boobs and codpieces. Especially that guy in the purple outfit, looks a lot like John Tesh without

more Ted >

tonight on P!
Olympia and The Red Head:
the hero and the harlot.
A P! Special, 9 p.m.

next week:
We're not telling -- But we promise you won't be let down by our ongoing peek into the world of POWERS and all things powerful. Y'all come back now.

▪help ▪about P! Online ▪site map ▪membership ▪newsletter

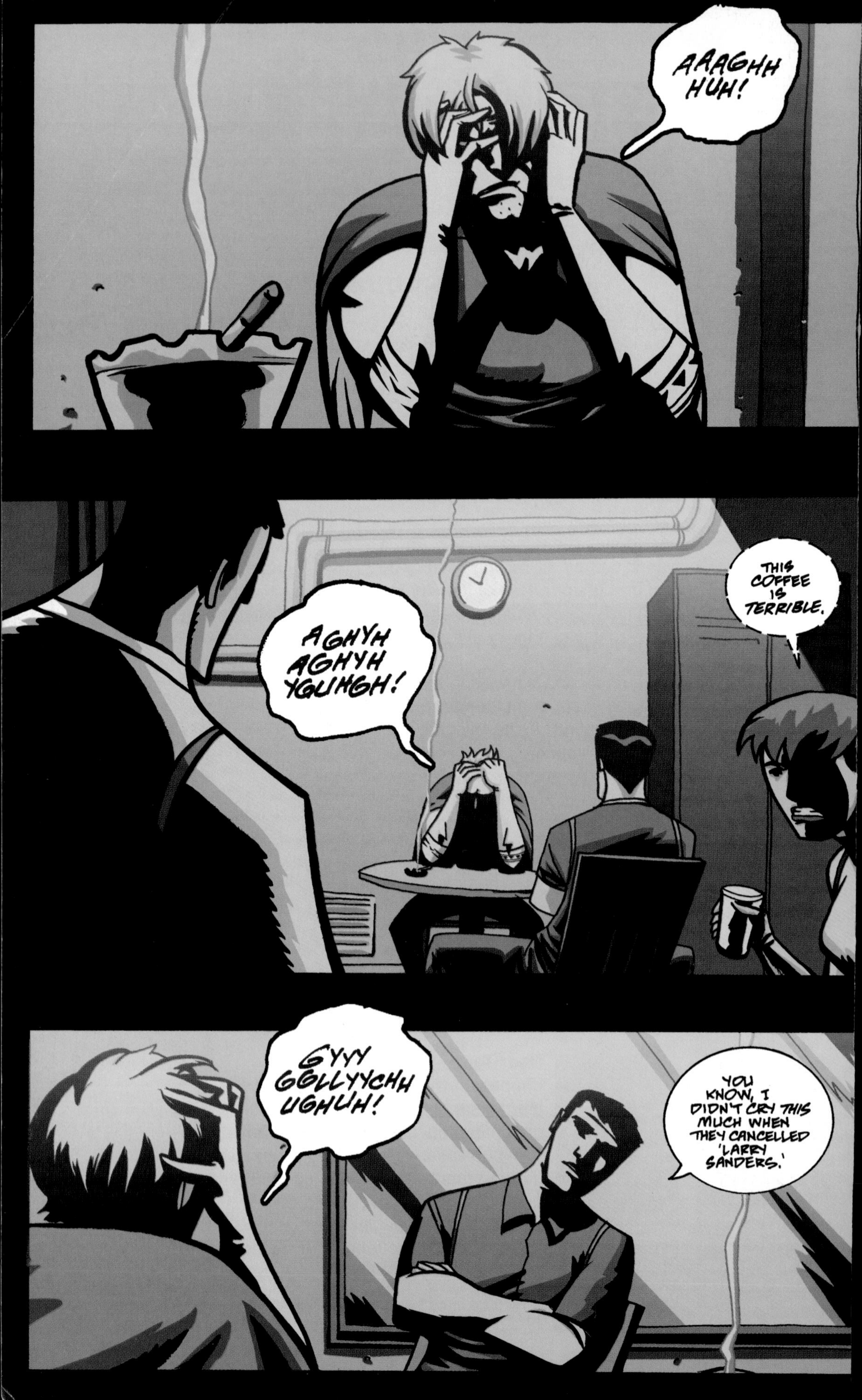
AAAGHH HUH!
AGHYH AGHYH YGUHGH!
THIS COFFEE IS TERRIBLE.
GYYY GGLLYYCHH UGHUH!
YOU KNOW, I DIDN'T CRY THIS MUCH WHEN THEY CANCELLED 'LARRY SANDERS.'

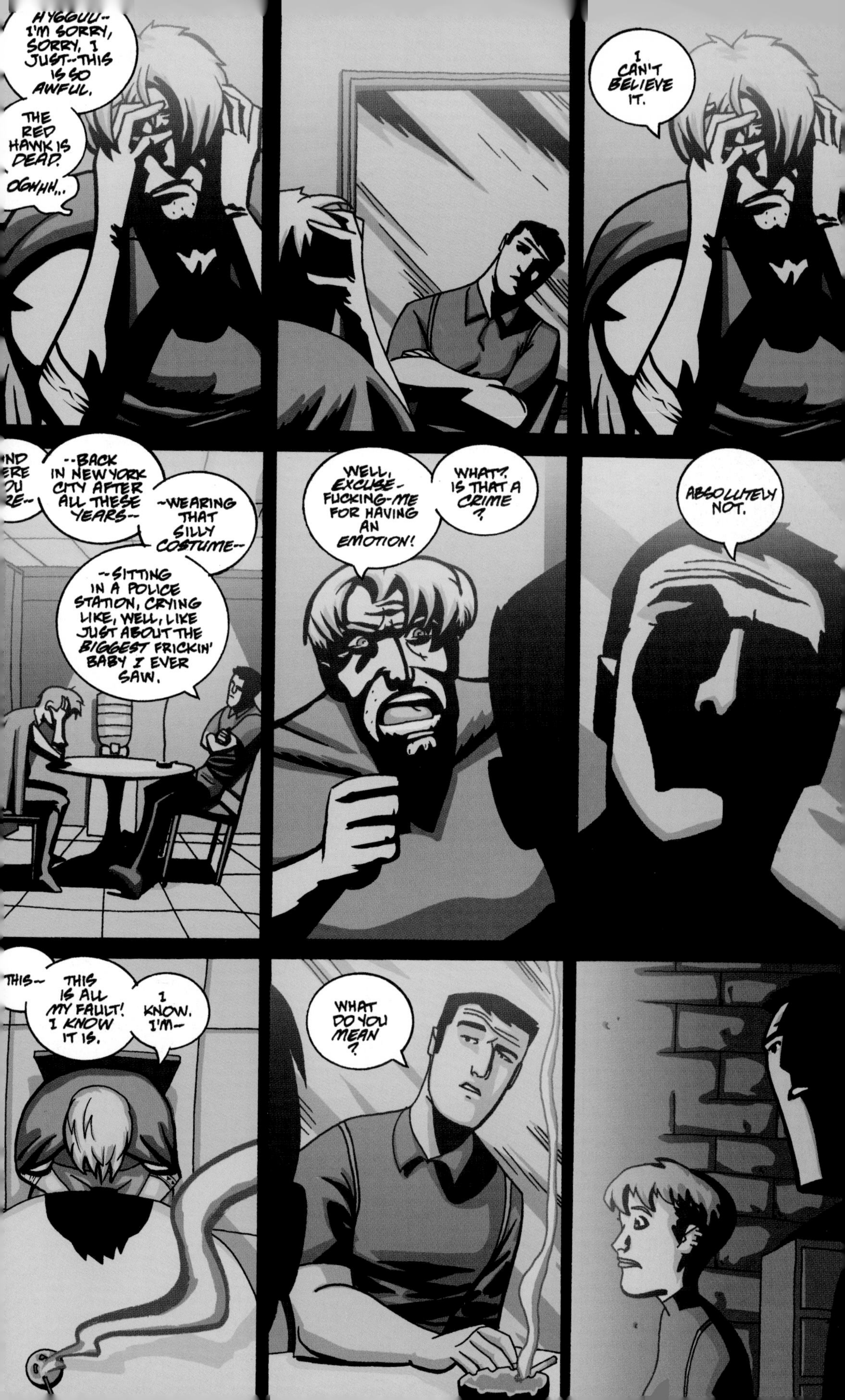
HYGGUU-- I'M SORRY, SORRY, I JUST--THIS IS SO AWFUL.
THE RED HAWK IS DEAD.
OGHHH...
I CAN'T BELIEVE IT.
--BACK IN NEW YORK CITY AFTER ALL THESE YEARS--
-WEARING THAT SILLY COSTUME--
--SITTING IN A POLICE STATION, CRYING LIKE, WELL, LIKE JUST ABOUT THE BIGGEST FRICKIN' BABY I EVER SAW.
WELL, EXCUSE-FUCKING-ME FOR HAVING AN EMOTION!
WHAT? IS THAT A CRIME?
ABSOLUTELY NOT.
THIS--
THIS IS ALL MY FAULT! I KNOW IT IS.
I KNOW. I'M--
WHAT DO YOU MEAN?

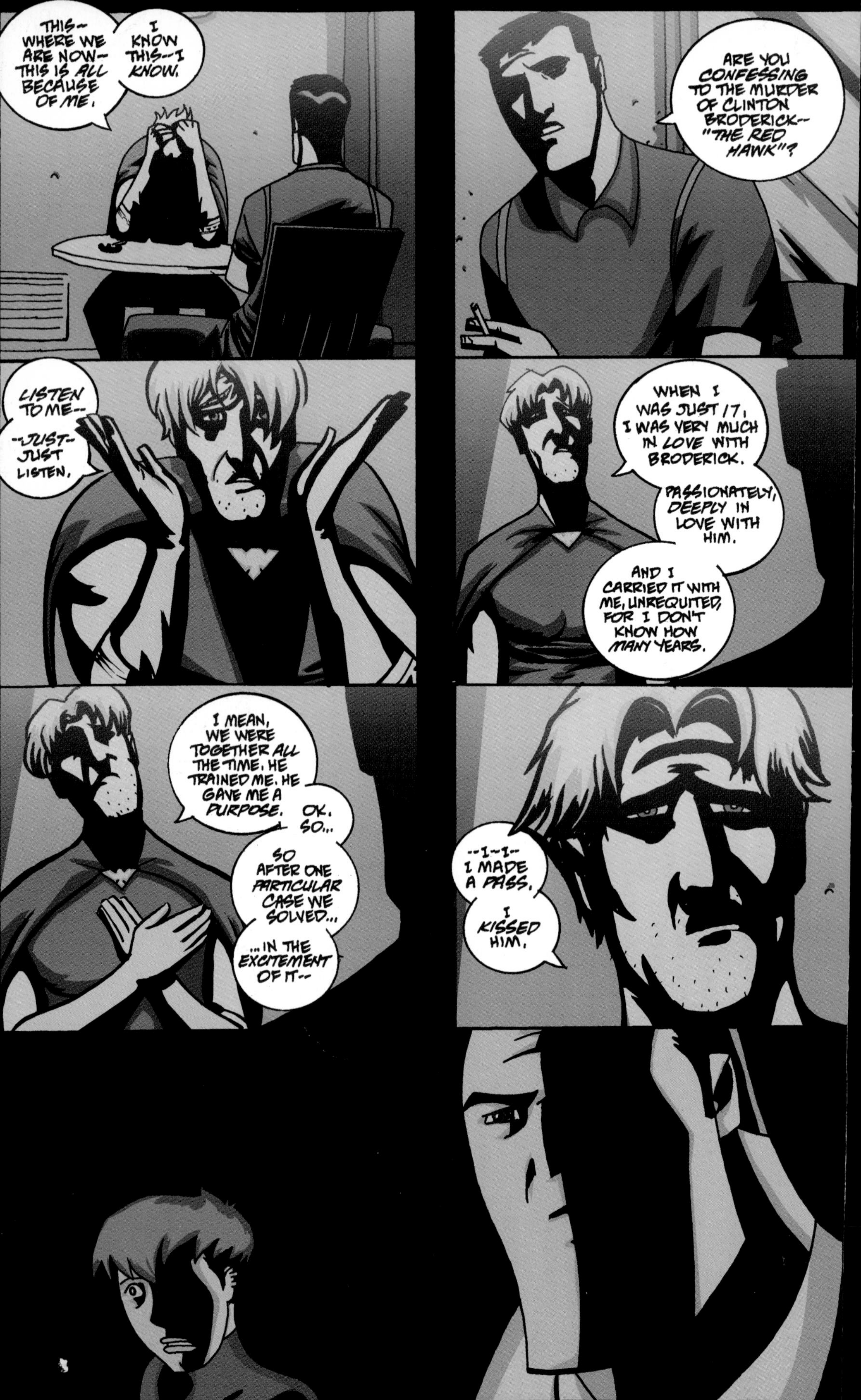
THIS-- WHERE WE ARE NOW-- THIS IS ALL BECAUSE OF ME.
I KNOW THIS--I KNOW.
ARE YOU CONFESSING TO THE MURDER OF CLINTON BRODERICK-- "THE RED HAWK"?
LISTEN TO ME--
--JUST-- JUST LISTEN.
WHEN I WAS JUST 17, I WAS VERY MUCH IN LOVE WITH BRODERICK.
PASSIONATELY, DEEPLY IN LOVE WITH HIM.
AND I CARRIED IT WITH ME, UNREQUITED, FOR I DON'T KNOW HOW MANY YEARS.
I MEAN, WE WERE TOGETHER ALL THE TIME. HE TRAINED ME. HE GAVE ME A PURPOSE.
OK. SO...
SO AFTER ONE PARTICULAR CASE WE SOLVED...
...IN THE EXCITEMENT OF IT--
--I--I-- I MADE A PASS.
I KISSED HIM.

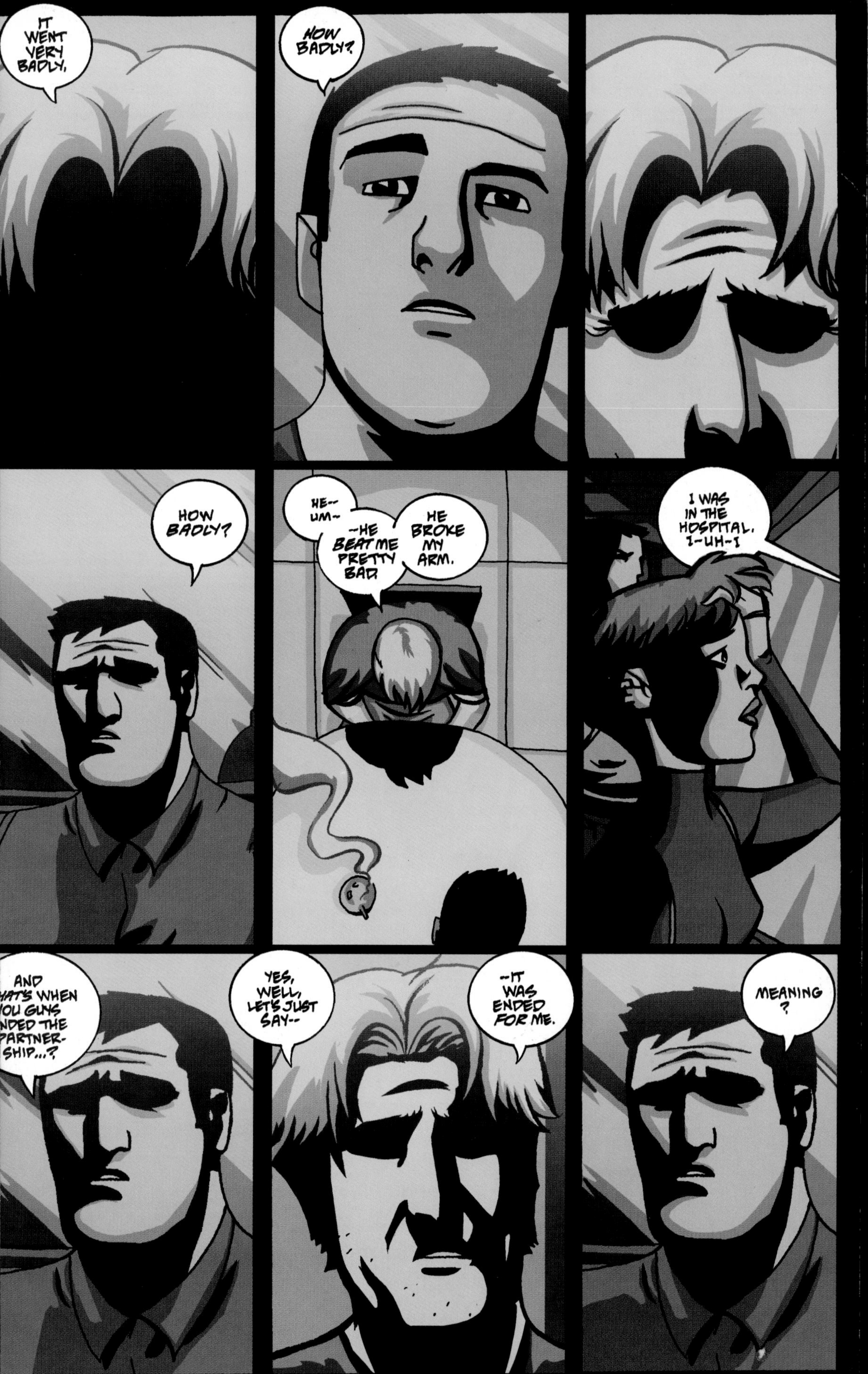
IT WENT VERY BADLY.
HOW BADLY?
HOW BADLY?
HE-- UM--
--HE BEAT ME PRETTY BAD.
HE BROKE MY ARM.
I WAS IN THE HOSPITAL. I--UH--I
AND THAT'S WHEN YOU GUYS ENDED THE PARTNERSHIP...?
YES, WELL, LET'S JUST SAY--
--IT WAS ENDED FOR ME.
MEANING?

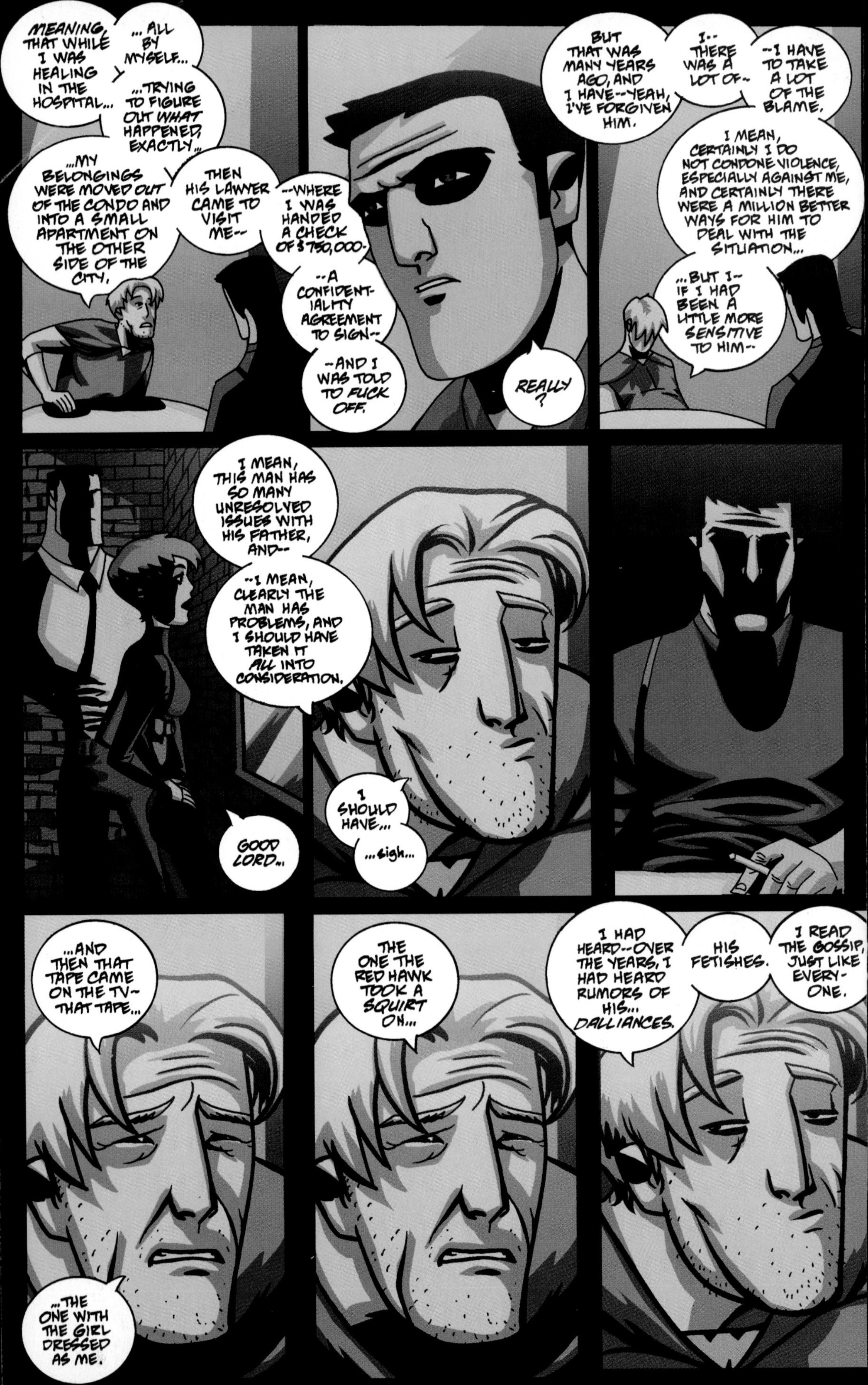
MEANING, THAT WHILE I WAS HEALING IN THE HOSPITAL...
...ALL BY MYSELF...
...TRYING TO FIGURE OUT WHAT HAPPENED, EXACTLY...
...MY BELONGINGS WERE MOVED OUT OF THE CONDO AND INTO A SMALL APARTMENT ON THE OTHER SIDE OF THE CITY.
THEN HIS LAWYER CAME TO VISIT ME--
--WHERE I WAS HANDED A CHECK OF $750,000-
--A CONFIDENTIALITY AGREEMENT TO SIGN--
--AND I WAS TOLD TO FUCK OFF.
REALLY?
BUT THAT WAS MANY YEARS AGO, AND I HAVE--YEAH, I'VE FORGIVEN HIM.
I-- THERE WAS A LOT OF--
--I HAVE TO TAKE A LOT OF THE BLAME.
I MEAN, CERTAINLY I DO NOT CONDONE VIOLENCE, ESPECIALLY AGAINST ME, AND CERTAINLY THERE WERE A MILLION BETTER WAYS FOR HIM TO DEAL WITH THE SITUATION...
...BUT I-- IF I HAD BEEN A LITTLE MORE SENSITIVE TO HIM--
I MEAN, THIS MAN HAS SO MANY UNRESOLVED ISSUES WITH HIS FATHER, AND--
--I MEAN, CLEARLY THE MAN HAS PROBLEMS, AND I SHOULD HAVE TAKEN IT ALL INTO CONSIDERATION.
GOOD LORD...
I SHOULD HAVE...
...sigh...
...AND THEN THAT TAPE CAME ON THE TV-- THAT TAPE...
...THE ONE WITH THE GIRL DRESSED AS ME.
THE ONE THE RED HAWK TOOK A SQUIRT ON...
I HAD HEARD--OVER THE YEARS, I HAD HEARD RUMORS OF HIS... DALLIANCES.
HIS FETISHES.
I READ THE GOSSIP, JUST LIKE EVERYONE.

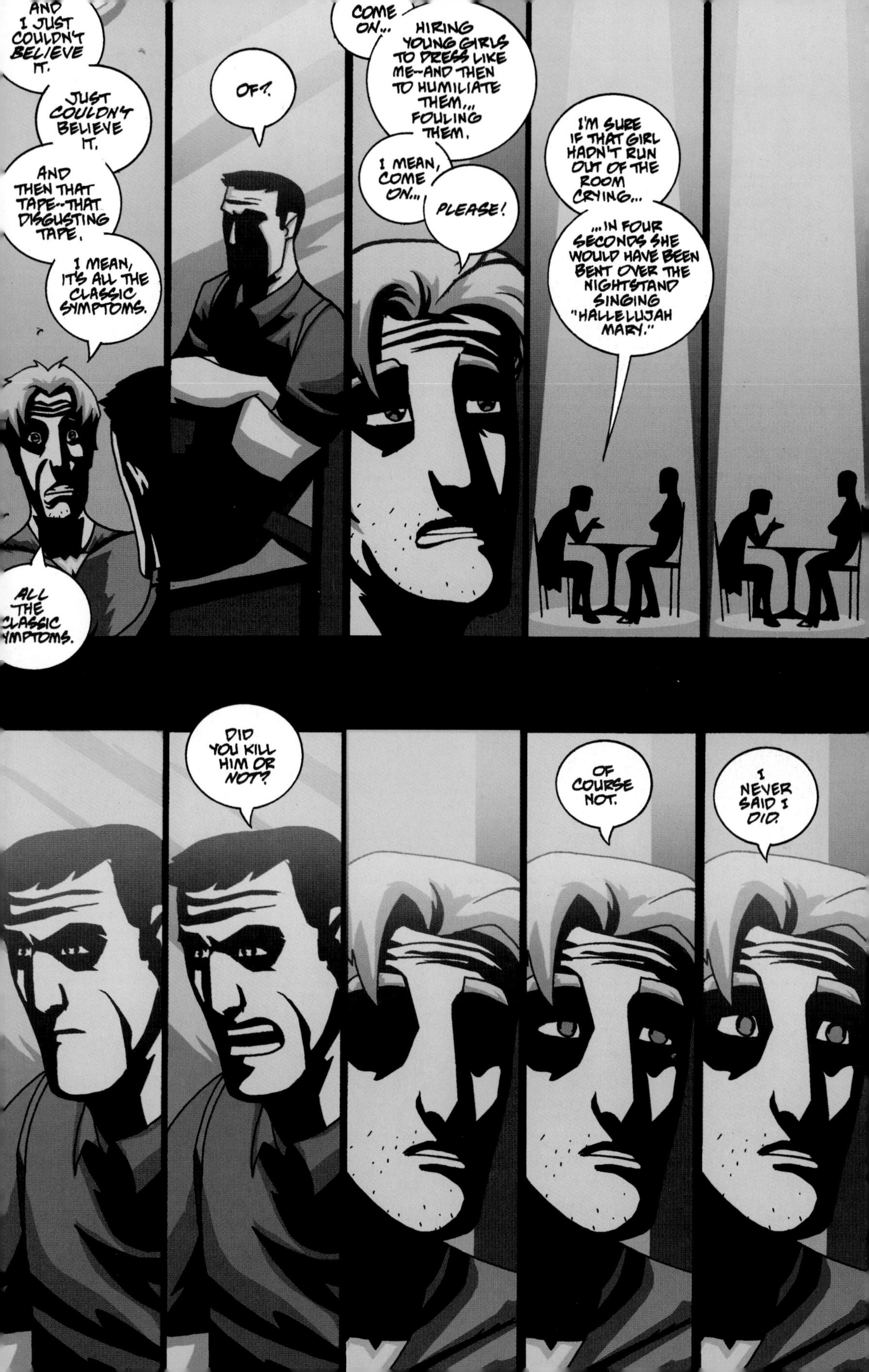
AND I JUST COULDN'T BELIEVE IT.
JUST COULDN'T BELIEVE IT.
AND THEN THAT TAPE--THAT DISGUSTING TAPE.
I MEAN, IT'S ALL THE CLASSIC SYMPTOMS.
ALL THE CLASSIC SYMPTOMS.
OF?
COME ON...
HIRING YOUNG GIRLS TO DRESS LIKE ME--AND THEN TO HUMILIATE THEM... FOULING THEM.
I MEAN, COME ON...
PLEASE!
I'M SURE IF THAT GIRL HADN'T RUN OUT OF THE ROOM CRYING...
...IN FOUR SECONDS SHE WOULD HAVE BEEN BENT OVER THE NIGHTSTAND SINGING "HALLELUJAH MARY."
DID YOU KILL HIM OR NOT?
OF COURSE NOT.
I NEVER SAID I DID.

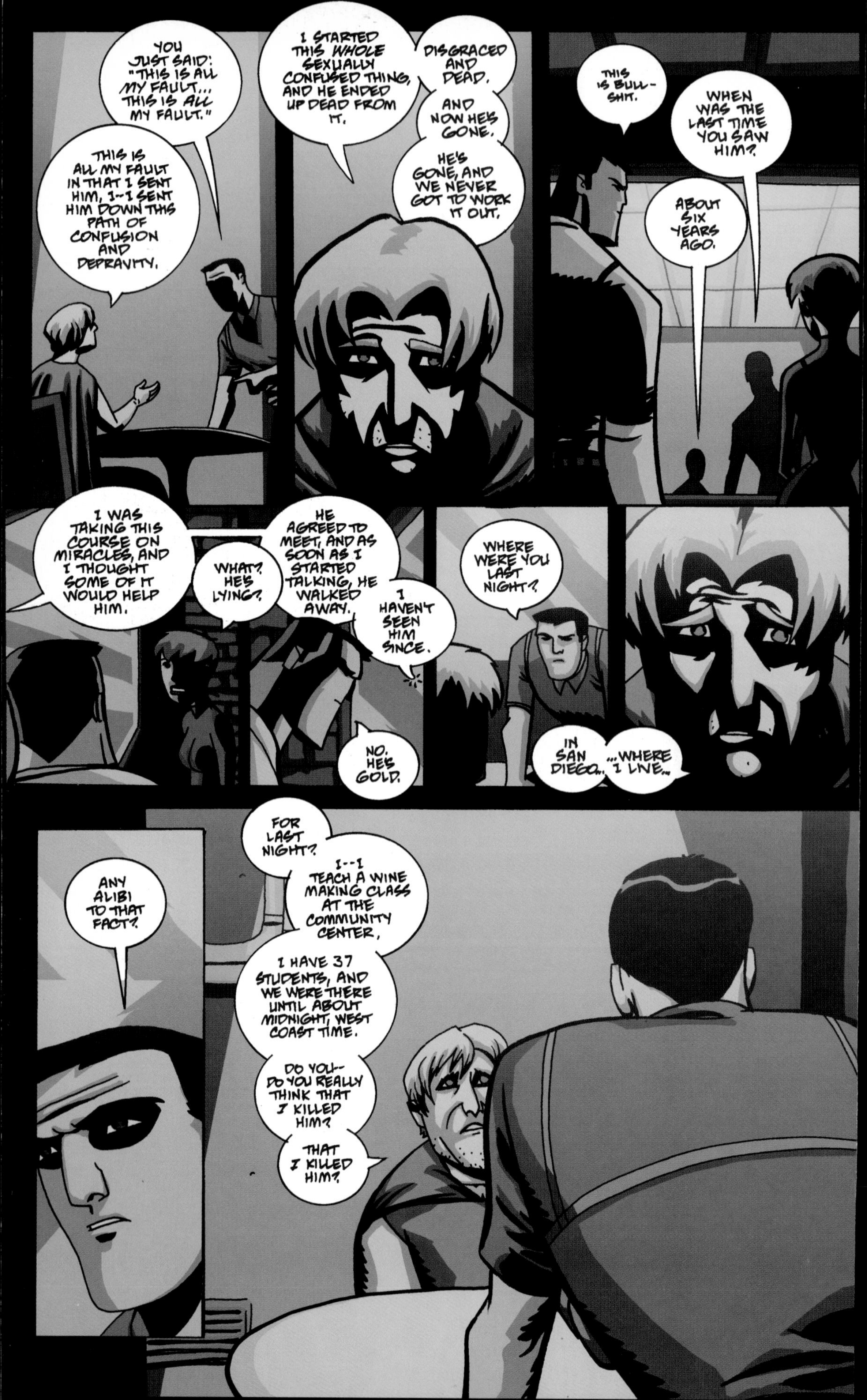

YOU JUST SAID: "THIS IS ALL MY FAULT... THIS IS ALL MY FAULT."
THIS IS ALL MY FAULT IN THAT I SENT HIM, I--I SENT HIM DOWN THIS PATH OF CONFUSION AND DEPRAVITY.
I STARTED THIS WHOLE SEXUALLY CONFUSED THING, AND HE ENDED UP DEAD FROM IT.
DISGRACED AND DEAD.
AND NOW HE'S GONE.
HE'S GONE, AND WE NEVER GOT TO WORK IT OUT.
THIS IS BULL-SHIT.
WHEN WAS THE LAST TIME YOU SAW HIM?
ABOUT SIX YEARS AGO.
I WAS TAKING THIS COURSE ON MIRACLES, AND I THOUGHT SOME OF IT WOULD HELP HIM.
WHAT? HE'S LYING?
HE AGREED TO MEET, AND AS SOON AS I STARTED TALKING, HE WALKED AWAY.
I HAVEN'T SEEN HIM SINCE.
NO. HE'S GOLD.
WHERE WERE YOU LAST NIGHT?
IN SAN DIEGO...
...WHERE I LIVE...
ANY ALIBI TO THAT FACT?
FOR LAST NIGHT?
I--I TEACH A WINE MAKING CLASS AT THE COMMUNITY CENTER.
I HAVE 37 STUDENTS, AND WE WERE THERE UNTIL ABOUT MIDNIGHT, WEST COAST TIME.
DO YOU-- DO YOU REALLY THINK THAT I KILLED HIM?
THAT I KILLED HIM?

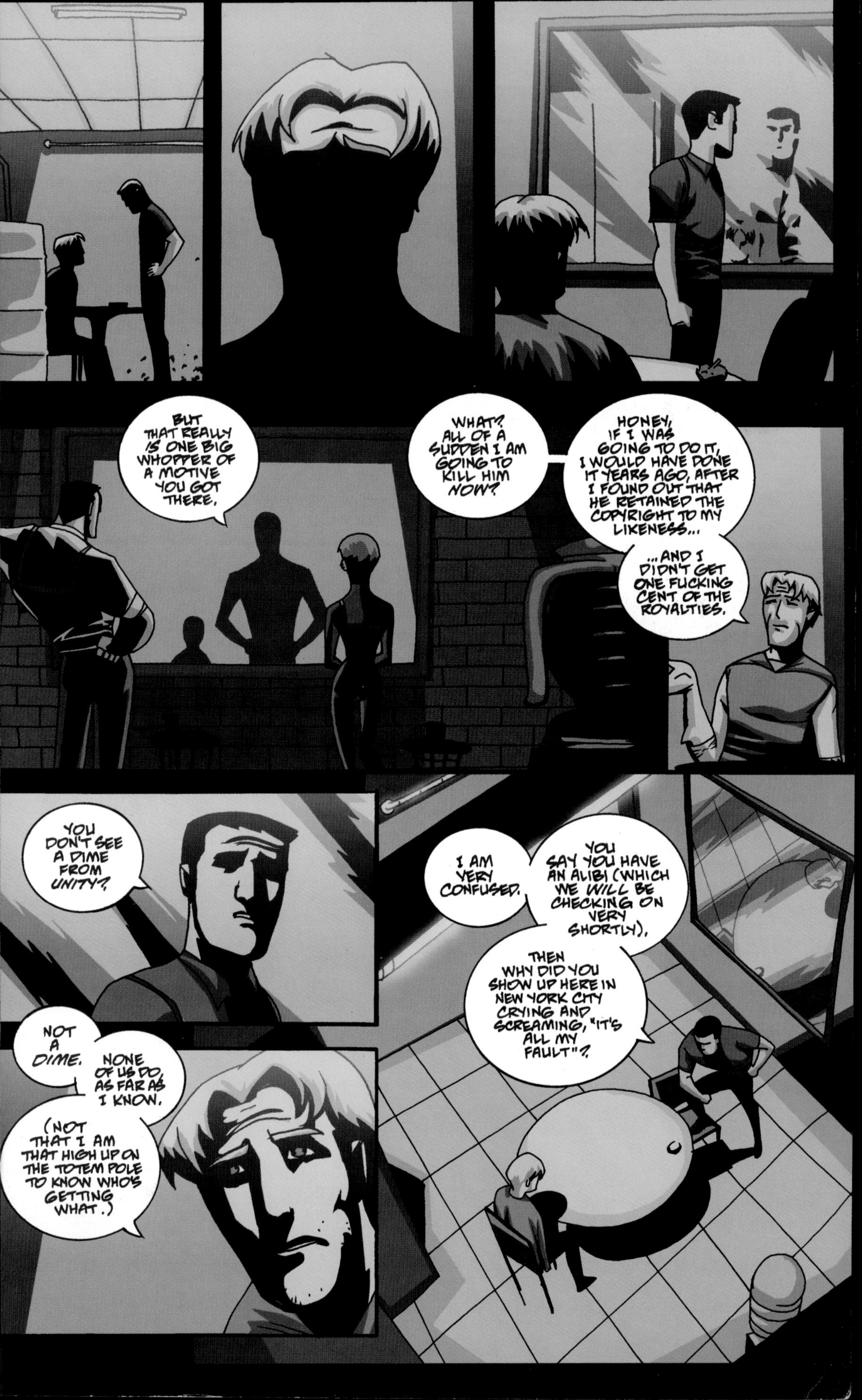
BUT THAT REALLY IS ONE BIG WHOPPER OF A MOTIVE YOU GOT THERE.
WHAT? ALL OF A SUDDEN I AM GOING TO KILL HIM NOW?
HONEY, IF I WAS GOING TO DO IT, I WOULD HAVE DONE IT YEARS AGO, AFTER I FOUND OUT THAT HE RETAINED THE COPYRIGHT TO MY LIKENESS...
...AND I DIDN'T GET ONE FUCKING CENT OF THE ROYALTIES.
YOU DON'T SEE A DIME FROM UNITY?
NOT A DIME.
NONE OF US DO, AS FAR AS I KNOW.
(NOT THAT I AM THAT HIGH UP ON THE TOTEM POLE TO KNOW WHO'S GETTING WHAT.)
I AM VERY CONFUSED.
YOU SAY YOU HAVE AN ALIBI (WHICH WE WILL BE CHECKING ON VERY SHORTLY),
THEN WHY DID YOU SHOW UP HERE IN NEW YORK CITY CRYING AND SCREAMING, "IT'S ALL MY FAULT"?

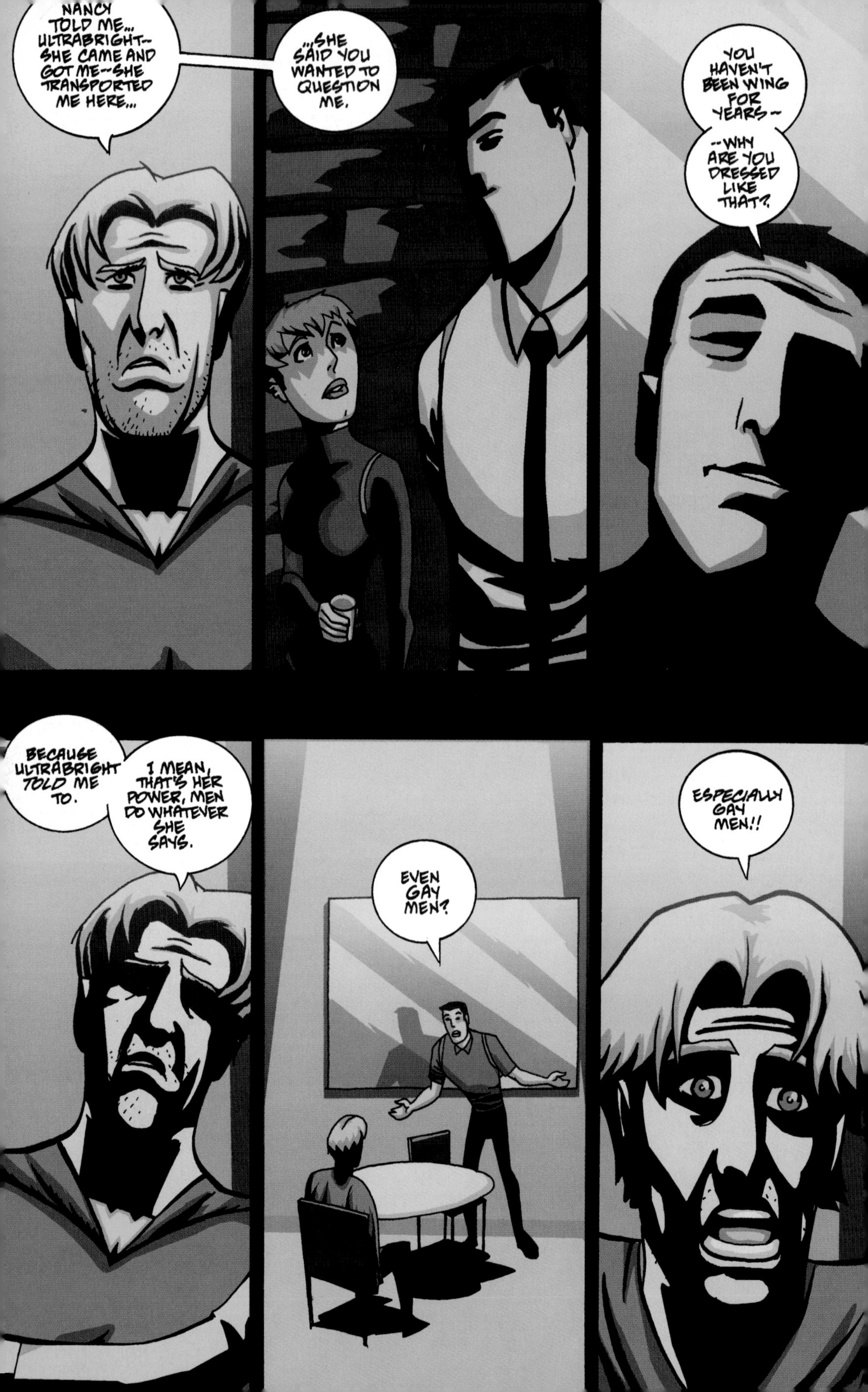
NANCY TOLD ME... ULTRABRIGHT-- SHE CAME AND GOT ME--SHE TRANSPORTED ME HERE...
...SHE SAID YOU WANTED TO QUESTION ME.
YOU HAVEN'T BEEN WING FOR YEARS--
--WHY ARE YOU DRESSED LIKE THAT?
BECAUSE ULTRABRIGHT TOLD ME TO.
I MEAN, THAT'S HER POWER, MEN DO WHATEVER SHE SAYS.
EVEN GAY MEN?
ESPECIALLY GAY MEN!!

GOSSIP CONTENTS

- Under The Cape
- Costume Closet
- Ask Alisa
- Two Mikes Talkin'

POWERS NEWS

FIRST LOOK: Men, Masks & Money

Flying in Skirts: A different view

Wall Street perks up on Powers Products

Gloves or Gauntlets? Fall fashion show

FRESH FACES

New Book Reviews: Flyin' High;
Life in the ultra-fast lane -- its perks, pains, and police photos

Ted's Tasty Tidbits:
The saddest, sickest and stupidest Powers stories in the news from around the globe

Powerballs:
Just how level is the playing field with superheroes suiting up? A P! Sports Extra

Guns 'n' Glamor:
The latest in urban personal protection vests, coordinating cool colors and kevlar

THE HIT LIST

Today's Best Bets:
- Pep Weider's *New Powers Workout*
- Ice-P's *Powertown*
- *Speedfreek* newest McD bobblehead

Ted Robinson's
Under The Cape

This is where the Dirty Dish gets dumped

Catch Ted Robinson on *P! News Live*
Tuesdays at 4:30 p.m. PT and
Sundays at 2:30 a.m and 7 p.m. PT

A Bird in the Hand

Well, "it takes all kinds" is the saying, but a picture that crossed your faithful dirt digger's desk this week is one for the records.

A truly uncanny member of one of America's quirkiest supercombos seems to love leather for more than just his costume.

According to this surprisingly well-lit pictorial essay I am looking at right now, it seems he also likes to have members of the opposite sex look for their car keys...up to the elbow.

They say a picture says a thousand words, but the only word that comes to my mind is, "Yowch!

Good Help Is So Hard to Find

Dear Ted:
I love your column, and log on every day. Thanks for the scoop on The Solar Sentinel and Titania.

Which reminded me of something I never hear about -- the crappy way Powers treat their sidekicks.
I, myself, saw Solar Sentinel close the elevator doors on his partner, Brightboy, just so Solar could score with three female fans between floors at a Powers Convention. That night, Brightboy slept in the lobby, waiting for his partner to trip his circuits with some

more Ted >

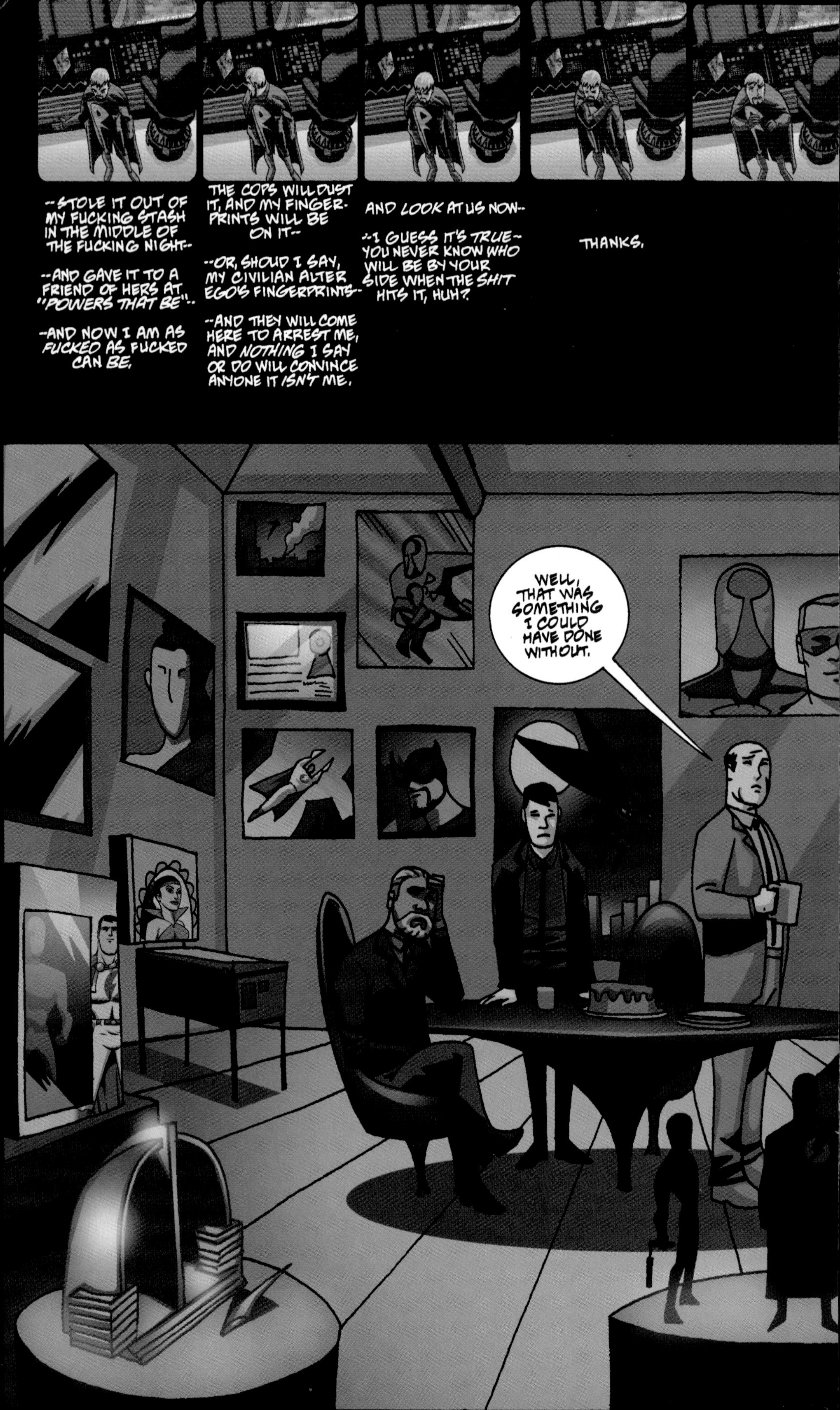
--STOLE IT OUT OF MY FUCKING STASH IN THE MIDDLE OF THE FUCKING NIGHT--
--AND GAVE IT TO A FRIEND OF HERS AT "POWERS THAT BE"--
--AND NOW I AM AS FUCKED AS FUCKED CAN BE.
THE COPS WILL DUST IT, AND MY FINGER-PRINTS WILL BE ON IT--
--OR, SHOUD I SAY, MY CIVILIAN ALTER EGO'S FINGERPRINTS--
--AND THEY WILL COME HERE TO ARREST ME, AND NOTHING I SAY OR DO WILL CONVINCE ANYONE IT ISN'T ME.
AND LOOK AT US NOW--
--I GUESS IT'S TRUE--YOU NEVER KNOW WHO WILL BE BY YOUR SIDE WHEN THE SHIT HITS IT, HUH?
THANKS.
WELL, THAT WAS SOMETHING I COULD HAVE DONE WITHOUT.

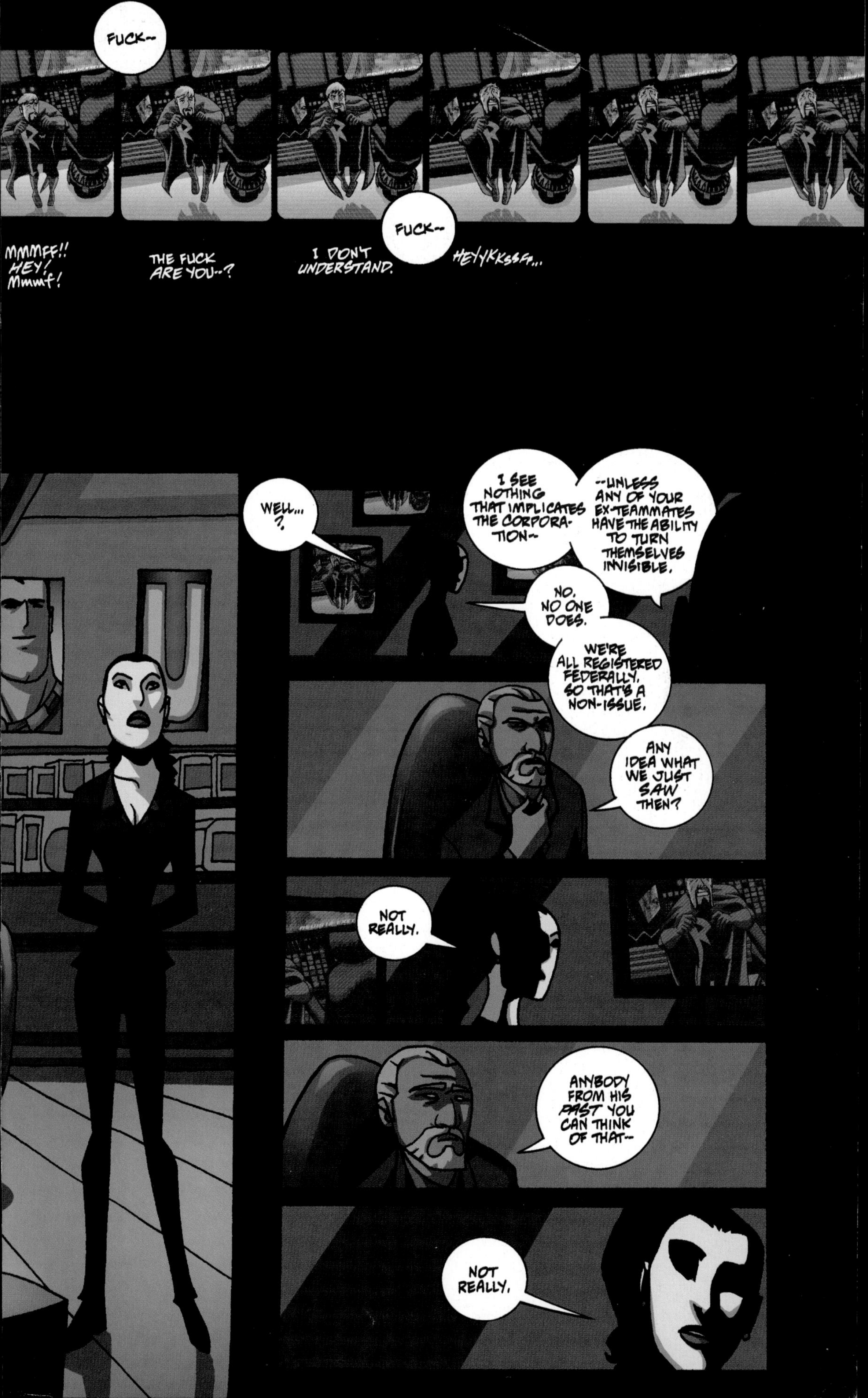
FUCK--
MMMFF!! HEY! Mmmf!
THE FUCK ARE YOU--?
I DON'T UNDERSTAND.
FUCK--
HEYYKKssff...
WELL... ?
I SEE NOTHING THAT IMPLICATES THE CORPORATION--
--UNLESS ANY OF YOUR EX-TEAMMATES HAVE THE ABILITY TO TURN THEMSELVES INVISIBLE.
NO. NO ONE DOES.
WE'RE ALL REGISTERED FEDERALLY, SO THAT'S A NON-ISSUE.
ANY IDEA WHAT WE JUST SAW THEN?
NOT REALLY.
ANYBODY FROM HIS PAST YOU CAN THINK OF THAT--
NOT REALLY.

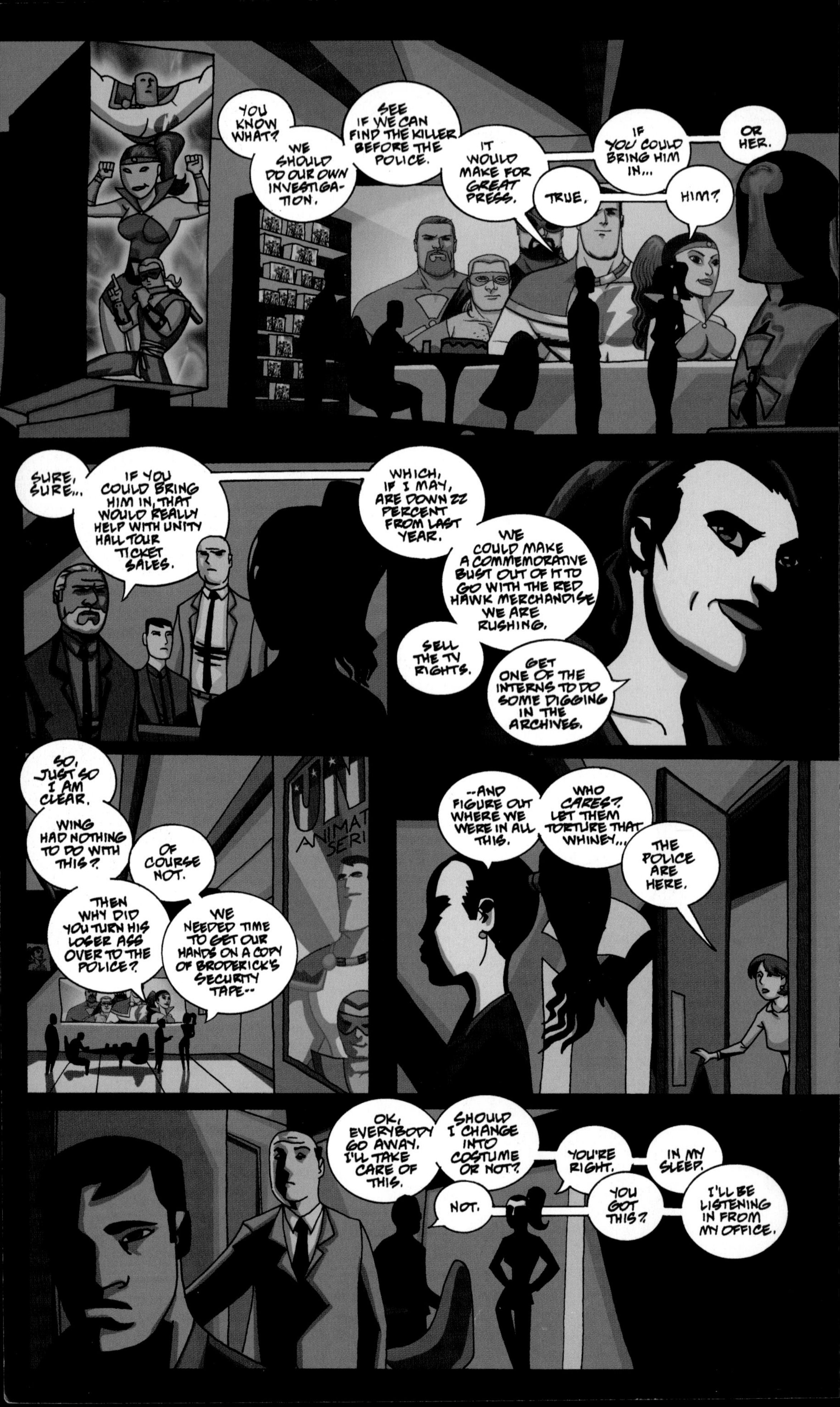
YOU KNOW WHAT?
WE SHOULD DO OUR OWN INVESTIGATION.
SEE IF WE CAN FIND THE KILLER BEFORE THE POLICE.
IT WOULD MAKE FOR GREAT PRESS.
TRUE.
IF YOU COULD BRING HIM IN...
HIM?
OR HER.
SURE, SURE...
IF YOU COULD BRING HIM IN, THAT WOULD REALLY HELP WITH UNITY HALL TOUR TICKET SALES.
WHICH, IF I MAY, ARE DOWN 22 PERCENT FROM LAST YEAR.
WE COULD MAKE A COMMEMORATIVE BUST OUT OF IT TO GO WITH THE RED HAWK MERCHANDISE WE ARE RUSHING.
SELL THE TV RIGHTS.
GET ONE OF THE INTERNS TO DO SOME DIGGING IN THE ARCHIVES.
SO, JUST SO I AM CLEAR.
WING HAD NOTHING TO DO WITH THIS?
OF COURSE NOT.
THEN WHY DID YOU TURN HIS LOSER ASS OVER TO THE POLICE?
WE NEEDED TIME TO GET OUR HANDS ON A COPY OF BRODERICK'S SECURITY TAPE--
--AND FIGURE OUT WHERE WE WERE IN ALL THIS.
WHO CARES? LET THEM TORTURE THAT WHINEY...
THE POLICE ARE HERE.
OK, EVERYBODY GO AWAY. I'LL TAKE CARE OF THIS.
SHOULD I CHANGE INTO COSTUME OR NOT?
NOT.
YOU'RE RIGHT.
YOU GOT THIS?
IN MY SLEEP.
I'LL BE LISTENING IN FROM MY OFFICE.

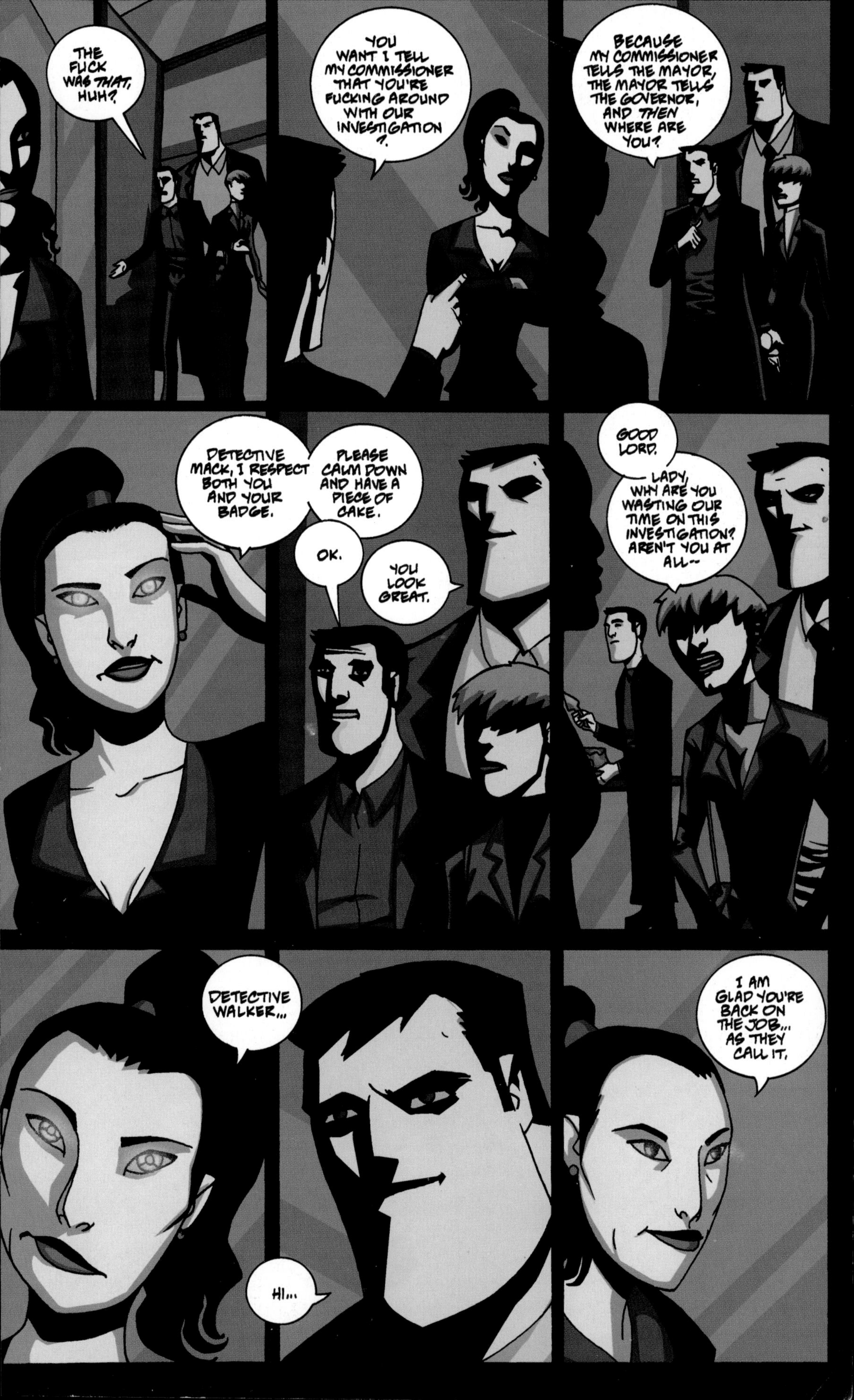
THE FUCK WAS THAT, HUH?
YOU WANT I TELL MY COMMISSIONER THAT YOU'RE FUCKING AROUND WITH OUR INVESTIGATION?
BECAUSE MY COMMISSIONER TELLS THE MAYOR, THE MAYOR TELLS THE GOVERNOR, AND THEN WHERE ARE YOU?
DETECTIVE MACK, I RESPECT BOTH YOU AND YOUR BADGE.
PLEASE CALM DOWN AND HAVE A PIECE OF CAKE.
OK.
YOU LOOK GREAT.
GOOD LORD.
LADY, WHY ARE YOU WASTING OUR TIME ON THIS INVESTIGATION? AREN'T YOU AT ALL--
DETECTIVE WALKER...
HI...
I AM GLAD YOU'RE BACK ON THE JOB... AS THEY CALL IT.

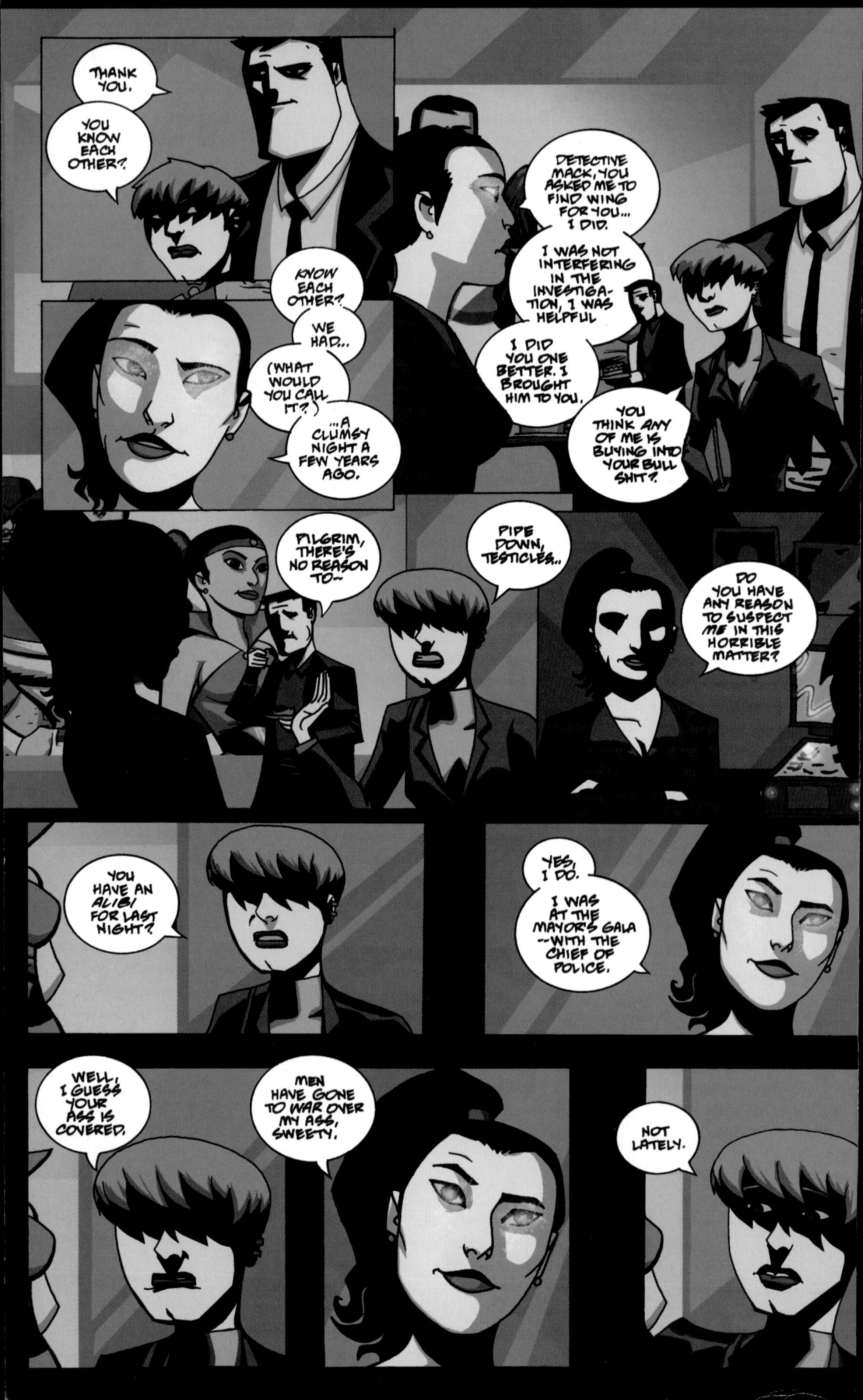
THANK YOU.
YOU KNOW EACH OTHER?
KNOW EACH OTHER?
WE HAD...
(WHAT WOULD YOU CALL IT?)
...A CLUMSY NIGHT A FEW YEARS AGO.
DETECTIVE MACK, YOU ASKED ME TO FIND WING FOR YOU... I DID.
I WAS NOT INTERFERING IN THE INVESTIGATION, I WAS HELPFUL
I DID YOU ONE BETTER. I BROUGHT HIM TO YOU.
YOU THINK ANY OF ME IS BUYING INTO YOUR BULL SHIT?
PILGRIM, THERE'S NO REASON TO--
PIPE DOWN, TESTICLES...
DO YOU HAVE ANY REASON TO SUSPECT ME IN THIS HORRIBLE MATTER?
YOU HAVE AN ALIBI FOR LAST NIGHT?
YES, I DO.
I WAS AT THE MAYOR'S GALA --WITH THE CHIEF OF POLICE.
WELL, I GUESS YOUR ASS IS COVERED.
MEN HAVE GONE TO WAR OVER MY ASS, SWEETY.
NOT LATELY.

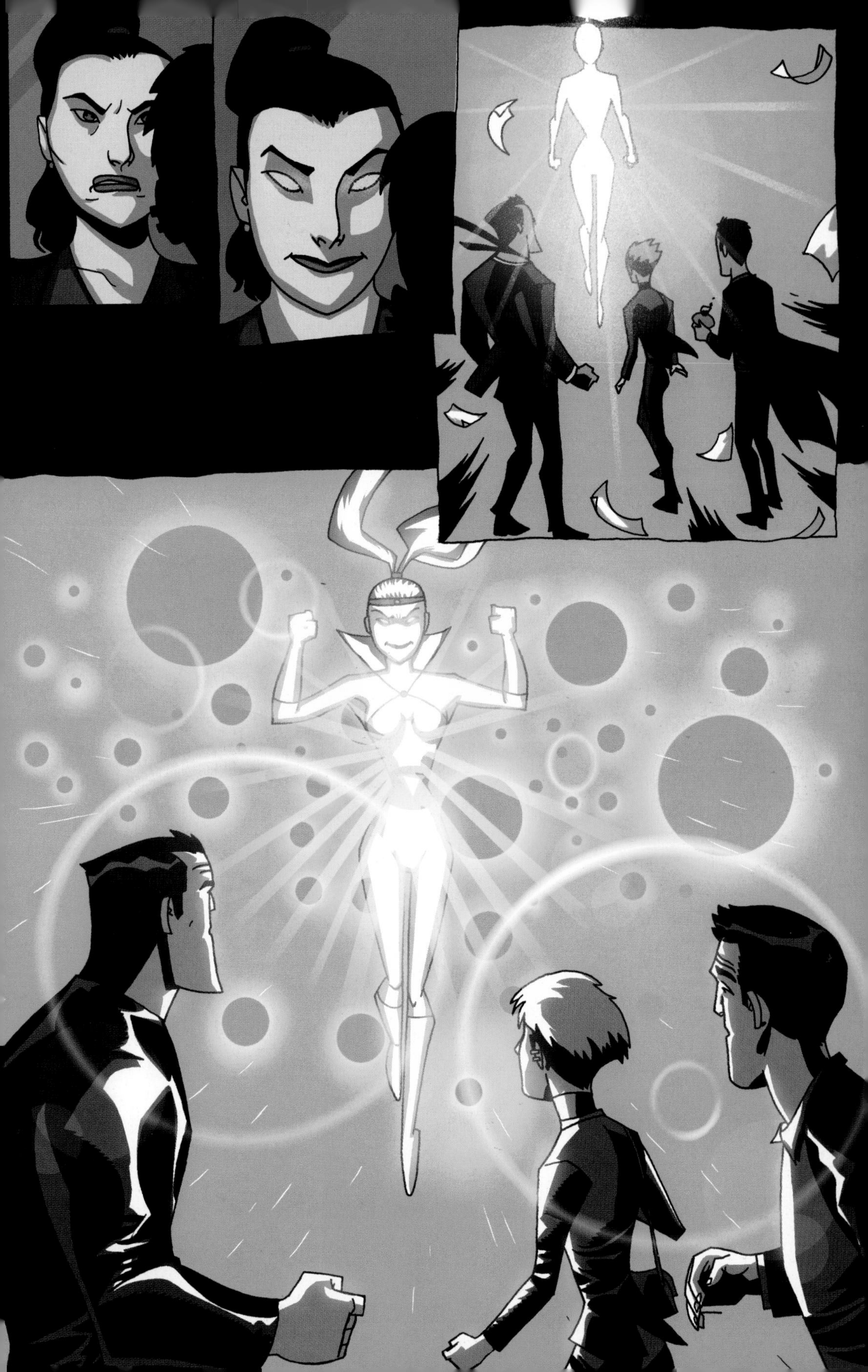

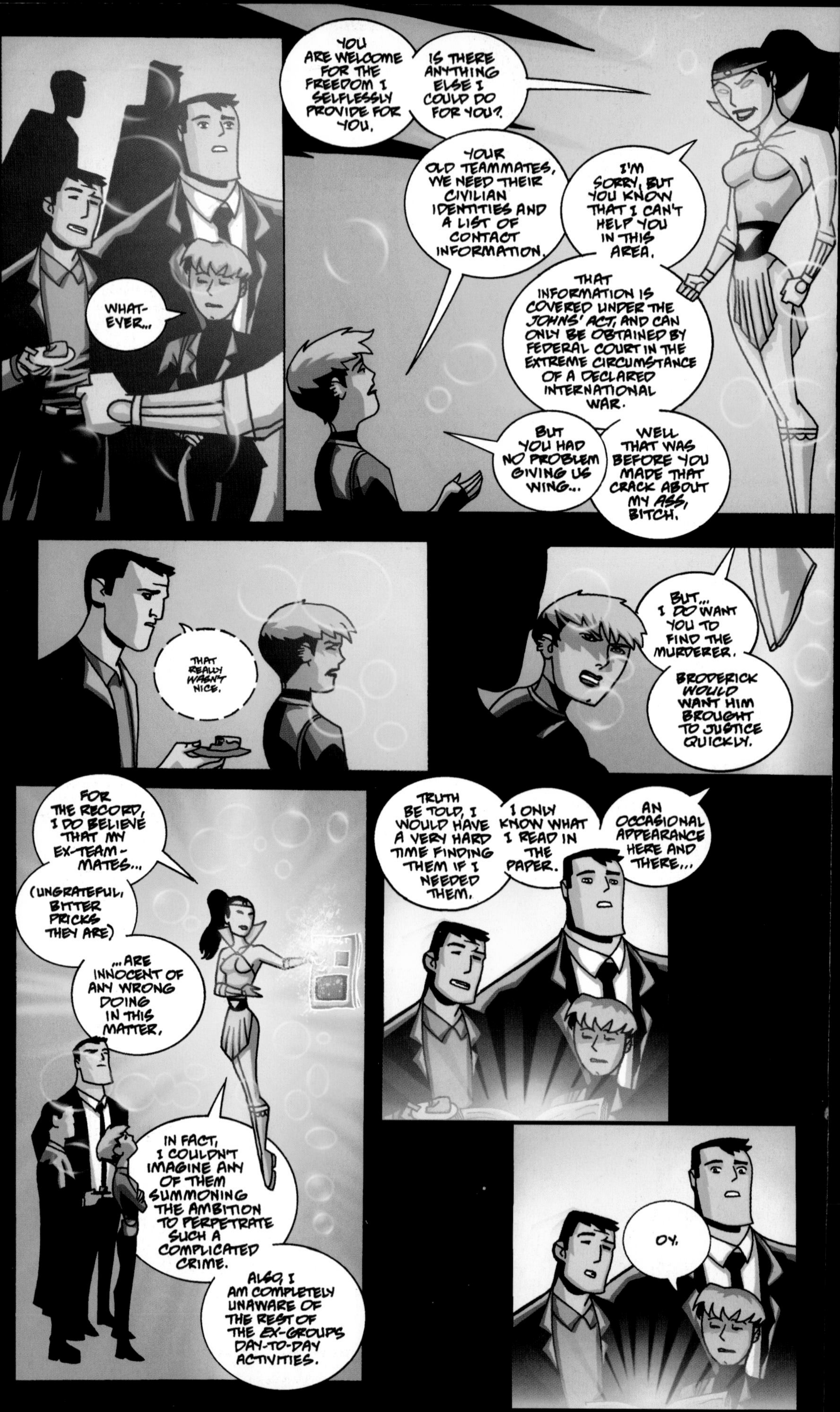
YOU ARE WELCOME FOR THE FREEDOM I SELFLESSLY PROVIDE FOR YOU.
IS THERE ANYTHING ELSE I COULD DO FOR YOU?
WHAT-EVER...
YOUR OLD TEAMMATES, WE NEED THEIR CIVILIAN IDENTITIES AND A LIST OF CONTACT INFORMATION.
I'M SORRY, BUT YOU KNOW THAT I CAN'T HELP YOU IN THIS AREA.
THAT INFORMATION IS COVERED UNDER THE JOHNS' ACT, AND CAN ONLY BE OBTAINED BY FEDERAL COURT IN THE EXTREME CIRCUMSTANCE OF A DECLARED INTERNATIONAL WAR.
BUT YOU HAD NO PROBLEM GIVING US WING...
WELL THAT WAS BEFORE YOU MADE THAT CRACK ABOUT MY ASS, BITCH.
THAT REALLY WASN'T NICE.
BUT... I DO WANT YOU TO FIND THE MURDERER.
BRODERICK WOULD WANT HIM BROUGHT TO JUSTICE QUICKLY.
FOR THE RECORD, I DO BELIEVE THAT MY EX-TEAM-MATES...
(UNGRATEFUL, BITTER PRICKS THEY ARE)
...ARE INNOCENT OF ANY WRONG DOING IN THIS MATTER.
IN FACT, I COULDN'T IMAGINE ANY OF THEM SUMMONING THE AMBITION TO PERPETRATE SUCH A COMPLICATED CRIME.
ALSO, I AM COMPLETELY UNAWARE OF THE REST OF THE EX-GROUP'S DAY-TO-DAY ACTIVITIES.
TRUTH BE TOLD, I WOULD HAVE A VERY HARD TIME FINDING THEM IF I NEEDED THEM.
I ONLY KNOW WHAT I READ IN THE PAPER.
AN OCCASIONAL APPEARANCE HERE AND THERE...
OY.

P!online!

Dateline: The Big Apple

SAFE SOPHISTICATED SENSUAL BLONDES FUN HOT EXCITING ROMANTIC BRUNETTES STIMULATING AFFORDABLE DISCREET SATISFYING REDHEADS

We do it all for you—where, when, and how you like it.

Rentadate.com

Get Our Free Newsletter > search go

▪HOME ▪NEWS ▪GOSSIP ▪REVIEWS ▪CELEBS ▪CHAT

GOSSIP CONTENTS

- Under The Cape
- Costume Closet
- Ask Alisa
- Two Mikes Talkin'

POWERS NEWS

FIRST LOOK: X-ray vision vs. Miranda

Mighty M'Timbu injured in Labonza

Dow flies high on Powers, Inc. trading

Luxuriant leather & silk cowls for Xmas

FRESH FACES

New Book Reviews: FirePower: *Memoirs of the late British hero, Neville "Firefly" Newton*

Ted's Tasty Tidbits: *The strangest, silliest, sexiest, and stupidest Powers stories in the news this week*

Bionic Bettie: *Prescription-only sexual surrogate stimulates gay and feminist backlash*

Powers:The Musical: *Casting begins for extremely well-endowed m/f dancers and singers*

THE HIT LIST

Today's Best Bets:

- Nick Neutron's *Powerman* still #1
- *U.N.C.L.E.* redux
- Ice-P starts filming *Gutshot* in Moscow

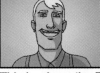

Ted Robinson's Under The Cape

This is where the Dirty Dish gets dumped

Catch Ted Robinson on *P! News Live*
Tuesdays at 4:30 p.m. PT and
Sundays at 2:30 a.m and 7 p.m. PT

Love in the Afternoon

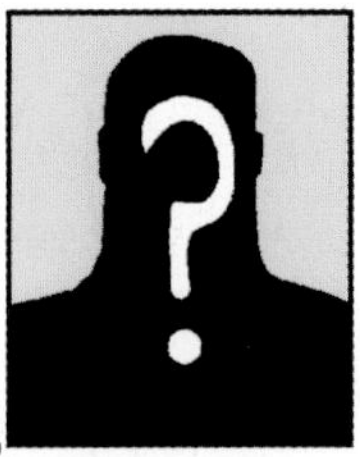

A certain Dark Avenger from across the waters somehow linked up with one of his biggest fans on none other than the information super-highway. It seems many of these online communications got quite hot, quite heavy, and very much into the hands of the woman's unsuspecting husband at home.

After reading the explicit cyber-escapades between his cheatin' wife and the bigger-than-life cowl-and-cape, the husband decided to strike back by publishing the transcripts on the message board of the Dark Avenger's very own home page.

Sure, it wasn't up for long, but one thing about the Internet is that things tend to float around on it for quite a long time.

After reading through the steamy transcript, all I can tell you is that our Dark Avenger is certainly not the world's greatest one-handed typist.

Fond Memories of ... Whom?

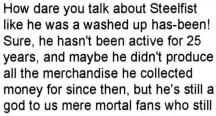

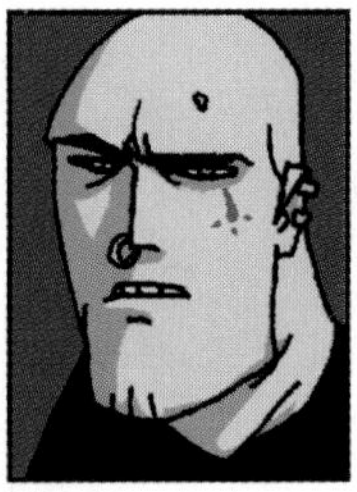

Dear Ted:

How dare you talk about Steelfist like he was a washed up has-been! Sure, he hasn't been active for 25 years, and maybe he didn't produce all the merchandise he collected money for since then, but he's still a god to us mere mortal fans who still

more Ted >

▪help ▪about P! Online ▪site map ▪membership ▪newsletter

tonight on P

Powers' Plastic Surgeon: Nips, tucks and big, big bucks! A P! 2-hour Exclusive, Starting at 8 p.m.

Faster Than a Speeding Bullet?
We can help.
Call 1-800-PROLONG

Eat Lots, Lose Weight, Get Babes!
GUARANTEED SAFE, SURE AND EASY.
CALL TONY AT EATWELL.COM/EASY

POWERS pics pay BIG bucks! Send us yours now! Confidential, and in cash. P!Online.net Click on job search.

next week:

Whip me, beat me, show me your Powers. Kinks and Crimefighters go fist in gauntlet, so to speak. We'll show you the public court records and the hidden police files, plus Whiz Kid's private, personal video diary. Tune in tomorrow.

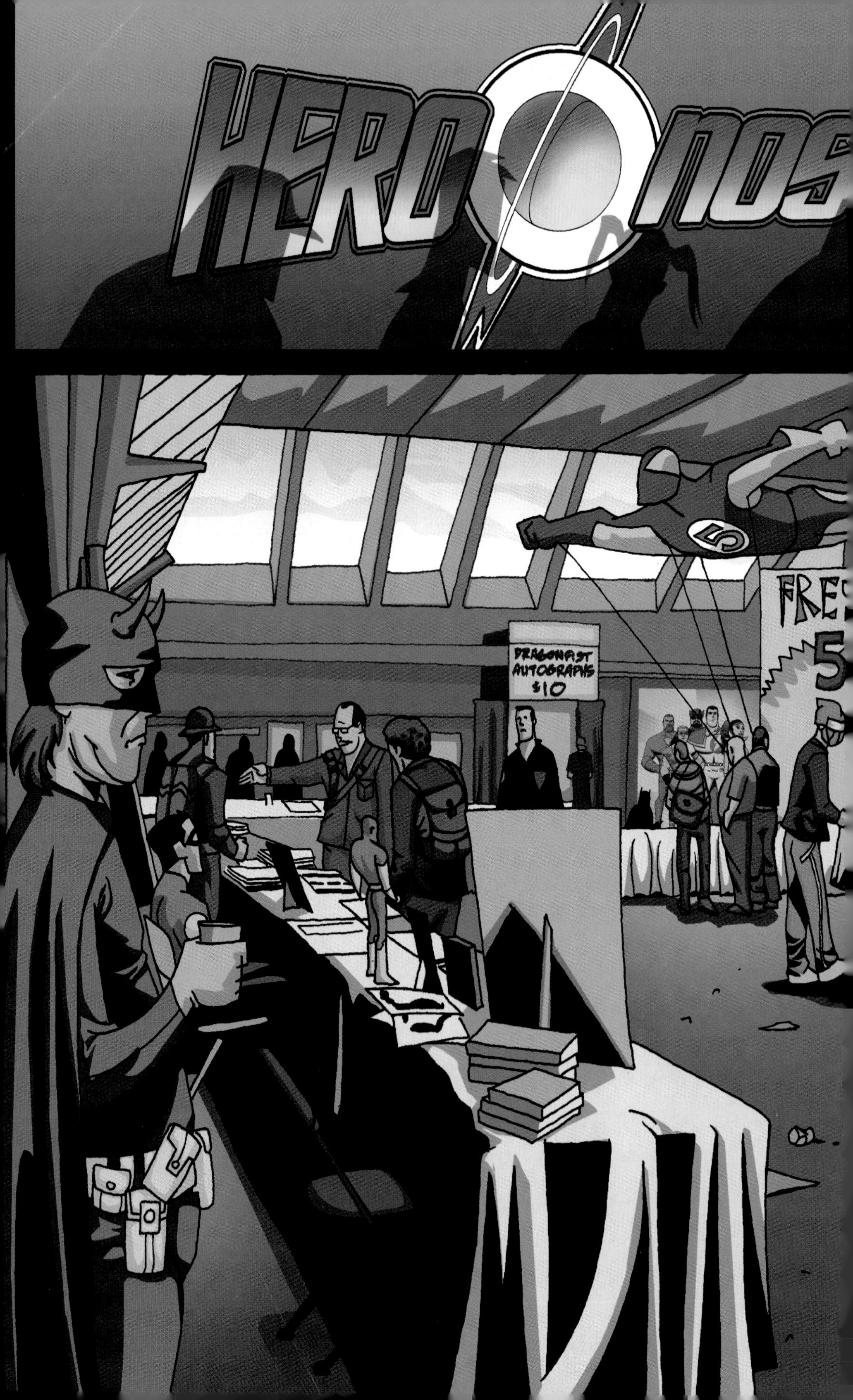
HERO
DRAGONFIST AUTOGRAPHS $10

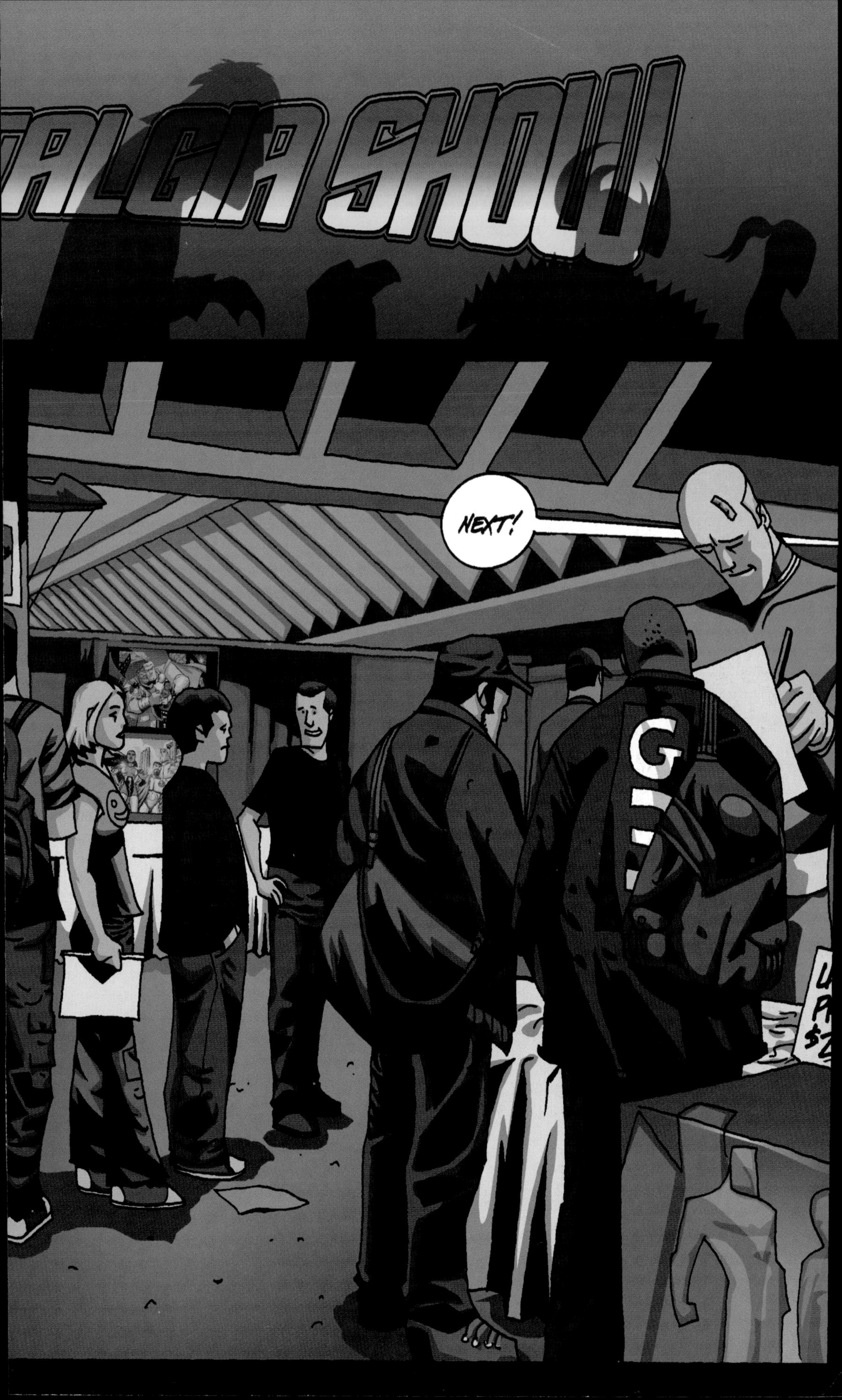
NEXT!

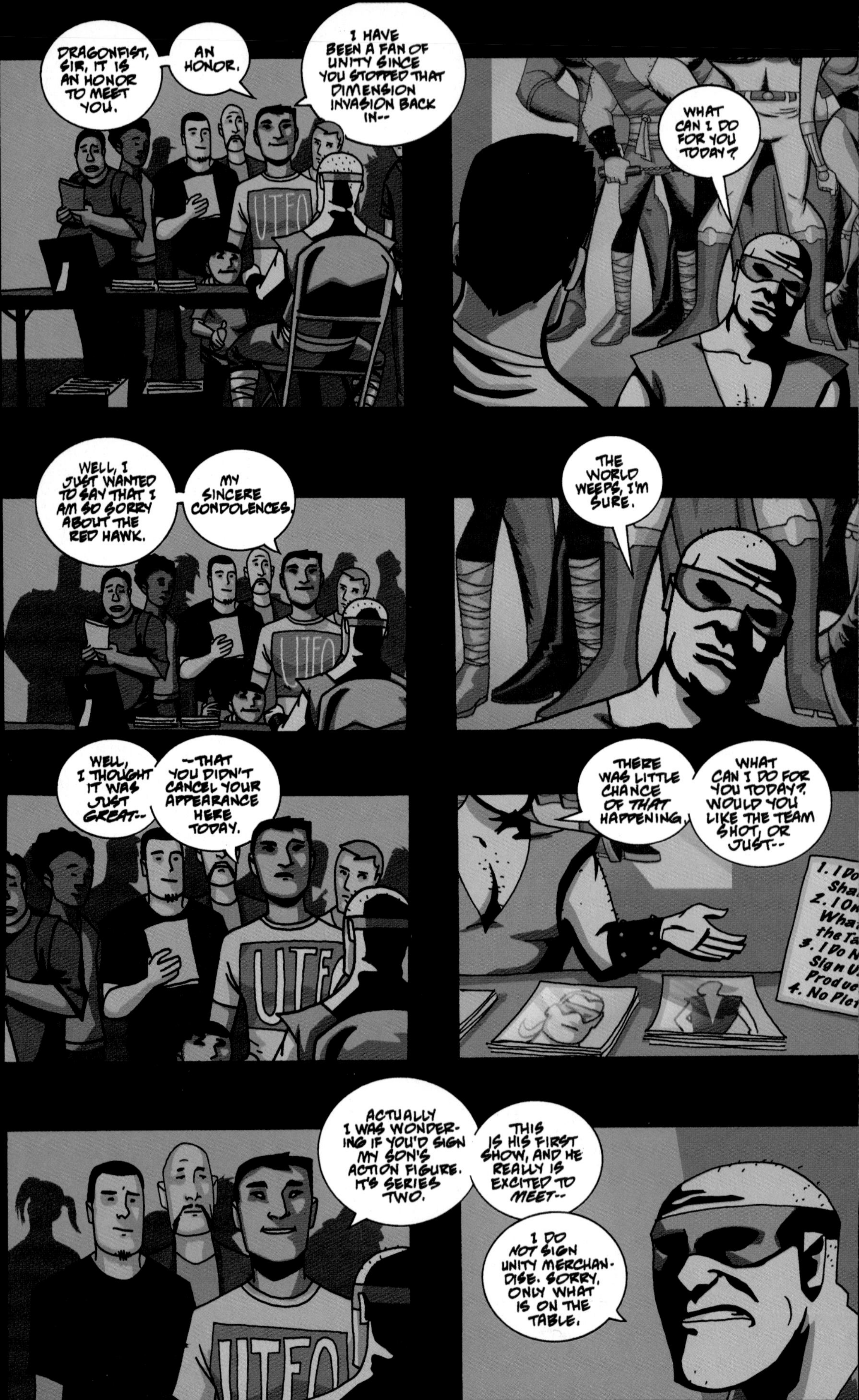
DRAGONFIST, SIR, IT IS AN HONOR TO MEET YOU.
AN HONOR.
I HAVE BEEN A FAN OF UNITY SINCE YOU STOPPED THAT DIMENSION INVASION BACK IN--
WHAT CAN I DO FOR YOU TODAY?
WELL, I JUST WANTED TO SAY THAT I AM SO SORRY ABOUT THE RED HAWK.
MY SINCERE CONDOLENCES.
THE WORLD WEEPS, I'M SURE.
WELL, I THOUGHT IT WAS JUST GREAT--
--THAT YOU DIDN'T CANCEL YOUR APPEARANCE HERE TODAY.
THERE WAS LITTLE CHANCE OF THAT HAPPENING.
WHAT CAN I DO FOR YOU TODAY? WOULD YOU LIKE THE TEAM SHOT, OR JUST--
ACTUALLY I WAS WONDERING IF YOU'D SIGN MY SON'S ACTION FIGURE. IT'S SERIES TWO.
THIS IS HIS FIRST SHOW, AND HE REALLY IS EXCITED TO MEET--
I DO NOT SIGN UNITY MERCHANDISE. SORRY, ONLY WHAT IS ON THE TABLE.

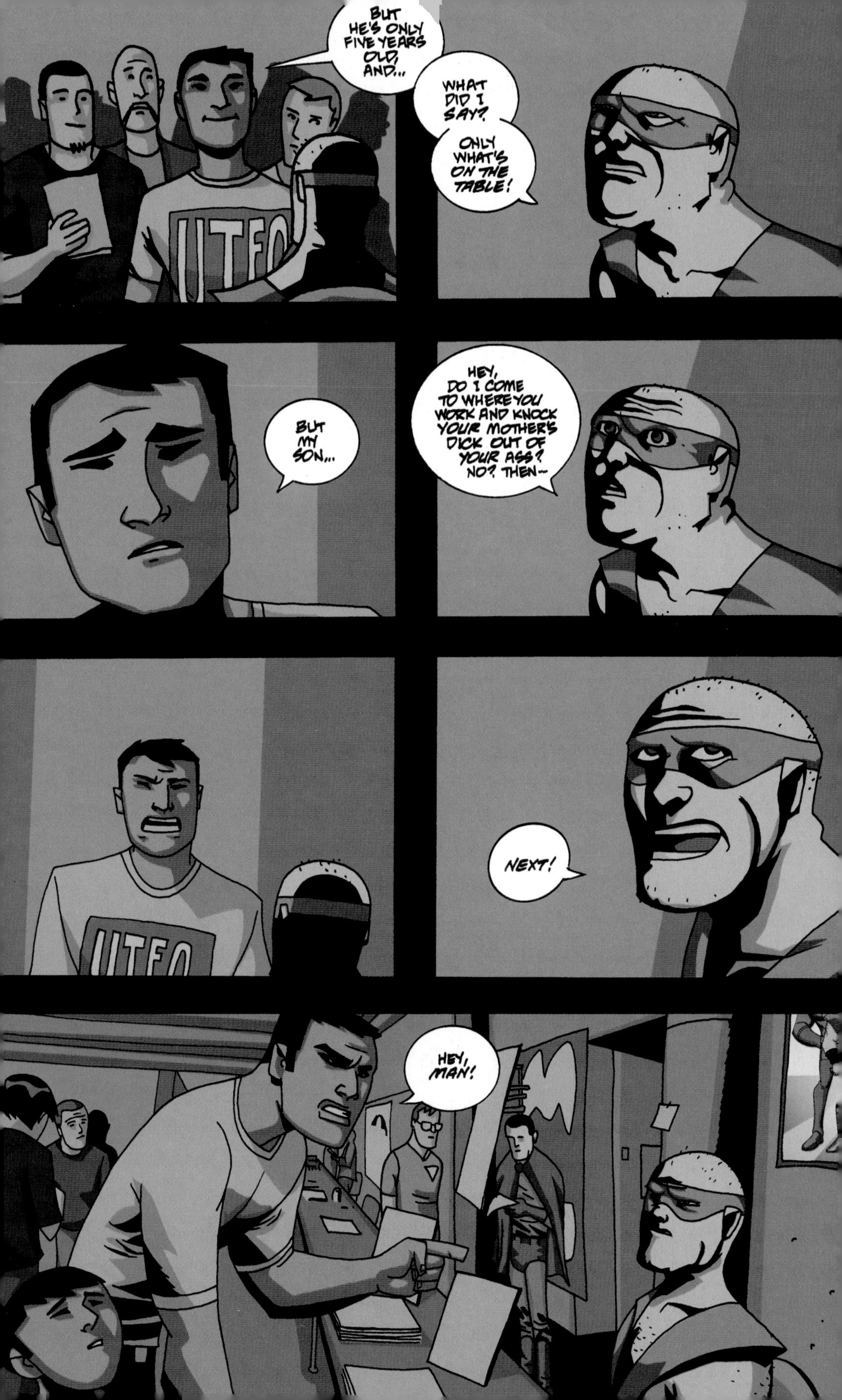

BUT HE'S ONLY FIVE YEARS OLD, AND...
UTFO
WHAT DID I SAY?
ONLY WHAT'S ON THE TABLE!
BUT MY SON...
HEY, DO I COME TO WHERE YOU WORK AND KNOCK YOUR MOTHER'S DICK OUT OF YOUR ASS? NO? THEN--
UTFO
NEXT!
HEY, MAN!

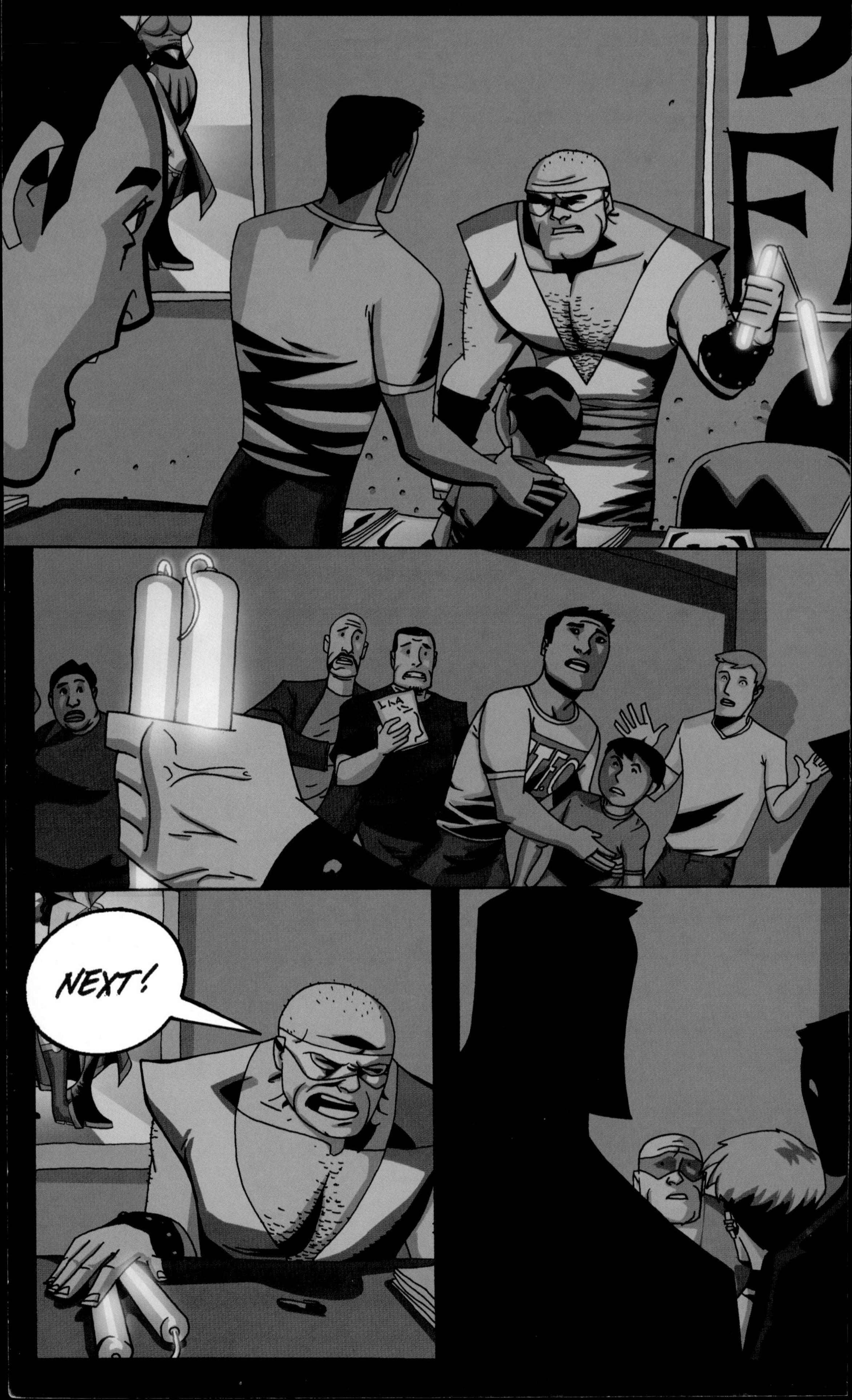
NEXT!

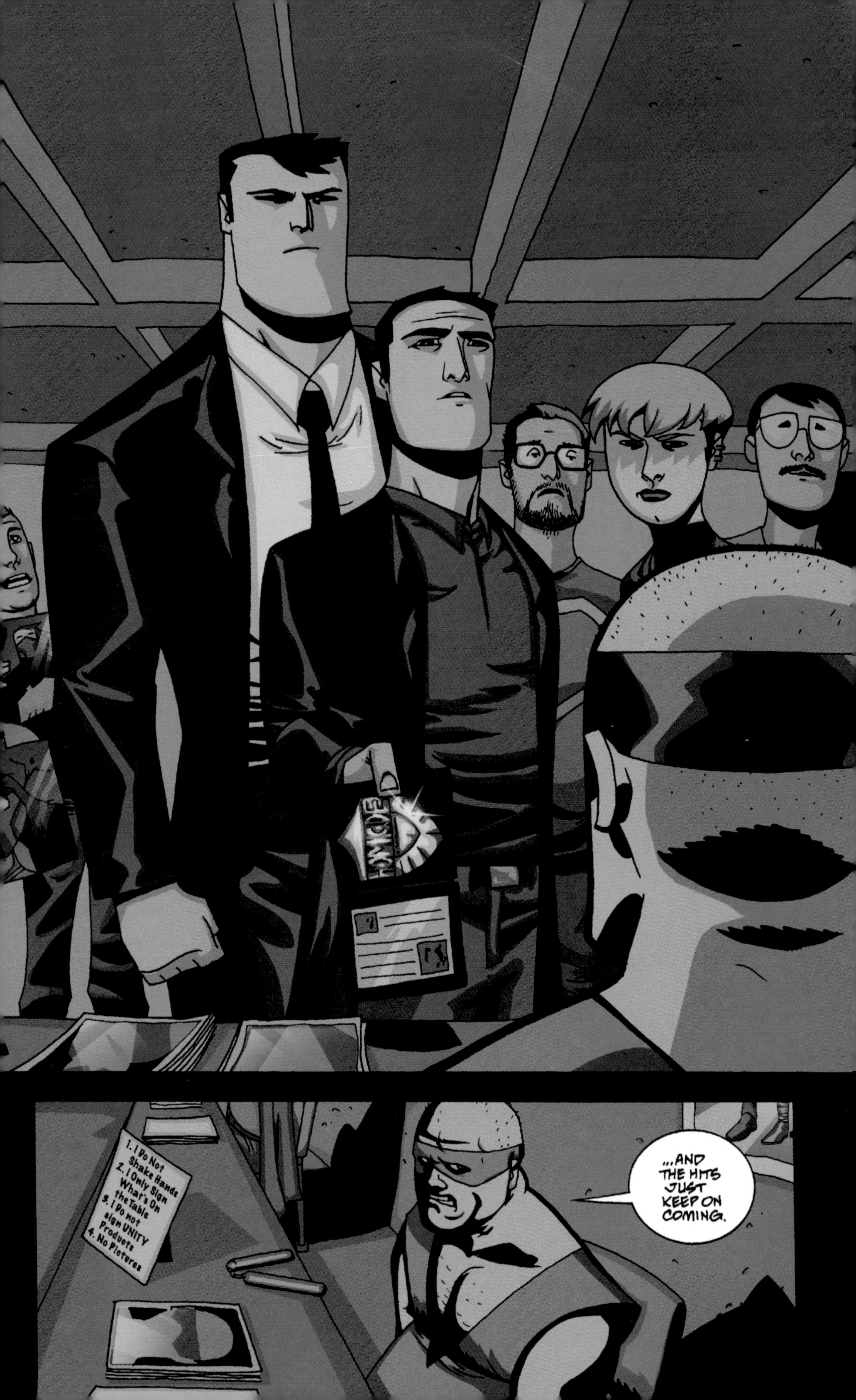
1. I Do Not Shake Hands
2. I Only Sign What's On the Table
3. I Do not sign UNITY Products
4. No Pictures
...AND THE HITS JUST KEEP ON COMING.

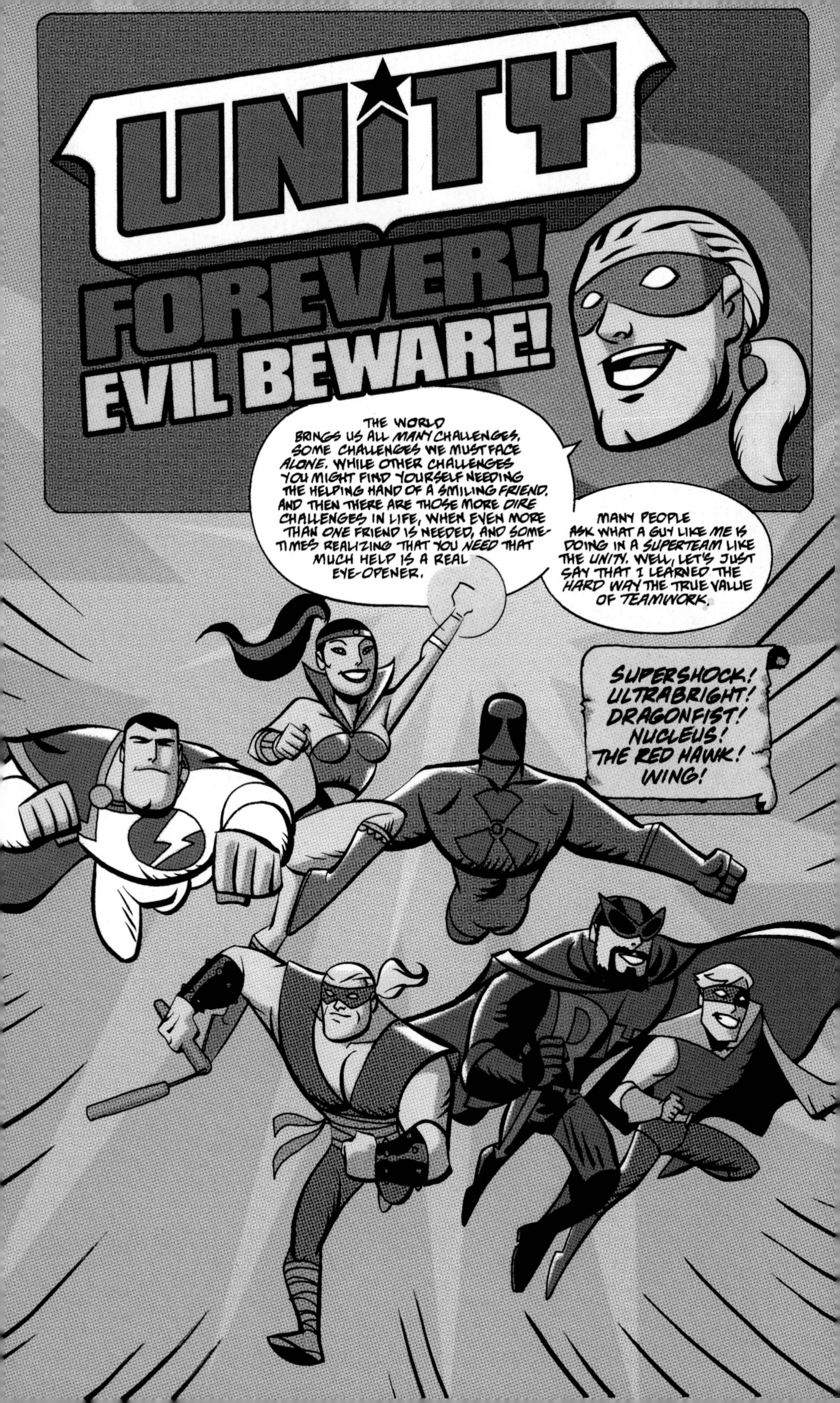
UNITY
FOREVER!
EVIL BEWARE!
THE WORLD BRINGS US ALL MANY CHALLENGES. SOME CHALLENGES WE MUST FACE ALONE. WHILE OTHER CHALLENGES YOU MIGHT FIND YOURSELF NEEDING THE HELPING HAND OF A SMILING FRIEND. AND THEN THERE ARE THOSE MORE DIRE CHALLENGES IN LIFE, WHEN EVEN MORE THAN ONE FRIEND IS NEEDED, AND SOMETIMES REALIZING THAT YOU NEED THAT MUCH HELP IS A REAL EYE-OPENER.
MANY PEOPLE ASK WHAT A GUY LIKE ME IS DOING IN A SUPERTEAM LIKE THE UNITY. WELL, LET'S JUST SAY THAT I LEARNED THE HARD WAY THE TRUE VALUE OF TEAMWORK.
SUPERSHOCK! ULTRABRIGHT! DRAGONFIST! NUCLEUS! THE RED HAWK! WING!

UNITY HALL, MANHATTAN.

THE REGULAR UNITY ROLL CALL MEETING STARTS EVEN THOUGH ONE OF ITS COLORFUL MEMBERS IS MISSING.

WELL, EVERYONE IS HERE BUT DRAGON-FIST, SO I GUESS WE WILL HAVE TO ASSUME THAT HE IS KNEE-DEEP IN ONE OF HIS OWN CASES.

OK, SO WHAT'S THE FIRST ORDER OF UNITY BUSINESS?

ACTUALLY, THAT WOULD BE ME, YOU STUCK UP PIECE OF SHIT!

FIRST POINT OF ORDER IS YOU CAN TAKE THIS SHIT TEAM AND SHOVE IT UP YOUR TEENY, TINY DICKHOLE!

WHAT !?!!

THIS IS AN OUTRAGE!

SIT DOWN, ULTRADYKE.

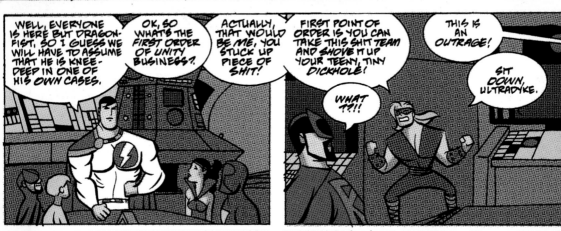

I AM SICK OF ALL OF THIS!! ALL OF YOU AND ALL OF THIS!

ARE YOU RESIGNING FROM UNITY?

YOU CAN'T BE SERIOUS.

OH, I'M SERIOUS.

CAN I ASK WHY?

THIS ENTIRE TEAM--THIS-- IT'S ALL GOTTEN OUT OF HAND.

WHO CHOSE US TO BE THE VOICE OF A GENERATION?

EVERYWHERE I GO, PEOPLE ARE TALKING ABOUT US LIKE WE'RE RELIGIOUS FIGURES OR SOMETHING.

OR, WORSE, THEY TALK ABOUT US LIKE WE'RE FUCKIN' CARTOON CHARACTERS!!

I'M SICK OF IT, AND TRUTH BE TOLD, I AM MORE THAN SICK OF YOU GUYS!!

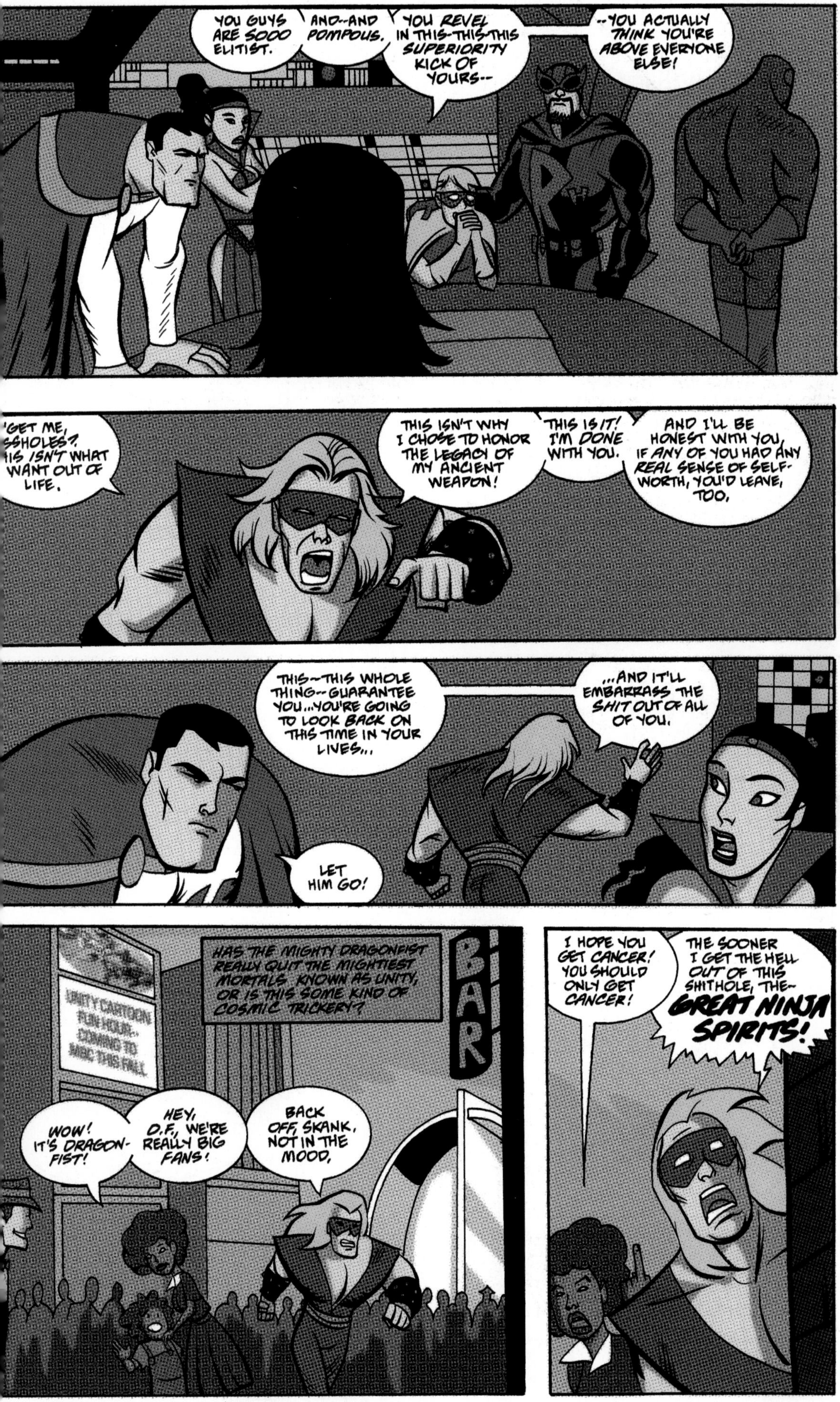

YOU GUYS ARE SOOO ELITIST.
AND--AND POMPOUS.
YOU REVEL IN THIS-THIS-THIS SUPERIORITY KICK OF YOURS--
--YOU ACTUALLY THINK YOU'RE ABOVE EVERYONE ELSE!
'GET ME, SSHOLES? HIS ISN'T WHAT WANT OUT OF LIFE.
THIS ISN'T WHY I CHOSE TO HONOR THE LEGACY OF MY ANCIENT WEAPON!
THIS IS IT! I'M DONE WITH YOU.
AND I'LL BE HONEST WITH YOU, IF ANY OF YOU HAD ANY REAL SENSE OF SELF-WORTH, YOU'D LEAVE, TOO.
THIS--THIS WHOLE THING--GUARANTEE YOU...YOU'RE GOING TO LOOK BACK ON THIS TIME IN YOUR LIVES...
...AND IT'LL EMBARRASS THE SHIT OUT OF ALL OF YOU.
LET HIM GO!
HAS THE MIGHTY DRAGONFIST REALLY QUIT THE MIGHTIEST MORTALS KNOWN AS UNITY, OR IS THIS SOME KIND OF COSMIC TRICKERY?
UNITY CARTOON FUN HOUR-- COMING TO MBC THIS FALL
BAR
WOW! IT'S DRAGON-FIST!
HEY, D.F., WE'RE REALLY BIG FANS!
BACK OFF, SKANK, NOT IN THE MOOD.
I HOPE YOU GET CANCER! YOU SHOULD ONLY GET CANCER!
THE SOONER I GET THE HELL OUT OF THIS SHITHOLE, THE--
GREAT NINJA SPIRITS!

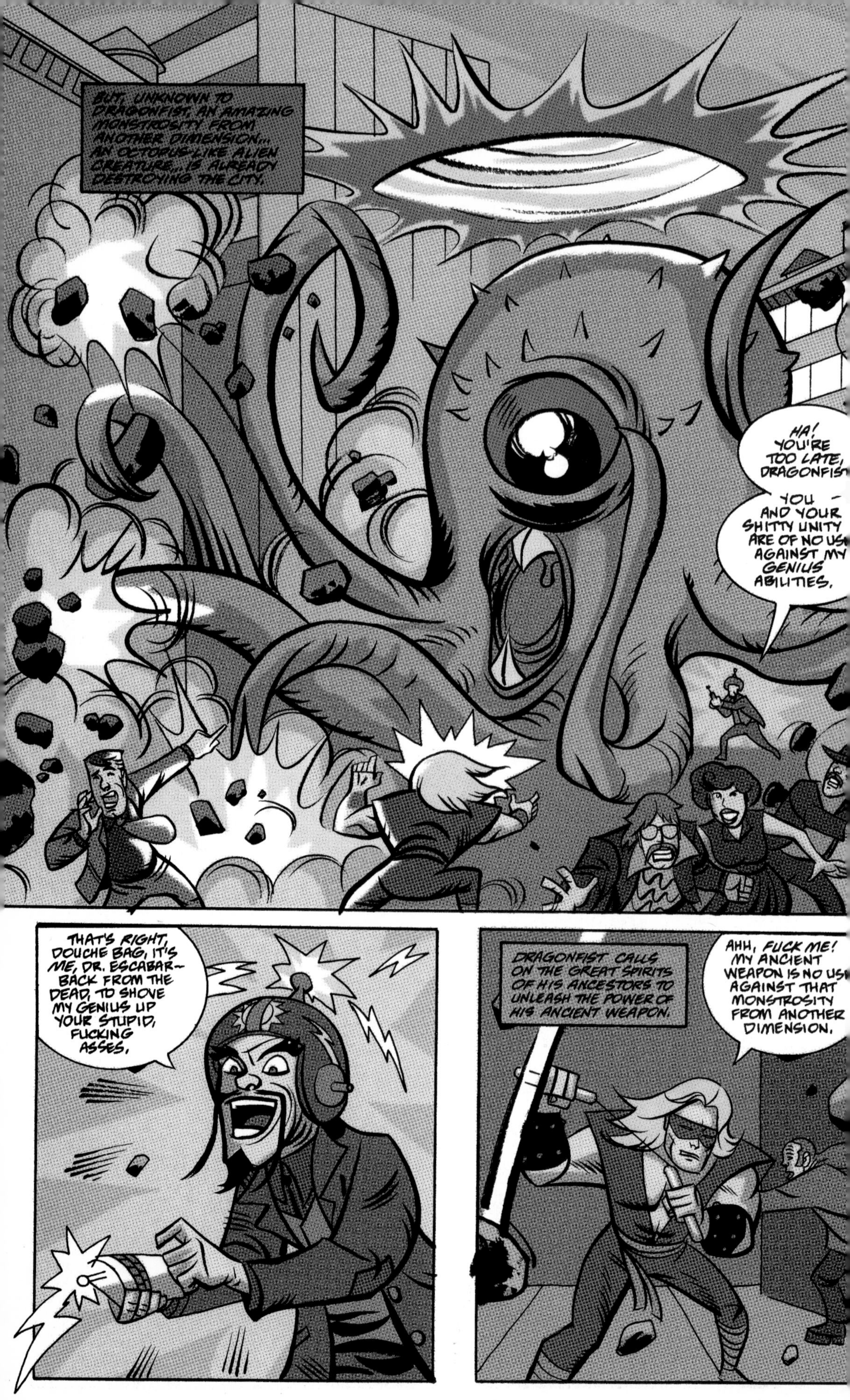
BUT, UNKNOWN TO DRAGONFIST, AN AMAZING MONSTROSITY FROM ANOTHER DIMENSION... AN OCTOPUS-LIKE ALIEN CREATURE... IS ALREADY DESTROYING THE CITY.
HA! YOU'RE TOO LATE, DRAGONFIS
YOU AND YOUR SHITTY UNITY ARE OF NO US AGAINST MY GENIUS ABILITIES.
THAT'S RIGHT, DOUCHE BAG, IT'S ME, DR. ESCABAR-- BACK FROM THE DEAD, TO SHOVE MY GENIUS UP YOUR STUPID, FUCKING ASSES.
DRAGONFIST CALLS ON THE GREAT SPIRITS OF HIS ANCESTORS TO UNLEASH THE POWER OF HIS ANCIENT WEAPON.
AHH, FUCK ME! MY ANCIENT WEAPON IS NO US AGAINST THAT MONSTROSITY FROM ANOTHER DIMENSION.

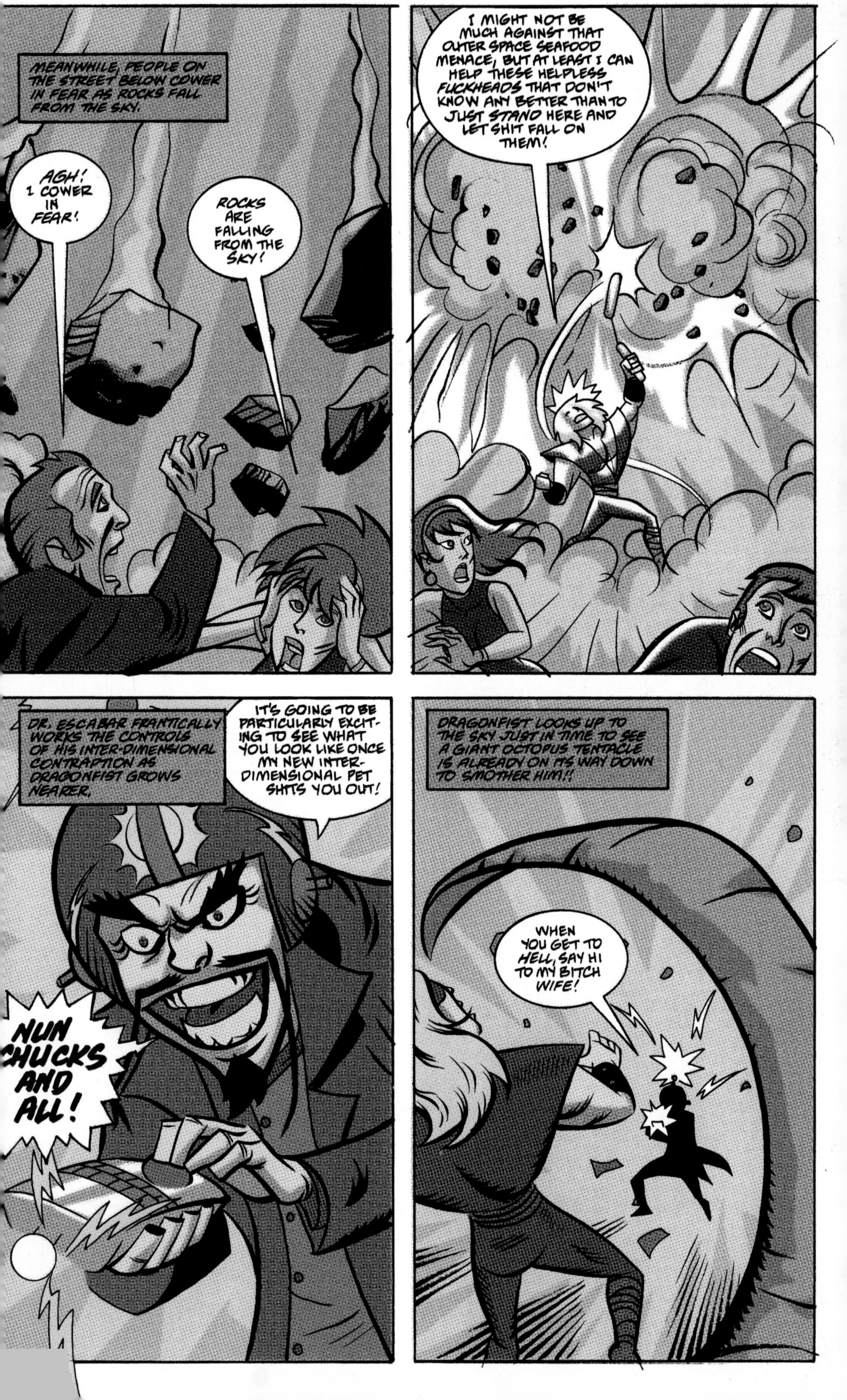
MEANWHILE, PEOPLE ON THE STREET BELOW COWER IN FEAR AS ROCKS FALL FROM THE SKY.
AGH! I COWER IN FEAR!
ROCKS ARE FALLING FROM THE SKY!
I MIGHT NOT BE MUCH AGAINST THAT OUTER SPACE SEAFOOD MENACE, BUT AT LEAST I CAN HELP THESE HELPLESS FUCKHEADS THAT DON'T KNOW ANY BETTER THAN TO JUST STAND HERE AND LET SHIT FALL ON THEM!
DR. ESCABAR FRANTICALLY WORKS THE CONTROLS OF HIS INTER-DIMENSIONAL CONTRAPTION AS DRAGONFIST GROWS NEARER.
IT'S GOING TO BE PARTICULARLY EXCITING TO SEE WHAT YOU LOOK LIKE ONCE MY NEW INTER-DIMENSIONAL PET SHITS YOU OUT!
NUN CHUCKS AND ALL!
DRAGONFIST LOOKS UP TO THE SKY JUST IN TIME TO SEE A GIANT OCTOPUS TENTACLE IS ALREADY ON ITS WAY DOWN TO SMOTHER HIM!!
WHEN YOU GET TO HELL, SAY HI TO MY BITCH WIFE!

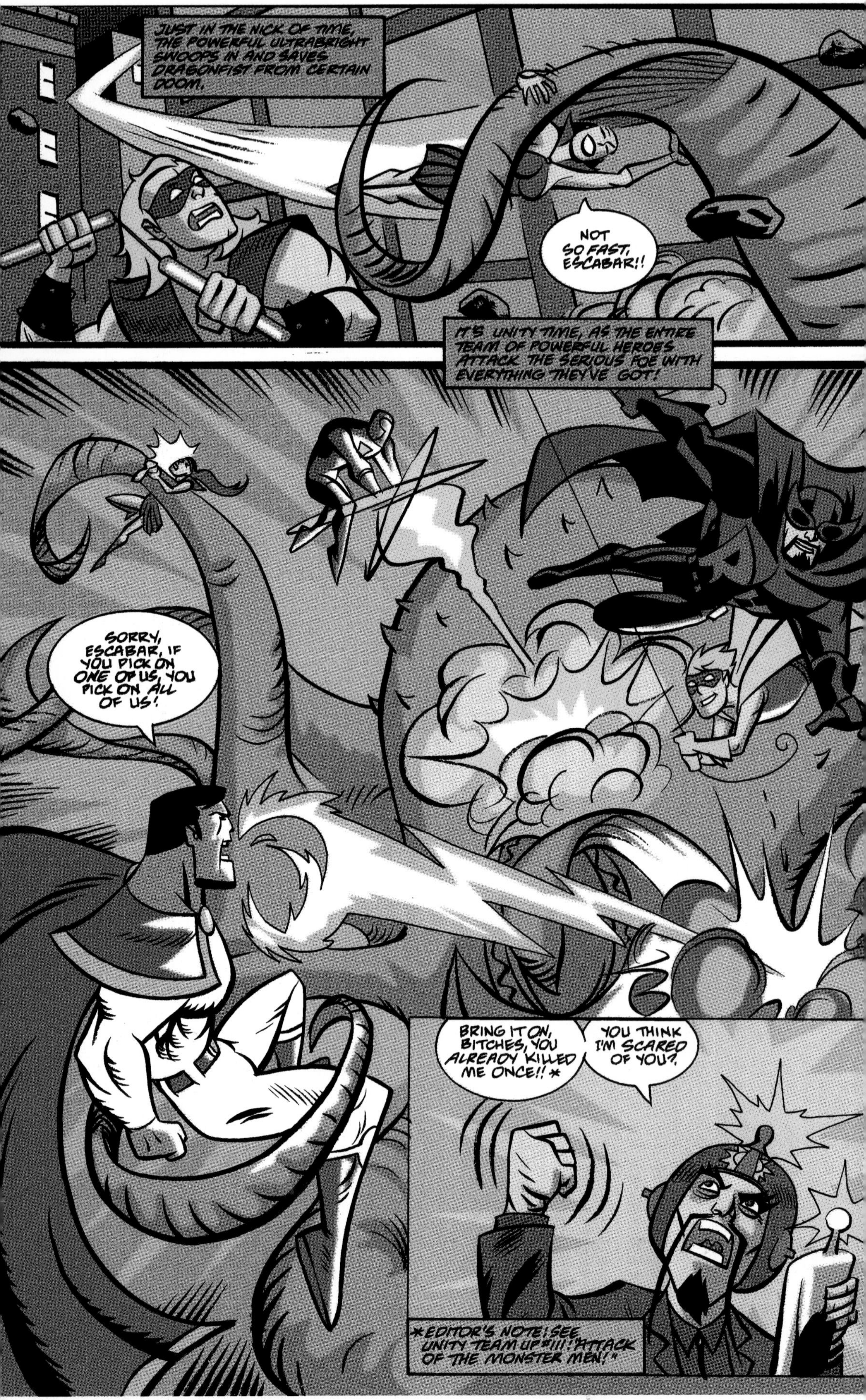
JUST IN THE NICK OF TIME, THE POWERFUL ULTRABRIGHT SWOOPS IN AND SAVES DRAGONFIST FROM CERTAIN DOOM.
NOT SO FAST, ESCABAR!!
IT'S UNITY TIME, AS THE ENTIRE TEAM OF POWERFUL HEROES ATTACK THE SERIOUS FOE WITH EVERYTHING THEY'VE GOT!
SORRY, ESCABAR, IF YOU PICK ON ONE OF US, YOU PICK ON ALL OF US!
BRING IT ON, BITCHES, YOU ALREADY KILLED ME ONCE!! *
YOU THINK I'M SCARED OF YOU?
*EDITOR'S NOTE: SEE UNITY TEAM UP #111! "ATTACK OF THE MONSTER MEN!"

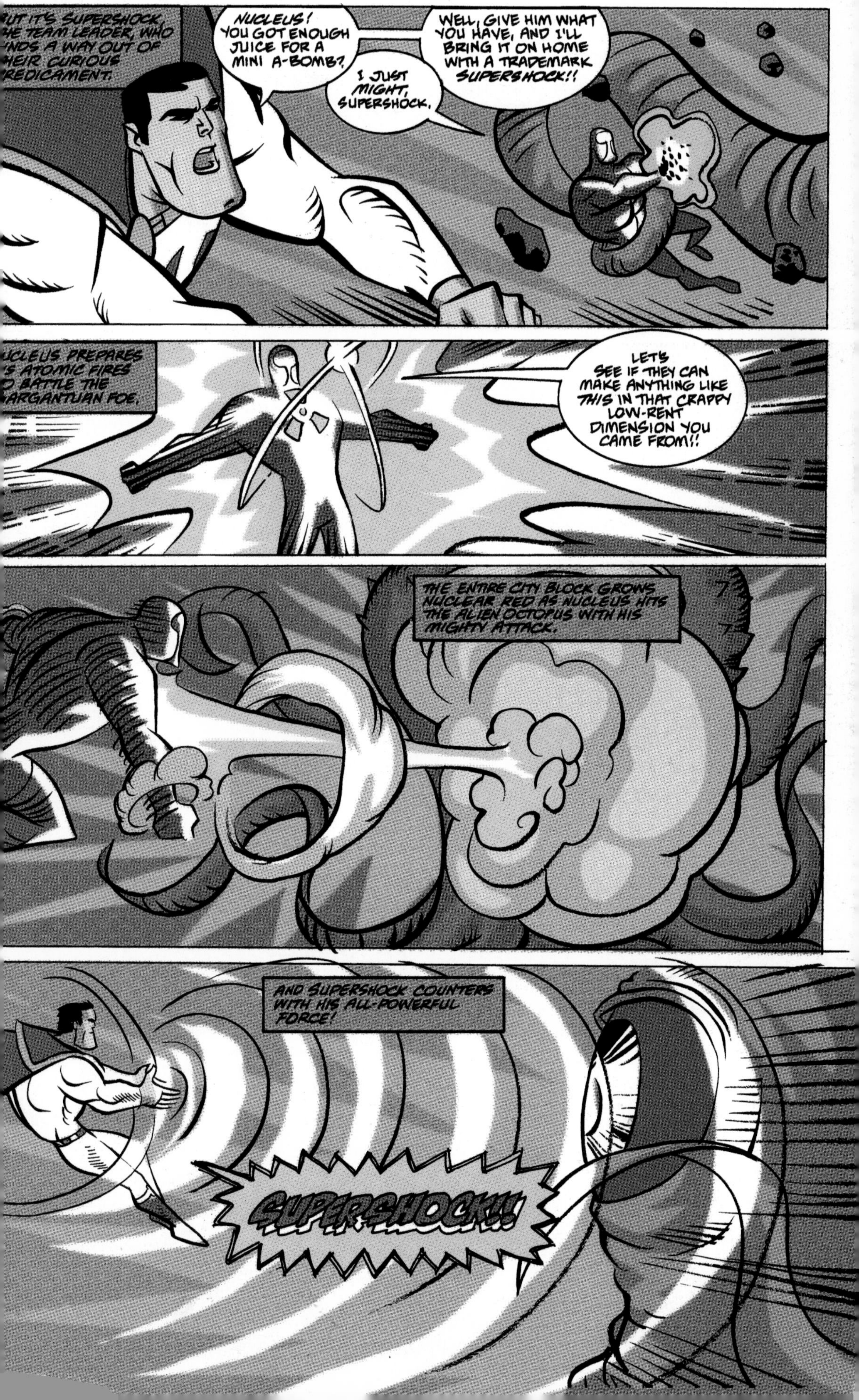
UT IT'S SUPERSHOCK, HE TEAM LEADER, WHO INDS A WAY OUT OF HEIR CURIOUS PREDICAMENT.
NUCLEUS! YOU GOT ENOUGH JUICE FOR A MINI A-BOMB?
I JUST MIGHT, SUPERSHOCK.
WELL, GIVE HIM WHAT YOU HAVE, AND I'LL BRING IT ON HOME WITH A TRADEMARK SUPERSHOCK!!
UCLEUS PREPARES S ATOMIC FIRES O BATTLE THE ARGANTUAN FOE.
LET'S SEE IF THEY CAN MAKE ANYTHING LIKE THIS IN THAT CRAPPY LOW-RENT DIMENSION YOU CAME FROM!!
THE ENTIRE CITY BLOCK GROWS NUCLEAR RED AS NUCLEUS HITS THE ALIEN OCTOPUS WITH HIS MIGHTY ATTACK.
AND SUPERSHOCK COUNTERS WITH HIS ALL-POWERFUL FORCE!
SUPERSHOCK!!

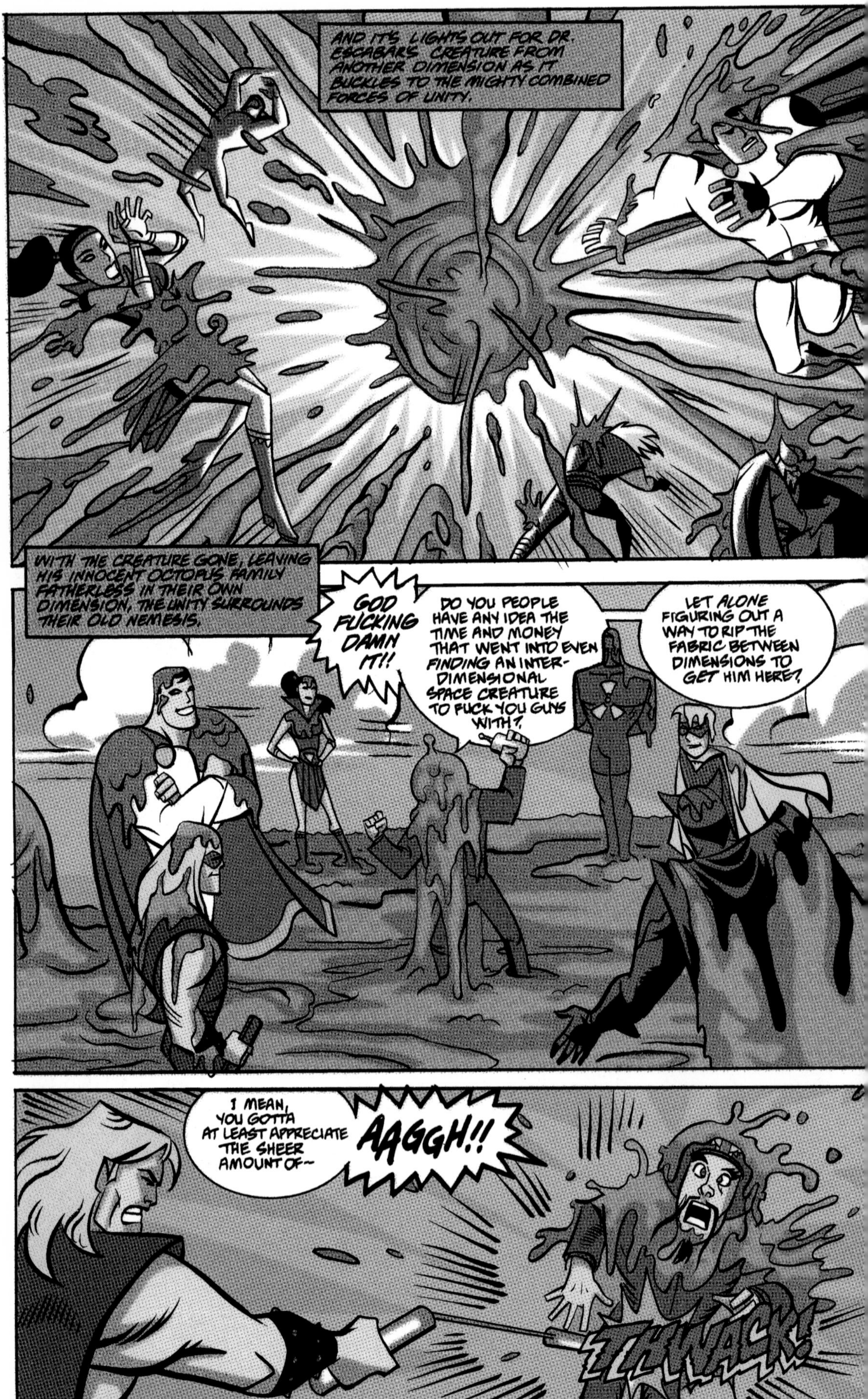
AND IT'S LIGHTS OUT FOR DR. ESCABAR'S CREATURE FROM ANOTHER DIMENSION AS IT BUCKLES TO THE MIGHTY COMBINED FORCES OF UNITY.
WITH THE CREATURE GONE, LEAVING HIS INNOCENT OCTOPUS FAMILY FATHERLESS IN THEIR OWN DIMENSION, THE UNITY SURROUNDS THEIR OLD NEMESIS.
GOD FUCKING DAMN IT!!
DO YOU PEOPLE HAVE ANY IDEA THE TIME AND MONEY THAT WENT INTO EVEN FINDING AN INTER-DIMENSIONAL SPACE CREATURE TO FUCK YOU GUYS WITH?.
LET ALONE FIGURING OUT A WAY TO RIP THE FABRIC BETWEEN DIMENSIONS TO GET HIM HERE?
I MEAN, YOU GOTTA AT LEAST APPRECIATE THE SHEER AMOUNT OF--
AAGGH!!
THWACK!

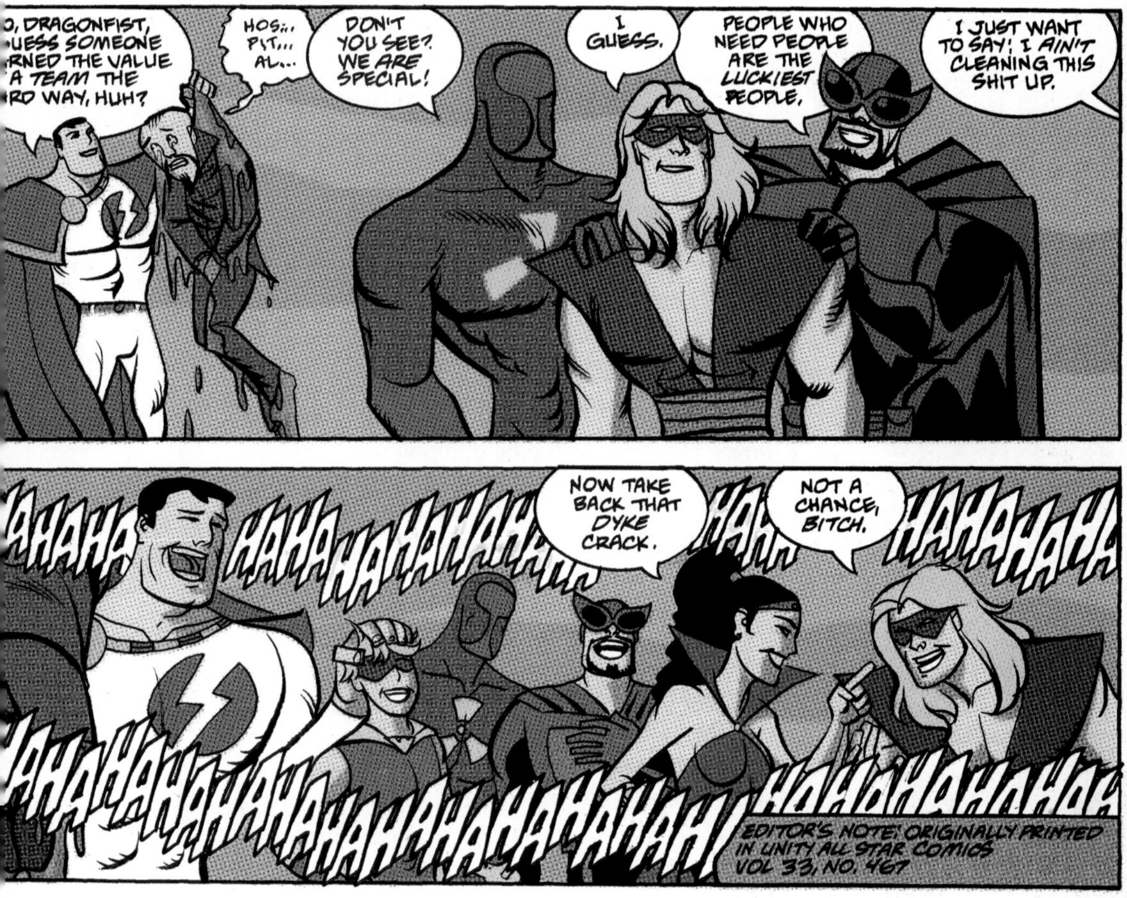
O, DRAGONFIST, UESS SOMEONE RNED THE VALUE A TEAM THE RD WAY, HUH?
HOS... PIT... AL...
DON'T YOU SEE? WE ARE SPECIAL!
I GUESS.
PEOPLE WHO NEED PEOPLE ARE THE LUCKIEST PEOPLE.
I JUST WANT TO SAY: I AIN'T CLEANING THIS SHIT UP.
AHAHA HAHAHAHAHAHAHAH
NOW TAKE BACK THAT DYKE CRACK.
NOT A CHANCE, BITCH.
HAHAHAHA
HAHAHAHAHAHAHAHAHAHAHAHAHAH!
HAHAHAHAHAHAHAH
EDITOR'S NOTE: ORIGINALLY PRINTED IN UNITY ALL STAR COMICS VOL 33, NO. 467

Puzzle BOXES can you find the 6 *Lucky* DUCKS

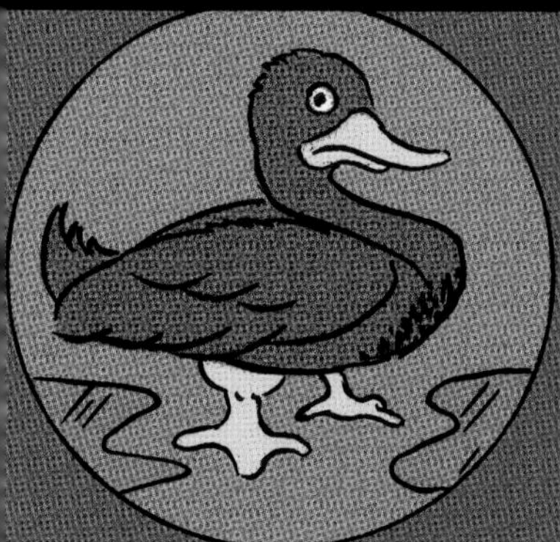

S	H	K	C	U	F
L	T	G	N	D	W
W	S	O	O	R	O
O	H	O	R	A	L
F	I	S	C	K	B
O	T	E	H	E	L

THE NAMES OF (6) LARGE *Lucky Ducks* ARE HIDDEN IN THE BOXES. CAPTURE THE FEATHERED WATER BIRDS BY DRAWING A CONTINUOUS LINE TO CONNECT THE LETTERS OF EACH NAME YOU ARE LOOKING FOR. YOU MAY GO UP OR DOWN, RIGHT OR LEFT, OR CORNER-TO-CORNER. EACH NAME YOU'RE SEEKING BEGINS WITH A WHITE LETTER.

CAN YOU CATCH ALL (6) OF THE *Lucky Ducks* BEFORE THEY FLY SOUTH FOR THE WINTER?

The **Answers** HERON-STORK-FOWL-GOOSE-DRAKE-SWAN

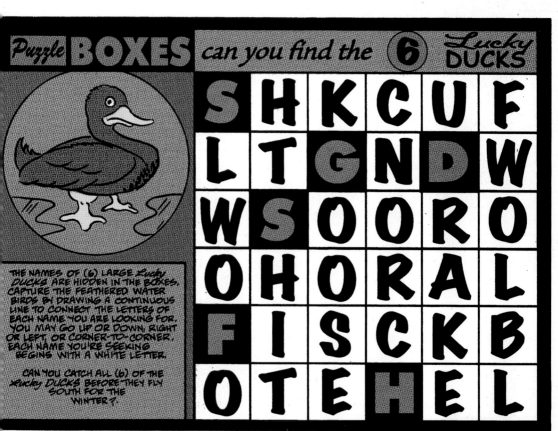

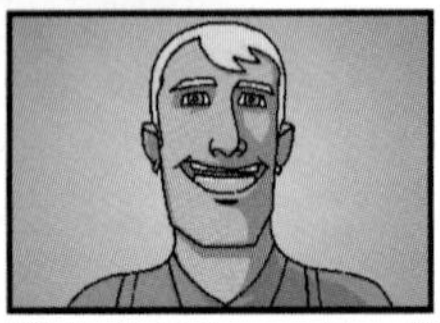

Ted Robinson's Under The Cape

This is where the Dirty Dish gets dumped

Catch Ted Robinson on *P! News Live* Tuesdays at 4:30 p.m. PT and Sundays at 2:30 a.m and 7 p.m. PT

Professing Your Lust

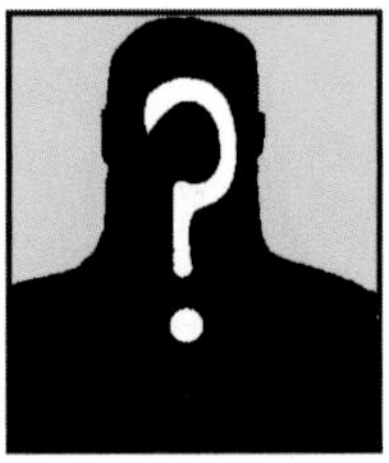

Word around the campfire is, back in the good old days of a high-profile SUPERTEAM, two of the most memorable members were having a not-so-secret super team-up under the sheets.

Well, it was a secret until the fateful day when they decided to go for what the kids call a little "quickie" on one of the expensive super-communication consoles that connect the team headquarters to the capital of every country in the world.

What our two little super-powered paramours didn't know was that during one of their bump-and-grind sessions, they accidentally hit a button sending their screams of passion out "live" to all the heads of state on this planet, and maybe beyond.

According to our sources, the leaders of the world all sat quietly and listened to the sounds of "love in the afternoon" for over forty-five minutes, and the offending couple never knew.

Forty-five minutes? Someone should tell these two the definition of the word "quickie" on this planet.

Pretty-as-a-Picture Powers

Dear Ted:

Have you noticed how Grimlock keeps getting younger and younger in his publicity photos? And when did he get the dog he was petting in *Powers For The People Magazine*? I mean, the Grecian Formula is just too

more Ted >

tonight on
The Chairman's Champion:
Powers in the People's Republic of China
P! Reports; 8-9 p.

next week
We've got the goods:
The Sting and Sparkle's hot honeymoon pic and a scoop on who else was in the bridal chamber...what the butler saw!

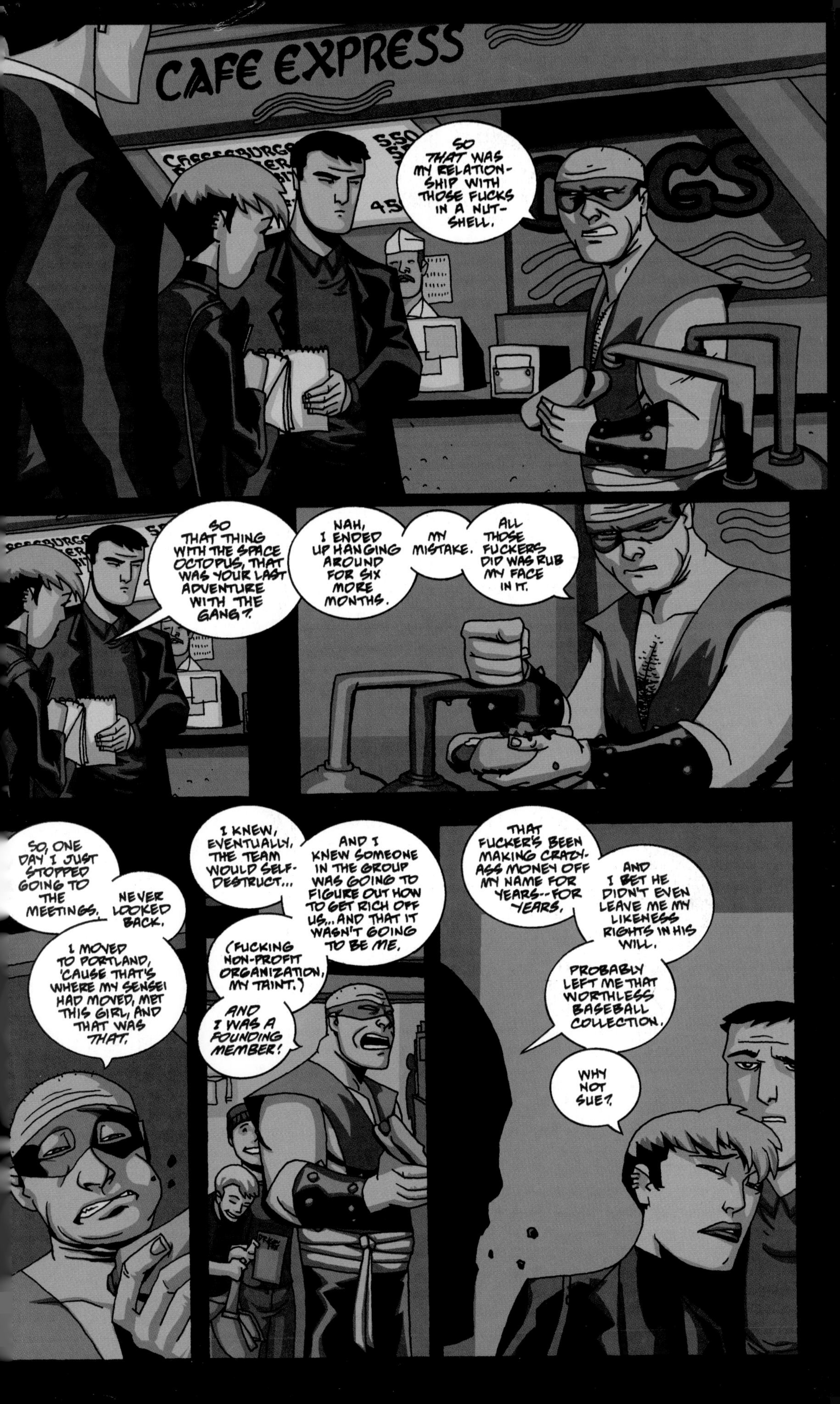
CAFE EXPRESS
SO THAT WAS MY RELATIONSHIP WITH THOSE FUCKS IN A NUTSHELL.
SO THAT THING WITH THE SPACE OCTOPUS, THAT WAS YOUR LAST ADVENTURE WITH THE GANG?
NAH, I ENDED UP HANGING AROUND FOR SIX MORE MONTHS.
MY MISTAKE.
ALL THOSE FUCKERS DID WAS RUB MY FACE IN IT.
SO, ONE DAY I JUST STOPPED GOING TO THE MEETINGS.
NEVER LOOKED BACK.
I MOVED TO PORTLAND, 'CAUSE THAT'S WHERE MY SENSEI HAD MOVED, MET THIS GIRL, AND THAT WAS THAT.
I KNEW, EVENTUALLY, THE TEAM WOULD SELF-DESTRUCT...
AND I KNEW SOMEONE IN THE GROUP WAS GOING TO FIGURE OUT HOW TO GET RICH OFF US... AND THAT IT WASN'T GOING TO BE ME.
(FUCKING NON-PROFIT ORGANIZATION, MY TAINT.)
AND I WAS A FOUNDING MEMBER!
THAT FUCKER'S BEEN MAKING CRAZY-ASS MONEY OFF MY NAME FOR YEARS--FOR YEARS.
AND I BET HE DIDN'T EVEN LEAVE ME MY LIKENESS RIGHTS IN HIS WILL.
PROBABLY LEFT ME THAT WORTHLESS BASEBALL COLLECTION.
WHY NOT SUE?

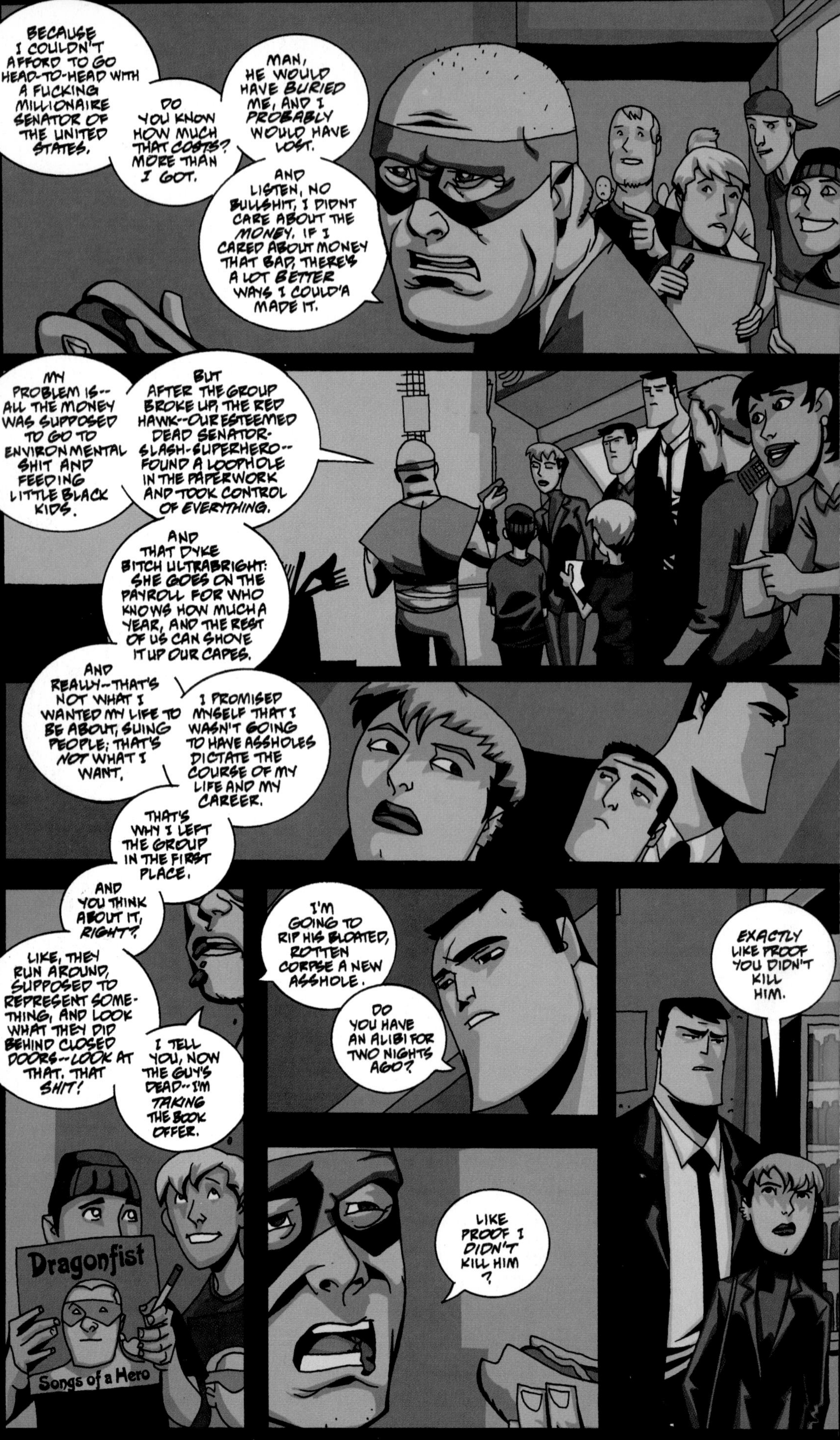
BECAUSE I COULDN'T AFFORD TO GO HEAD-TO-HEAD WITH A FUCKING MILLIONAIRE SENATOR OF THE UNITED STATES.
DO YOU KNOW HOW MUCH THAT COSTS? MORE THAN I GOT.
MAN, HE WOULD HAVE BURIED ME, AND I PROBABLY WOULD HAVE LOST.
AND LISTEN, NO BULLSHIT, I DIDNT CARE ABOUT THE MONEY. IF I CARED ABOUT MONEY THAT BAD, THERE'S A LOT BETTER WAYS I COULD'A MADE IT.
MY PROBLEM IS-- ALL THE MONEY WAS SUPPOSED TO GO TO ENVIRONMENTAL SHIT AND FEEDING LITTLE BLACK KIDS.
BUT AFTER THE GROUP BROKE UP, THE RED HAWK--OUR ESTEEMED DEAD SENATOR-SLASH-SUPERHERO--FOUND A LOOPHOLE IN THE PAPERWORK AND TOOK CONTROL OF EVERYTHING.
AND THAT DYKE BITCH ULTRABRIGHT: SHE GOES ON THE PAYROLL FOR WHO KNOWS HOW MUCH A YEAR, AND THE REST OF US CAN SHOVE IT UP OUR CAPES.
AND REALLY--THAT'S NOT WHAT I WANTED MY LIFE TO BE ABOUT, SUING PEOPLE; THAT'S NOT WHAT I WANT.
I PROMISED MYSELF THAT I WASN'T GOING TO HAVE ASSHOLES DICTATE THE COURSE OF MY LIFE AND MY CAREER.
THAT'S WHY I LEFT THE GROUP IN THE FIRST PLACE.
AND YOU THINK ABOUT IT, RIGHT?
LIKE, THEY RUN AROUND, SUPPOSED TO REPRESENT SOMETHING, AND LOOK WHAT THEY DID BEHIND CLOSED DOORS--LOOK AT THAT. THAT SHIT!
I TELL YOU, NOW THE GUY'S DEAD--I'M TAKING THE BOOK OFFER.
Dragonfist
Songs of a Hero
I'M GOING TO RIP HIS BLOATED, ROTTEN CORPSE A NEW ASSHOLE.
DO YOU HAVE AN ALIBI FOR TWO NIGHTS AGO?
LIKE PROOF I DIDN'T KILL HIM?
EXACTLY LIKE PROOF YOU DIDN'T KILL HIM.

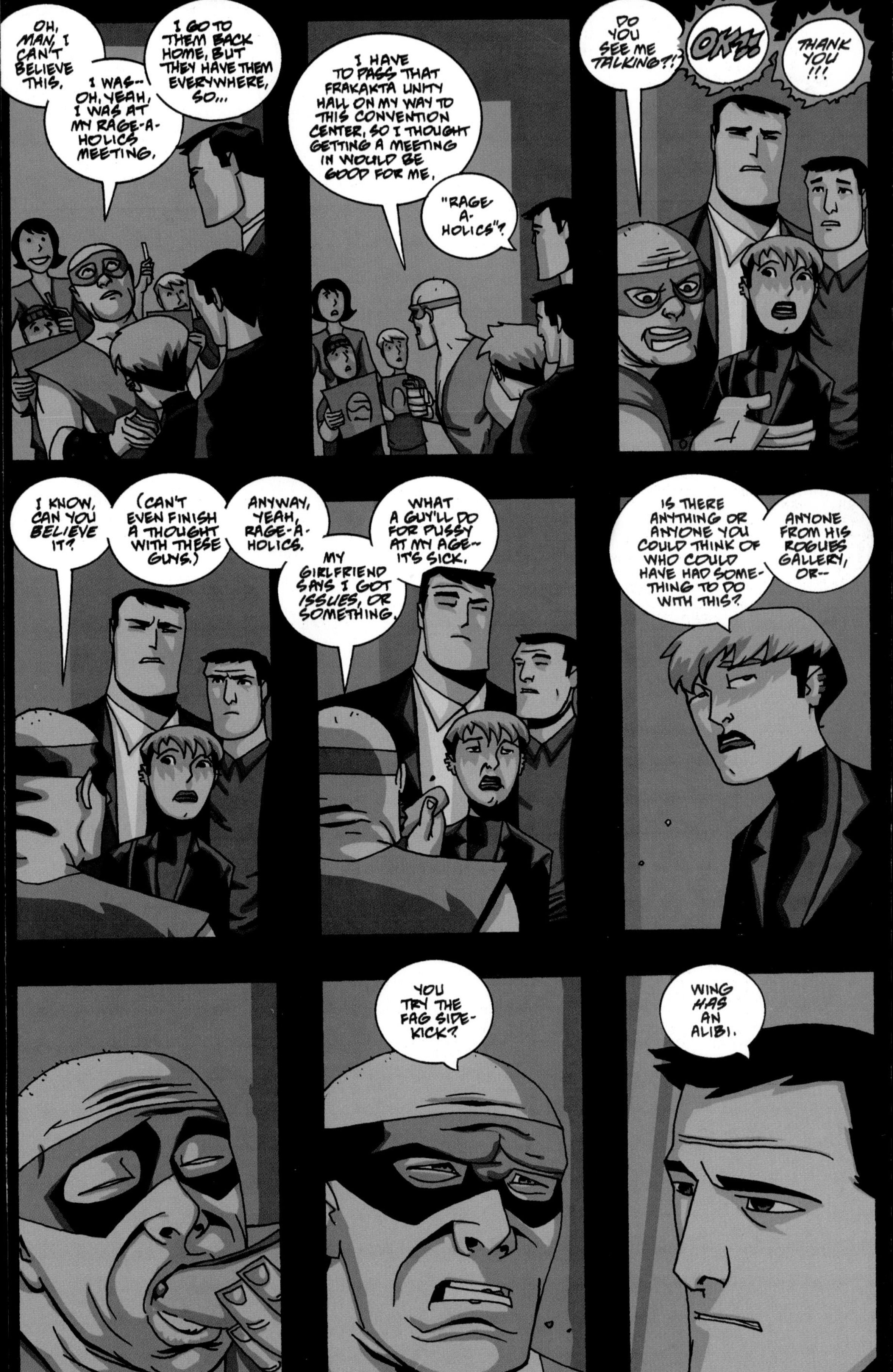
OH, MAN, I CAN'T BELIEVE THIS.
I WAS-- OH, YEAH, I WAS AT MY RAGE-A-HOLICS MEETING.
I GO TO THEM BACK HOME, BUT THEY HAVE THEM EVERYWHERE, SO...
I HAVE TO PASS THAT FRAKAKTA UNITY HALL ON MY WAY TO THIS CONVENTION CENTER, SO I THOUGHT GETTING A MEETING IN WOULD BE GOOD FOR ME.
"RAGE-A-HOLICS"?
DO YOU SEE ME TALKING?!
OK!!
THANK YOU!!!
I KNOW, CAN YOU BELIEVE IT?
(CAN'T EVEN FINISH A THOUGHT WITH THESE GUYS.)
ANYWAY, YEAH, RAGE-A-HOLICS.
MY GIRLFRIEND SAYS I GOT ISSUES, OR SOMETHING.
WHAT A GUY'LL DO FOR PUSSY AT MY AGE-- IT'S SICK.
IS THERE ANYTHING OR ANYONE YOU COULD THINK OF WHO COULD HAVE HAD SOMETHING TO DO WITH THIS?
ANYONE FROM HIS ROGUES GALLERY, OR--
YOU TRY THE FAG SIDEKICK?
WING HAS AN ALIBI.

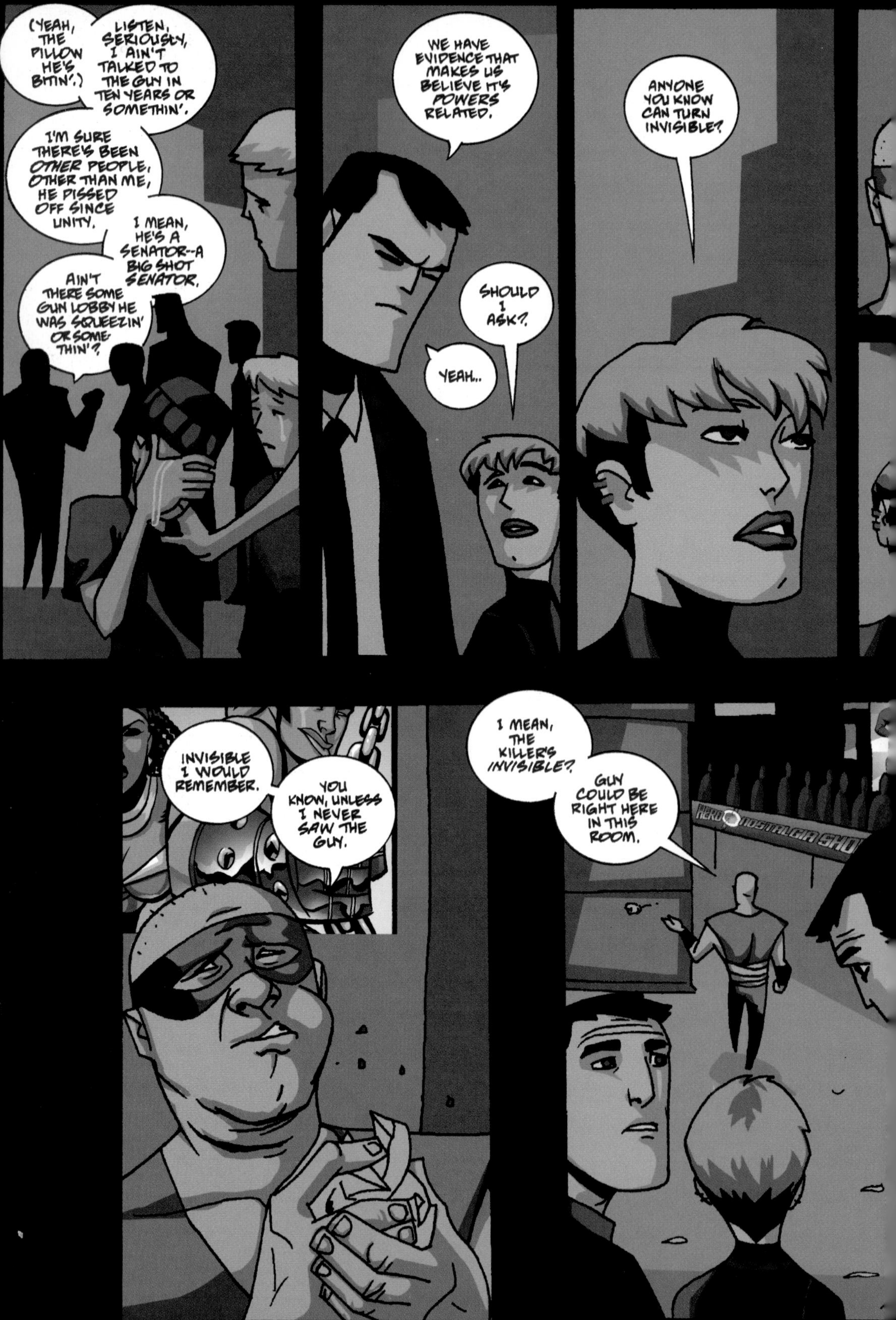
(YEAH, THE PILLOW HE'S BITIN'.)
LISTEN, SERIOUSLY, I AIN'T TALKED TO THE GUY IN TEN YEARS OR SOMETHIN'.
I'M SURE THERE'S BEEN OTHER PEOPLE, OTHER THAN ME, HE PISSED OFF SINCE UNITY.
I MEAN, HE'S A SENATOR--A BIG SHOT SENATOR.
AIN'T THERE SOME GUN LOBBY HE WAS SQUEEZIN' OR SOMETHIN'?
WE HAVE EVIDENCE THAT MAKES US BELIEVE IT'S POWERS RELATED.
SHOULD I ASK?
YEAH...
ANYONE YOU KNOW CAN TURN INVISIBLE?
INVISIBLE I WOULD REMEMBER.
YOU KNOW, UNLESS I NEVER SAW THE GUY.
I MEAN, THE KILLER'S INVISIBLE?
GUY COULD BE RIGHT HERE IN THIS ROOM.

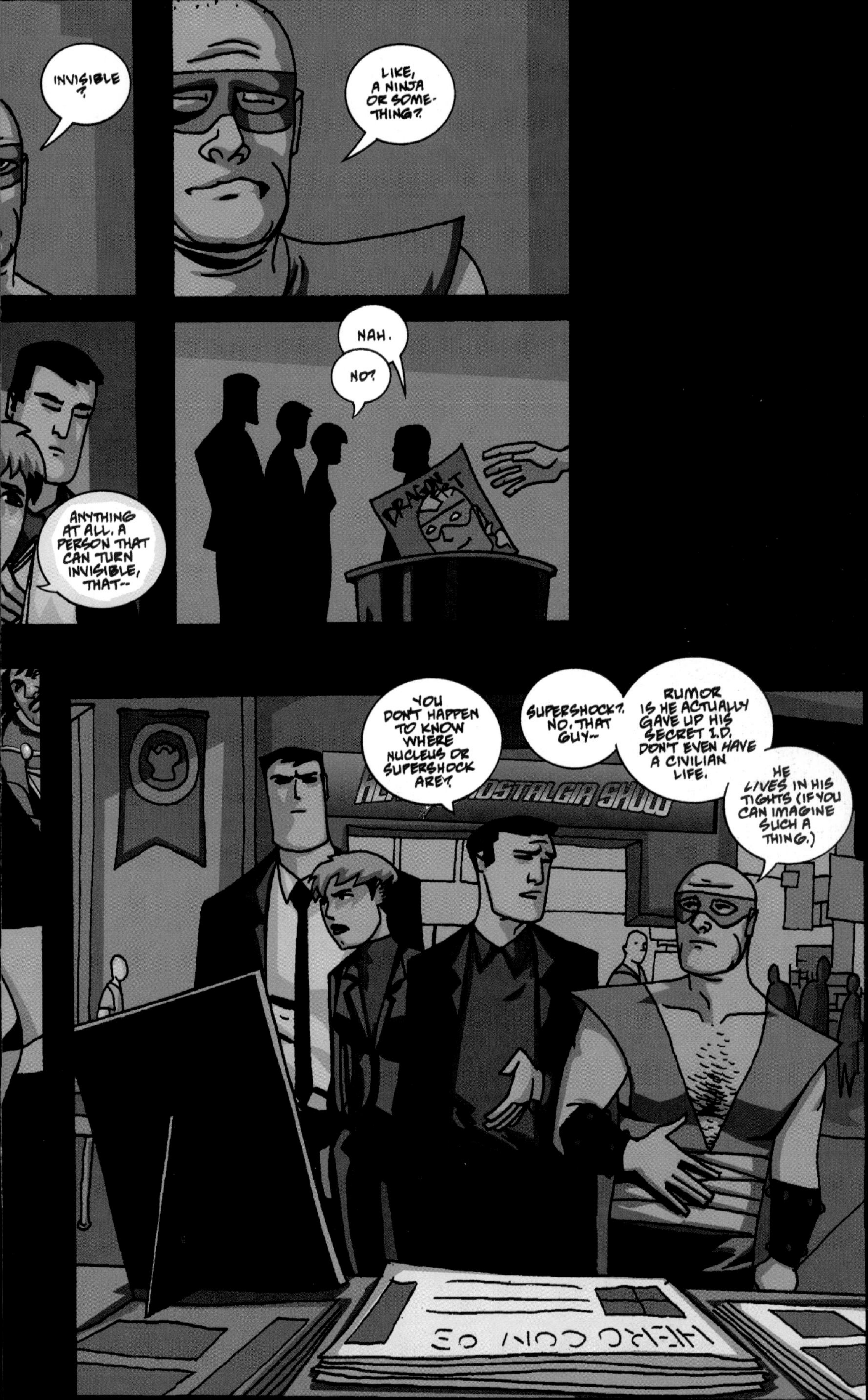
INVISIBLE?
LIKE, A NINJA OR SOME-THING?
NAH.
NO?
ANYTHING AT ALL. A PERSON THAT CAN TURN INVISIBLE, THAT--
DRAGON
YOU DON'T HAPPEN TO KNOW WHERE NUCLEUS OR SUPERSHOCK ARE?
SUPERSHOCK? NO. THAT GUY--
RUMOR IS HE ACTUALLY GAVE UP HIS SECRET I.D. DON'T EVEN HAVE A CIVILIAN LIFE.
HE LIVES IN HIS TIGHTS (IF YOU CAN IMAGINE SUCH A THING.)
NOSTALGIA SHOW
HERO CON 03

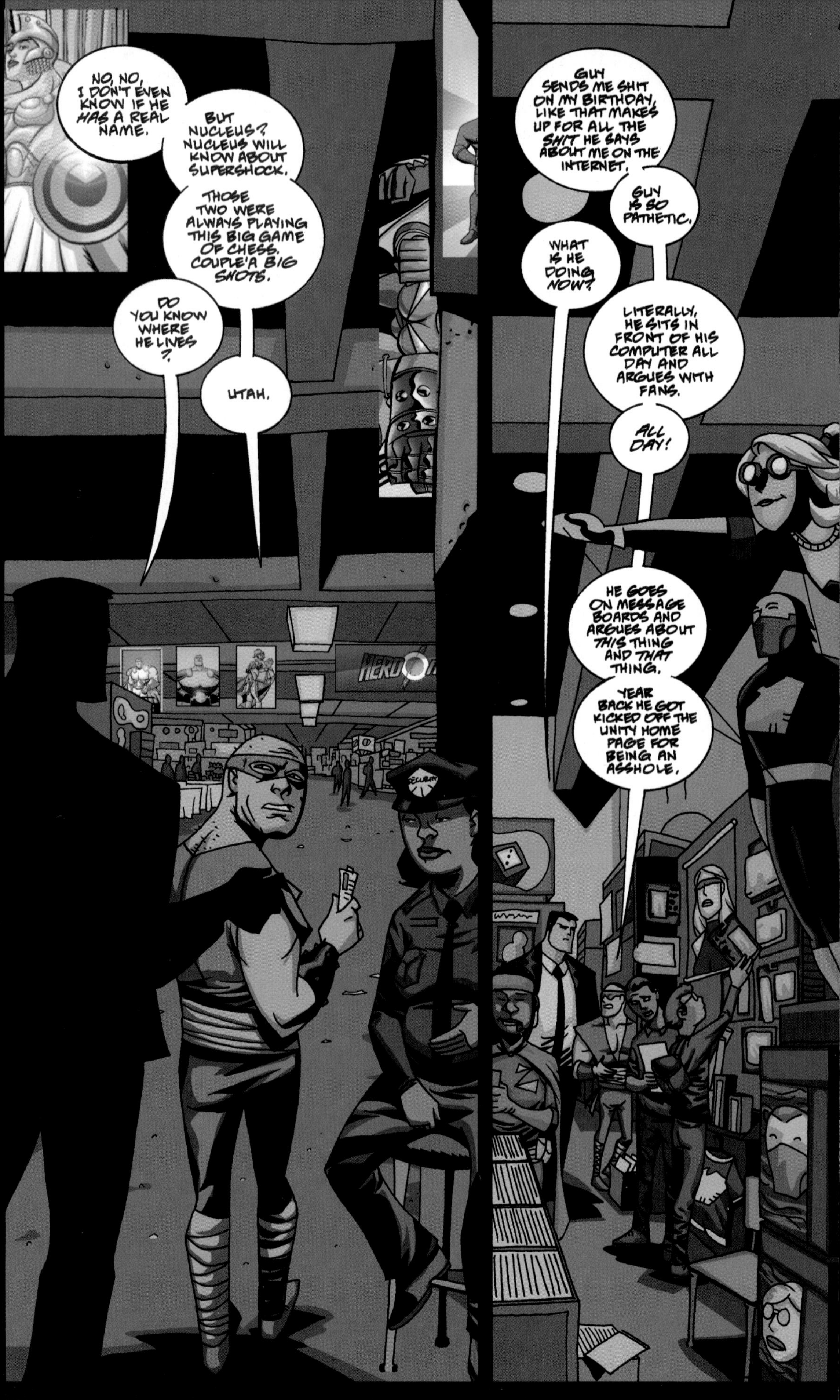
NO, NO, I DON'T EVEN KNOW IF HE HAS A REAL NAME.
BUT NUCLEUS? NUCLEUS WILL KNOW ABOUT SUPERSHOCK.
THOSE TWO WERE ALWAYS PLAYING THIS BIG GAME OF CHESS. COUPLE'A BIG SHOTS.
DO YOU KNOW WHERE HE LIVES?
UTAH.
GUY SENDS ME SHIT ON MY BIRTHDAY, LIKE THAT MAKES UP FOR ALL THE SHIT HE SAYS ABOUT ME ON THE INTERNET.
GUY IS SO PATHETIC.
WHAT IS HE DOING NOW?
LITERALLY, HE SITS IN FRONT OF HIS COMPUTER ALL DAY AND ARGUES WITH FANS.
ALL DAY!
HE GOES ON MESSAGE BOARDS AND ARGUES ABOUT THIS THING AND THAT THING.
YEAR BACK HE GOT KICKED OFF THE UNITY HOME PAGE FOR BEING AN ASSHOLE.

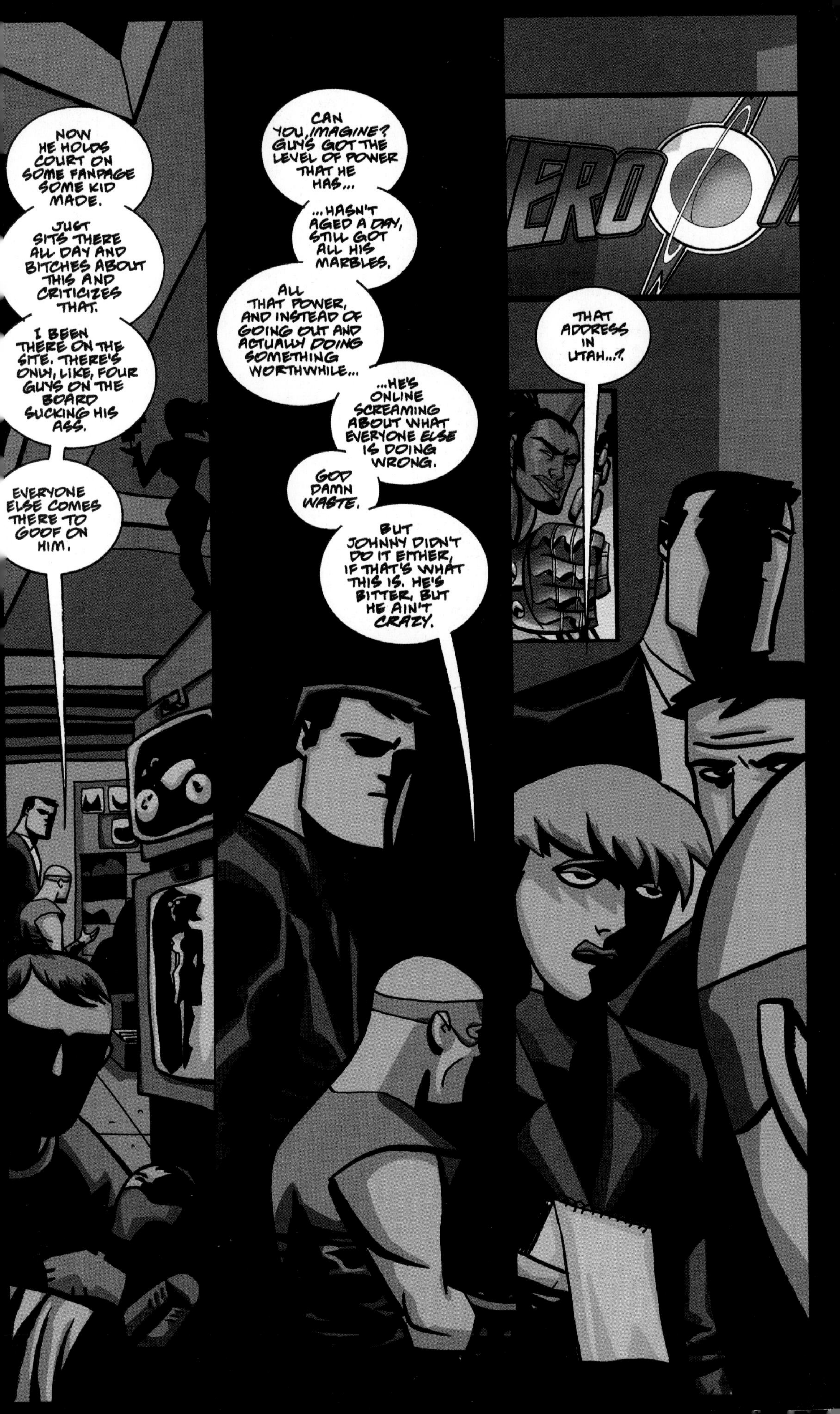
NOW HE HOLDS COURT ON SOME FANPAGE SOME KID MADE.
JUST SITS THERE ALL DAY AND BITCHES ABOUT THIS AND CRITICIZES THAT.
I BEEN THERE ON THE SITE. THERE'S ONLY, LIKE, FOUR GUYS ON THE BOARD SUCKING HIS ASS.
EVERYONE ELSE COMES THERE TO GOOF ON HIM.
CAN YOU, IMAGINE? GUY'S GOT THE LEVEL OF POWER THAT HE HAS...
...HASN'T AGED A DAY, STILL GOT ALL HIS MARBLES.
ALL THAT POWER, AND INSTEAD OF GOING OUT AND ACTUALLY DOING SOMETHING WORTHWHILE...
...HE'S ONLINE SCREAMING ABOUT WHAT EVERYONE ELSE IS DOING WRONG.
GOD DAMN WASTE.
BUT JOHNNY DIDN'T DO IT EITHER, IF THAT'S WHAT THIS IS. HE'S BITTER, BUT HE AIN'T CRAZY.
THAT ADDRESS IN UTAH...?

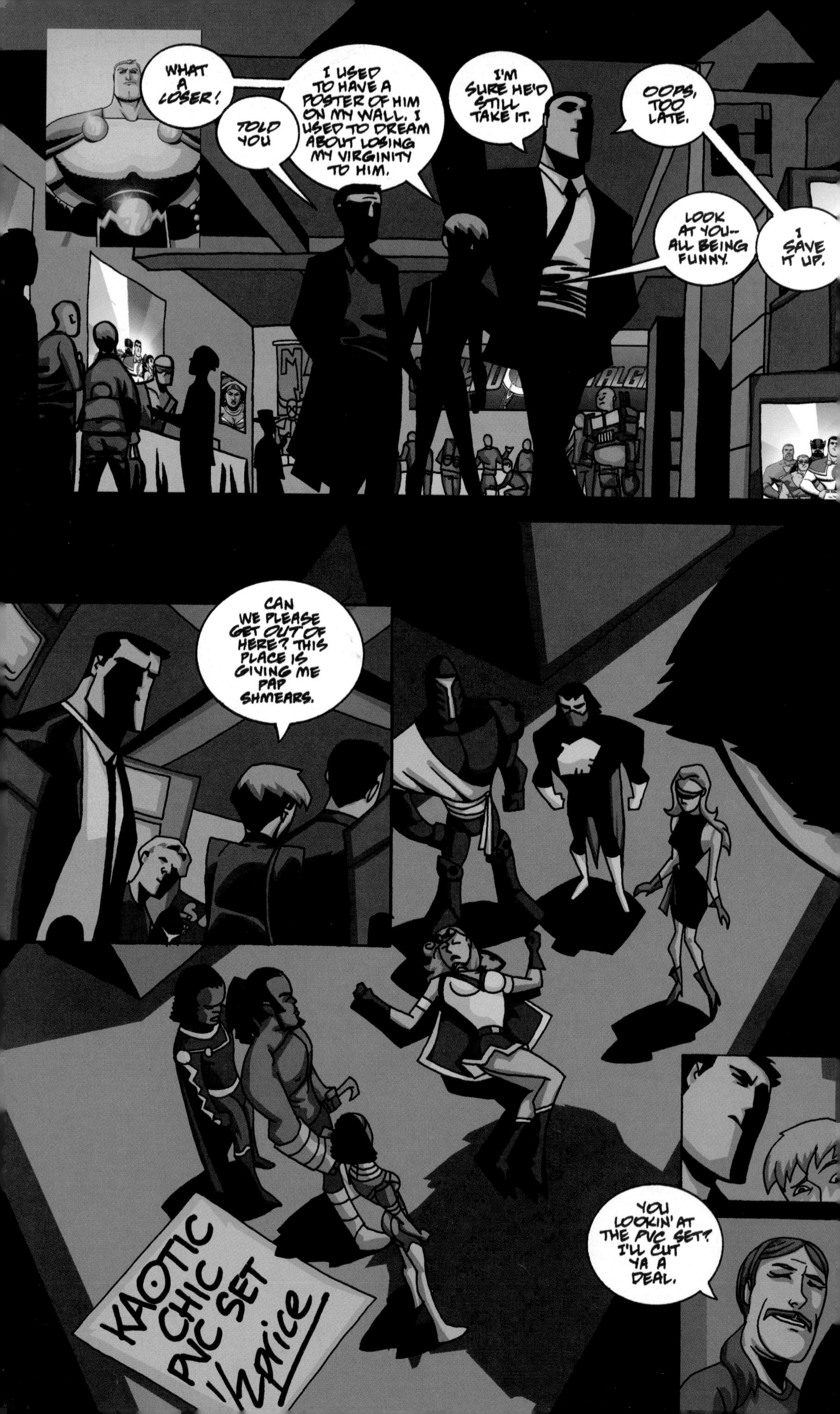
WHAT A LOSER!
TOLD YOU
I USED TO HAVE A POSTER OF HIM ON MY WALL. I USED TO DREAM ABOUT LOSING MY VIRGINITY TO HIM.
I'M SURE HE'D STILL TAKE IT.
OOPS, TOO LATE.
LOOK AT YOU-- ALL BEING FUNNY.
I SAVE IT UP.
CAN WE PLEASE GET OUT OF HERE? THIS PLACE IS GIVING ME PAP SHMEARS.
KAOTIC CHIC PVC SET ½ price
YOU LOOKIN' AT THE PVC SET? I'LL CUT YA A DEAL.

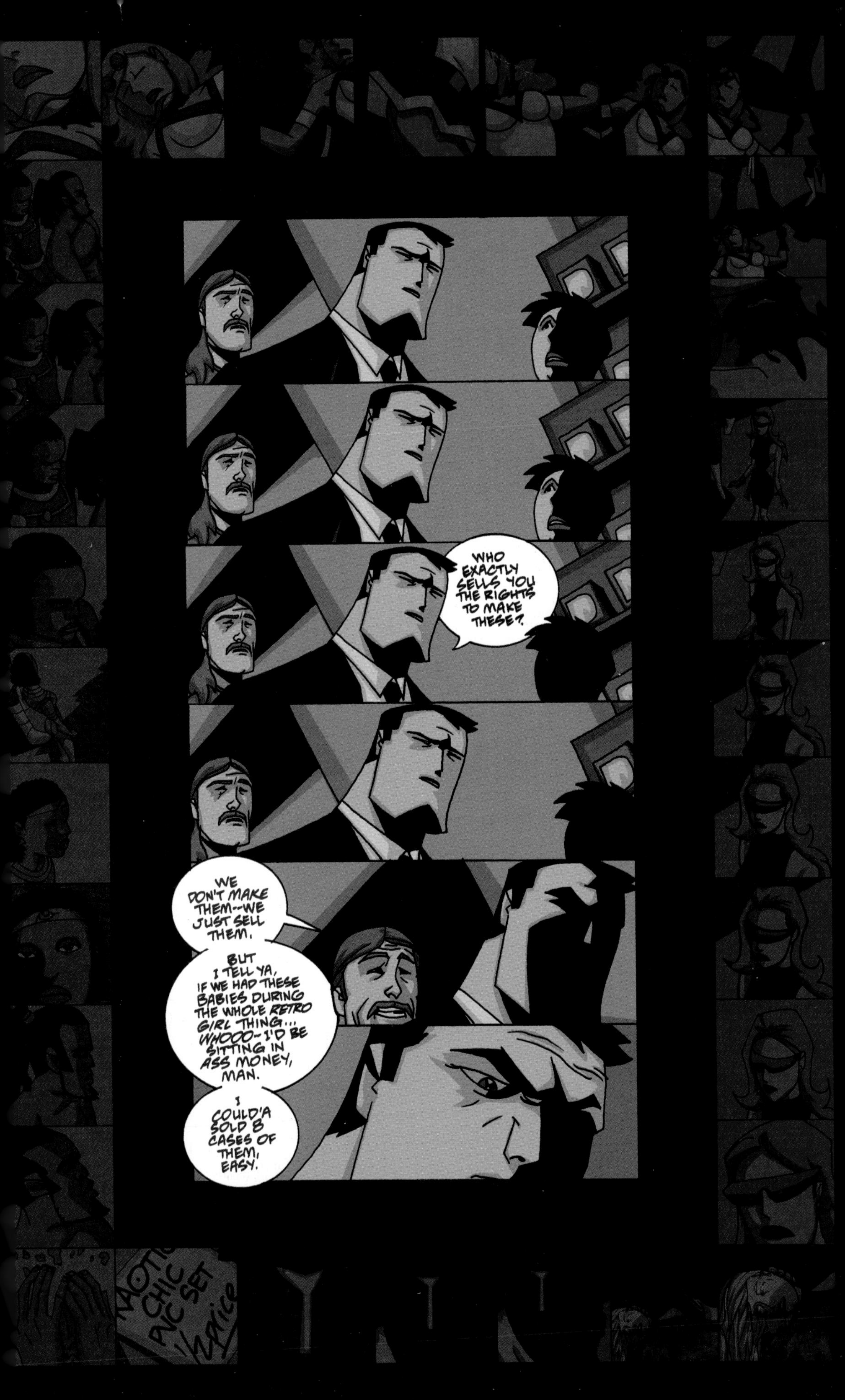
WHO EXACTLY SELLS YOU THE RIGHTS TO MAKE THESE?
WE DON'T MAKE THEM--WE JUST SELL THEM.
BUT I TELL YA, IF WE HAD THESE BABIES DURING THE WHOLE RETRO GIRL THING... WHOOO-I'D BE SITTING IN ASS MONEY, MAN.
I COULD'A SOLD 8 CASES OF THEM, EASY.

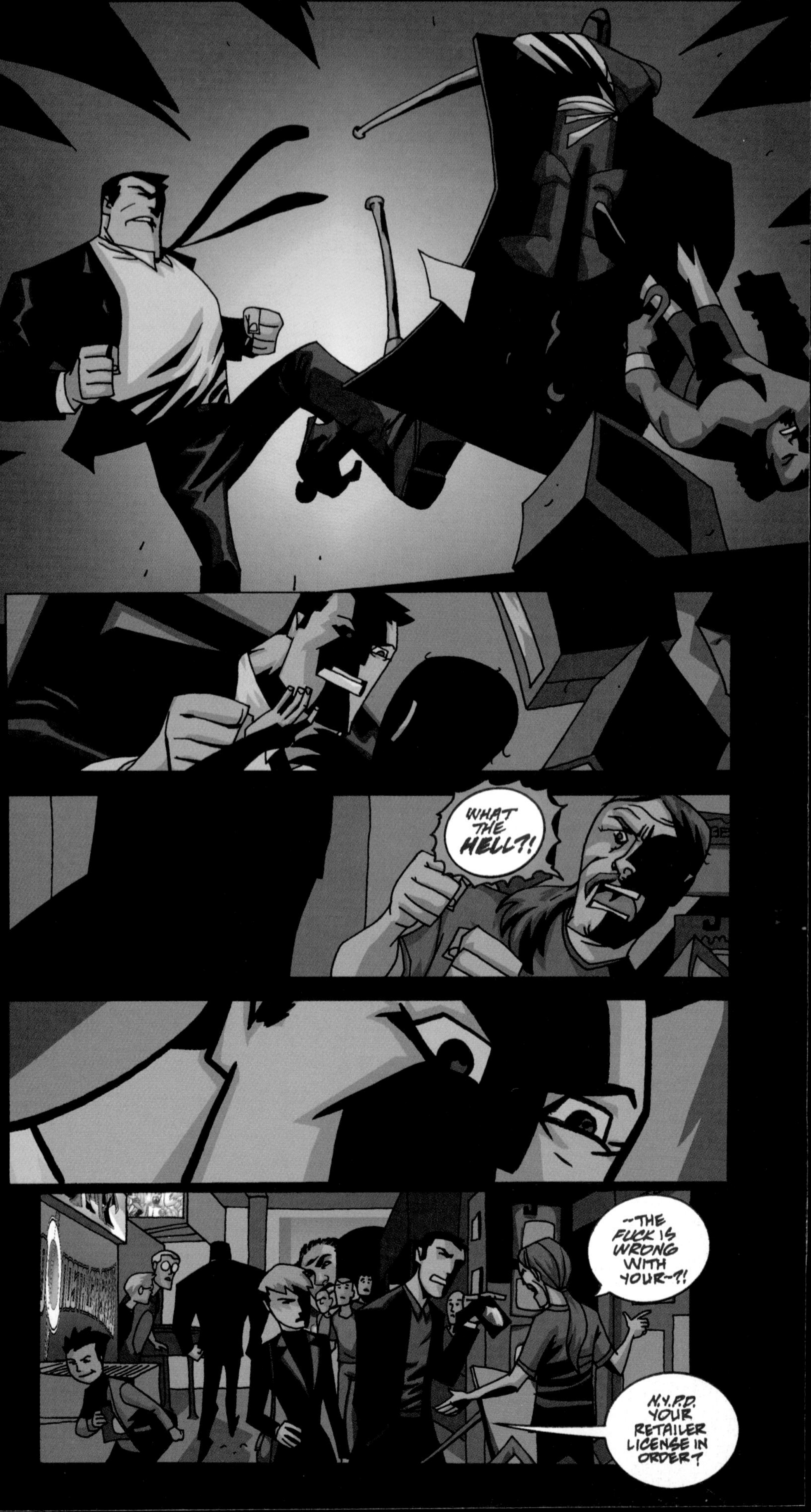
WHAT THE HELL?!
--THE FUCK IS WRONG WITH YOUR--?!
N.Y.P.D. YOUR RETAILER LICENSE IN ORDER?

P online!

Dateline: A Toddlin' Town

When you want it
Where you want it
How you want it
1-888-iwantit

Get Our Free Newsletter > search go

▪HOME ▪NEWS ▪GOSSIP ▪REVIEWS ▪CELEBS ▪CHAT

GOSSIP CONTENTS

- Under The Cape
- Costume Closet
- Ask Alisa
- Two Mikes Talkin'

POWERS NEWS

FIRST LOOK: Urban combat boutique

Twinkle's new breast implants

Powers Inc. opens new Petrograd store

Bomber strikes Unity sperm bank

FRESH FACES

New Book Reviews: **Lab Rats,** *the early experiments on the first Powers kids in the 1950s*

At the Movies: *Massimo Testi and Tiffany Topp return, in* ***Shockwave,*** *Unity thriller #7*

Graverobbing: *Why more and more Powers are choosing cremation in the Sun, the tragic truth*

Unbridled Powers: *Jimmy "Big Wadd" Homes tells all about his 25 years as the king of porn*

THE HIT LIST

Today's Best Bets

- *Bad Boys:* Powers in prison
- *Arnold* interviewed tonight on *Conan*
- Uma on *Oprah*

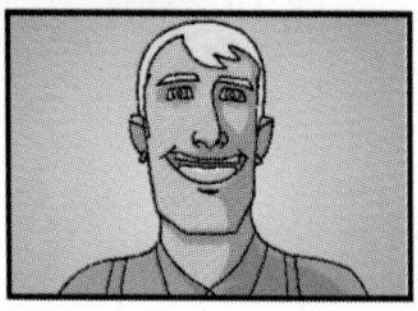

Ted Robinson's Under The Cape

This is where the Dirty Dish gets dumped

Catch Ted Robinson on *P! News Live* Tuesdays at 4:30 p.m. PT and Sundays at 2:30 a.m and 7 p.m. PT

Long-Distance Looney Tune

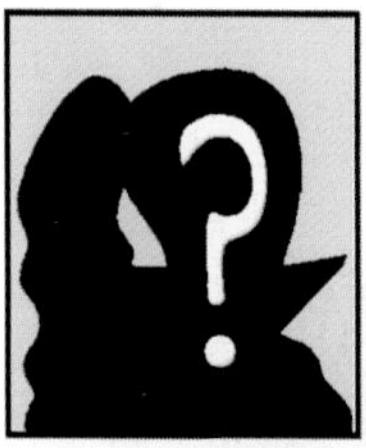

Word among the top dogs of the cape-wearing cavalcade is that one of the most boisterous female members of a once-popular, mostly male group found her romantic problems solved in the form of a long distance love affair that had her flying all the way from her hometown here in the States to the outbacks of Australia.

But after months of begging her rugged beau to move to America and marry her, she got her wish. He moved to the U.S. with the promise of love and a green card. But wouldn't you know it? The minute he arrived, the Golden Goddess freaked out and refused to talk to him -- leaving him stranded in this country with nowhere to live, no one to call, and no place to go.

Word is he ended up sleeping on the floor of some people he vaguely knew, dreaming of the life he almost had.

I Thought You Were Dead

Dear Ted:

When I was at the 2K2 NYPowersCon, there was a table in the back, and some guy with grey hair in a 60s-style jumpsuit open to the waist. My God, it was Stingray, and he kept trying to hit on the teenage daughters of the fans that came to his table, and he was trying to sell a reprint of some 20 year-old book

more Ted >

▪help ▪about P! Online ▪site map ▪membership ▪newsletter

Use of this page signifies your acceptance of the Privacy Policy and Terms of Use. Copyright (c) Jinxworld, Inc. All Rights Reserved

tonight on P

Whizzer on the Carpet: His first interview since rehab, with Maury. An exclusive P! Biography; 10 p.m

Cheerleaders On Your Desktop

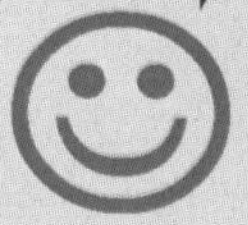

Sweet and sassy and shaking their pop-poms for your enjoyment. gogobooty.com

AMMO IN BULK LOTS

All Makes And Calibres. From .22 to 20mm. Discretion assured. Ask for P!O discount. gunsrus.net/cs

We pay cash for your POWERS photos. Quick and confidential. Sign on now! P!Online.net Click on job search.

next week:

Tickle My Elmo: Three single and available Powers cuties reveal what turns them on, how to make a good first impression, and your chances for getting lucky.

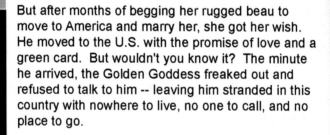

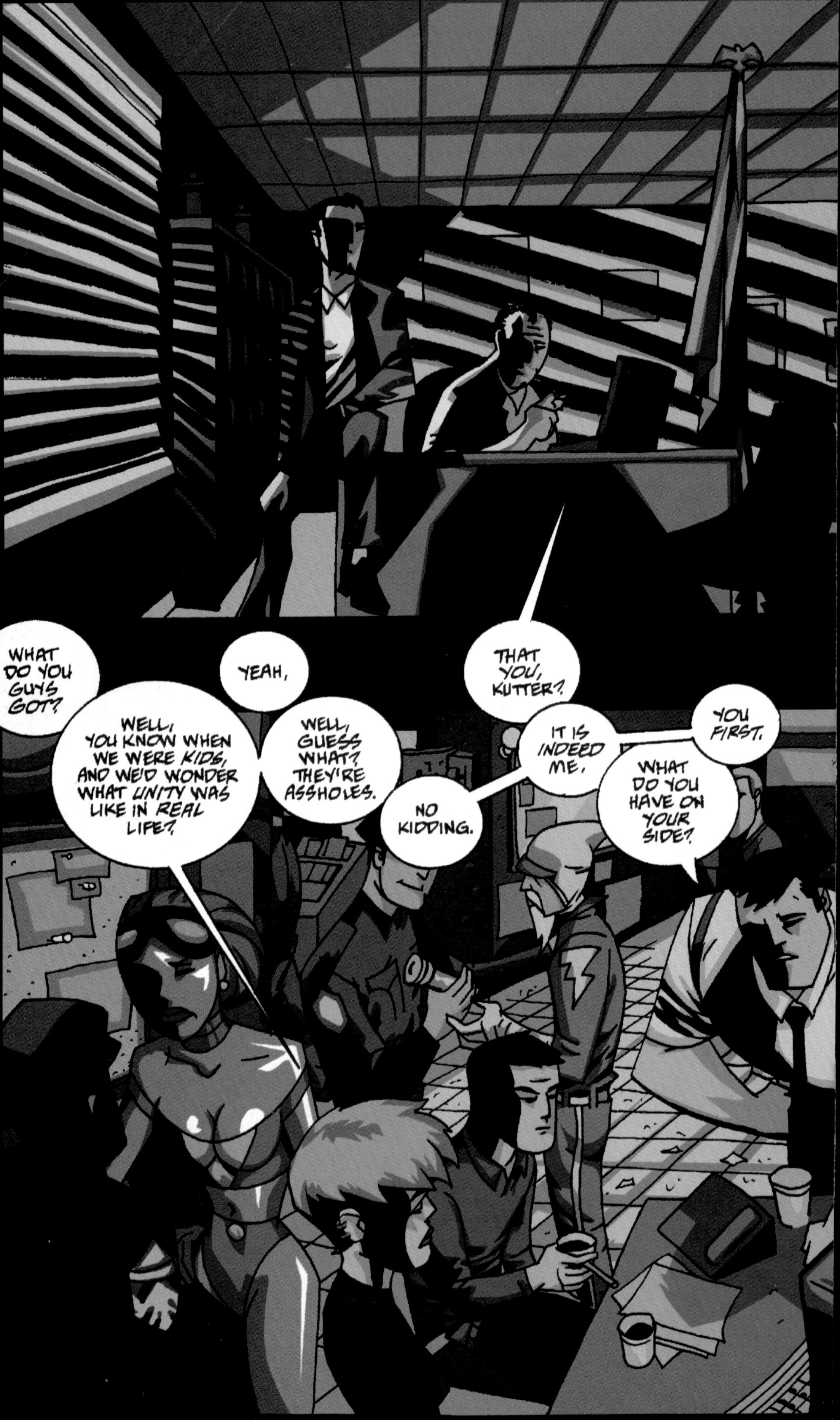
THAT YOU, KUTTER?
IT IS INDEED ME.
NO KIDDING.
WHAT DO YOU HAVE ON YOUR SIDE?
YOU FIRST.
WHAT DO YOU GUYS GOT?
YEAH,
WELL, YOU KNOW WHEN WE WERE KIDS, AND WE'D WONDER WHAT UNITY WAS LIKE IN REAL LIFE?
WELL, GUESS WHAT? THEY'RE ASSHOLES.

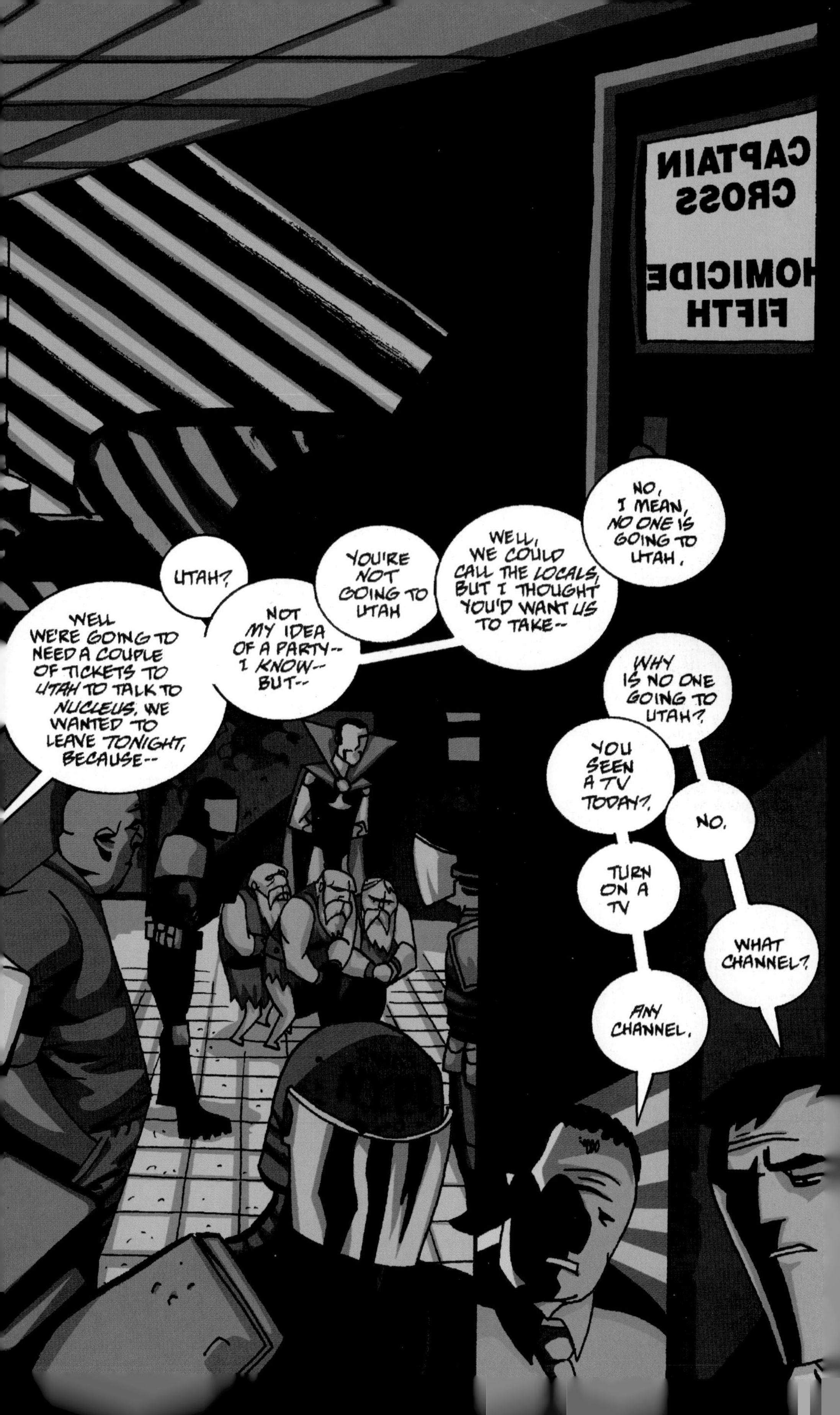
CAPTAIN CROSS
HOMICIDE FIFTH
WELL WE'RE GOING TO NEED A COUPLE OF TICKETS TO UTAH TO TALK TO NUCLEUS. WE WANTED TO LEAVE TONIGHT, BECAUSE--
UTAH?
NOT MY IDEA OF A PARTY-- I KNOW-- BUT--
YOU'RE NOT GOING TO UTAH
WELL, WE COULD CALL THE LOCALS, BUT I THOUGHT YOU'D WANT US TO TAKE--
NO, I MEAN, NO ONE IS GOING TO UTAH.
WHY IS NO ONE GOING TO UTAH?
YOU SEEN A TV TODAY?
NO.
TURN ON A TV
WHAT CHANNEL?
ANY CHANNEL.

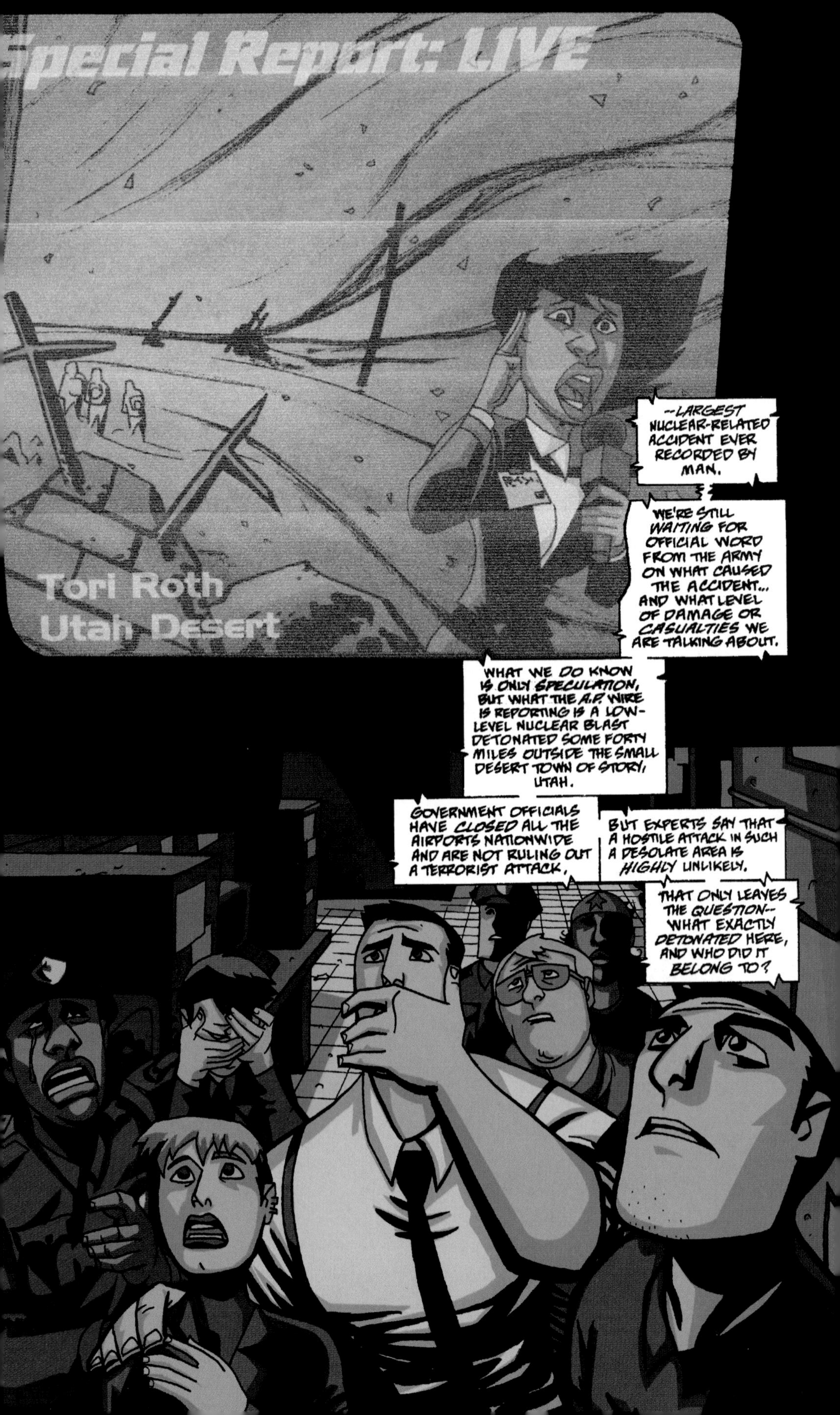
Special Report: LIVE
Tori Roth
Utah Desert
--LARGEST NUCLEAR-RELATED ACCIDENT EVER RECORDED BY MAN.
WE'RE STILL WAITING FOR OFFICIAL WORD FROM THE ARMY ON WHAT CAUSED THE ACCIDENT... AND WHAT LEVEL OF DAMAGE OR CASUALTIES WE ARE TALKING ABOUT.
WHAT WE DO KNOW IS ONLY SPECULATION, BUT WHAT THE A.P. WIRE IS REPORTING IS A LOW-LEVEL NUCLEAR BLAST DETONATED SOME FORTY MILES OUTSIDE THE SMALL DESERT TOWN OF STORY, UTAH.
GOVERNMENT OFFICIALS HAVE CLOSED ALL THE AIRPORTS NATIONWIDE AND ARE NOT RULING OUT A TERRORIST ATTACK,
BUT EXPERTS SAY THAT A HOSTILE ATTACK IN SUCH A DESOLATE AREA IS HIGHLY UNLIKELY.
THAT ONLY LEAVES THE QUESTION-- WHAT EXACTLY DETONATED HERE, AND WHO DID IT BELONG TO?

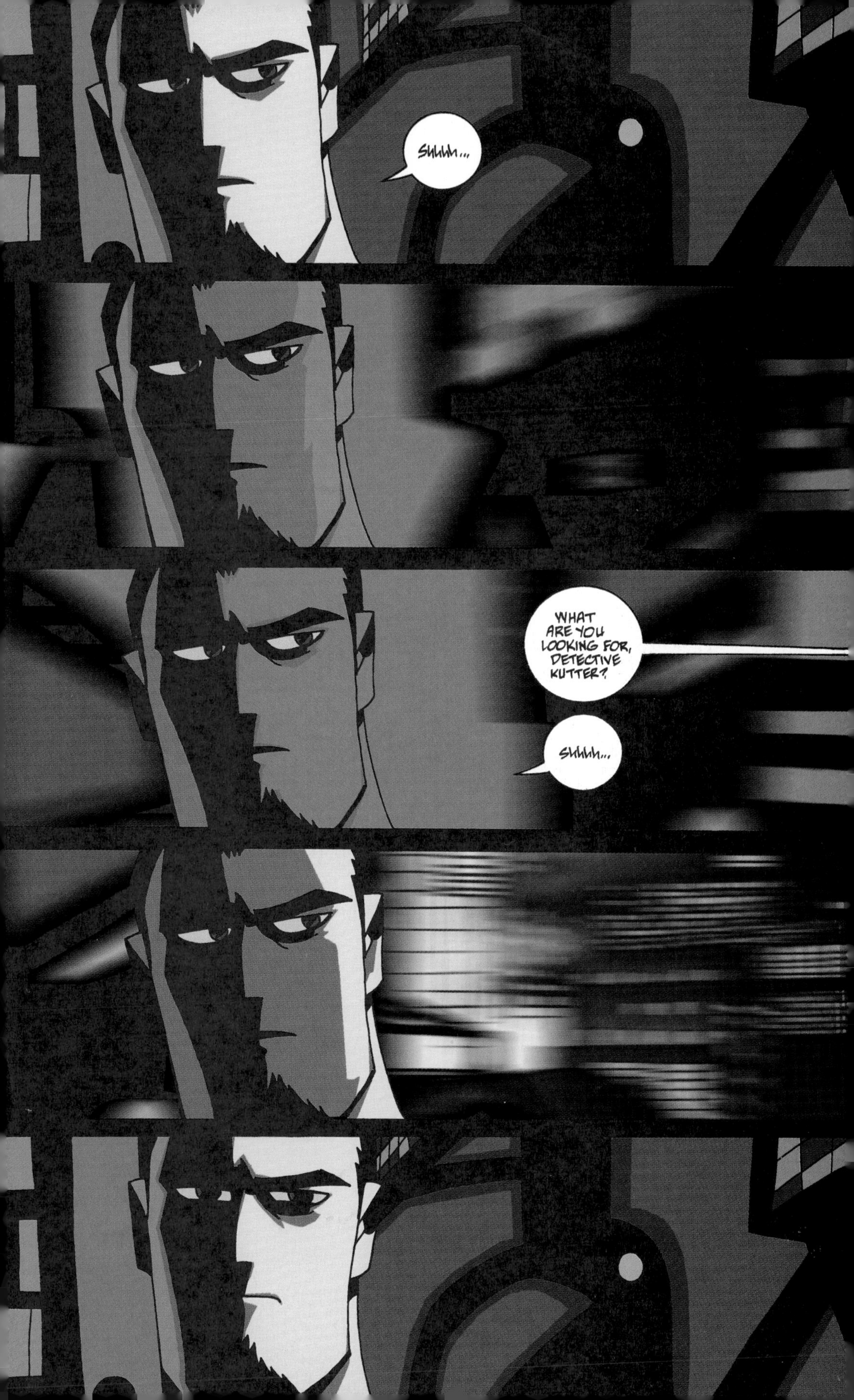
SHHHH...
WHAT ARE YOU LOOKING FOR, DETECTIVE KUTTER?
SHHHH...

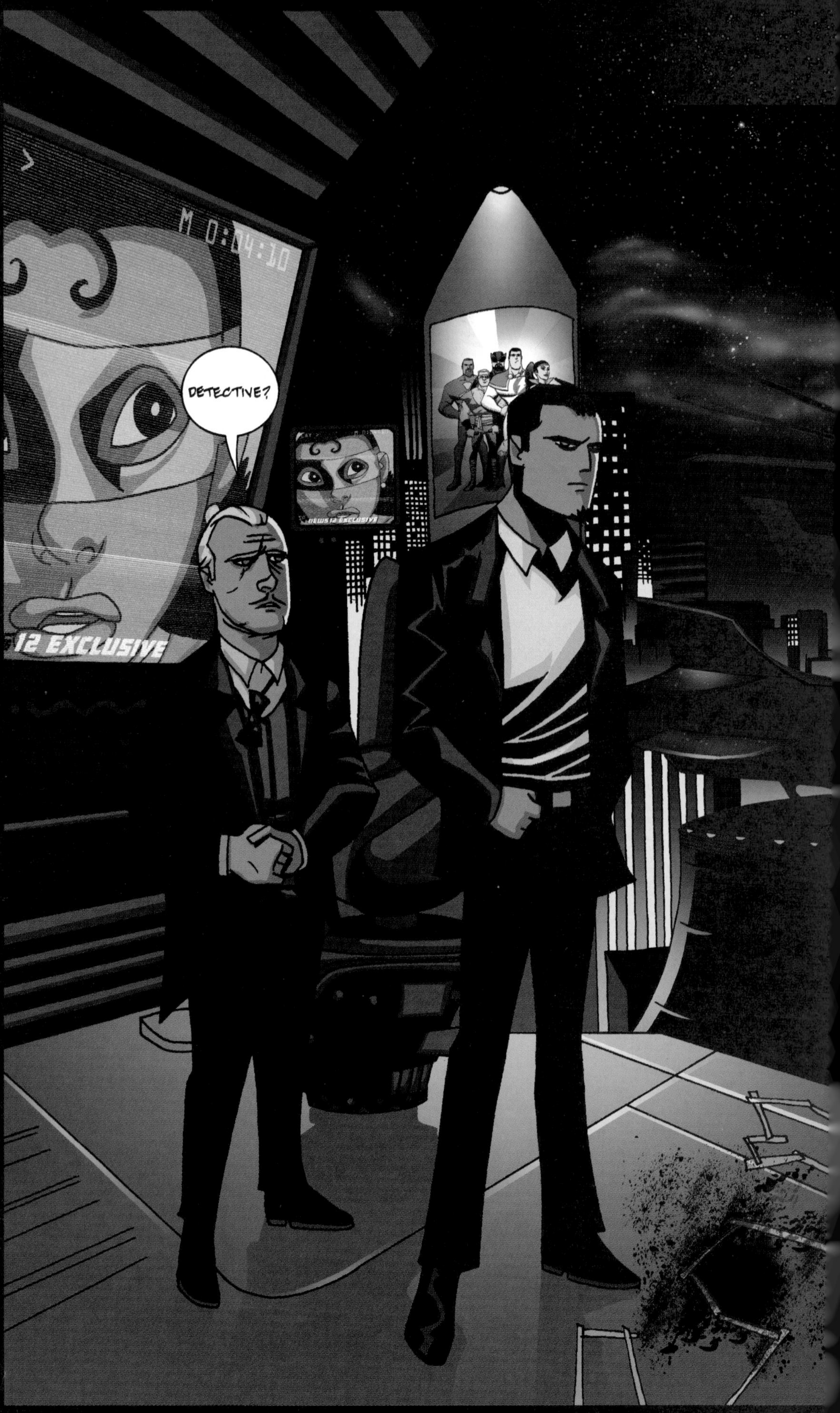
M 0:04:10
DETECTIVE?
12 EXCLUSIVE
NEWS 12 EXCLUSIVE

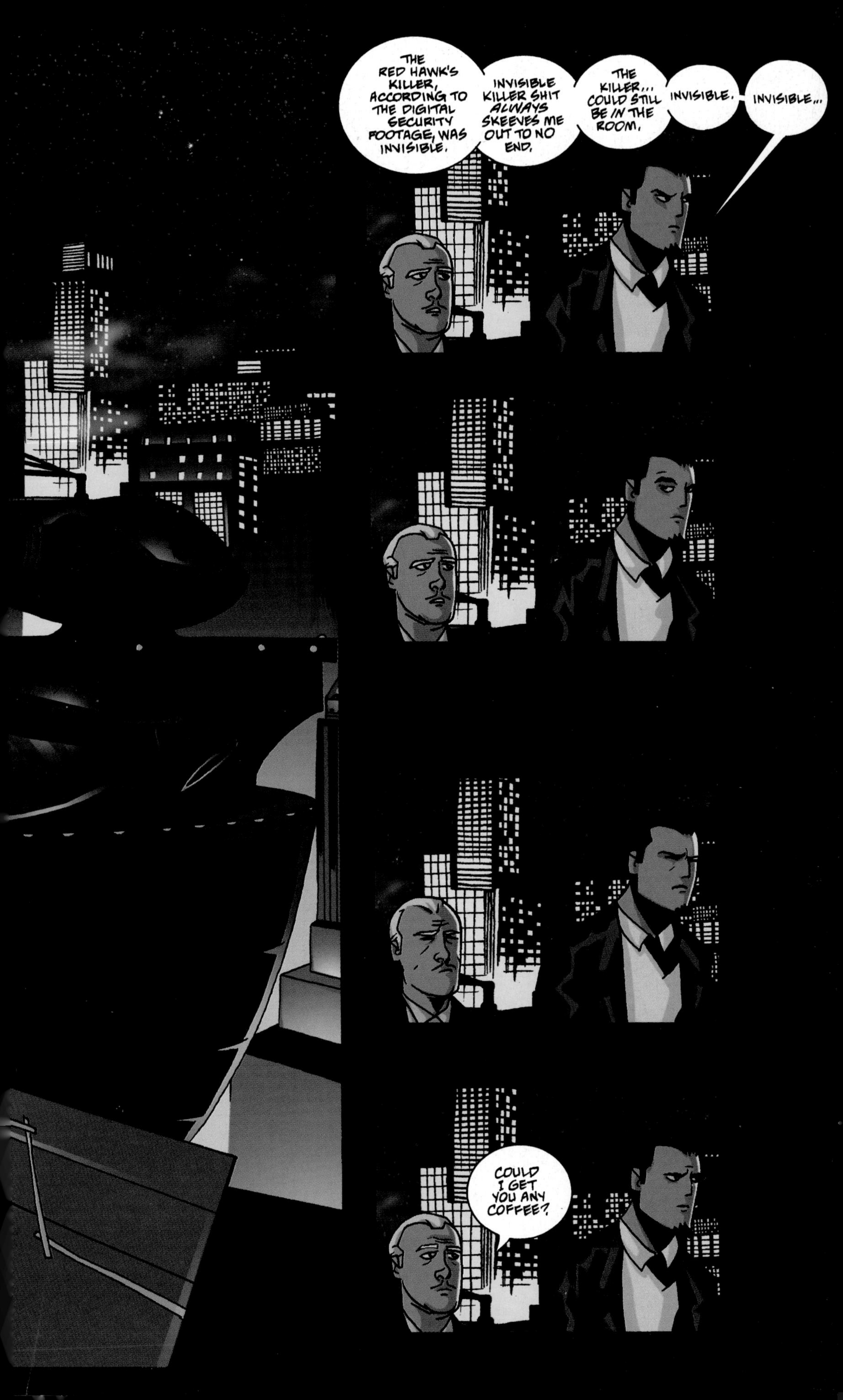
THE RED HAWK'S KILLER, ACCORDING TO THE DIGITAL SECURITY FOOTAGE, WAS INVISIBLE.
INVISIBLE KILLER SHIT ALWAYS SKEEVES ME OUT TO NO END.
THE KILLER... COULD STILL BE IN THE ROOM.
INVISIBLE.
INVISIBLE...
COULD I GET YOU ANY COFFEE?

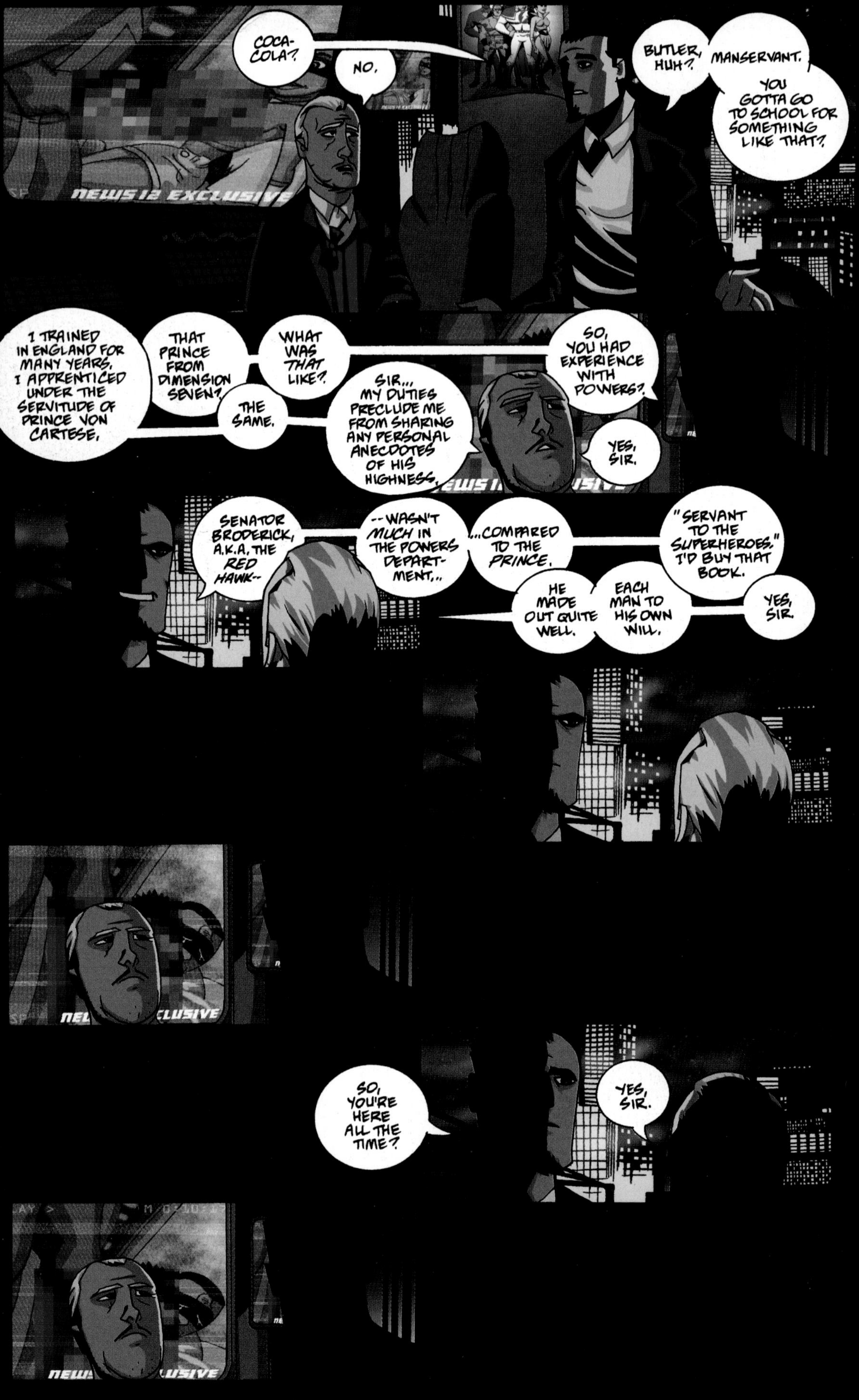
NEWS 12 EXCLUSIVE
COCA-COLA?
NO.
BUTLER, HUH?
MANSERVANT.
YOU GOTTA GO TO SCHOOL FOR SOMETHING LIKE THAT?
SO, YOU HAD EXPERIENCE WITH POWERS?
YES, SIR.
I TRAINED IN ENGLAND FOR MANY YEARS. I APPRENTICED UNDER THE SERVITUDE OF PRINCE VON CARTESE.
THAT PRINCE FROM DIMENSION SEVEN?
THE SAME.
WHAT WAS THAT LIKE?
SIR... MY DUTIES PRECLUDE ME FROM SHARING ANY PERSONAL ANECDOTES OF HIS HIGHNESS.
SENATOR BRODERICK, A.K.A. THE RED HAWK--
--WASN'T MUCH IN THE POWERS DEPARTMENT...
...COMPARED TO THE PRINCE.
HE MADE OUT QUITE WELL.
EACH MAN TO HIS OWN WILL.
"SERVANT TO THE SUPERHEROES." I'D BUY THAT BOOK.
YES, SIR.
CLUSIVE
SO, YOU'RE HERE ALL THE TIME?
YES, SIR.
CLUSIVE

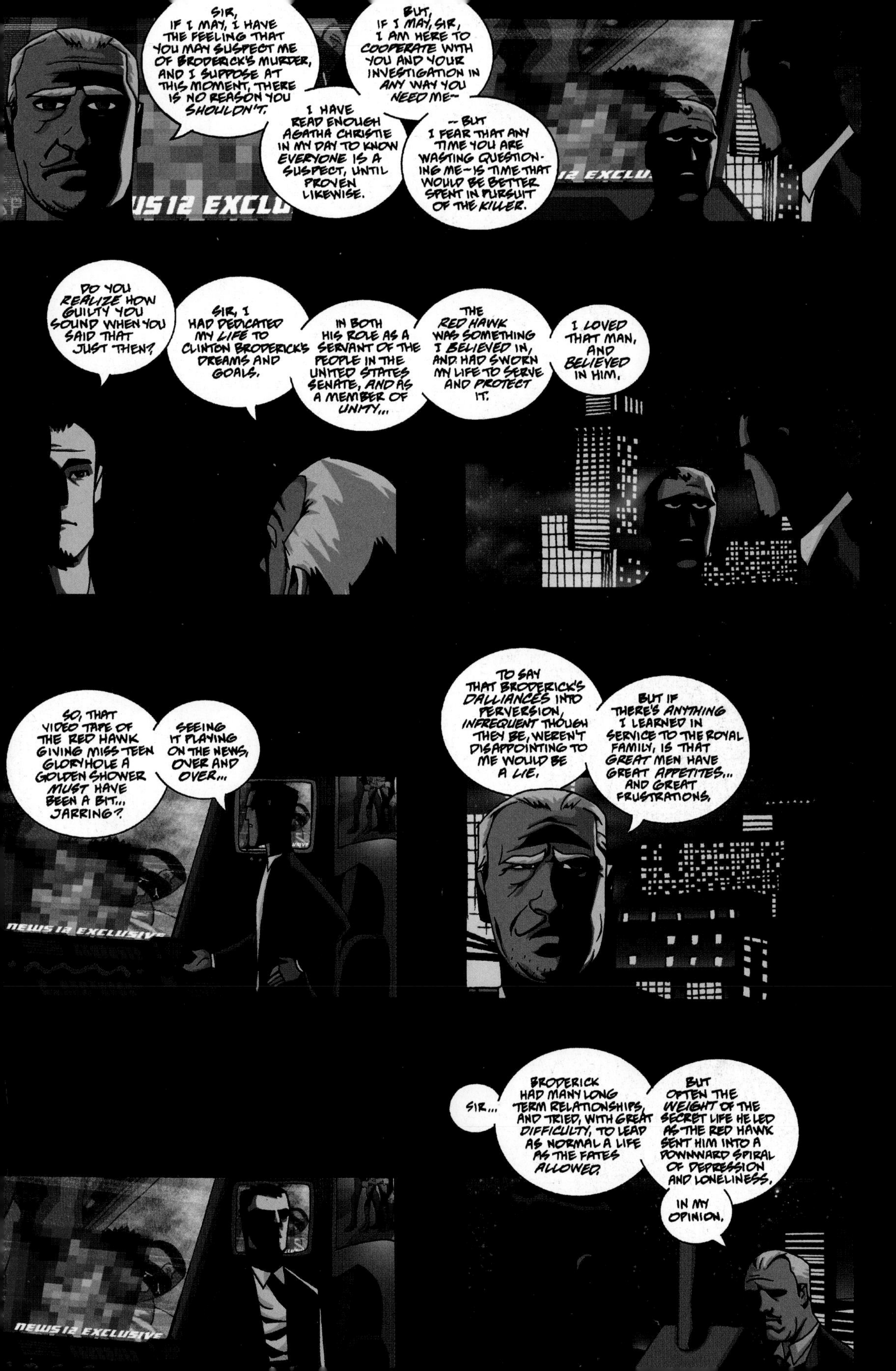
SIR, IF I MAY, I HAVE THE FEELING THAT YOU MAY SUSPECT ME OF BRODERICK'S MURDER, AND I SUPPOSE AT THIS MOMENT, THERE IS NO REASON YOU SHOULDN'T.
I HAVE READ ENOUGH AGATHA CHRISTIE IN MY DAY TO KNOW EVERYONE IS A SUSPECT, UNTIL PROVEN LIKEWISE.
BUT, IF I MAY, SIR, I AM HERE TO COOPERATE WITH YOU AND YOUR INVESTIGATION IN ANY WAY YOU NEED ME--
-- BUT I FEAR THAT ANY TIME YOU ARE WASTING QUESTIONING ME--IS TIME THAT WOULD BE BETTER SPENT IN PURSUIT OF THE KILLER.
US 12 EXCLU
12 EXCLU
DO YOU REALIZE HOW GUILTY YOU SOUND WHEN YOU SAID THAT JUST THEN?
SIR, I HAD DEDICATED MY LIFE TO CLINTON BRODERICK'S DREAMS AND GOALS.
IN BOTH HIS ROLE AS A SERVANT OF THE PEOPLE IN THE UNITED STATES SENATE, AND AS A MEMBER OF UNITY...
THE RED HAWK WAS SOMETHING I BELIEVED IN, AND HAD SWORN MY LIFE TO SERVE AND PROTECT IT.
I LOVED THAT MAN, AND BELIEVED IN HIM.
SO, THAT VIDEO TAPE OF THE RED HAWK GIVING MISS TEEN GLORYHOLE A GOLDEN SHOWER MUST HAVE BEEN A BIT... JARRING?
SEEING IT PLAYING ON THE NEWS, OVER AND OVER...
NEWS 12 EXCLUSIVE
TO SAY THAT BRODERICK'S DALLIANCES INTO PERVERSION, INFREQUENT THOUGH THEY BE, WEREN'T DISAPPOINTING TO ME WOULD BE A LIE.
BUT IF THERE'S ANYTHING I LEARNED IN SERVICE TO THE ROYAL FAMILY, IS THAT GREAT MEN HAVE GREAT APPETITES... AND GREAT FRUSTRATIONS.
SIR...
BRODERICK HAD MANY LONG TERM RELATIONSHIPS, AND TRIED, WITH GREAT DIFFICULTY, TO LEAD AS NORMAL A LIFE AS THE FATES ALLOWED.
BUT OFTEN THE WEIGHT OF THE SECRET LIFE HE LED AS THE RED HAWK SENT HIM INTO A DOWNWARD SPIRAL OF DEPRESSION AND LONELINESS.
IN MY OPINION.
NEWS 12 EXCLUSIVE

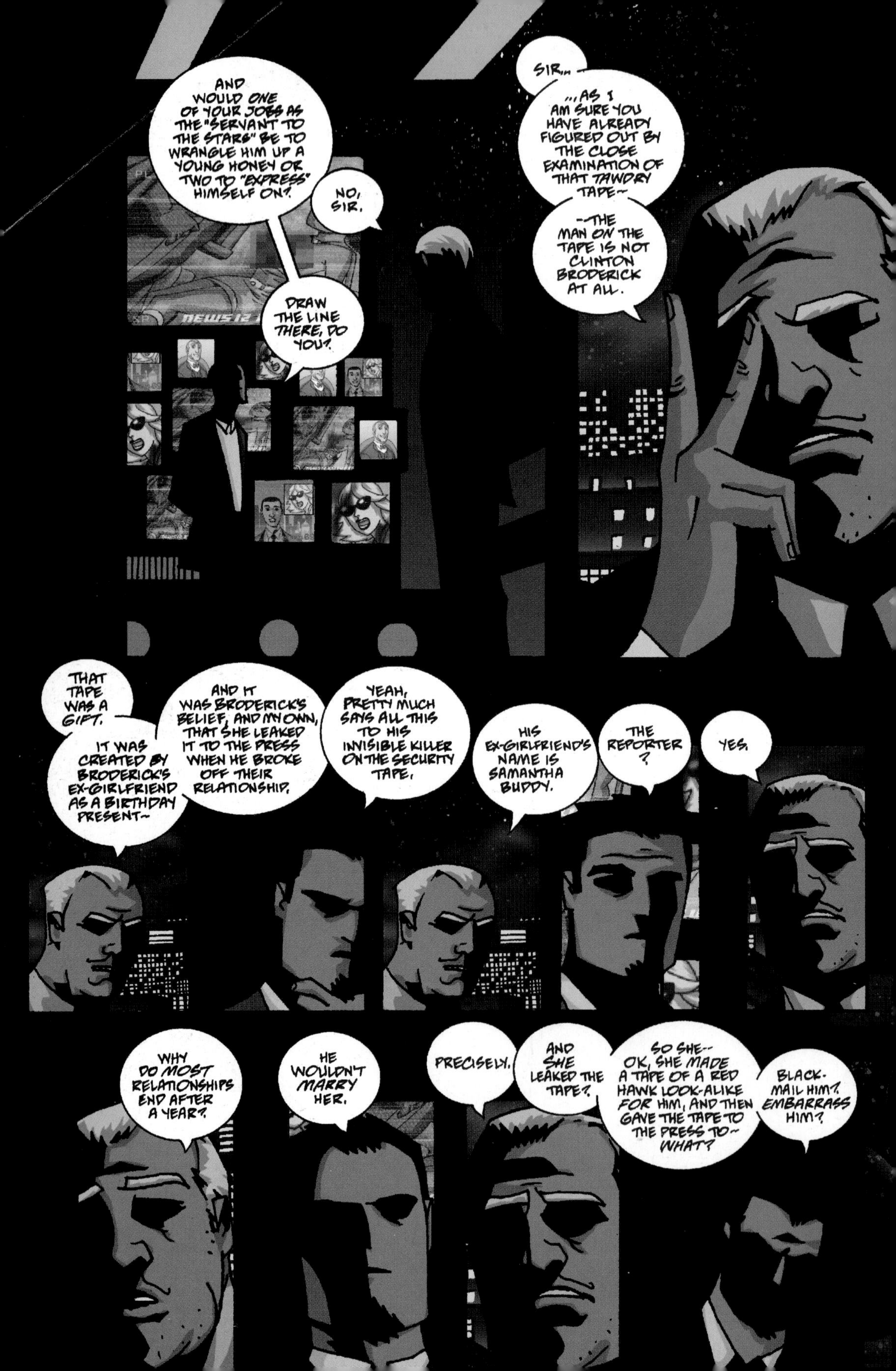

AND WOULD ONE OF YOUR JOBS AS THE "SERVANT TO THE STARS" BE TO WRANGLE HIM UP A YOUNG HONEY OR TWO TO "EXPRESS" HIMSELF ON?
NO, SIR.
DRAW THE LINE THERE, DO YOU?
SIR...
...AS I AM SURE YOU HAVE ALREADY FIGURED OUT BY THE CLOSE EXAMINATION OF THAT TAWDRY TAPE--
--THE MAN ON THE TAPE IS NOT CLINTON BRODERICK AT ALL.
THAT TAPE WAS A GIFT.
IT WAS CREATED BY BRODERICK'S EX-GIRLFRIEND AS A BIRTHDAY PRESENT--
AND IT WAS BRODERICK'S BELIEF, AND MY OWN, THAT SHE LEAKED IT TO THE PRESS WHEN HE BROKE OFF THEIR RELATIONSHIP.
YEAH, PRETTY MUCH SAYS ALL THIS TO HIS INVISIBLE KILLER ON THE SECURITY TAPE.
HIS EX-GIRLFRIEND'S NAME IS SAMANTHA BUDDY.
THE REPORTER?
YES.
WHY DO MOST RELATIONSHIPS END AFTER A YEAR?
HE WOULDN'T MARRY HER.
PRECISELY.
AND SHE LEAKED THE TAPE?
SO SHE-- OK, SHE MADE A TAPE OF A RED HAWK LOOK-ALIKE FOR HIM, AND THEN GAVE THE TAPE TO THE PRESS TO--WHAT?
BLACK-MAIL HIM? EMBARRASS HIM?

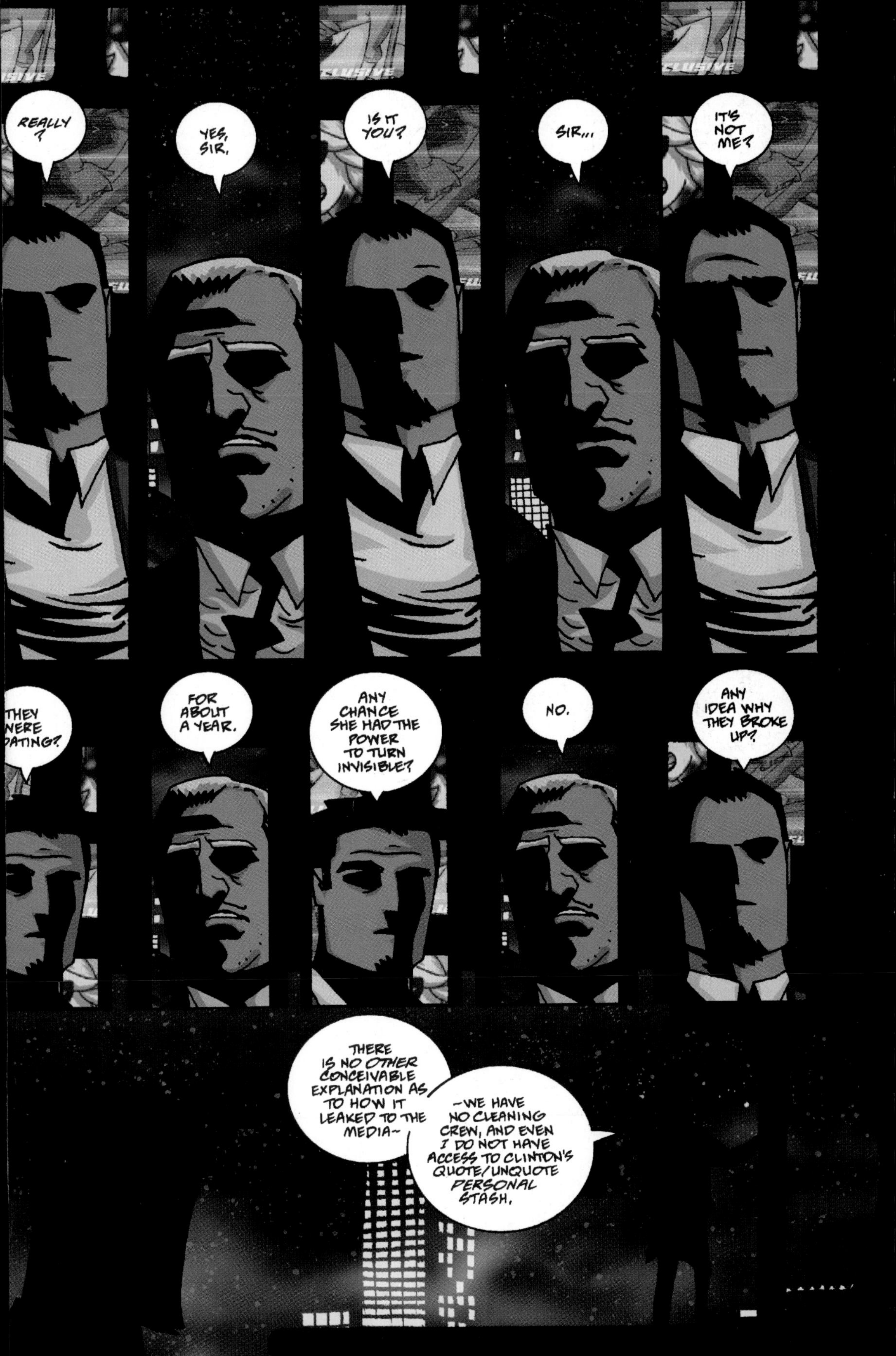
REALLY?
YES, SIR.
IS IT YOU?
SIR...
IT'S NOT ME?
THEY WERE DATING?
FOR ABOUT A YEAR.
ANY CHANCE SHE HAD THE POWER TO TURN INVISIBLE?
NO.
ANY IDEA WHY THEY BROKE UP?
THERE IS NO OTHER CONCEIVABLE EXPLANATION AS TO HOW IT LEAKED TO THE MEDIA~
~WE HAVE NO CLEANING CREW, AND EVEN I DO NOT HAVE ACCESS TO CLINTON'S QUOTE/UNQUOTE PERSONAL STASH.

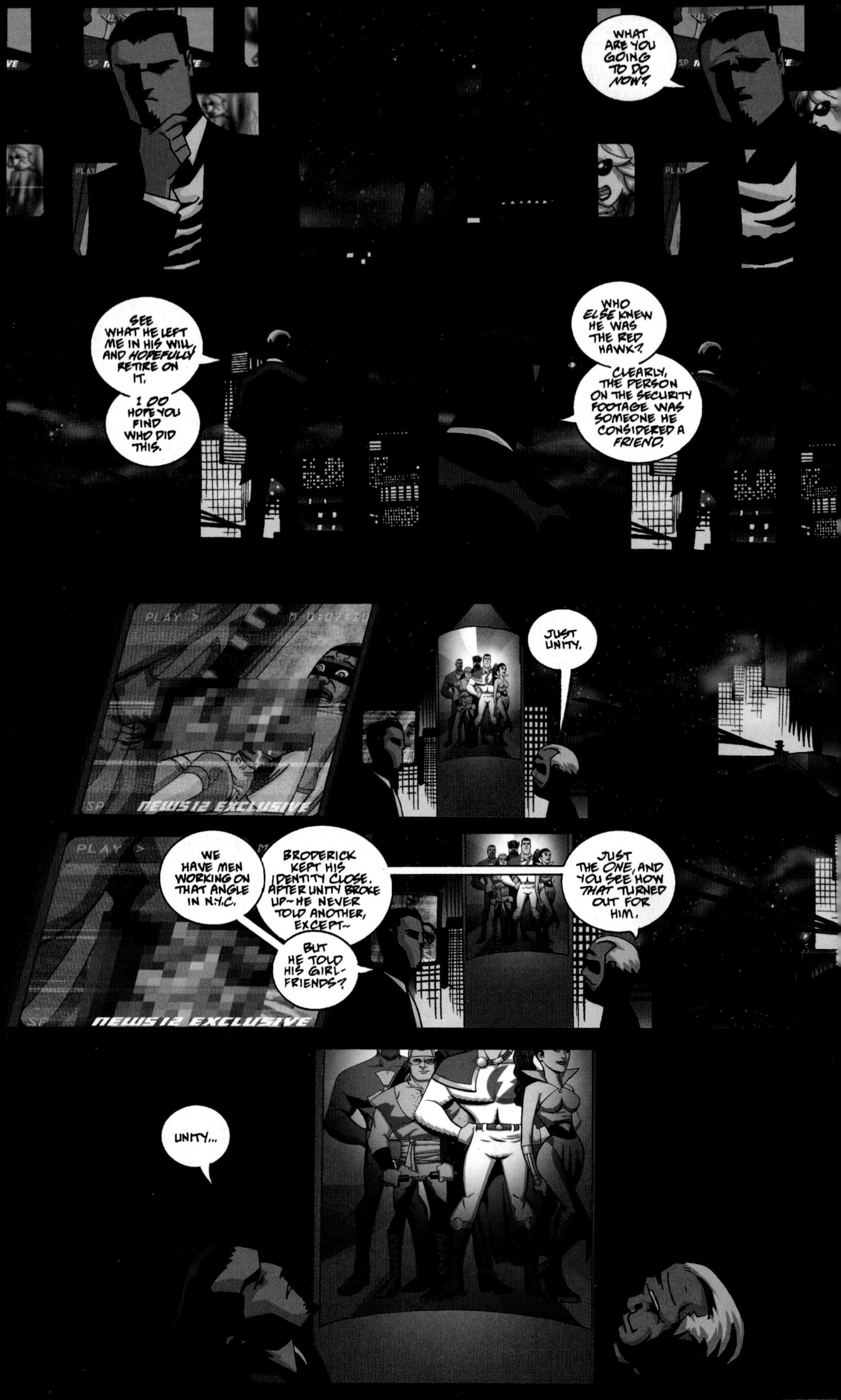
WHAT ARE YOU GOING TO DO NOW?
SEE WHAT HE LEFT ME IN HIS WILL, AND HOPEFULLY RETIRE ON IT.
I DO HOPE YOU FIND WHO DID THIS.
WHO ELSE KNEW HE WAS THE RED HAWK?
CLEARLY, THE PERSON ON THE SECURITY FOOTAGE WAS SOMEONE HE CONSIDERED A FRIEND.
PLAY >
NEWS 12 EXCLUSIVE
JUST UNITY.
PLAY >
WE HAVE MEN WORKING ON THAT ANGLE IN N.Y.C.
BRODERICK KEPT HIS IDENTITY CLOSE. AFTER UNITY BROKE UP-- HE NEVER TOLD ANOTHER, EXCEPT--
JUST THE ONE, AND YOU SEE HOW THAT TURNED OUT FOR HIM.
BUT HE TOLD HIS GIRLFRIENDS?
NEWS 12 EXCLUSIVE
UNITY...

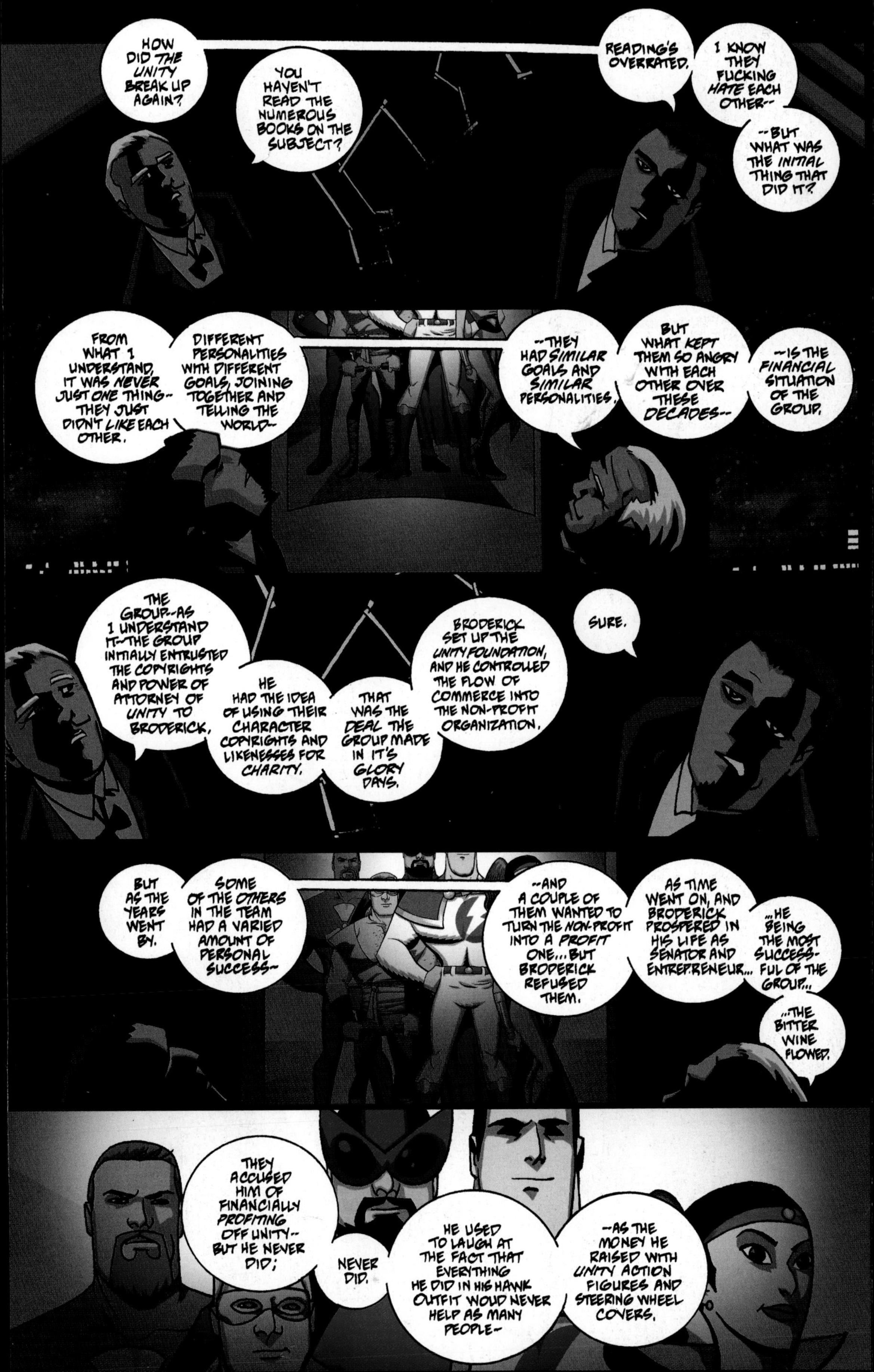
HOW DID THE UNITY BREAK UP AGAIN?
YOU HAVEN'T READ THE NUMEROUS BOOKS ON THE SUBJECT?
READING'S OVERRATED.
I KNOW THEY FUCKING HATE EACH OTHER--
--BUT WHAT WAS THE INITIAL THING THAT DID IT?
FROM WHAT I UNDERSTAND, IT WAS NEVER JUST ONE THING-- THEY JUST DIDN'T LIKE EACH OTHER.
DIFFERENT PERSONALITIES WITH DIFFERENT GOALS, JOINING TOGETHER AND TELLING THE WORLD--
--THEY HAD SIMILAR GOALS AND SIMILAR PERSONALITIES.
BUT WHAT KEPT THEM SO ANGRY WITH EACH OTHER OVER THESE DECADES--
--IS THE FINANCIAL SITUATION OF THE GROUP.
THE GROUP--AS I UNDERSTAND IT--THE GROUP INITIALLY ENTRUSTED THE COPYRIGHTS AND POWER OF ATTORNEY OF UNITY TO BRODERICK.
HE HAD THE IDEA OF USING THEIR CHARACTER COPYRIGHTS AND LIKENESSES FOR CHARITY.
THAT WAS THE DEAL THE GROUP MADE IN IT'S GLORY DAYS.
BRODERICK SET UP THE UNITY FOUNDATION, AND HE CONTROLLED THE FLOW OF COMMERCE INTO THE NON-PROFIT ORGANIZATION.
SURE.
BUT AS THE YEARS WENT BY.
SOME OF THE OTHERS IN THE TEAM HAD A VARIED AMOUNT OF PERSONAL SUCCESS--
--AND A COUPLE OF THEM WANTED TO TURN THE NON-PROFIT INTO A PROFIT ONE... BUT BRODERICK REFUSED THEM.
AS TIME WENT ON, AND BRODERICK PROSPERED IN HIS LIFE AS SENATOR AND ENTREPRENEUR...
...HE BEING THE MOST SUCCESSFUL OF THE GROUP...
...THE BITTER WINE FLOWED.
THEY ACCUSED HIM OF FINANCIALLY PROFITING OFF UNITY-- BUT HE NEVER DID;
NEVER DID.
HE USED TO LAUGH AT THE FACT THAT EVERYTHING HE DID IN HIS HAWK OUTFIT WOUD NEVER HELP AS MANY PEOPLE--
--AS THE MONEY HE RAISED WITH UNITY ACTION FIGURES AND STEERING WHEEL COVERS.

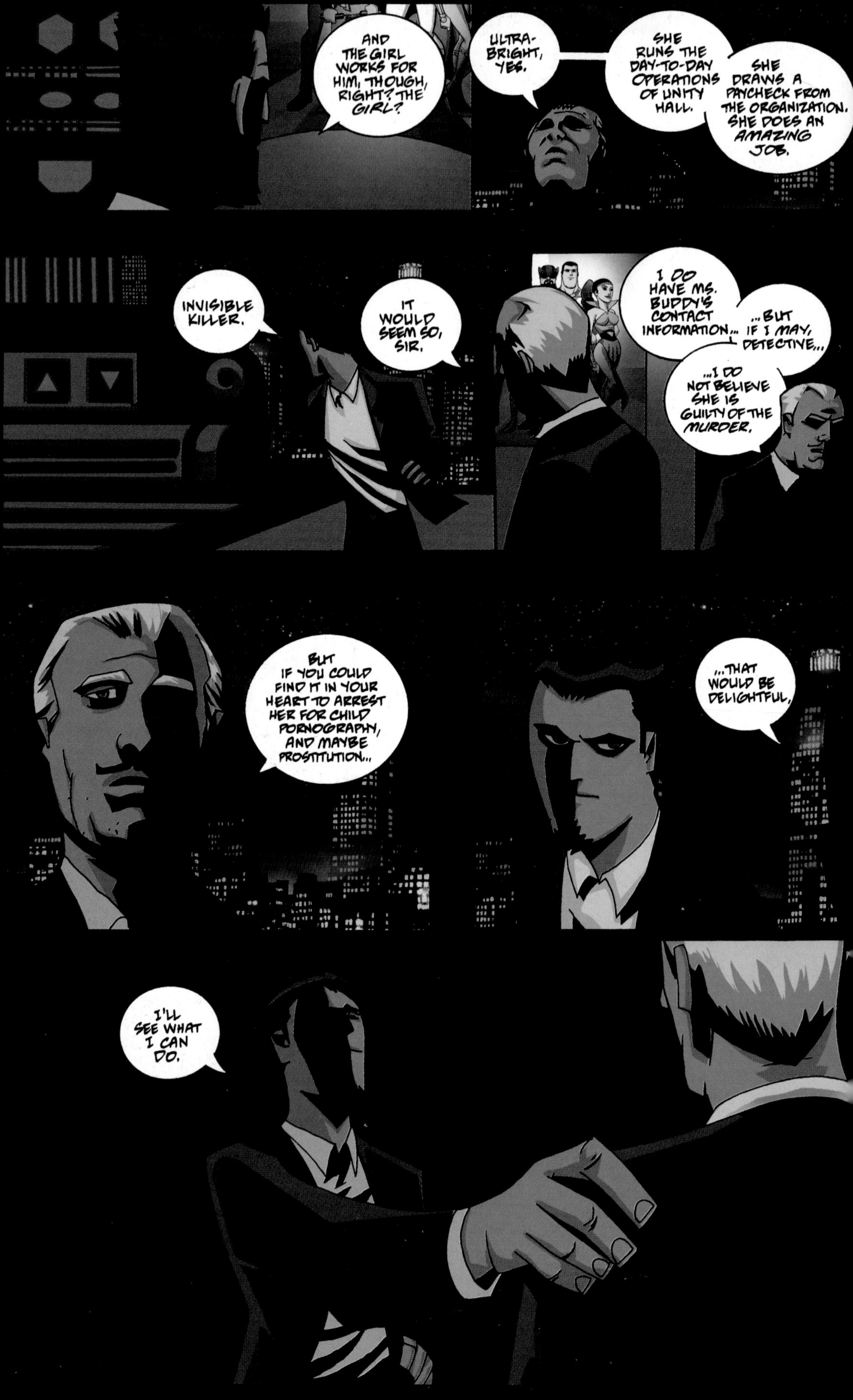
AND THE GIRL WORKS FOR HIM, THOUGH, RIGHT? THE GIRL?
ULTRA-BRIGHT, YES.
SHE RUNS THE DAY-TO-DAY OPERATIONS OF UNITY HALL.
SHE DRAWS A PAYCHECK FROM THE ORGANIZATION. SHE DOES AN AMAZING JOB.
INVISIBLE KILLER.
IT WOULD SEEM SO, SIR.
I DO HAVE MS. BUDDY'S CONTACT INFORMATION...
...BUT IF I MAY, DETECTIVE...
...I DO NOT BELIEVE SHE IS GUILTY OF THE MURDER.
BUT IF YOU COULD FIND IT IN YOUR HEART TO ARREST HER FOR CHILD PORNOGRAPHY, AND MAYBE PROSTITUTION...
...THAT WOULD BE DELIGHTFUL.
I'LL SEE WHAT I CAN DO.

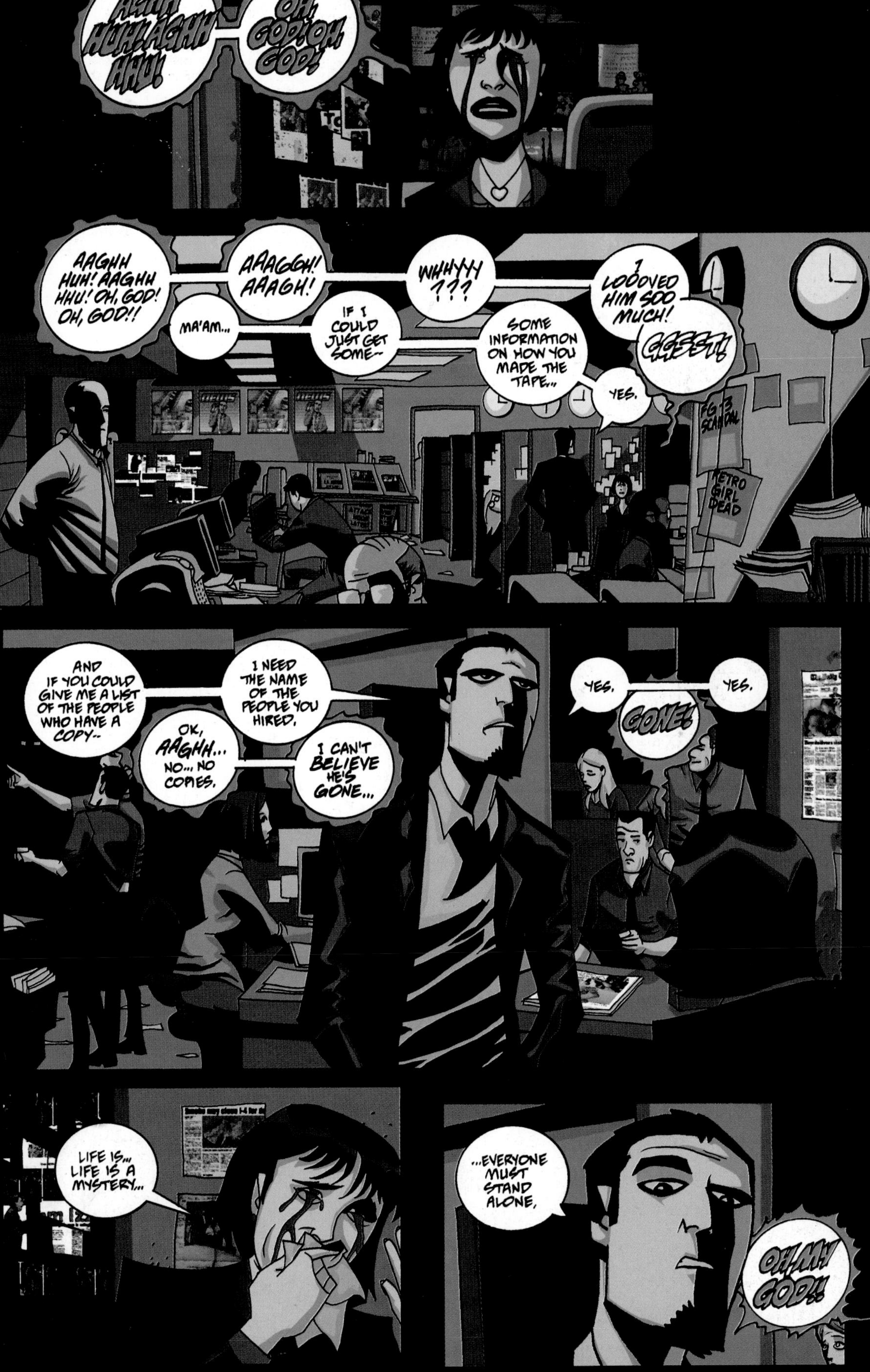
AGHH HUH! AGHH HHU!
OH, GOD! OH, GOD!
AAGHH HUH! AAGHH HHU! OH, GOD! OH, GOD!!
MA'AM...
AAAGGH! AAAGH!
IF I COULD JUST GET SOME--
WHHYYY ???
SOME INFORMATION ON HOW YOU MADE THE TAPE...
I LOOOVED HIM SOO MUCH!
YES.
FG-13 SCANDAL
RETRO GIRL DEAD
AND IF YOU COULD GIVE ME A LIST OF THE PEOPLE WHO HAVE A COPY--
OK, AAGHH... NO... NO COPIES.
I NEED THE NAME OF THE PEOPLE YOU HIRED.
I CAN'T BELIEVE HE'S GONE...
YES.
GONE!
YES.
LIFE IS... LIFE IS A MYSTERY...
...EVERYONE MUST STAND ALONE.
OH MY GOD!!

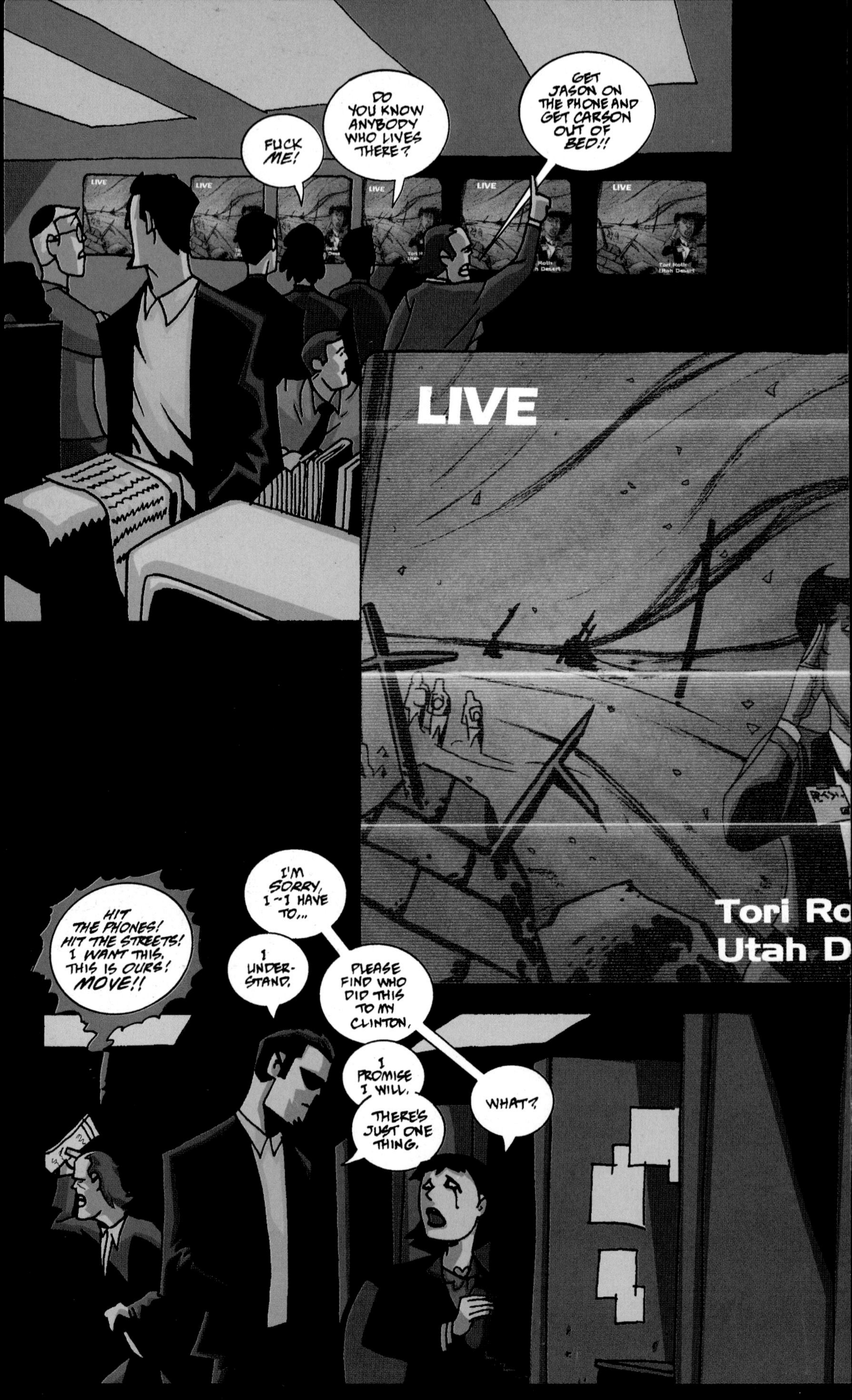
FUCK ME!
DO YOU KNOW ANYBODY WHO LIVES THERE?
GET JASON ON THE PHONE AND GET CARSON OUT OF BED!!
LIVE
LIVE
LIVE
LIVE
LIVE
Tori Rollr Utah Desert
LIVE
Tori Ro
Utah D
HIT THE PHONES! HIT THE STREETS! I WANT THIS. THIS IS OURS! MOVE!!
I'M SORRY, I--I HAVE TO...
I UNDER-STAND.
PLEASE FIND WHO DID THIS TO MY CLINTON.
I PROMISE I WILL.
THERE'S JUST ONE THING.
WHAT?

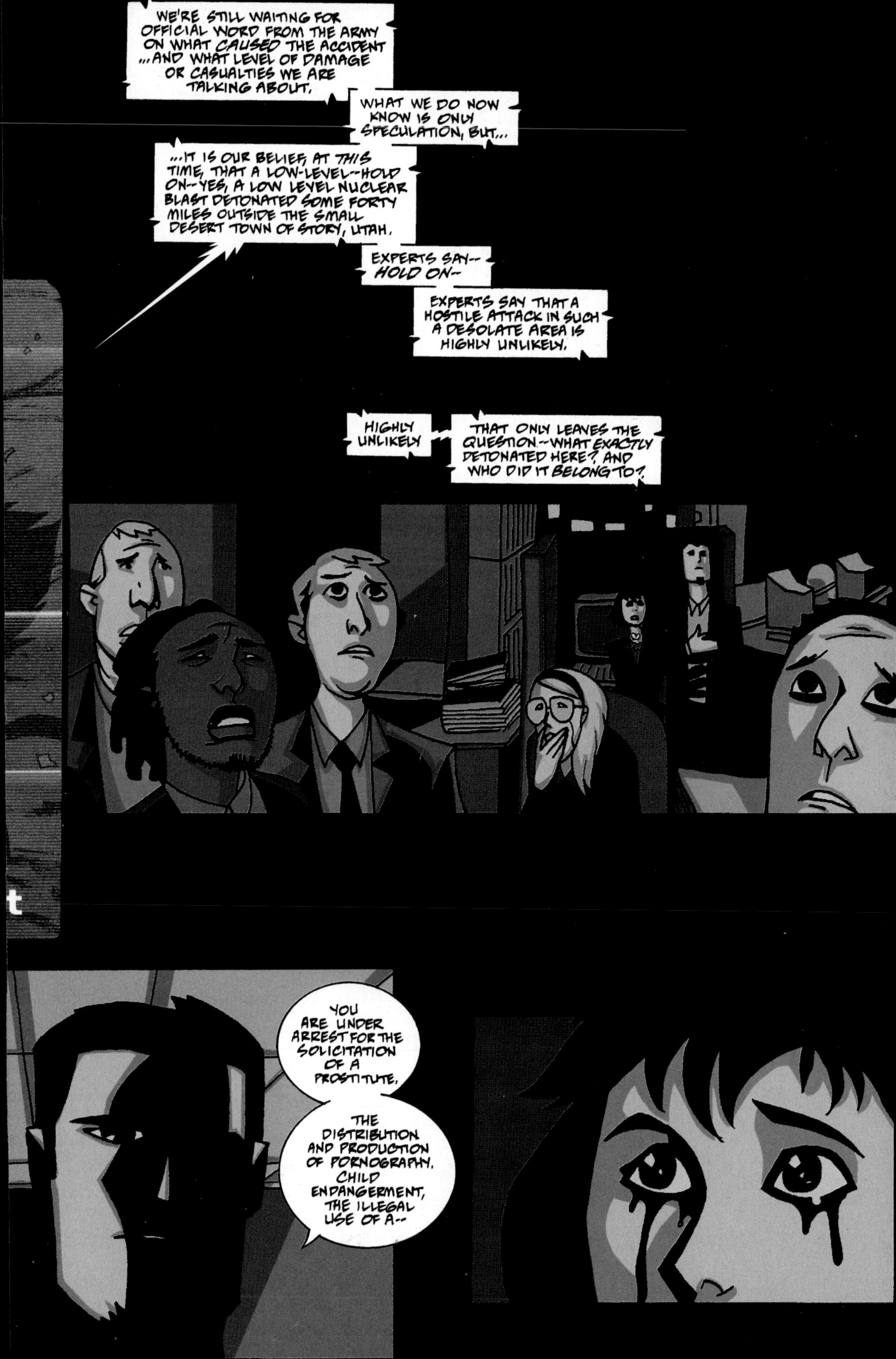
WE'RE STILL WAITING FOR OFFICIAL WORD FROM THE ARMY ON WHAT CAUSED THE ACCIDENT ...AND WHAT LEVEL OF DAMAGE OR CASUALTIES WE ARE TALKING ABOUT.
WHAT WE DO NOW KNOW IS ONLY SPECULATION, BUT...
...IT IS OUR BELIEF, AT THIS TIME, THAT A LOW-LEVEL--HOLD ON--YES, A LOW LEVEL NUCLEAR BLAST DETONATED SOME FORTY MILES OUTSIDE THE SMALL DESERT TOWN OF STORY, UTAH.
EXPERTS SAY-- HOLD ON--
EXPERTS SAY THAT A HOSTILE ATTACK IN SUCH A DESOLATE AREA IS HIGHLY UNLIKELY.
HIGHLY UNLIKELY
THAT ONLY LEAVES THE QUESTION--WHAT EXACTLY DETONATED HERE? AND WHO DID IT BELONG TO?
YOU ARE UNDER ARREST FOR THE SOLICITATION OF A PROSTITUTE.
THE DISTRIBUTION AND PRODUCTION OF PORNOGRAPHY. CHILD ENDANGERMENT, THE ILLEGAL USE OF A--

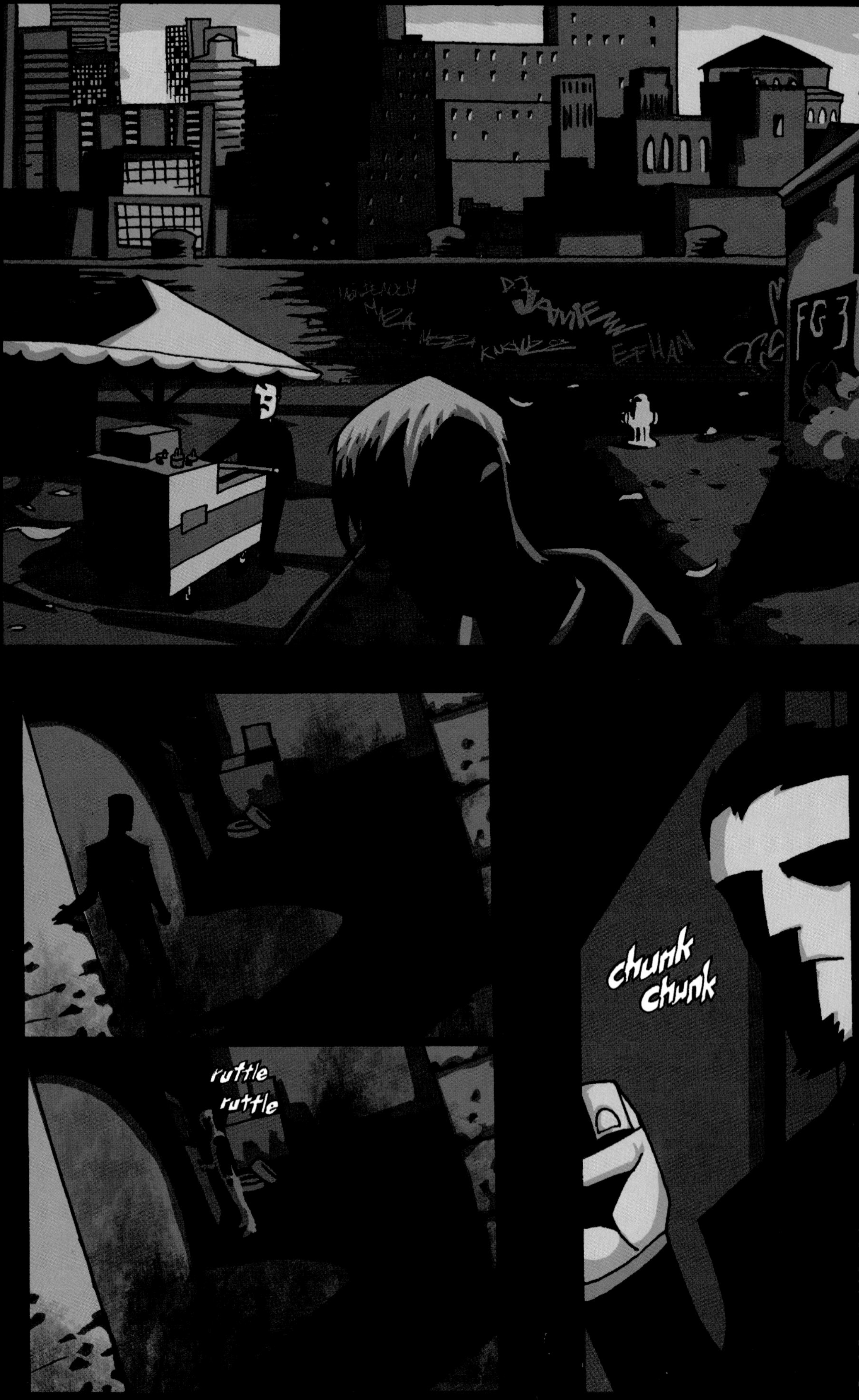
FG 3
chunk chunk
ruttle ruttle

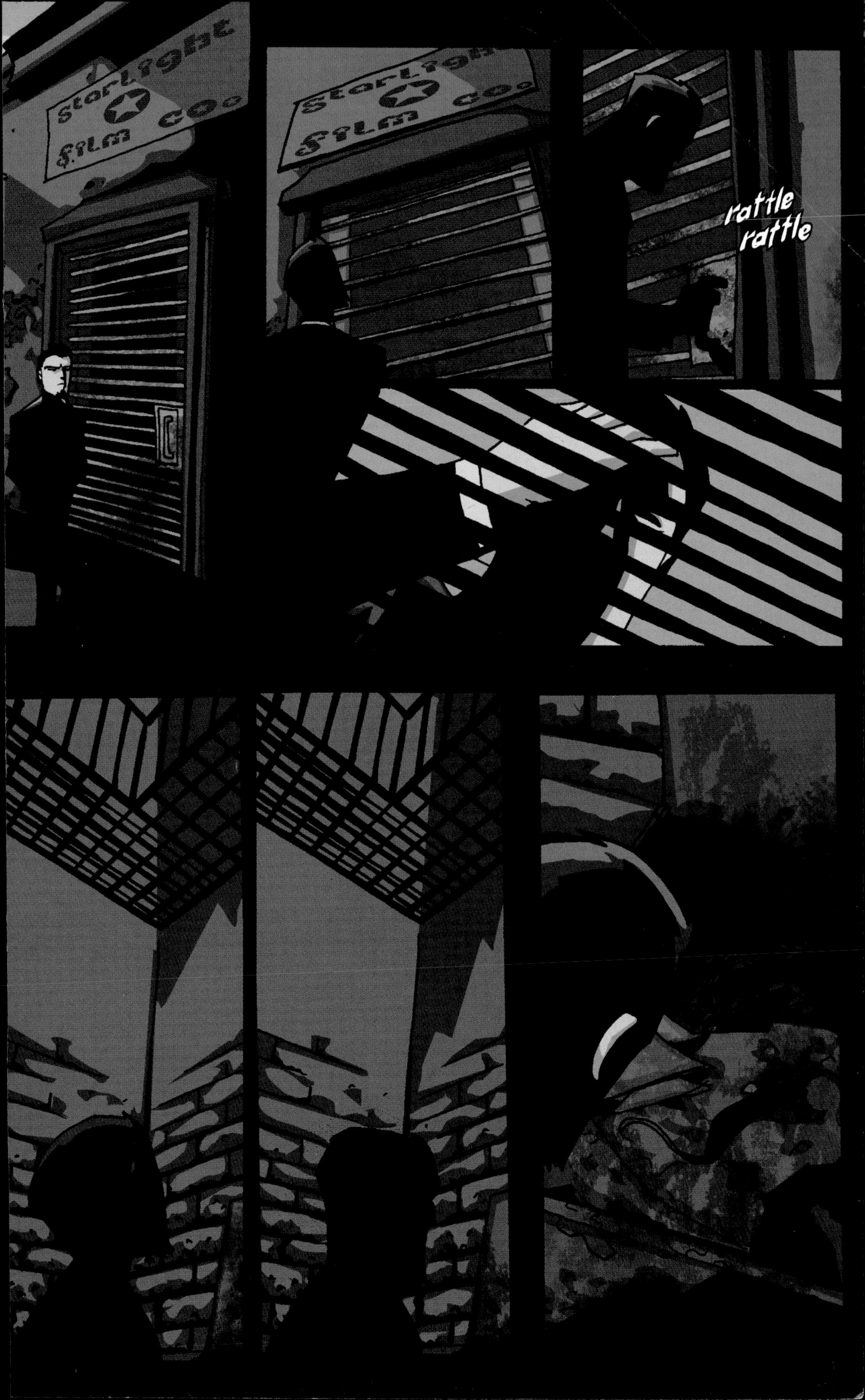
StarLight Film Co.
StarLight Film Co.
rattle rattle

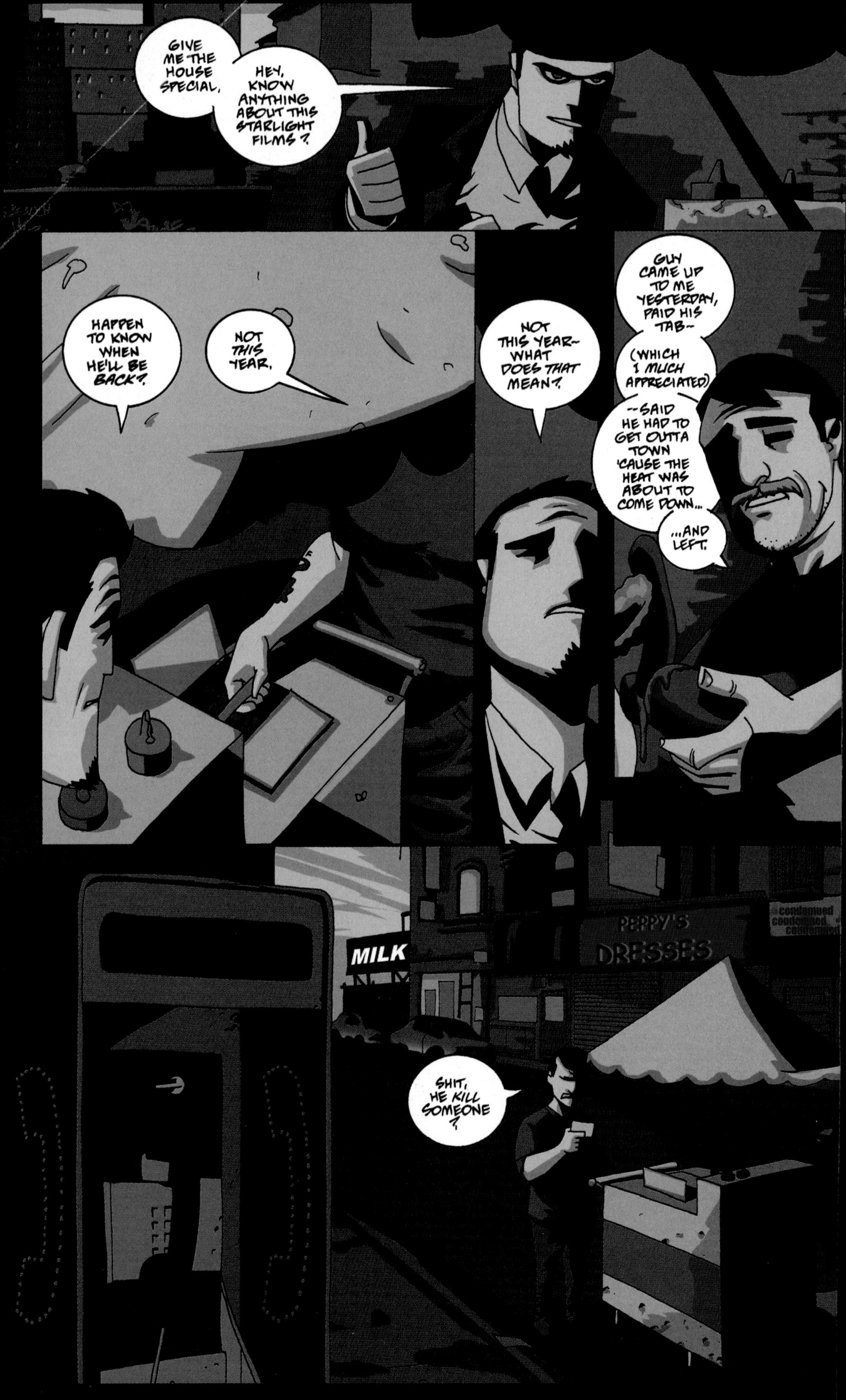
GIVE ME THE HOUSE SPECIAL.
HEY, KNOW ANYTHING ABOUT THIS STARLIGHT FILMS?
HAPPEN TO KNOW WHEN HE'LL BE BACK?
NOT THIS YEAR.
NOT THIS YEAR-- WHAT DOES THAT MEAN?
GUY CAME UP TO ME YESTERDAY, PAID HIS TAB--
(WHICH I MUCH APPRECIATED)
--SAID HE HAD TO GET OUTTA TOWN 'CAUSE THE HEAT WAS ABOUT TO COME DOWN...
...AND LEFT.
MILK
PEPPY'S
DRESSES
SHIT, HE KILL SOMEONE?

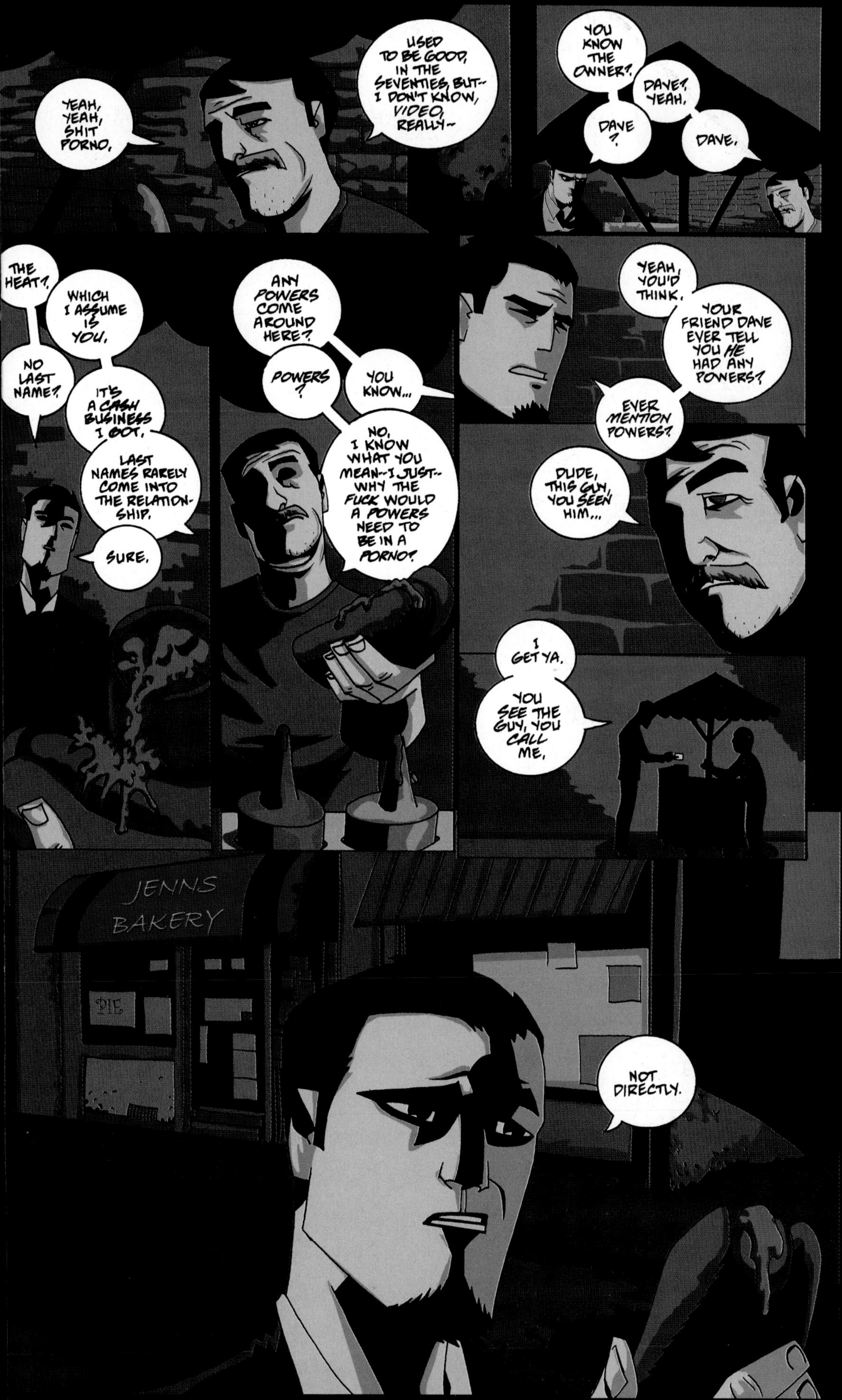
YEAH, YEAH, SHIT PORNO.
USED TO BE GOOD, IN THE SEVENTIES, BUT-- I DON'T KNOW, VIDEO, REALLY--
YOU KNOW THE OWNER?
DAVE?
DAVE? YEAH.
DAVE.
THE HEAT?
WHICH I ASSUME IS YOU.
NO LAST NAME?
IT'S A CASH BUSINESS I GOT.
LAST NAMES RARELY COME INTO THE RELATIONSHIP.
SURE.
ANY POWERS COME AROUND HERE?
POWERS?
YOU KNOW...
NO, I KNOW WHAT YOU MEAN--I JUST-- WHY THE FUCK WOULD A POWERS NEED TO BE IN A PORNO?
YEAH, YOU'D THINK.
YOUR FRIEND DAVE EVER TELL YOU HE HAD ANY POWERS?
EVER MENTION POWERS?
DUDE, THIS GUY, YOU SEEN HIM...
I GET YA.
YOU SEE THE GUY, YOU CALL ME.
JENNS BAKERY
PIE
NOT DIRECTLY.

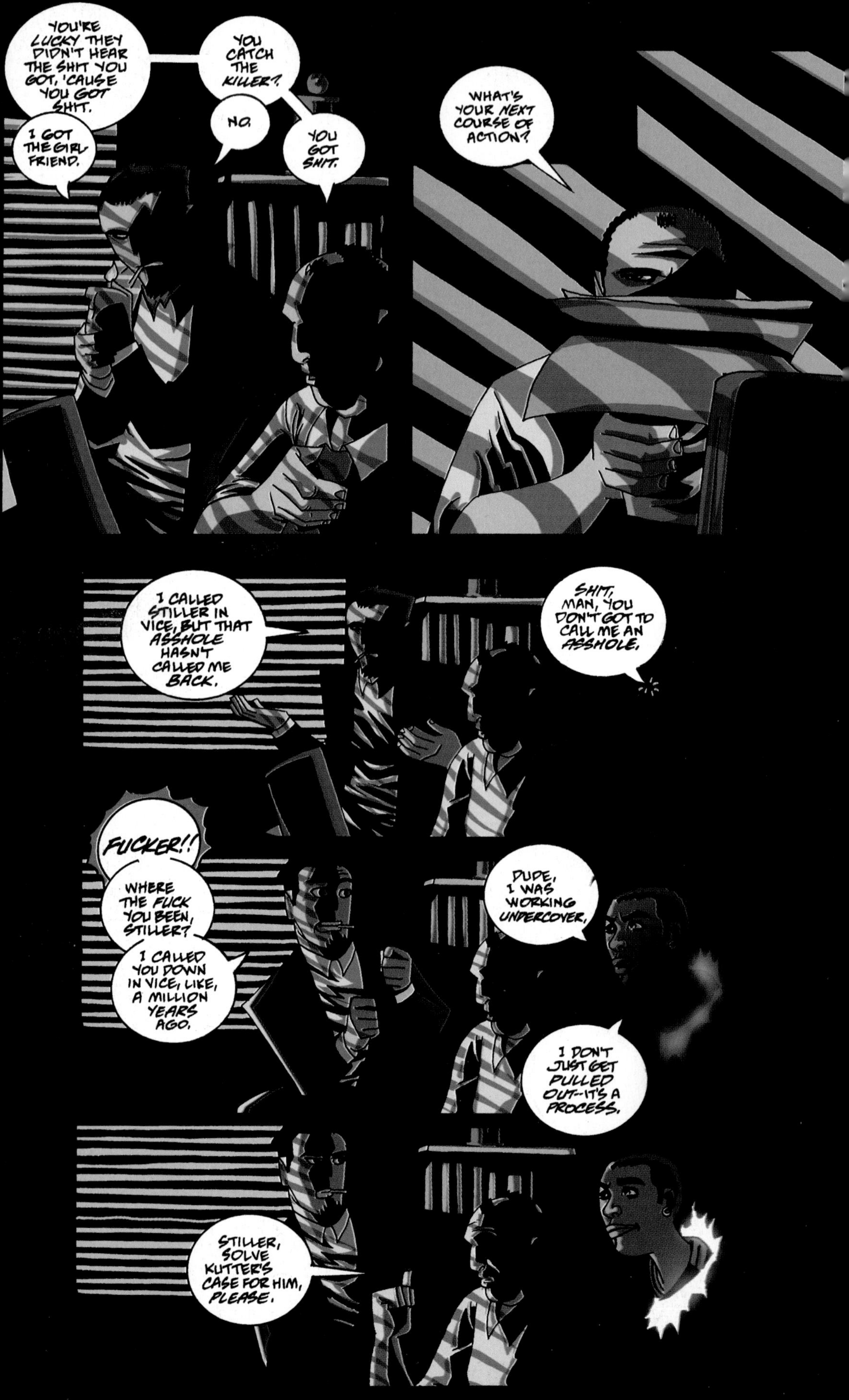
YOU'RE LUCKY THEY DIDN'T HEAR THE SHIT YOU GOT, 'CAUSE YOU GOT SHIT.
YOU CATCH THE KILLER?
I GOT THE GIRLFRIEND.
NO.
YOU GOT SHIT.
WHAT'S YOUR NEXT COURSE OF ACTION?
I CALLED STILLER IN VICE, BUT THAT ASSHOLE HASN'T CALLED ME BACK.
SHIT, MAN, YOU DON'T GOT TO CALL ME AN ASSHOLE.
FUCKER!!
WHERE THE FUCK YOU BEEN, STILLER?
I CALLED YOU DOWN IN VICE, LIKE, A MILLION YEARS AGO.
DUDE, I WAS WORKING UNDERCOVER.
I DON'T JUST GET PULLED OUT--IT'S A PROCESS.
STILLER, SOLVE KUTTER'S CASE FOR HIM, PLEASE.

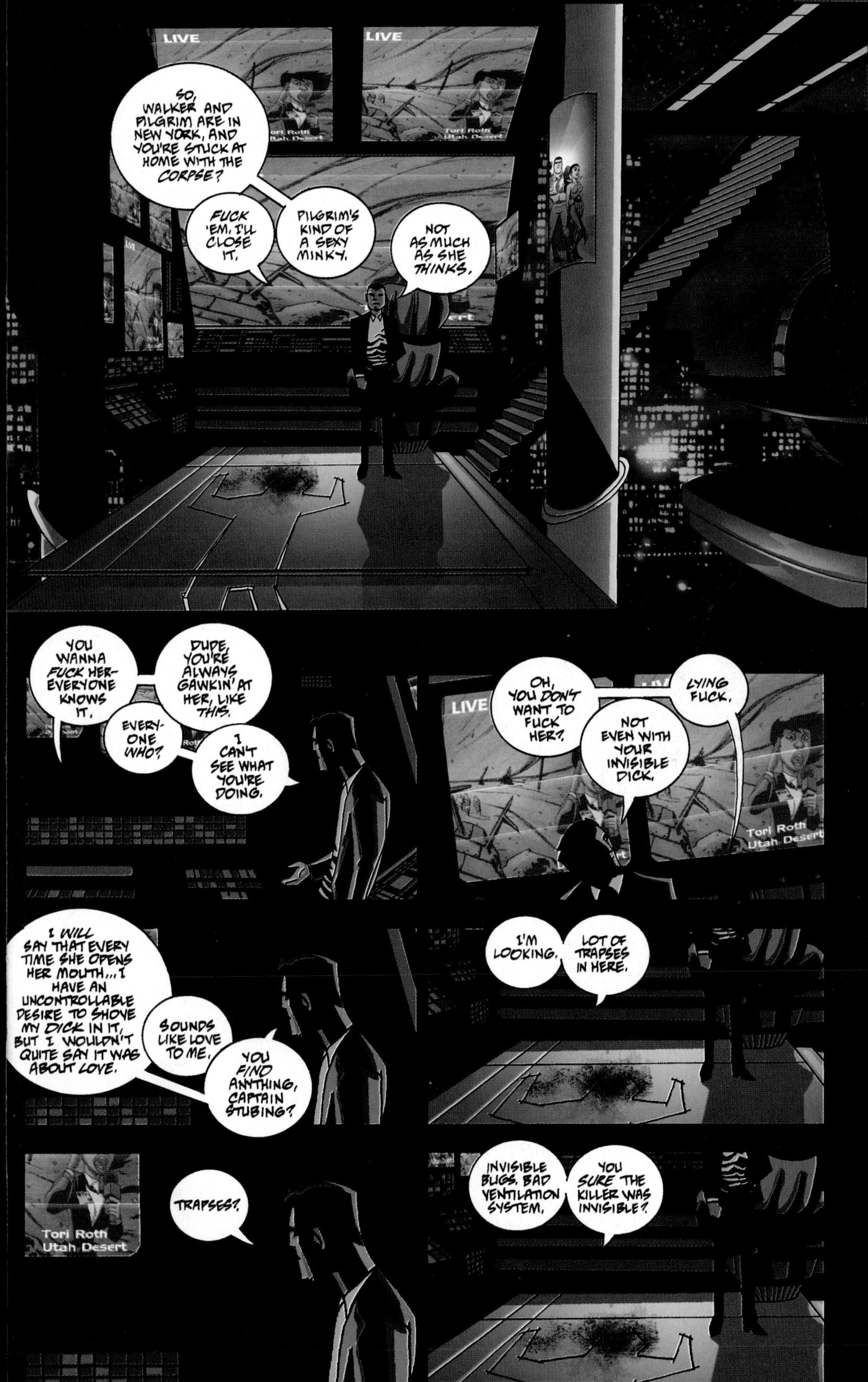
LIVE
LIVE
SO, WALKER AND PILGRIM ARE IN NEW YORK, AND YOU'RE STUCK AT HOME WITH THE CORPSE?
FUCK 'EM, I'LL CLOSE IT.
PILGRIM'S KIND OF A SEXY MINKY.
NOT AS MUCH AS SHE THINKS.
Tori Roth
Utah Desert
YOU WANNA FUCK HER-- EVERYONE KNOWS IT.
DUDE, YOU'RE ALWAYS GAWKIN' AT HER, LIKE THIS.
EVERY-ONE WHO?
I CAN'T SEE WHAT YOU'RE DOING.
OH, YOU DON'T WANT TO FUCK HER?
LYING FUCK.
NOT EVEN WITH YOUR INVISIBLE DICK.
LIVE
Tori Roth
Utah Desert
I WILL SAY THAT EVERY TIME SHE OPENS HER MOUTH... I HAVE AN UNCONTROLLABLE DESIRE TO SHOVE MY DICK IN IT, BUT I WOULDN'T QUITE SAY IT WAS ABOUT LOVE.
SOUNDS LIKE LOVE TO ME.
YOU FIND ANYTHING, CAPTAIN STUBING?
I'M LOOKING.
LOT OF TRAPSES IN HERE.
Tori Roth
Utah Desert
TRAPSES?
INVISIBLE BUGS. BAD VENTILATION SYSTEM.
YOU SURE THE KILLER WAS INVISIBLE?

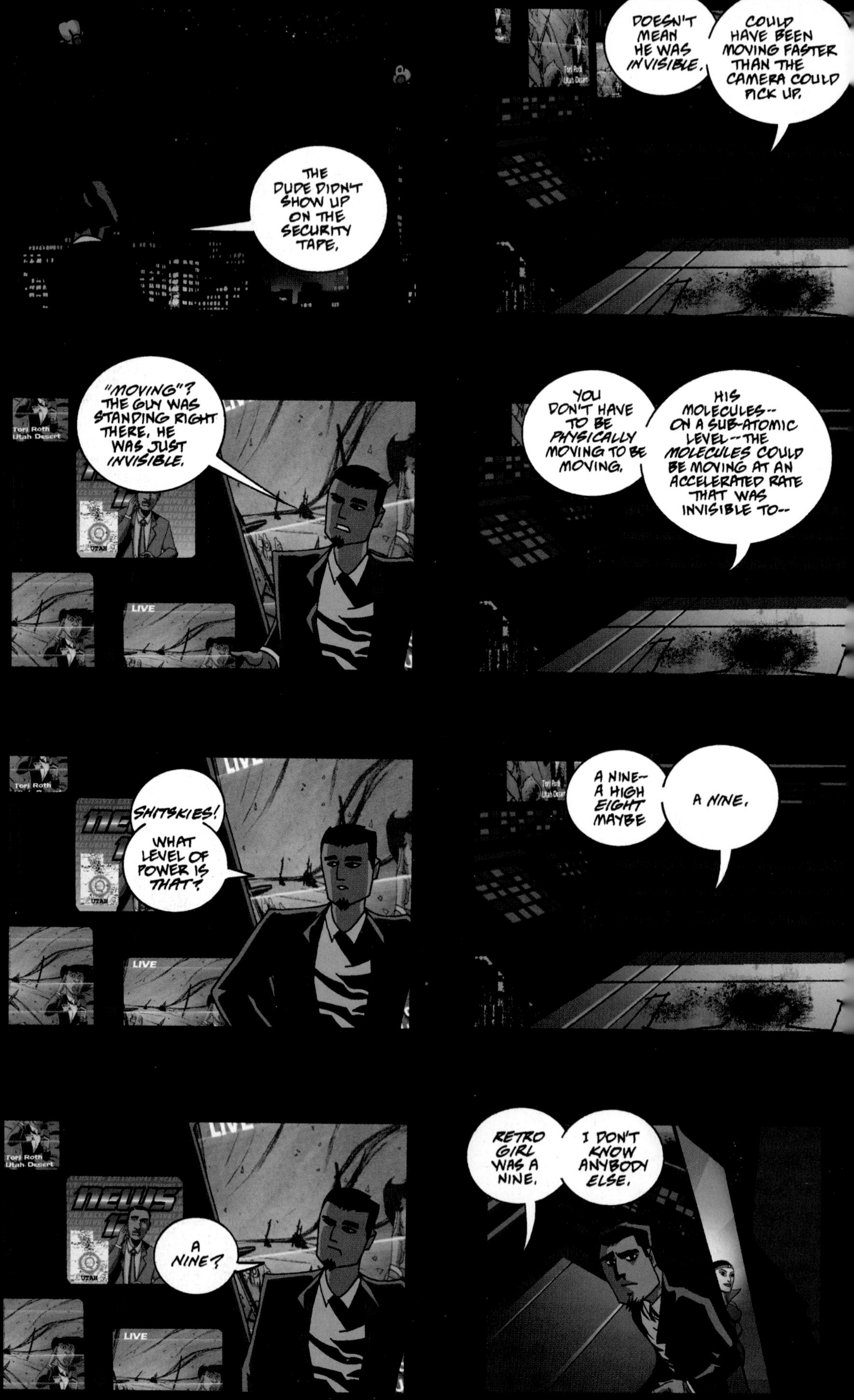

THE DUDE DIDN'T SHOW UP ON THE SECURITY TAPE.
DOESN'T MEAN HE WAS INVISIBLE.
COULD HAVE BEEN MOVING FASTER THAN THE CAMERA COULD PICK UP.
Tori Roth Utah Desert
"MOVING"? THE GUY WAS STANDING RIGHT THERE. HE WAS JUST INVISIBLE.
LIVE
YOU DON'T HAVE TO BE PHYSICALLY MOVING TO BE MOVING.
HIS MOLECULES-- ON A SUB-ATOMIC LEVEL-- THE MOLECULES COULD BE MOVING AT AN ACCELERATED RATE THAT WAS INVISIBLE TO--
SHITSKIES!
WHAT LEVEL OF POWER IS THAT?
A NINE-- A HIGH EIGHT MAYBE
A NINE.
A NINE?
RETRO GIRL WAS A NINE.
I DON'T KNOW ANYBODY ELSE.

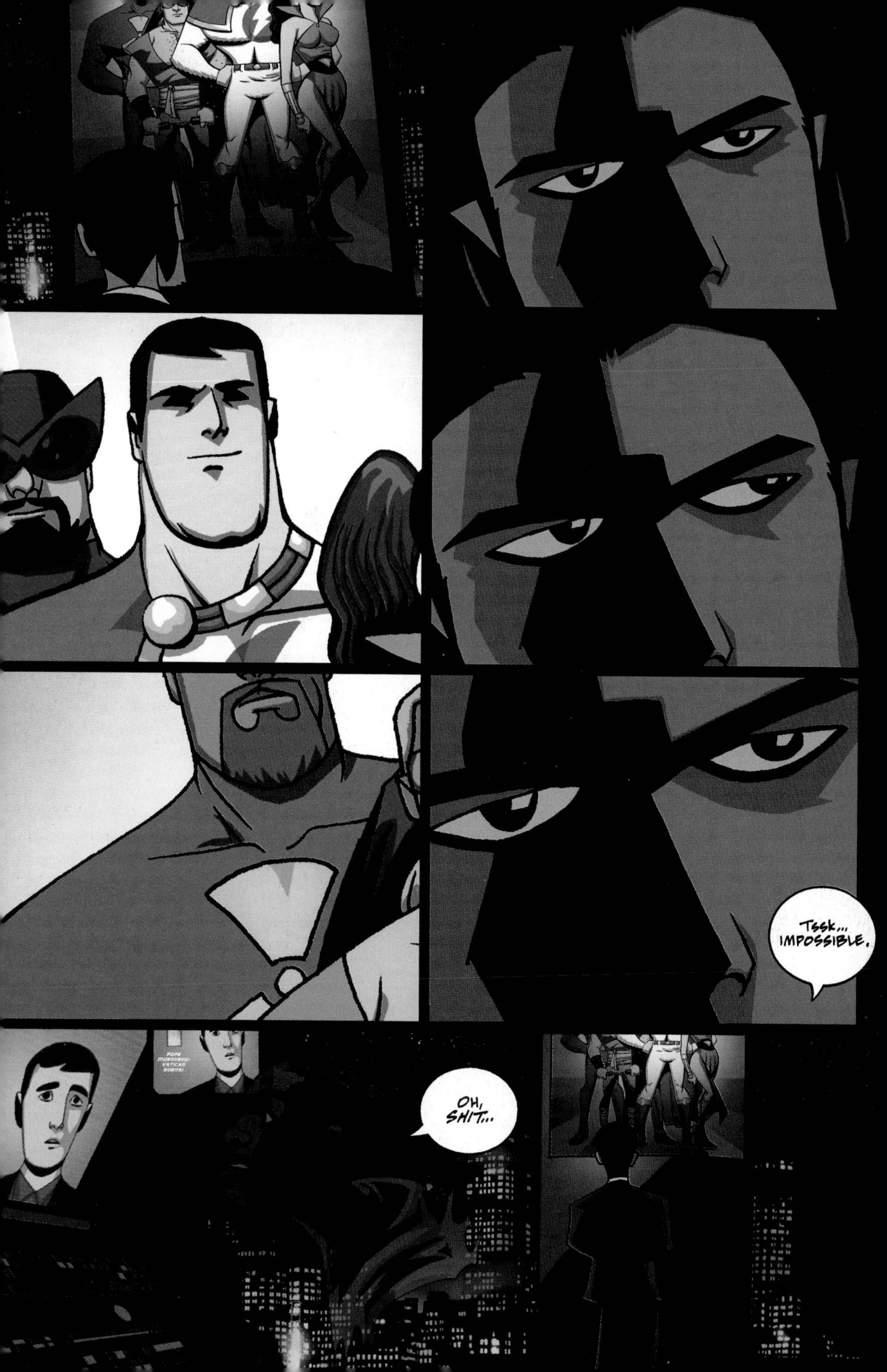
Tssk... IMPOSSIBLE.
OH, SHIT...

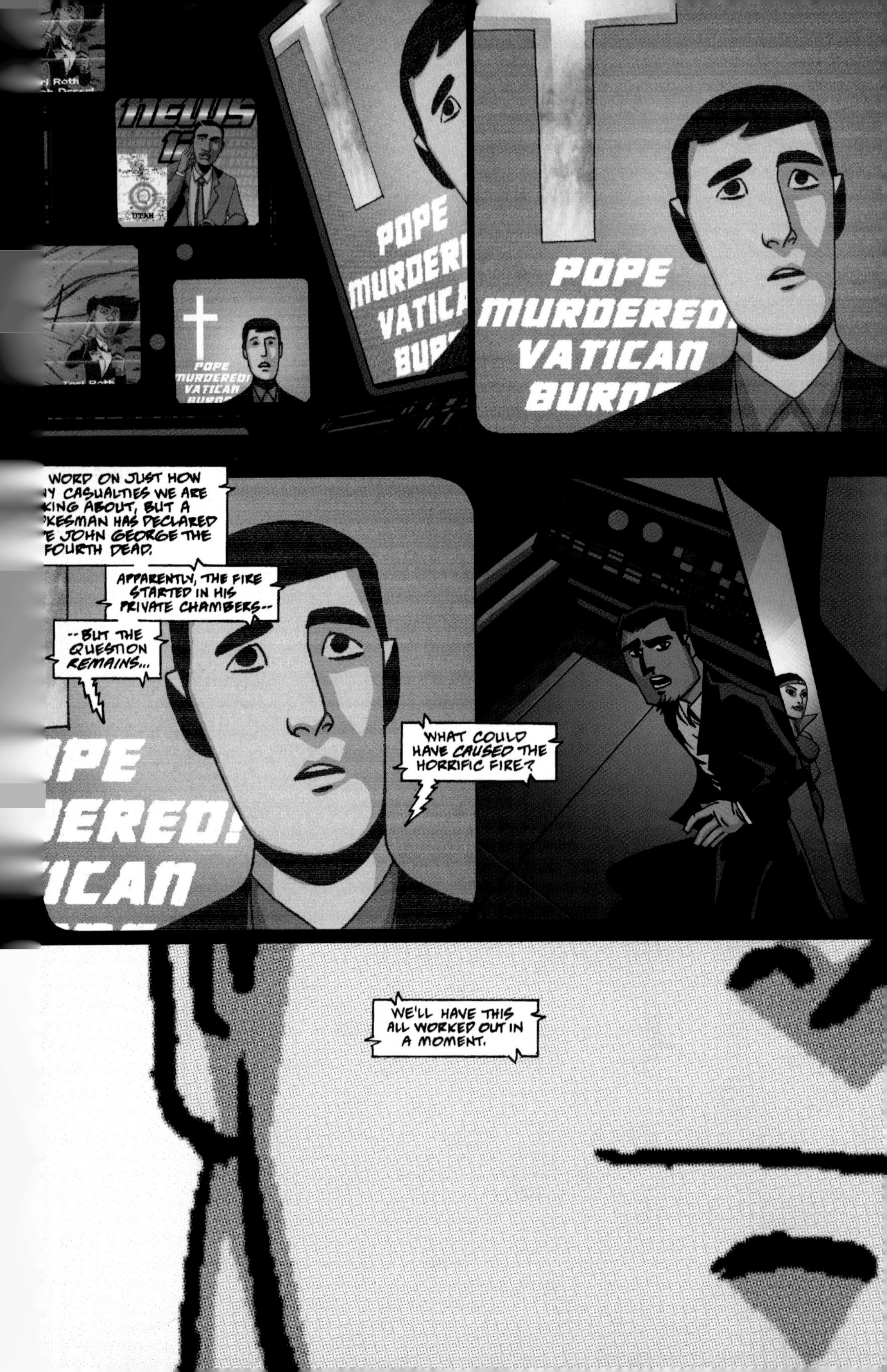
POPE MURDERED! VATICAN
WORD ON JUST HOW
NY CASUALTIES WE ARE
KING ABOUT, BUT A
OKESMAN HAS DECLARED
E JOHN GEORGE THE
FOURTH DEAD.
APPARENTLY, THE FIRE STARTED IN HIS PRIVATE CHAMBERS--
--BUT THE QUESTION REMAINS...
WHAT COULD HAVE CAUSED THE HORRIFIC FIRE?
WE'LL HAVE THIS ALL WORKED OUT IN A MOMENT.

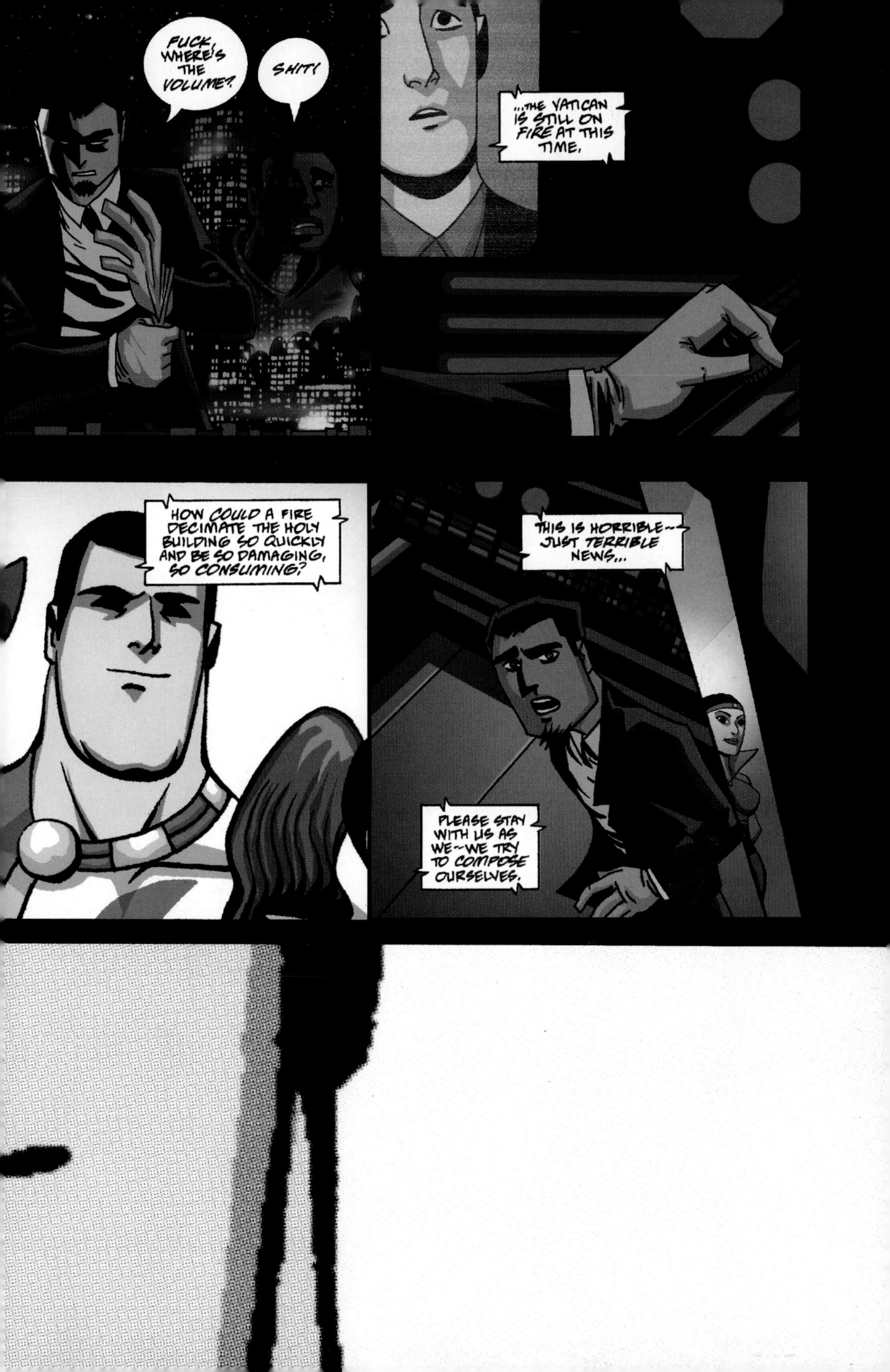
FUCK, WHERE'S THE VOLUME?
SHIT!
...THE VATICAN IS STILL ON FIRE AT THIS TIME.
HOW COULD A FIRE DECIMATE THE HOLY BUILDING SO QUICKLY AND BE SO DAMAGING, SO CONSUMING?
THIS IS HORRIBLE-- JUST TERRIBLE NEWS...
PLEASE STAY WITH US AS WE--WE TRY TO COMPOSE OURSELVES.

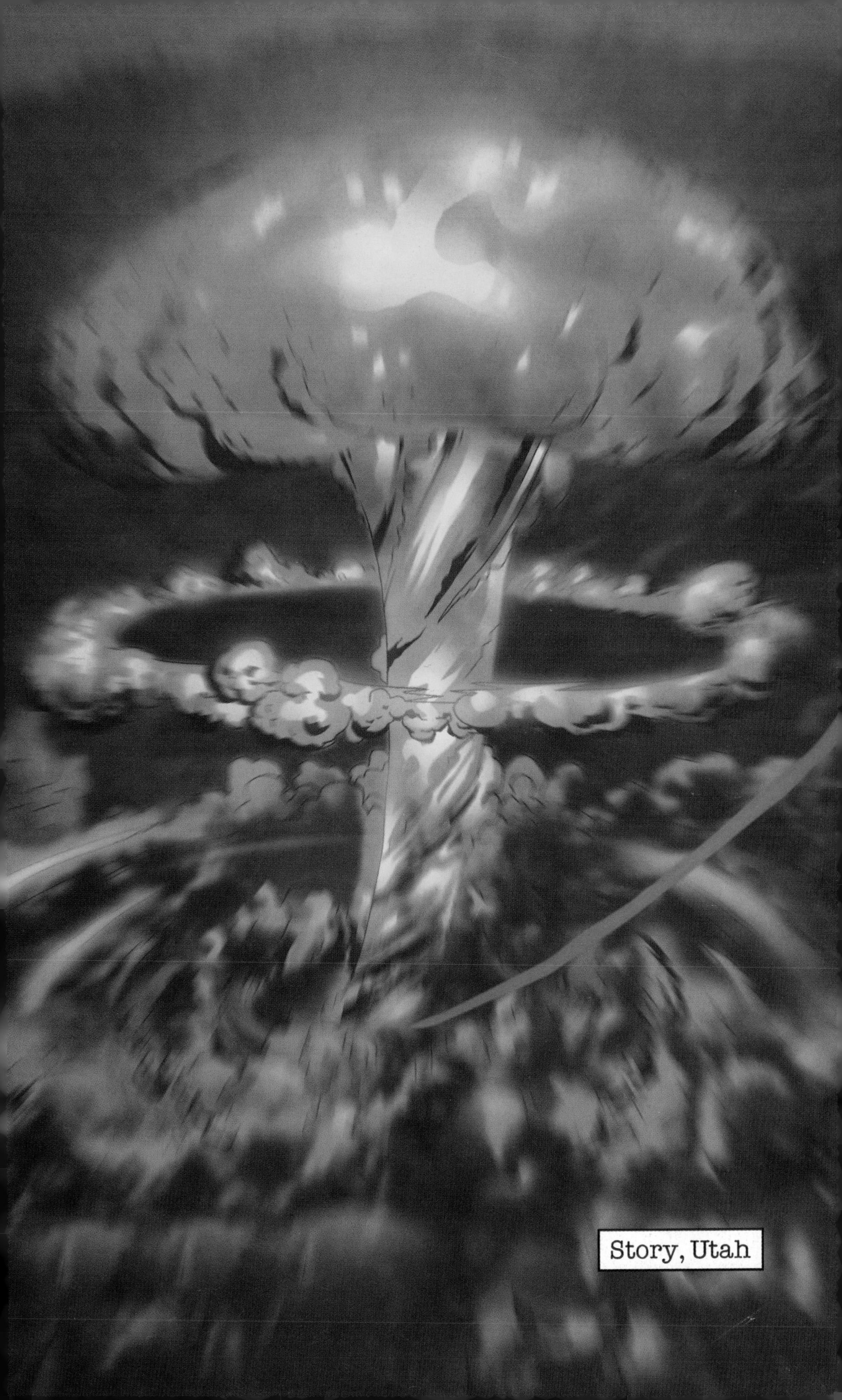
Story, Utah

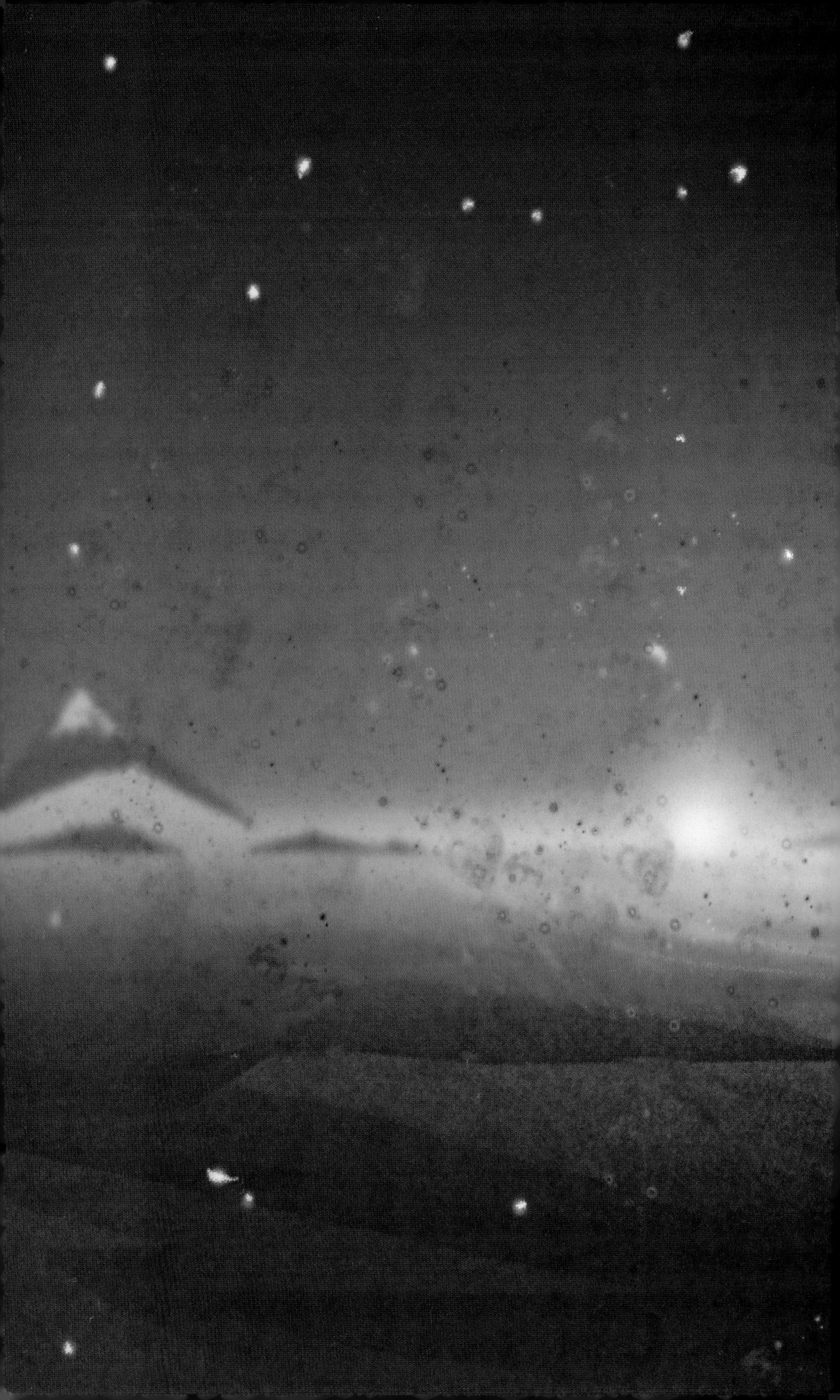

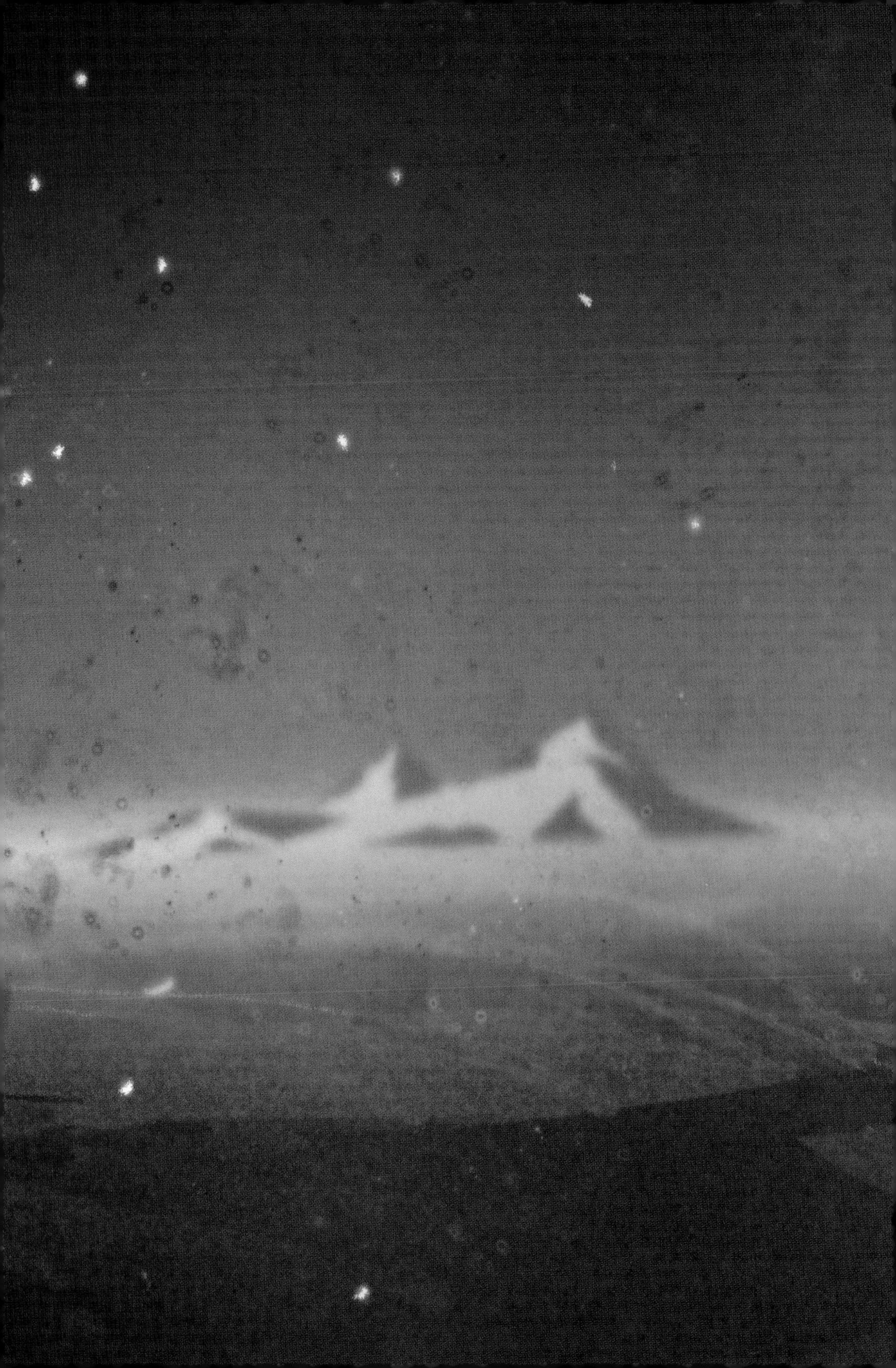

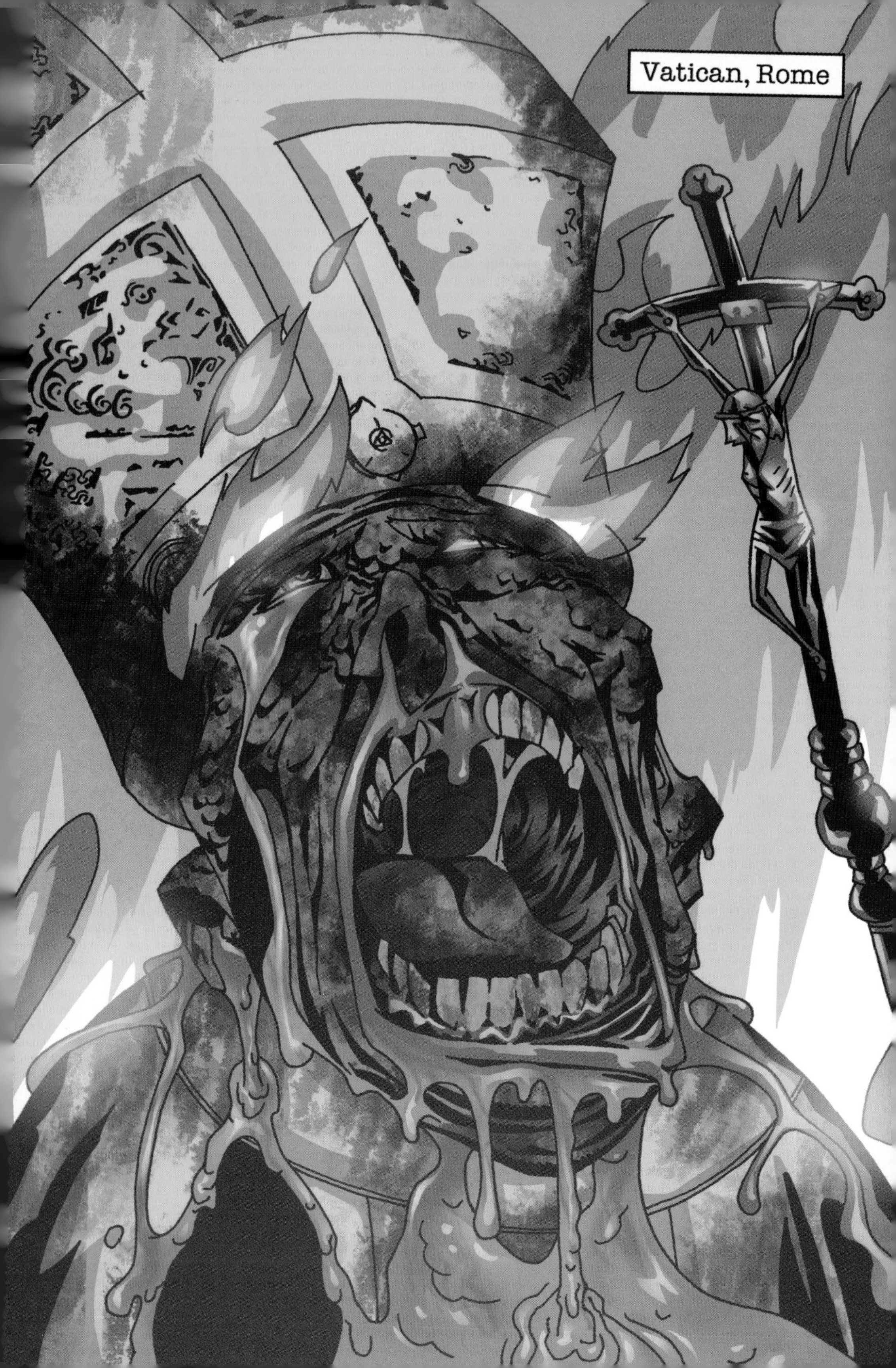
Vatican, Rome

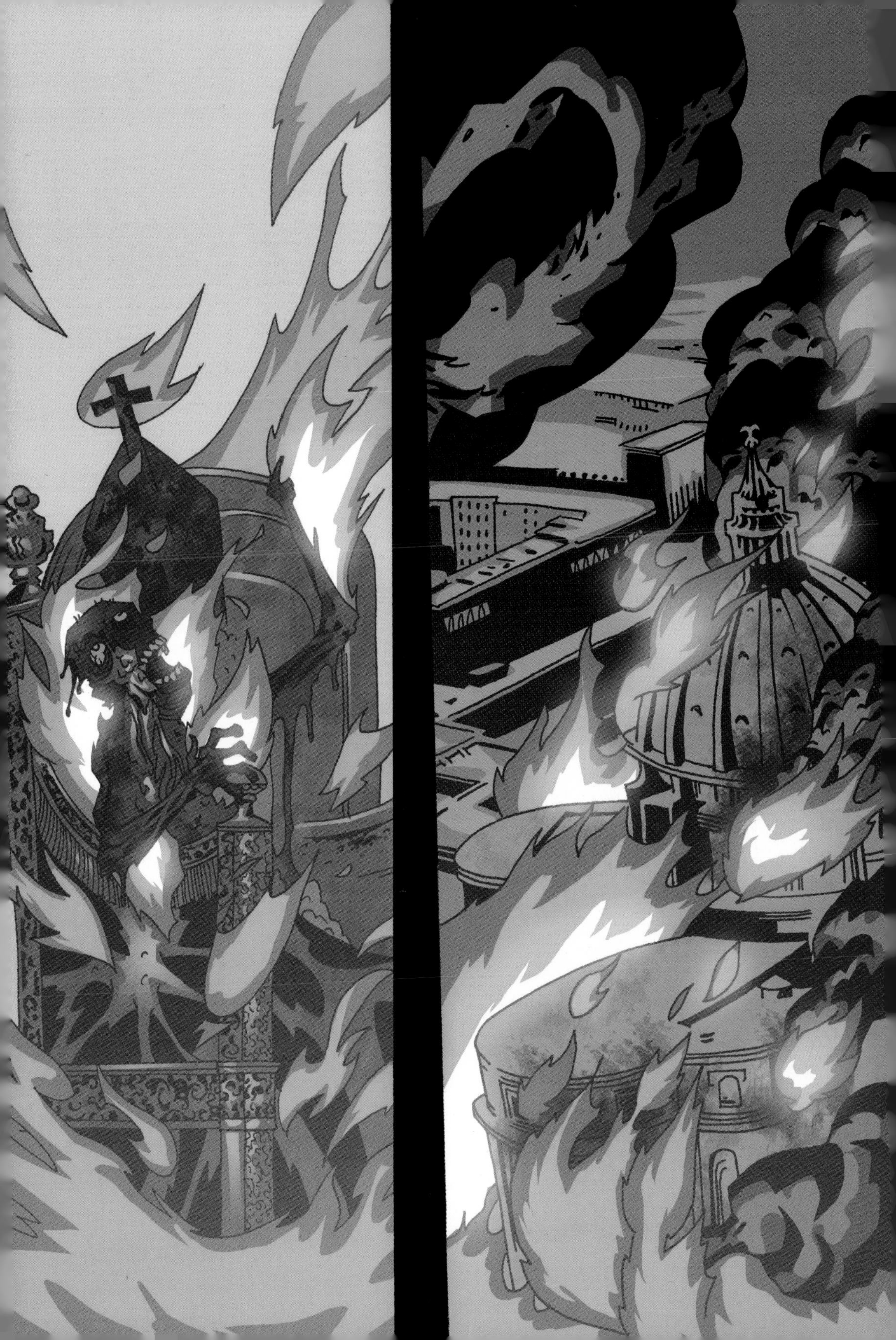

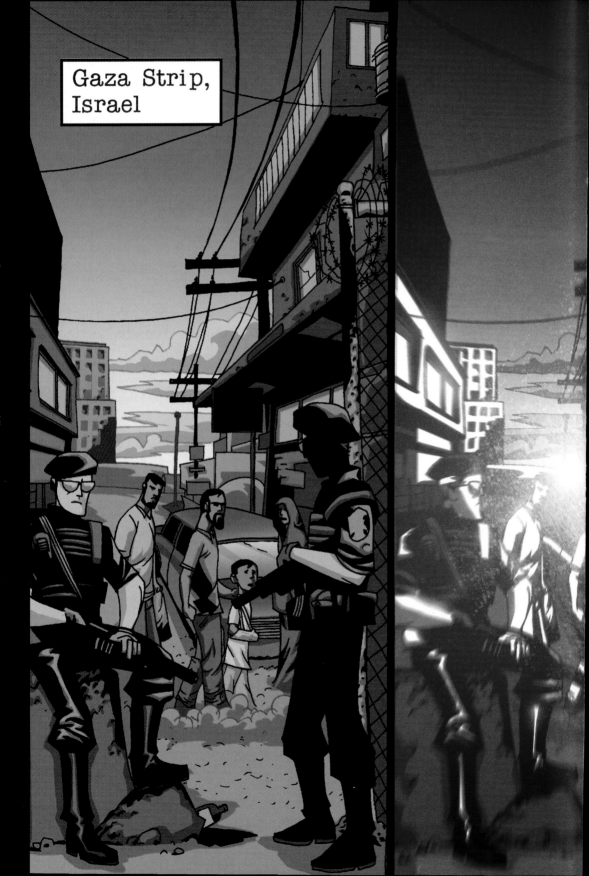

Gaza Strip,
Israel

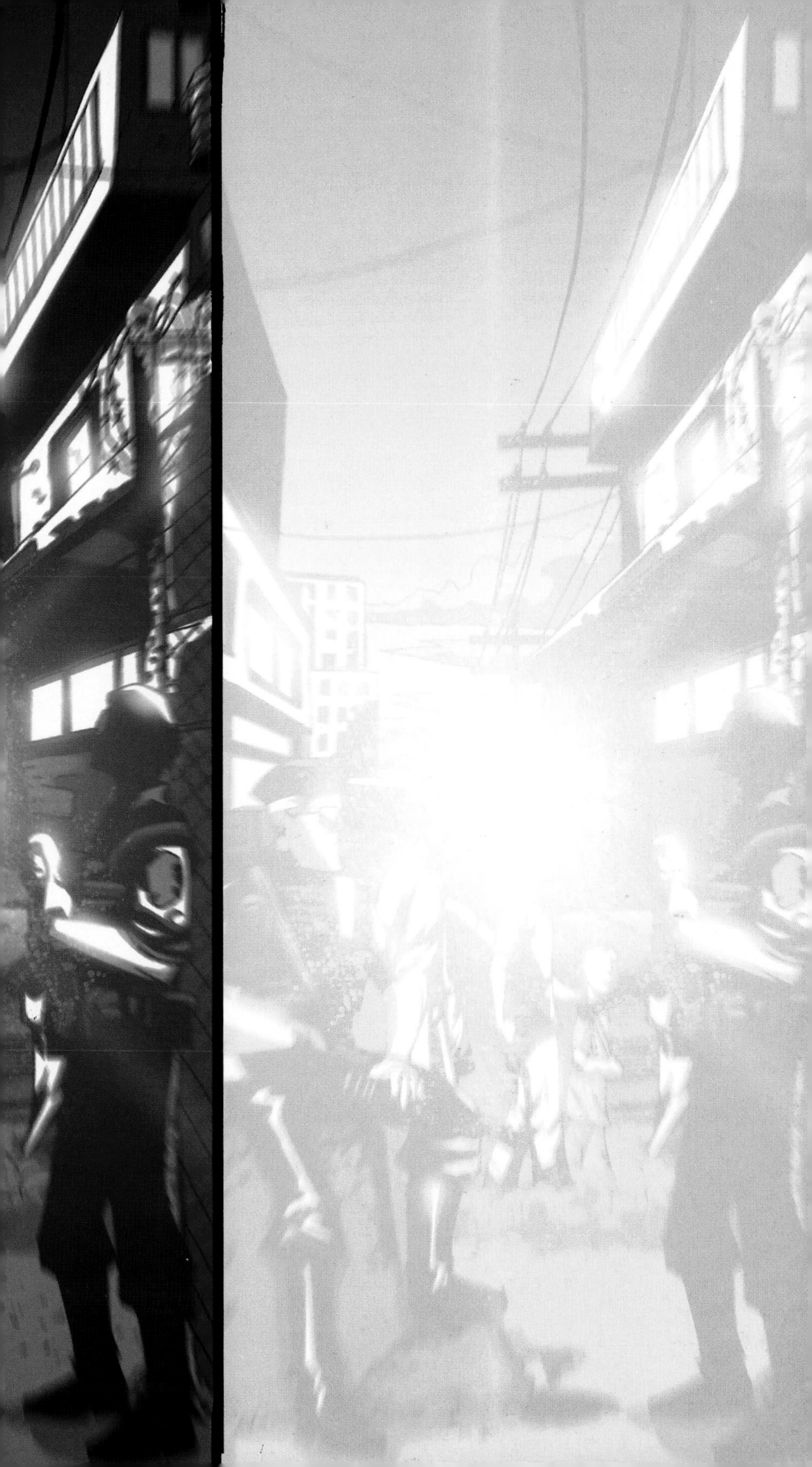

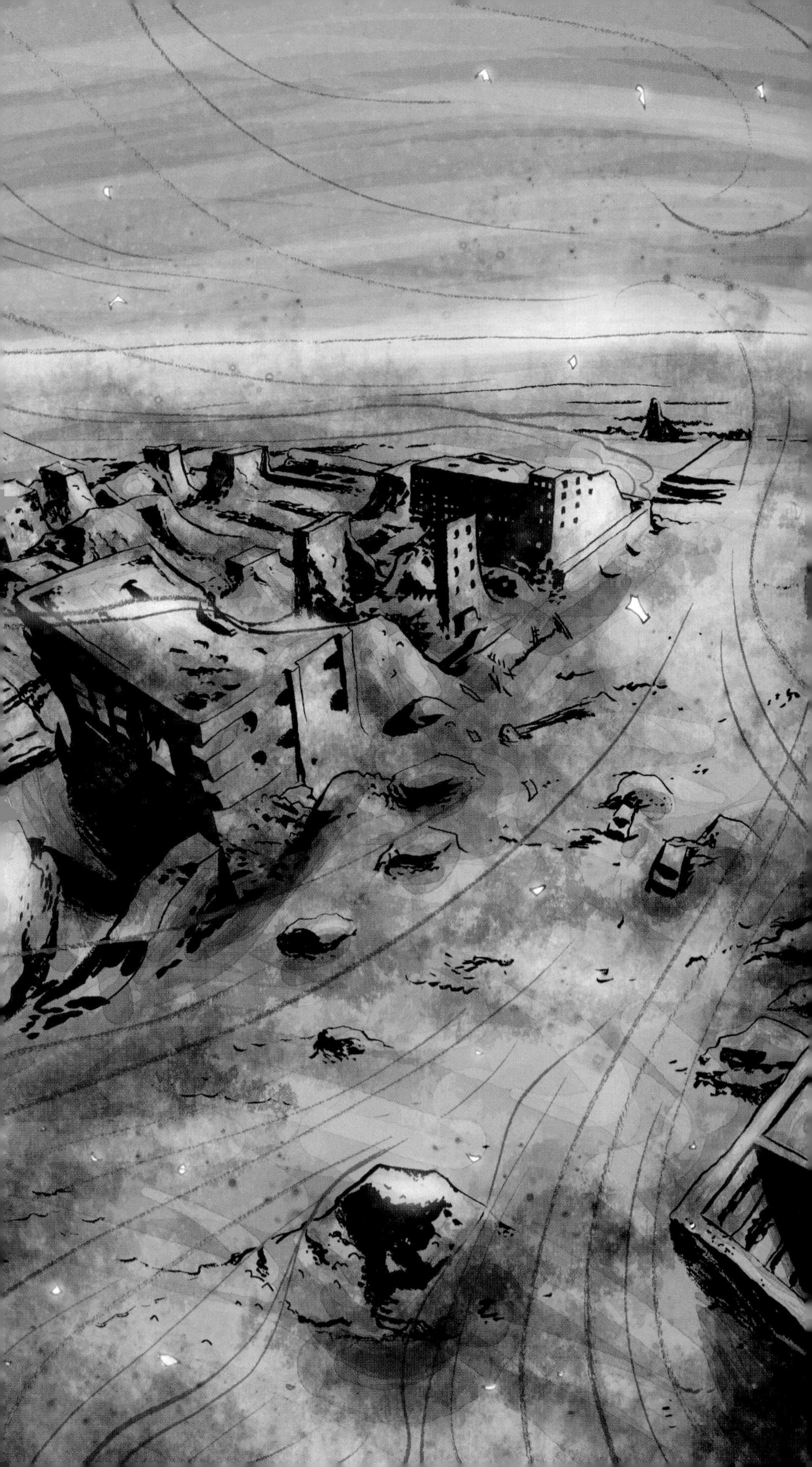

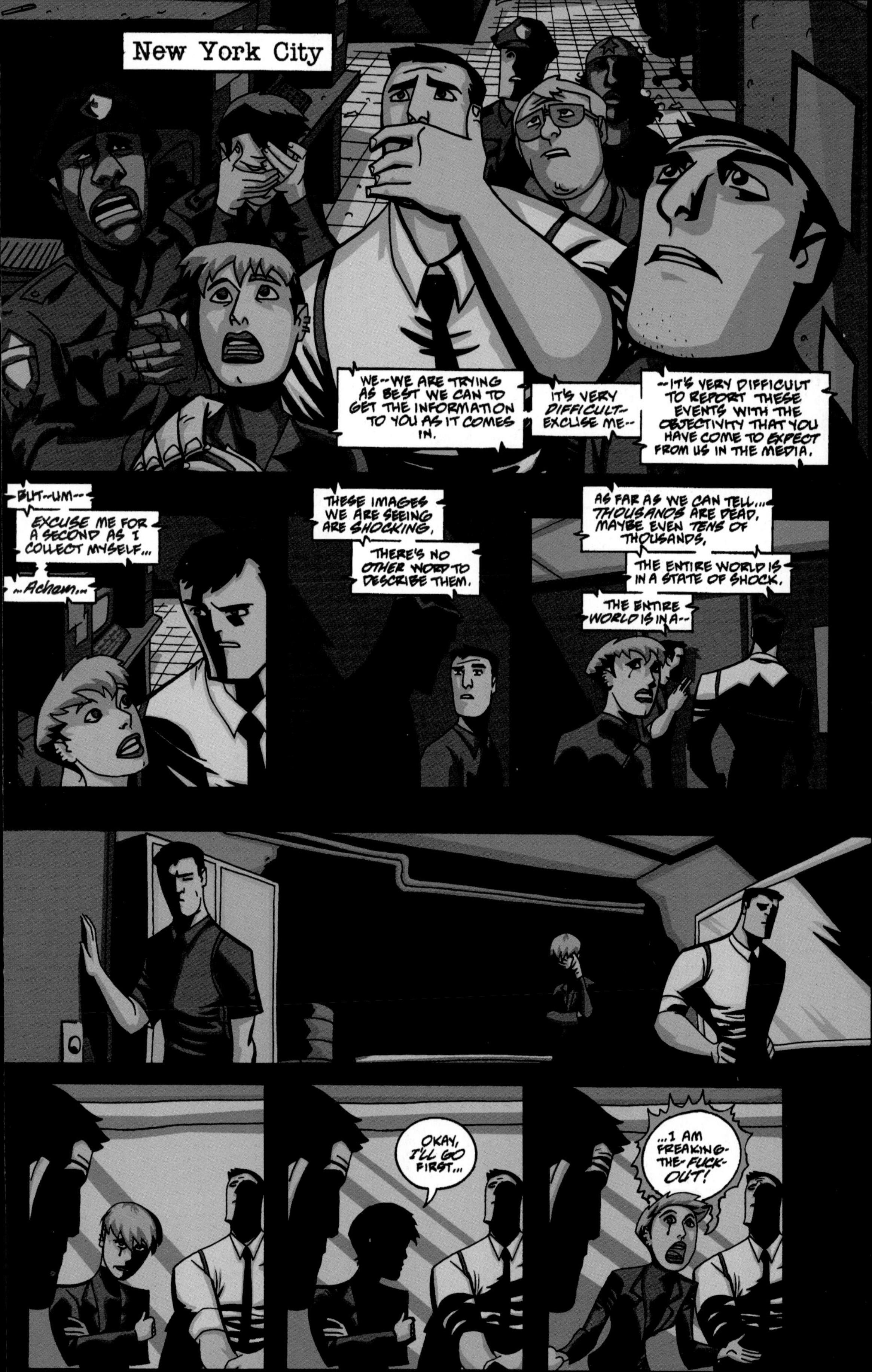
New York City
WE--WE ARE TRYING AS BEST WE CAN TO GET THE INFORMATION TO YOU AS IT COMES IN.
IT'S VERY DIFFICULT-- EXCUSE ME--
--IT'S VERY DIFFICULT TO REPORT THESE EVENTS WITH THE OBJECTIVITY THAT YOU HAVE COME TO EXPECT FROM US IN THE MEDIA.
BUT--UM--
EXCUSE ME FOR A SECOND AS I COLLECT MYSELF...
...Ahem...
THESE IMAGES WE ARE SEEING ARE SHOCKING.
THERE'S NO OTHER WORD TO DESCRIBE THEM.
AS FAR AS WE CAN TELL... THOUSANDS ARE DEAD, MAYBE EVEN TENS OF THOUSANDS.
THE ENTIRE WORLD IS IN A STATE OF SHOCK.
THE ENTIRE WORLD IS IN A--
OKAY, I'LL GO FIRST...
...I AM FREAKING-THE-FUCK-OUT!

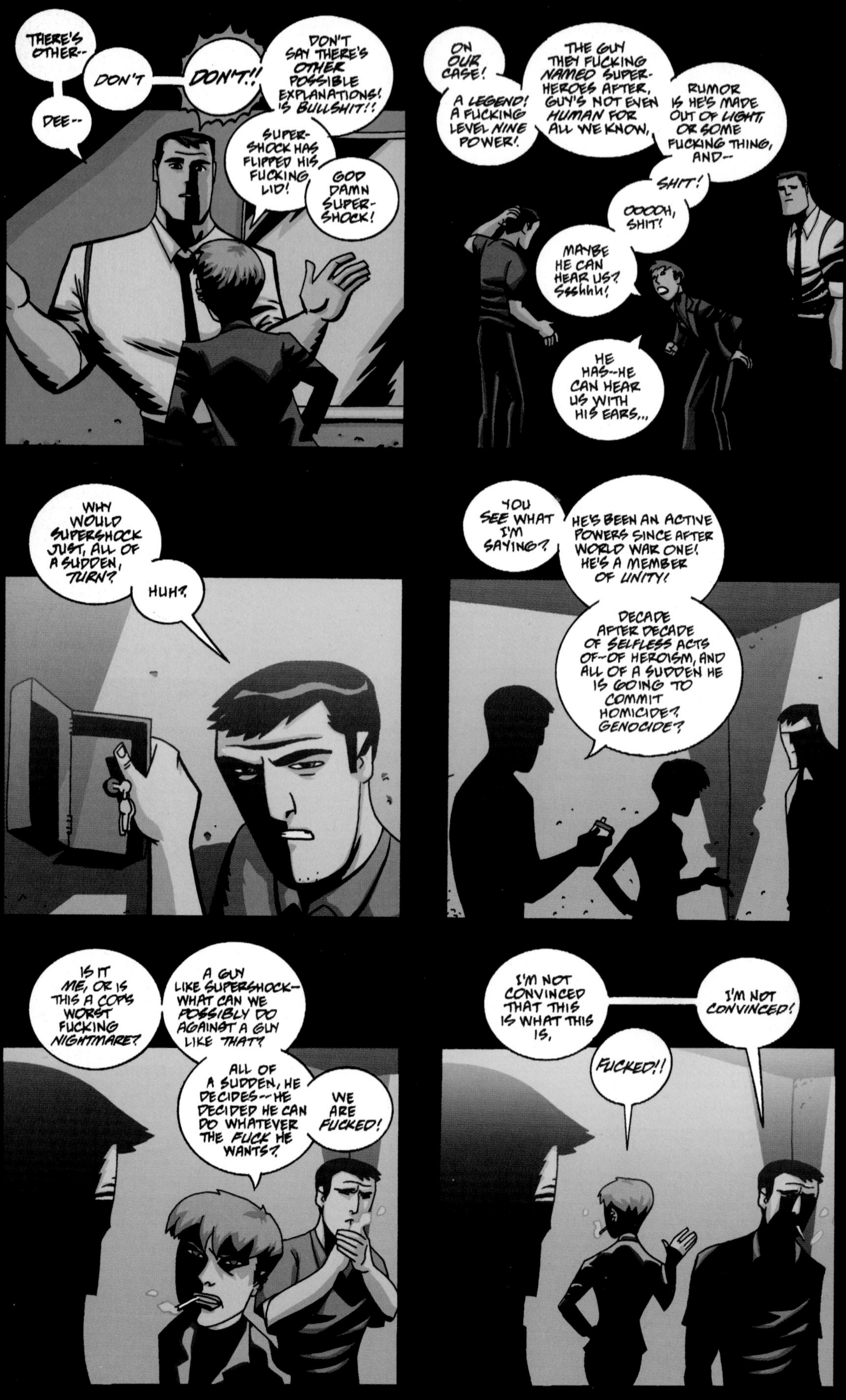
THERE'S OTHER--
DEE--
DON'T
DON'T!!
DON'T SAY THERE'S OTHER POSSIBLE EXPLANATIONS! 'S BULLSHIT!!
SUPER-SHOCK HAS FLIPPED HIS FUCKING LID!
GOD DAMN SUPER-SHOCK!
ON OUR CASE!
A LEGEND! A FUCKING LEVEL NINE POWER!
THE GUY THEY FUCKING NAMED SUPER-HEROES AFTER, GUY'S NOT EVEN HUMAN FOR ALL WE KNOW,
RUMOR IS HE'S MADE OUT OF LIGHT, OR SOME FUCKING THING, AND--
SHIT!
OOOOH, SHIT!
MAYBE HE CAN HEAR US? Ssshhh!
HE HAS--HE CAN HEAR US WITH HIS EARS...
WHY WOULD SUPERSHOCK JUST, ALL OF A SUDDEN, TURN?
HUH?
YOU SEE WHAT I'M SAYING?
HE'S BEEN AN ACTIVE POWERS SINCE AFTER WORLD WAR ONE! HE'S A MEMBER OF UNITY!
DECADE AFTER DECADE OF SELFLESS ACTS OF--OF HEROISM, AND ALL OF A SUDDEN HE IS GOING TO COMMIT HOMICIDE? GENOCIDE?
IS IT ME, OR IS THIS A COP'S WORST FUCKING NIGHTMARE?
A GUY LIKE SUPERSHOCK--WHAT CAN WE POSSIBLY DO AGAINST A GUY LIKE THAT?
ALL OF A SUDDEN, HE DECIDES--HE DECIDED HE CAN DO WHATEVER THE FUCK HE WANTS?
WE ARE FUCKED!
I'M NOT CONVINCED THAT THIS IS WHAT THIS IS,
I'M NOT CONVINCED!
FUCKED!!

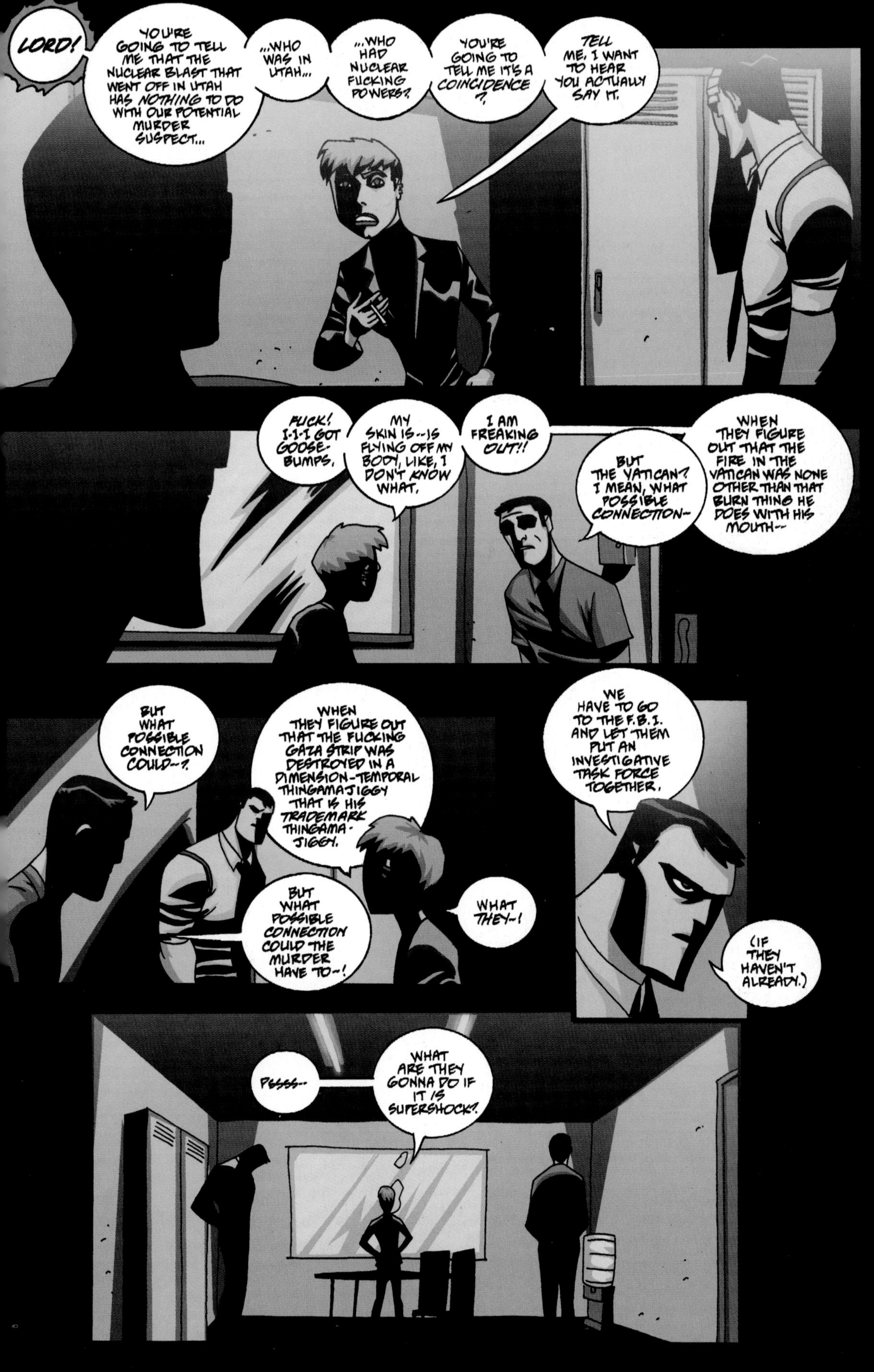
LORD!
YOU'RE GOING TO TELL ME THAT THE NUCLEAR BLAST THAT WENT OFF IN UTAH HAS NOTHING TO DO WITH OUR POTENTIAL MURDER SUSPECT...
...WHO WAS IN UTAH...
...WHO HAD NUCLEAR FUCKING POWERS?
YOU'RE GOING TO TELL ME IT'S A COINCIDENCE?
TELL ME, I WANT TO HEAR YOU ACTUALLY SAY IT.
FUCK! I-I-I GOT GOOSE-BUMPS.
MY SKIN IS--IS FLYING OFF MY BODY, LIKE, I DON'T KNOW WHAT.
I AM FREAKING OUT!!
BUT THE VATICAN? I MEAN, WHAT POSSIBLE CONNECTION--
WHEN THEY FIGURE OUT THAT THE FIRE IN THE VATICAN WAS NONE OTHER THAN THAT BURN THING HE DOES WITH HIS MOUTH--
BUT WHAT POSSIBLE CONNECTION COULD--?
WHEN THEY FIGURE OUT THAT THE FUCKING GAZA STRIP WAS DESTROYED IN A DIMENSION-TEMPORAL THINGAMAJIGGY THAT IS HIS TRADEMARK THINGAMA-JIGGY.
BUT WHAT POSSIBLE CONNECTION COULD THE MURDER HAVE TO--!
WHAT THEY--!
WE HAVE TO GO TO THE F.B.I. AND LET THEM PUT AN INVESTIGATIVE TASK FORCE TOGETHER.
(IF THEY HAVEN'T ALREADY.)
PSSSS--
WHAT ARE THEY GONNA DO IF IT IS SUPERSHOCK?

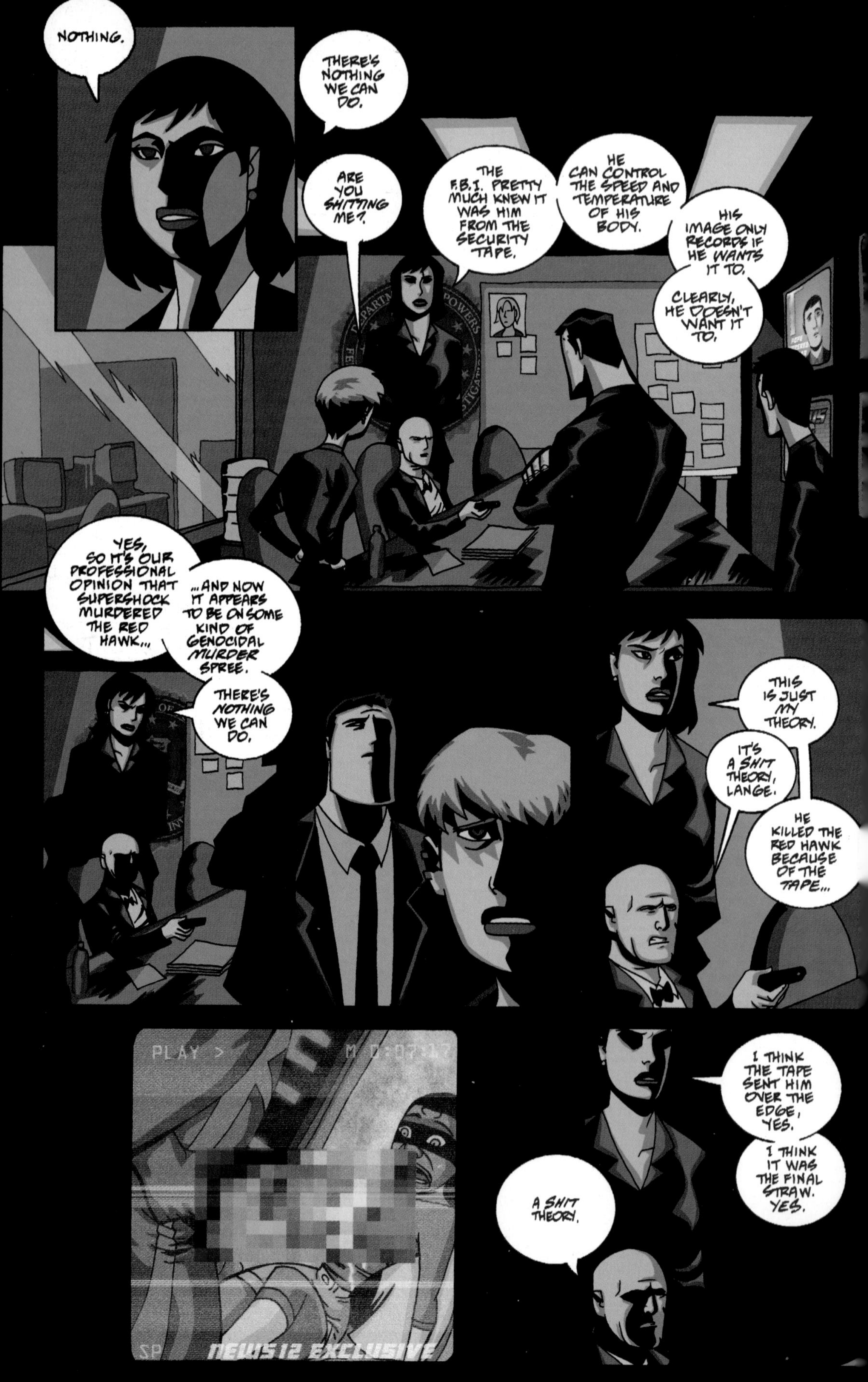
NOTHING.
THERE'S NOTHING WE CAN DO.
ARE YOU SHITTING ME?
THE F.B.I. PRETTY MUCH KNEW IT WAS HIM FROM THE SECURITY TAPE.
HE CAN CONTROL THE SPEED AND TEMPERATURE OF HIS BODY.
HIS IMAGE ONLY RECORDS IF HE WANTS IT TO.
CLEARLY, HE DOESN'T WANT IT TO.
YES, SO IT'S OUR PROFESSIONAL OPINION THAT SUPERSHOCK MURDERED THE RED HAWK...
...AND NOW IT APPEARS TO BE ON SOME KIND OF GENOCIDAL MURDER SPREE.
THERE'S NOTHING WE CAN DO.
THIS IS JUST MY THEORY.
IT'S A SHIT THEORY, LANGE.
HE KILLED THE RED HAWK BECAUSE OF THE TAPE...
PLAY >
NEWS 12 EXCLUSIVE
I THINK THE TAPE SENT HIM OVER THE EDGE, YES.
I THINK IT WAS THE FINAL STRAW. YES.
A SHIT THEORY.

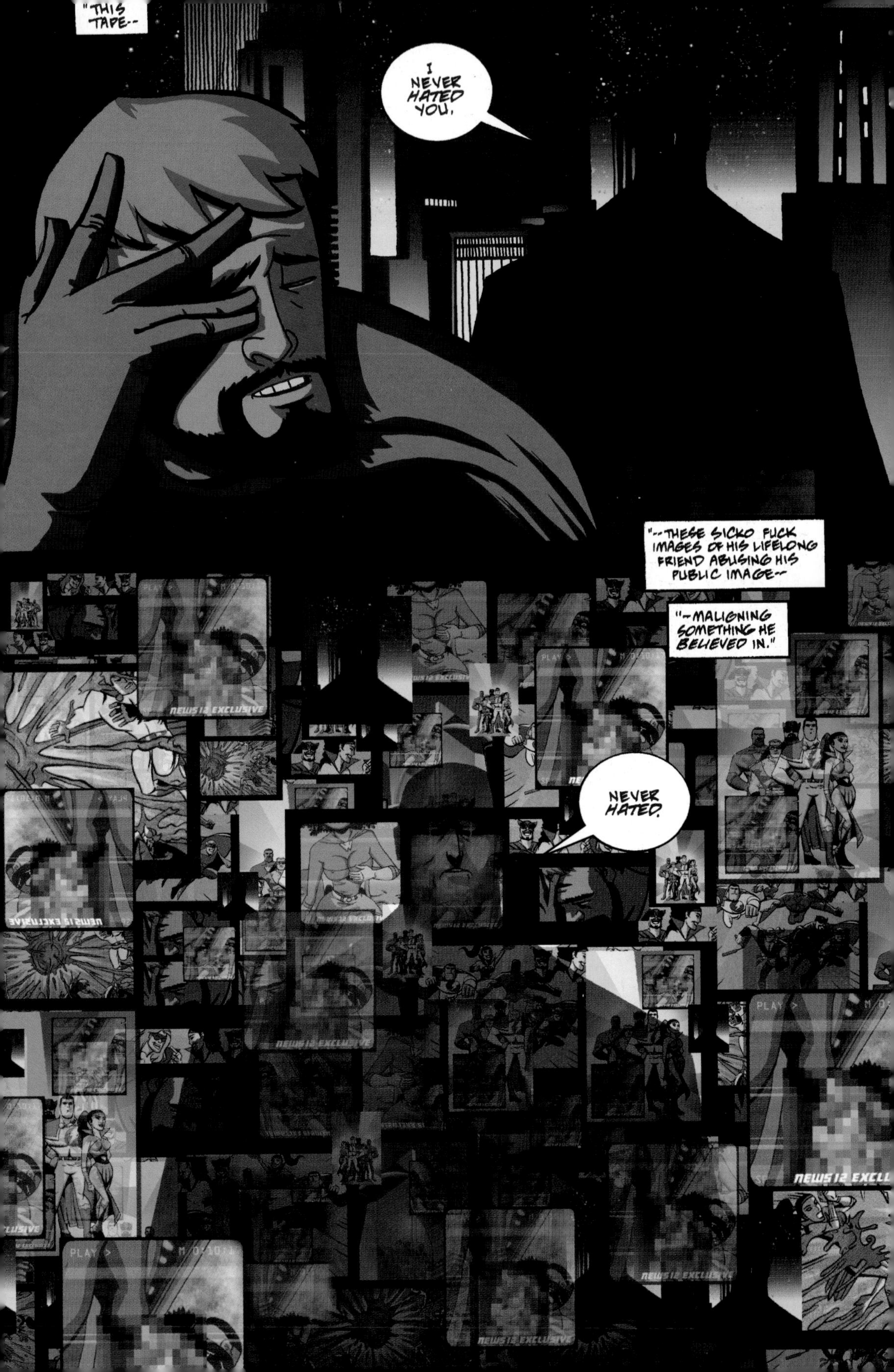
"THIS TAPE--
I NEVER HATED YOU.
"--THESE SICKO FUCK IMAGES OF HIS LIFELONG FRIEND ABUSING HIS PUBLIC IMAGE--
"--MALIGNING SOMETHING HE BELIEVED IN."
NEVER HATED.
NEWS 12 EXCLUSIVE
PLAY >

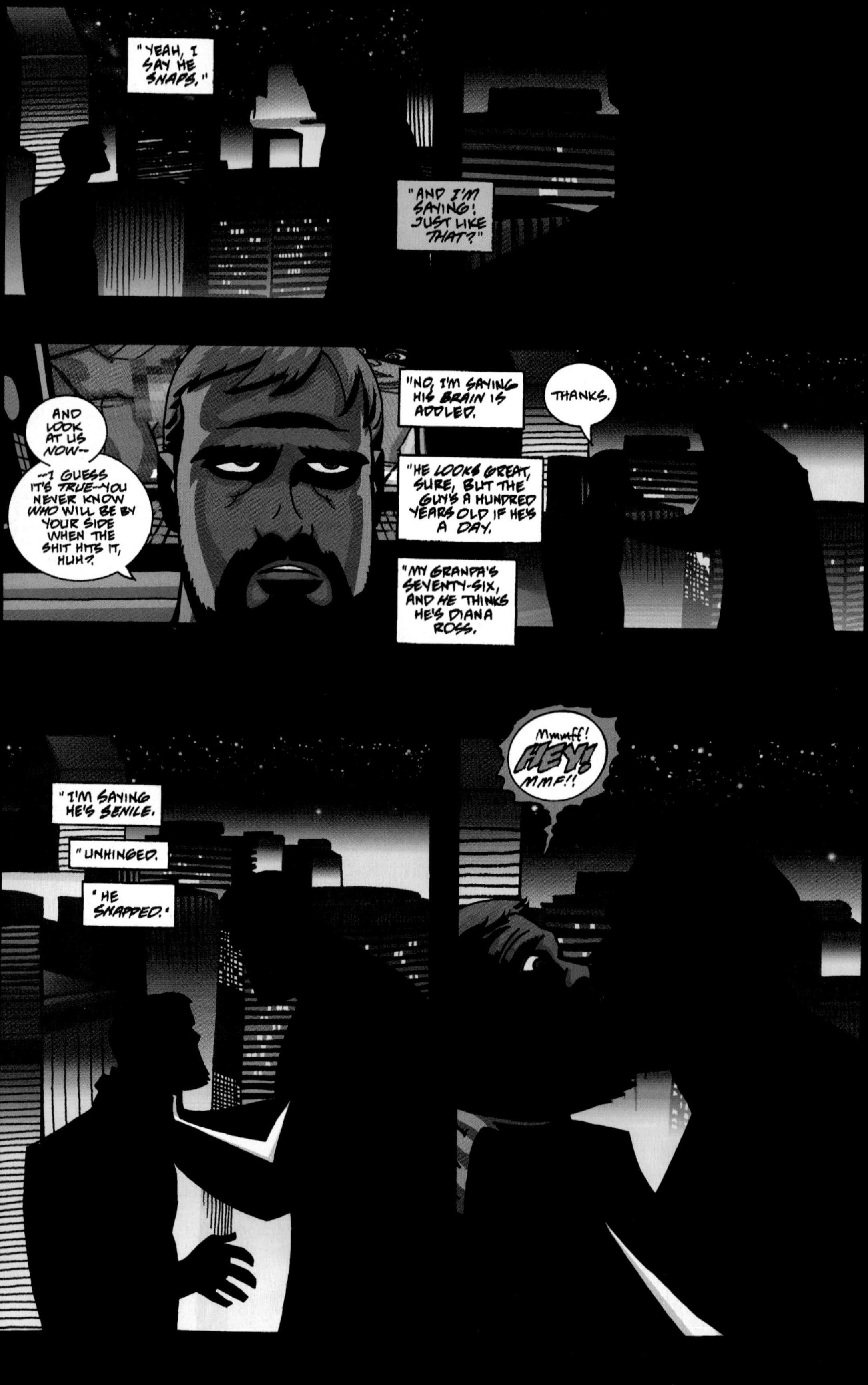
"YEAH, I SAY HE SNAPS."
"AND I'M SAYING! JUST LIKE THAT?"
AND LOOK AT US NOW--
--I GUESS IT'S TRUE--YOU NEVER KNOW WHO WILL BE BY YOUR SIDE WHEN THE SHIT HITS IT, HUH?
"NO, I'M SAYING HIS BRAIN IS ADDLED.
"HE LOOKS GREAT, SURE, BUT THE GUY'S A HUNDRED YEARS OLD IF HE'S A DAY.
"MY GRANPA'S SEVENTY-SIX, AND HE THINKS HE'S DIANA ROSS.
THANKS.
"I'M SAYING HE'S SENILE.
"UNHINGED.
"HE SNAPPED."
Mmmff! HEY! MMF!!

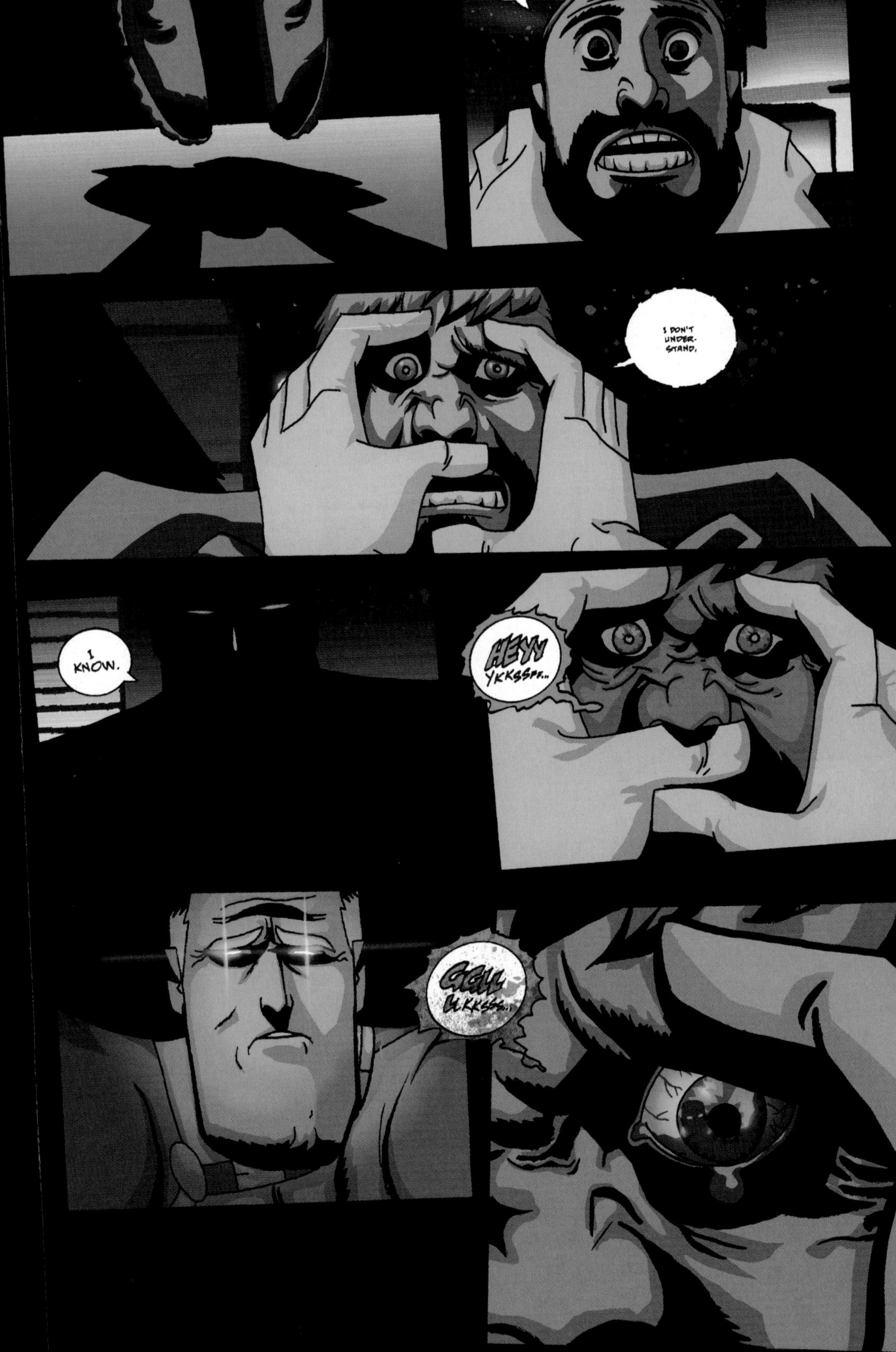
I DON'T UNDER-STAND.
I KNOW.
HEYN YKKSSFF...
GGLL LLKKSSS..

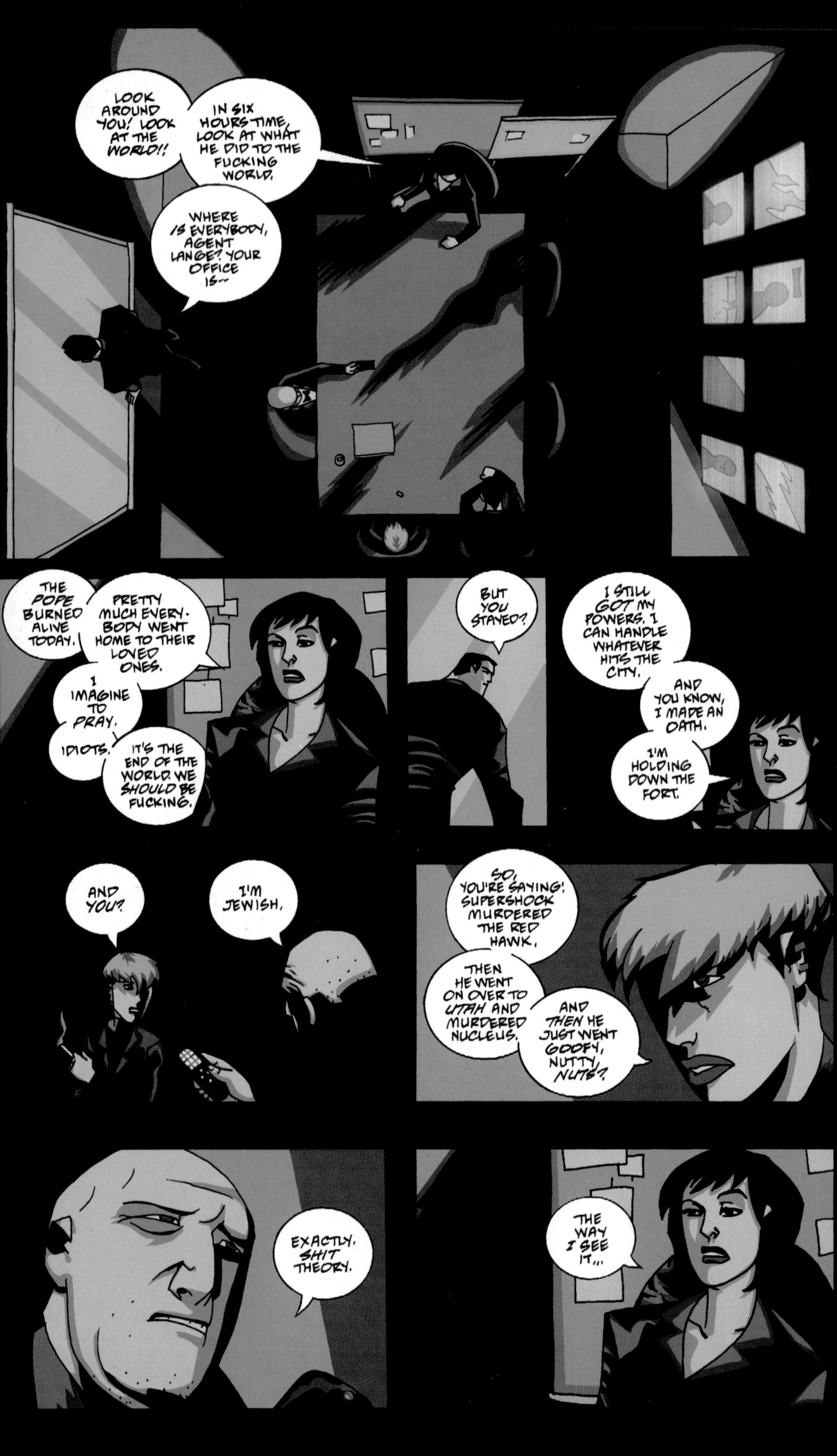
LOOK AROUND YOU! LOOK AT THE WORLD!!
IN SIX HOURS TIME, LOOK AT WHAT HE DID TO THE FUCKING WORLD.
WHERE IS EVERYBODY, AGENT LANGE? YOUR OFFICE IS--
THE POPE BURNED ALIVE TODAY.
PRETTY MUCH EVERY-BODY WENT HOME TO THEIR LOVED ONES.
I IMAGINE TO PRAY.
IDIOTS.
IT'S THE END OF THE WORLD. WE SHOULD BE FUCKING.
BUT YOU STAYED?
I STILL GOT MY POWERS. I CAN HANDLE WHATEVER HITS THE CITY.
AND YOU KNOW, I MADE AN OATH.
I'M HOLDING DOWN THE FORT.
AND YOU?
I'M JEWISH.
SO, YOU'RE SAYING: SUPERSHOCK MURDERED THE RED HAWK.
THEN HE WENT ON OVER TO UTAH AND MURDERED NUCLEUS.
AND THEN HE JUST WENT GOOFY, NUTTY, NUTS?
EXACTLY. SHIT THEORY.
THE WAY I SEE IT...

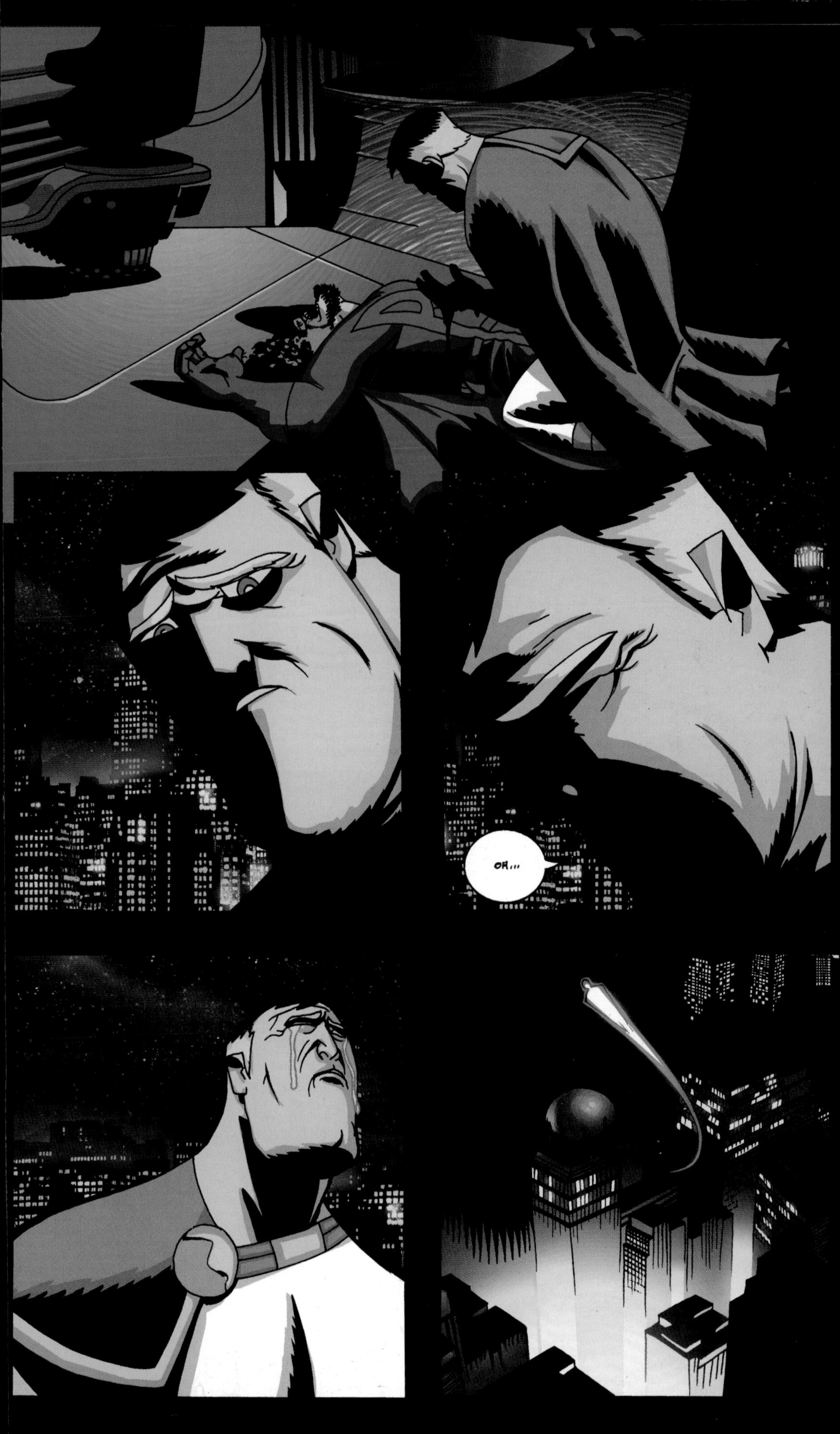
OR...

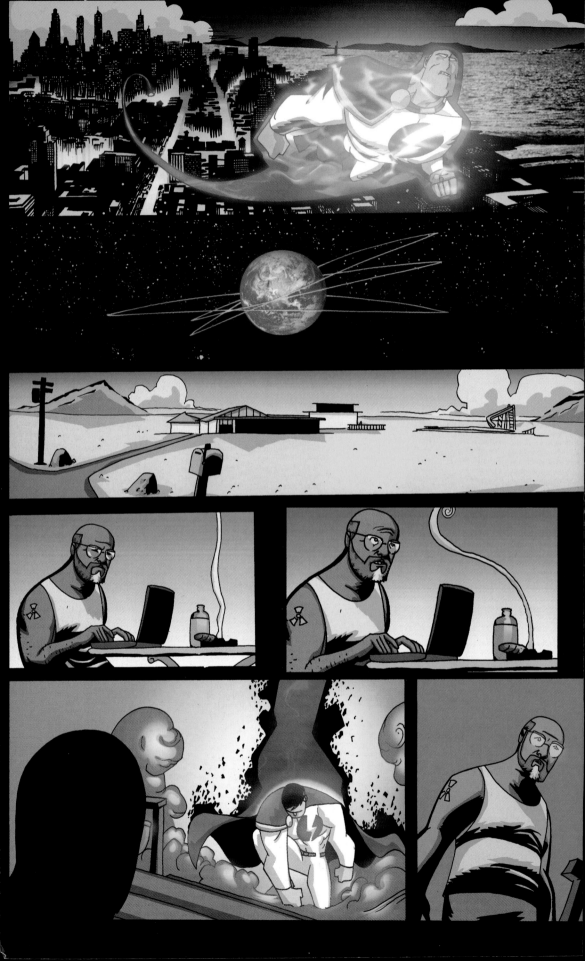

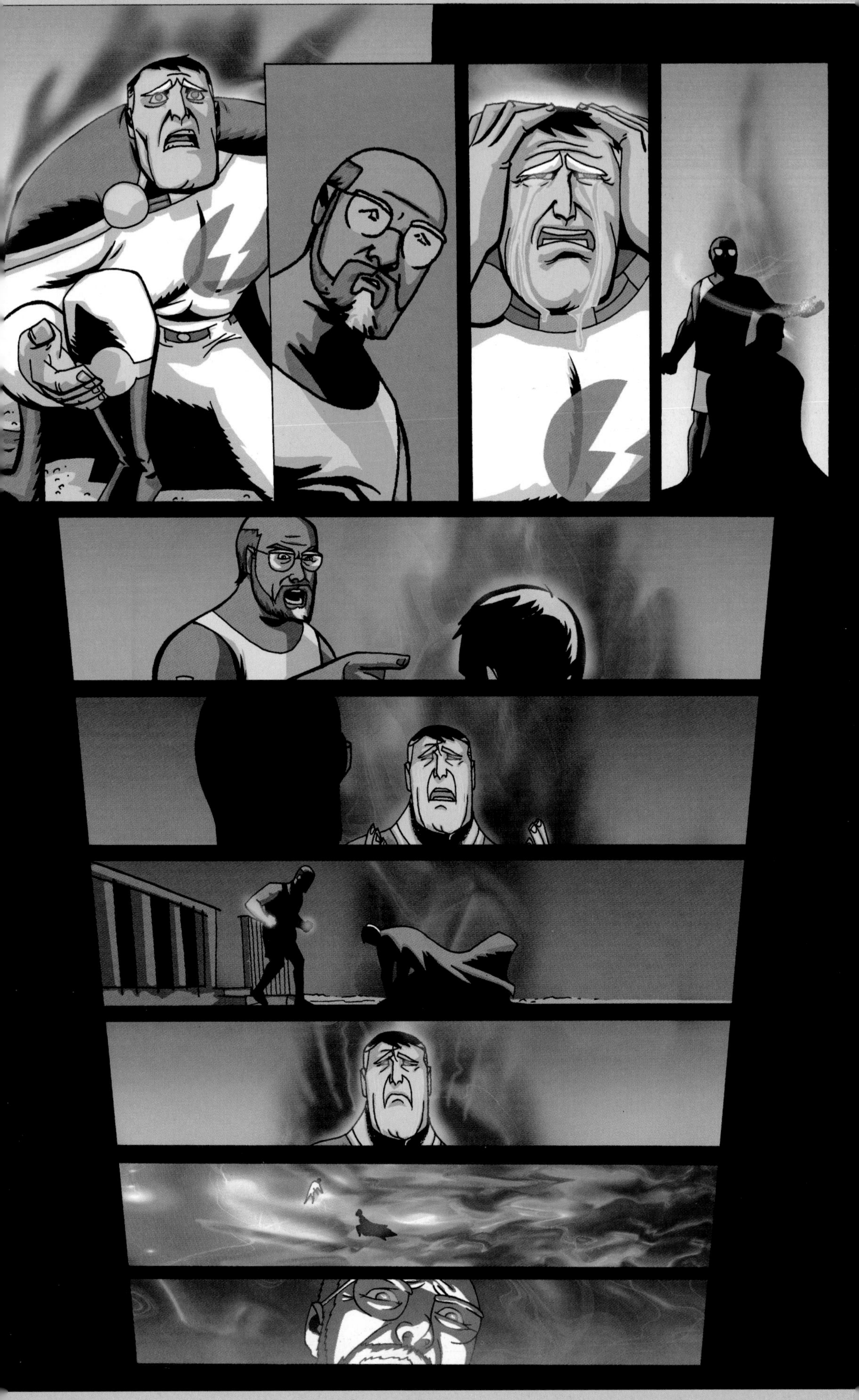

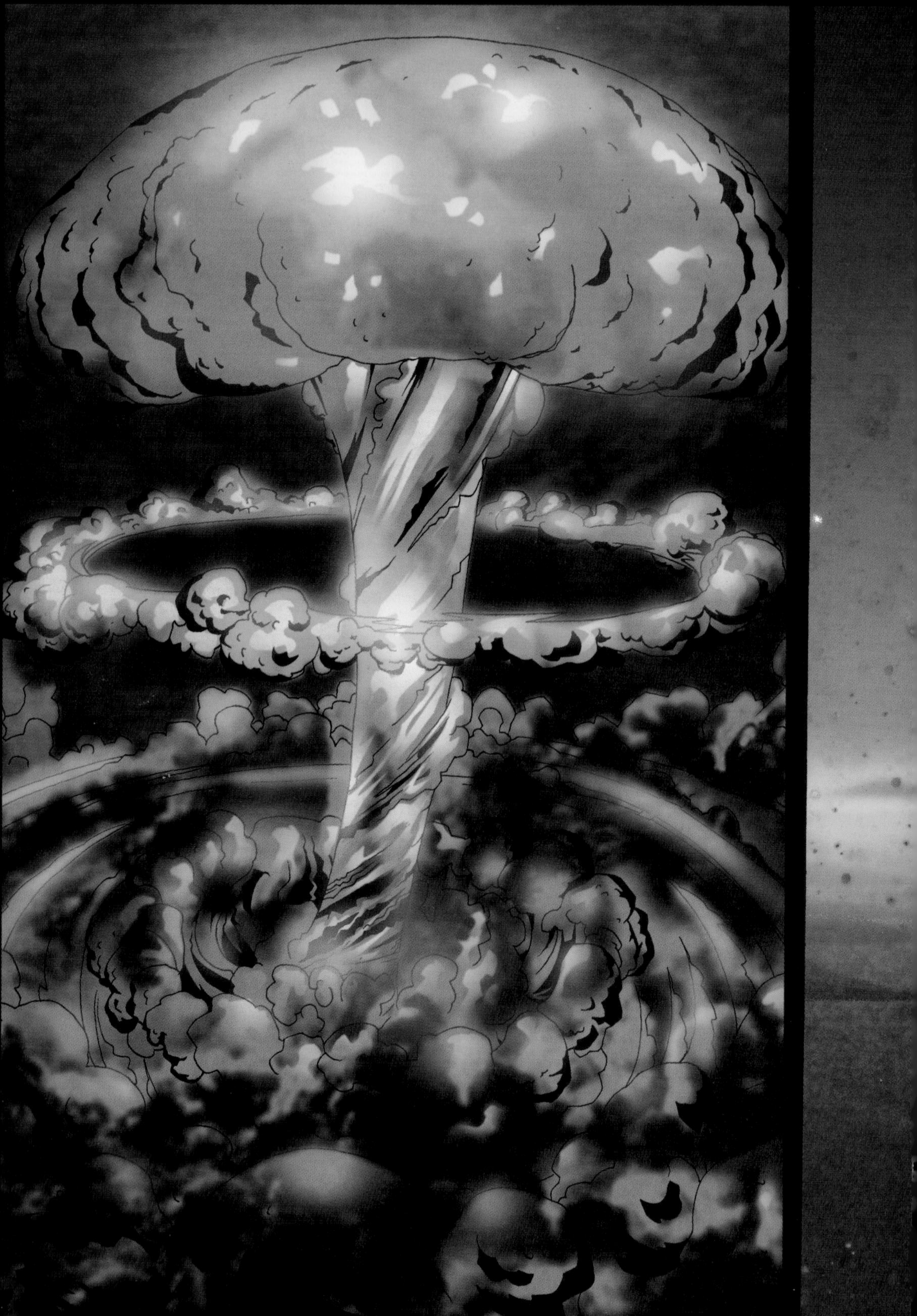

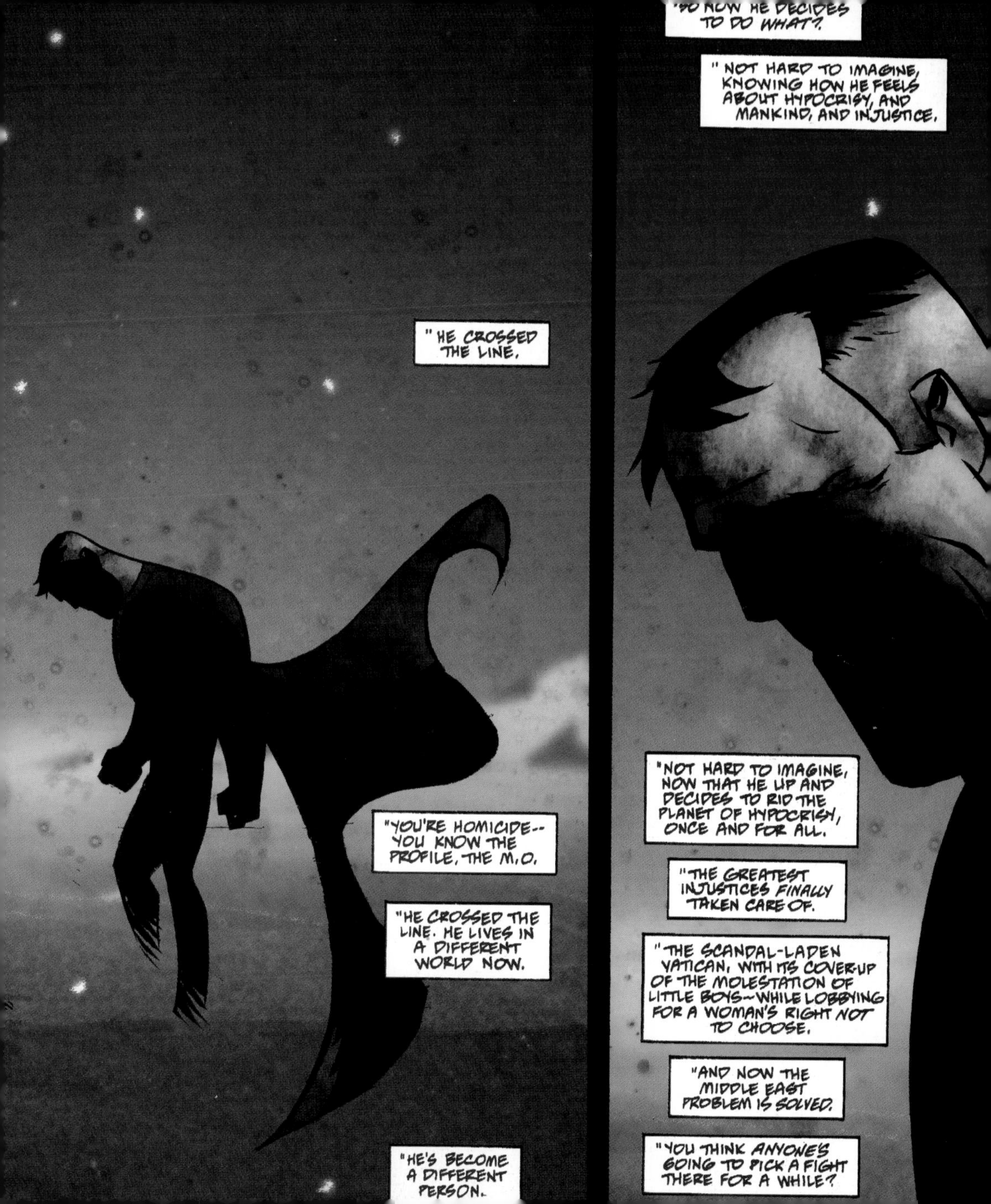
"HE CROSSED THE LINE.
"YOU'RE HOMICIDE-- YOU KNOW THE PROFILE, THE M.O.
"HE CROSSED THE LINE. HE LIVES IN A DIFFERENT WORLD NOW.
"HE'S BECOME A DIFFERENT PERSON.
"SO NOW HE DECIDES TO DO WHAT?
"NOT HARD TO IMAGINE, KNOWING HOW HE FEELS ABOUT HYPOCRISY, AND MANKIND, AND INJUSTICE.
"NOT HARD TO IMAGINE, NOW THAT HE UP AND DECIDES TO RID THE PLANET OF HYPOCRISY, ONCE AND FOR ALL.
"THE GREATEST INJUSTICES FINALLY TAKEN CARE OF.
"THE SCANDAL-LADEN VATICAN, WITH ITS COVER-UP OF THE MOLESTATION OF LITTLE BOYS--WHILE LOBBYING FOR A WOMAN'S RIGHT NOT TO CHOOSE.
"AND NOW THE MIDDLE EAST PROBLEM IS SOLVED.
"YOU THINK ANYONE'S GOING TO PICK A FIGHT THERE FOR A WHILE?

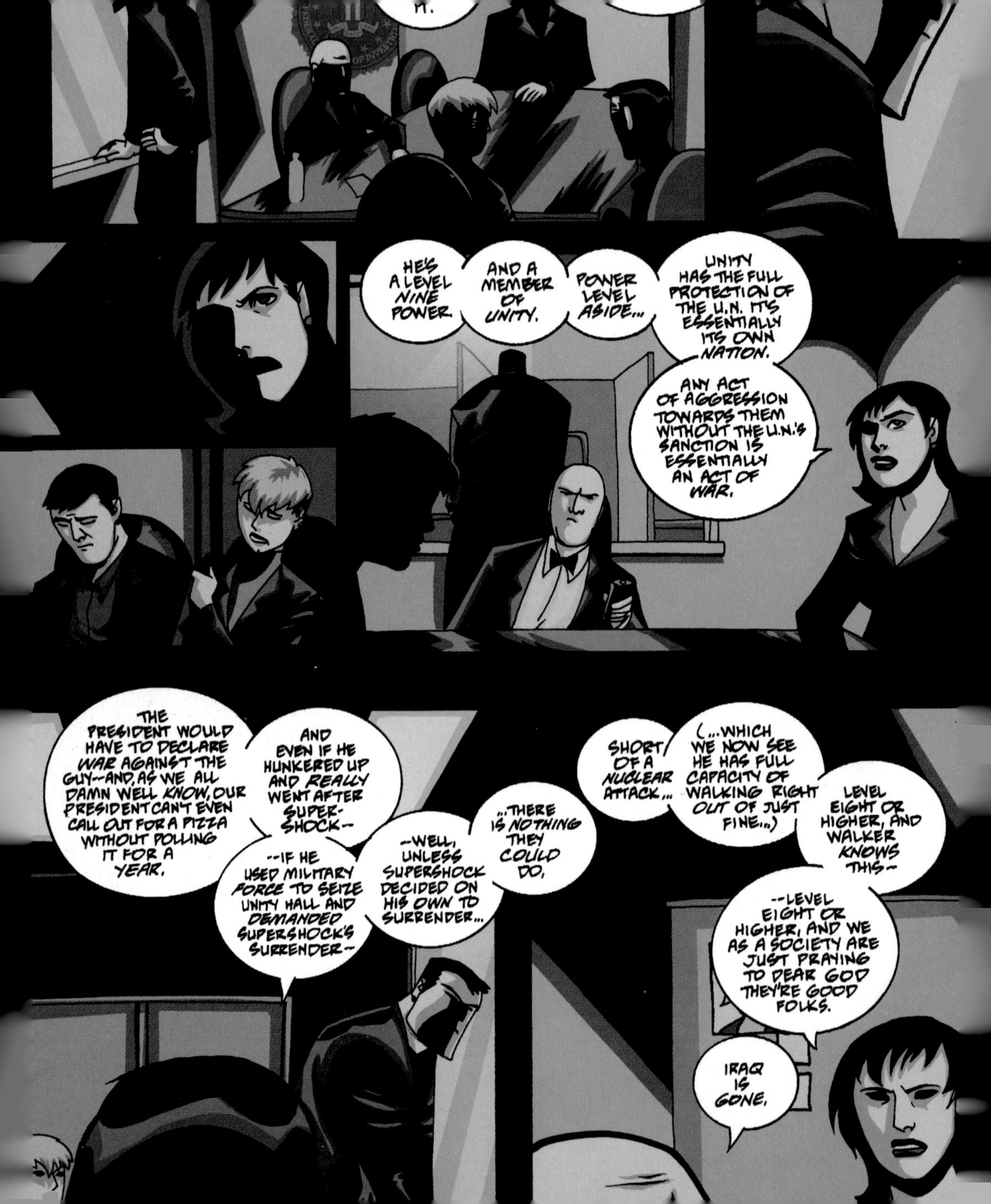

IT.
HE'S A LEVEL NINE POWER.
AND A MEMBER OF UNITY.
POWER LEVEL ASIDE...
UNITY HAS THE FULL PROTECTION OF THE U.N. IT'S ESSENTIALLY ITS OWN NATION.
ANY ACT OF AGGRESSION TOWARDS THEM WITHOUT THE U.N.'S SANCTION IS ESSENTIALLY AN ACT OF WAR.
THE PRESIDENT WOULD HAVE TO DECLARE WAR AGAINST THE GUY--AND, AS WE ALL DAMN WELL KNOW, OUR PRESIDENT CAN'T EVEN CALL OUT FOR A PIZZA WITHOUT POLLING IT FOR A YEAR.
AND EVEN IF HE HUNKERED UP AND REALLY WENT AFTER SUPER-SHOCK--
--IF HE USED MILITARY FORCE TO SEIZE UNITY HALL AND DEMANDED SUPERSHOCK'S SURRENDER--
--WELL, UNLESS SUPERSHOCK DECIDED ON HIS OWN TO SURRENDER...
...THERE IS NOTHING THEY COULD DO.
SHORT OF A NUCLEAR ATTACK...
(...WHICH WE NOW SEE HE HAS FULL CAPACITY OF WALKING RIGHT OUT OF JUST FINE...)
LEVEL EIGHT OR HIGHER, AND WALKER KNOWS THIS--
--LEVEL EIGHT OR HIGHER, AND WE AS A SOCIETY ARE JUST PRAYING TO DEAR GOD THEY'RE GOOD FOLKS.
IRAQ IS GONE.

US AS WE TRY TO GET A FOOTHOLD ON THE EVENTS THAT ARE UNFOLDING.

WE ARE GETTING CONFLICTING REPORTS FROM NUMEROUS SOURCES AS TO WHAT MAY BE BEHIND THESE TRULY *HORRIFIC*, EARTH-SHATTERING EVENTS.

WE ARE RECEIVING INTERNATIONAL REPORTS THAT DECLARE EVERYTHING FROM AN ALIEN INVASION TO THE END OF THE WORLD AS WE *KNOW* IT.

NEWS 12

EXCLUSIVE

NEWS 12 EXCLUSIVE

TERRORISM, OF COURSE, HAS *NOT* BEEN RULED OUT...

...NOR HAS THE TERRIFYING IDEA THAT A LONE, HIGH-LEVEL, SUPERPOWER MIGHT BE THE CAUSE OF THIS.

TO BELIEVE THAT THE CAPITAL OF BAGHDAD IS GONE--

--WIPED OFF THE *MAP*, AS IF IT NEVER EXISTED.

NEWS 12

NEWS 12 EXCLUSIVE

IT IS NO MORE.

WE ARE ALL AWAITING WORD FROM THE PRESIDENT--

--BUT IT MIGHT JUST BE THAT THE PRESIDENT HAS BEEN *TAKEN*--

--WE IMAGINE-- ALONG WITH THE JOINT CHIEFS OF STAFF, TO A SECRET LOCATION--A SAFE HOUSE.

WE ARE GOING TO GO BACK LIVE TO VATICAN CITY, WHERE LOCAL NEWS COVERAGE IS SUPPLYING US WITH FOOTAGE OF THE--

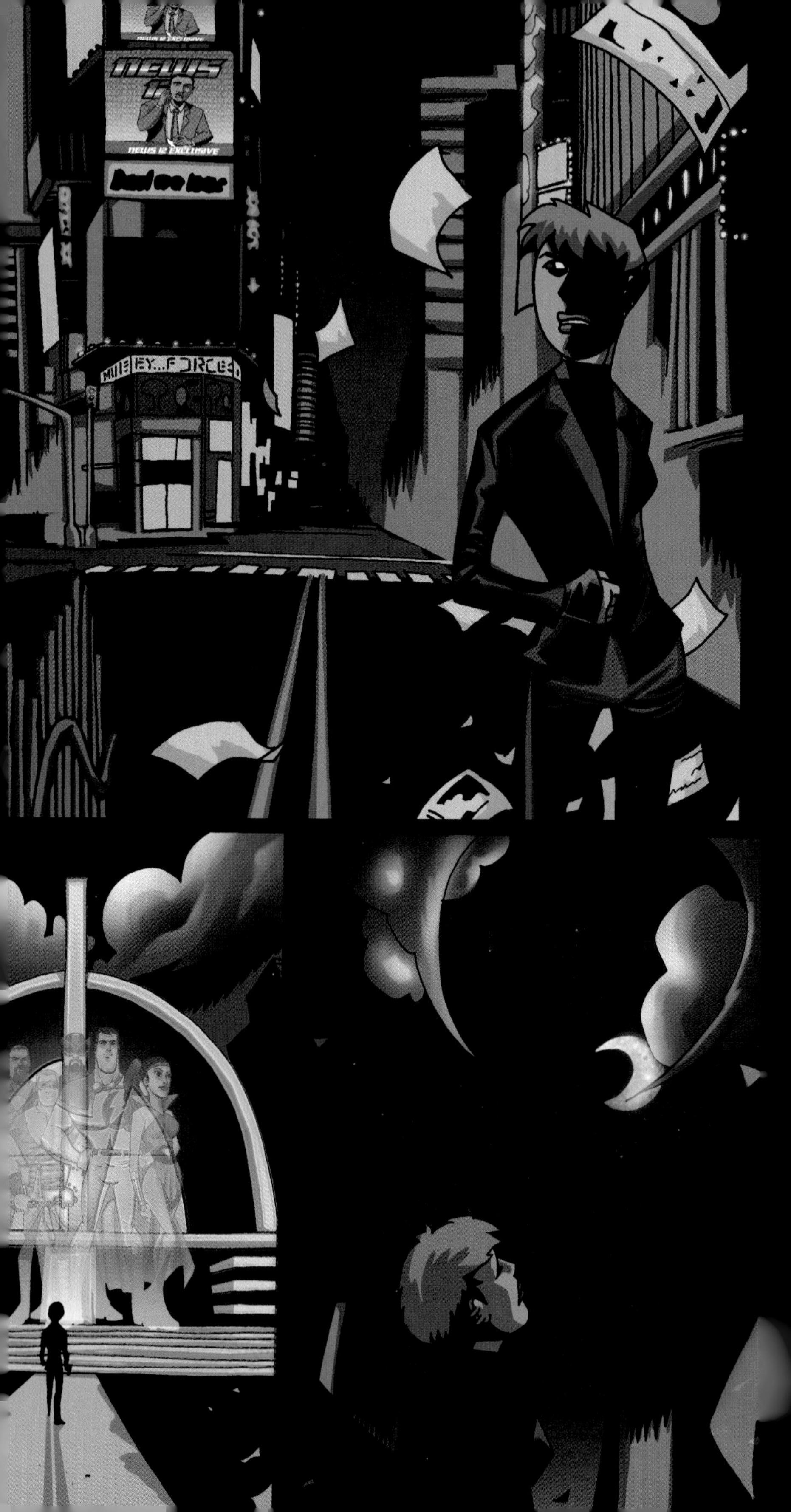
NEWS 12 EXCLUSIVE
NEWS 12
NEWS 12 EXCLUSIVE

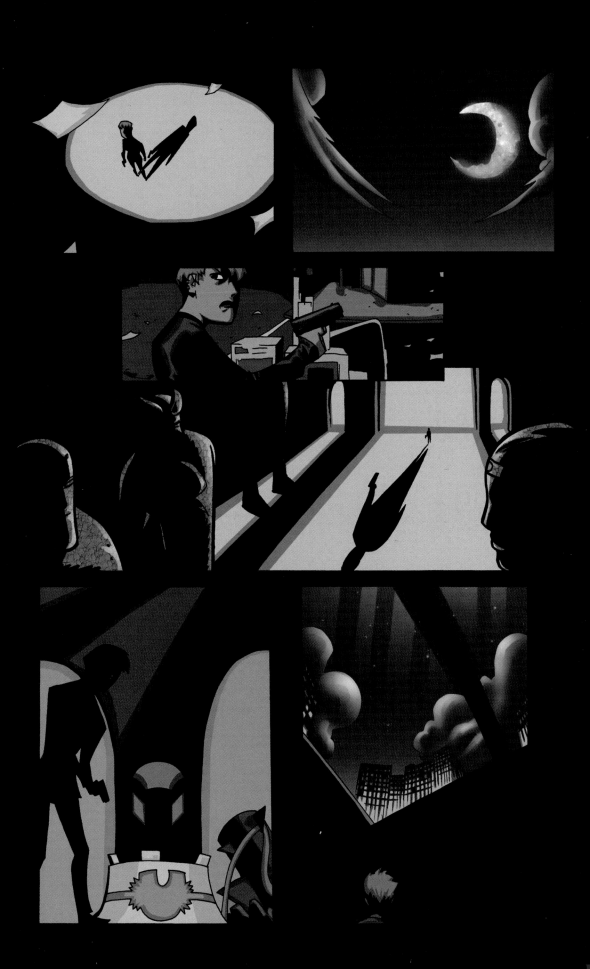

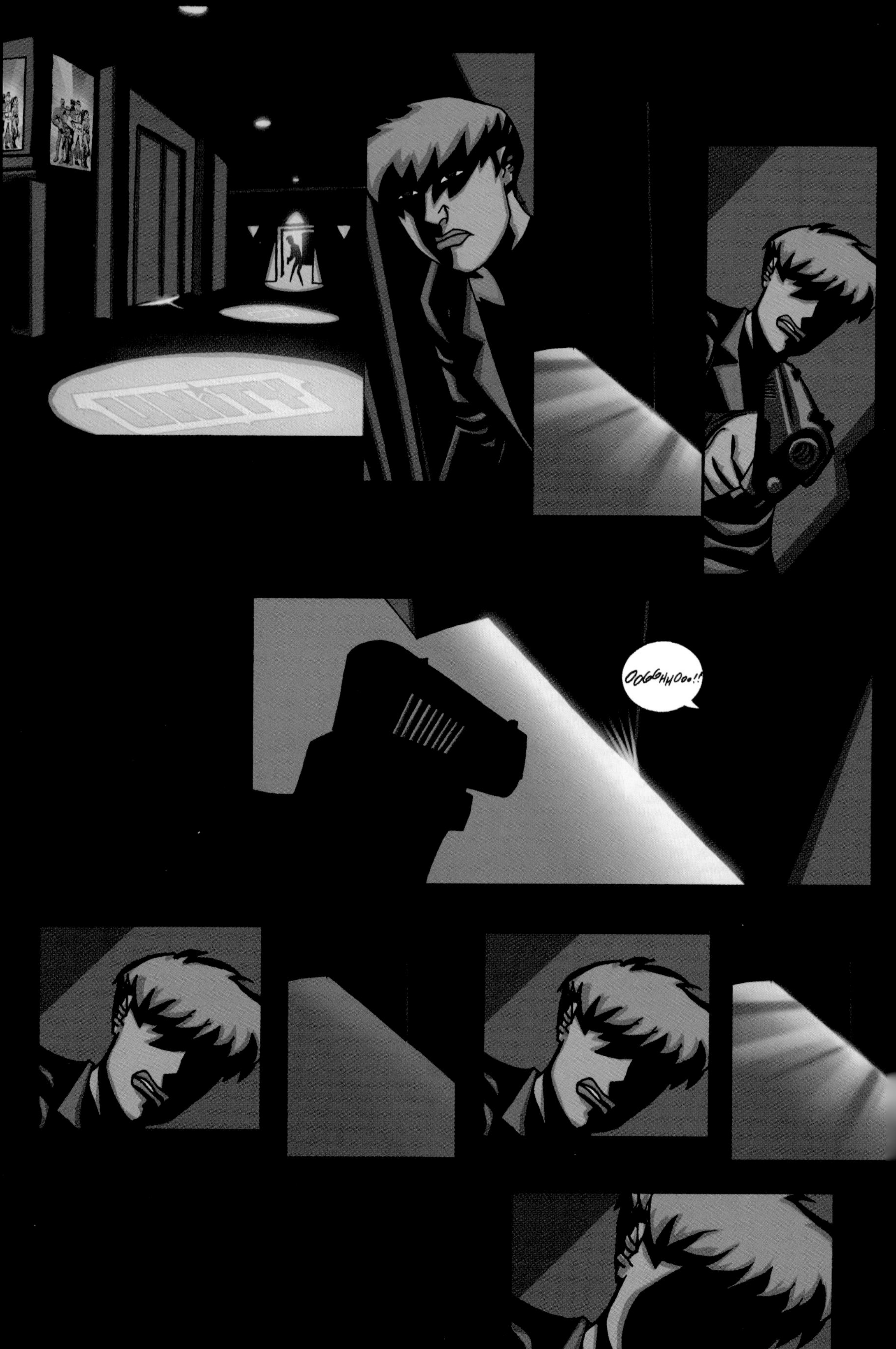
UNITY
OOGGHHOoo!!

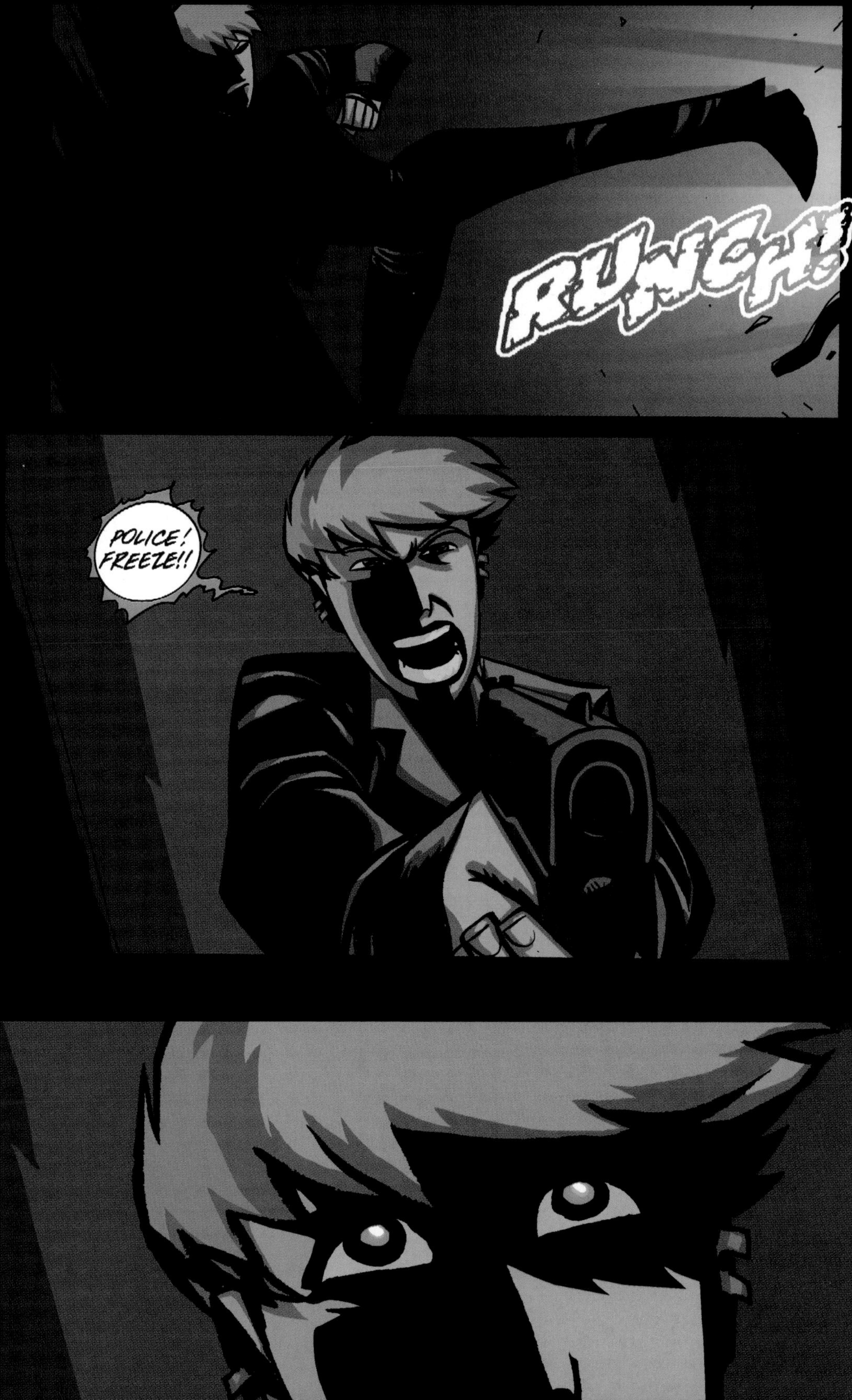
RUNCH!
POLICE! FREEZE!!

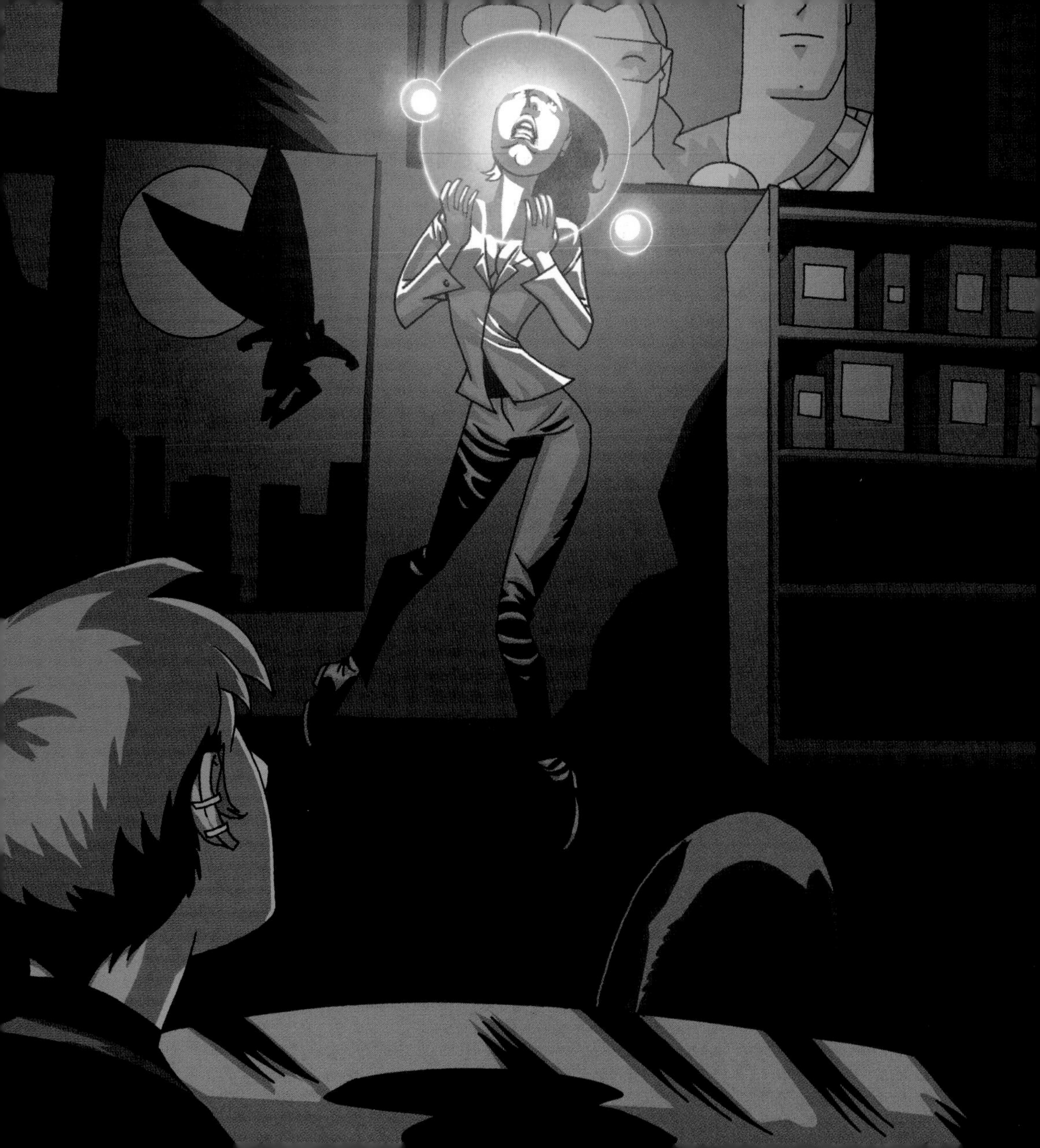

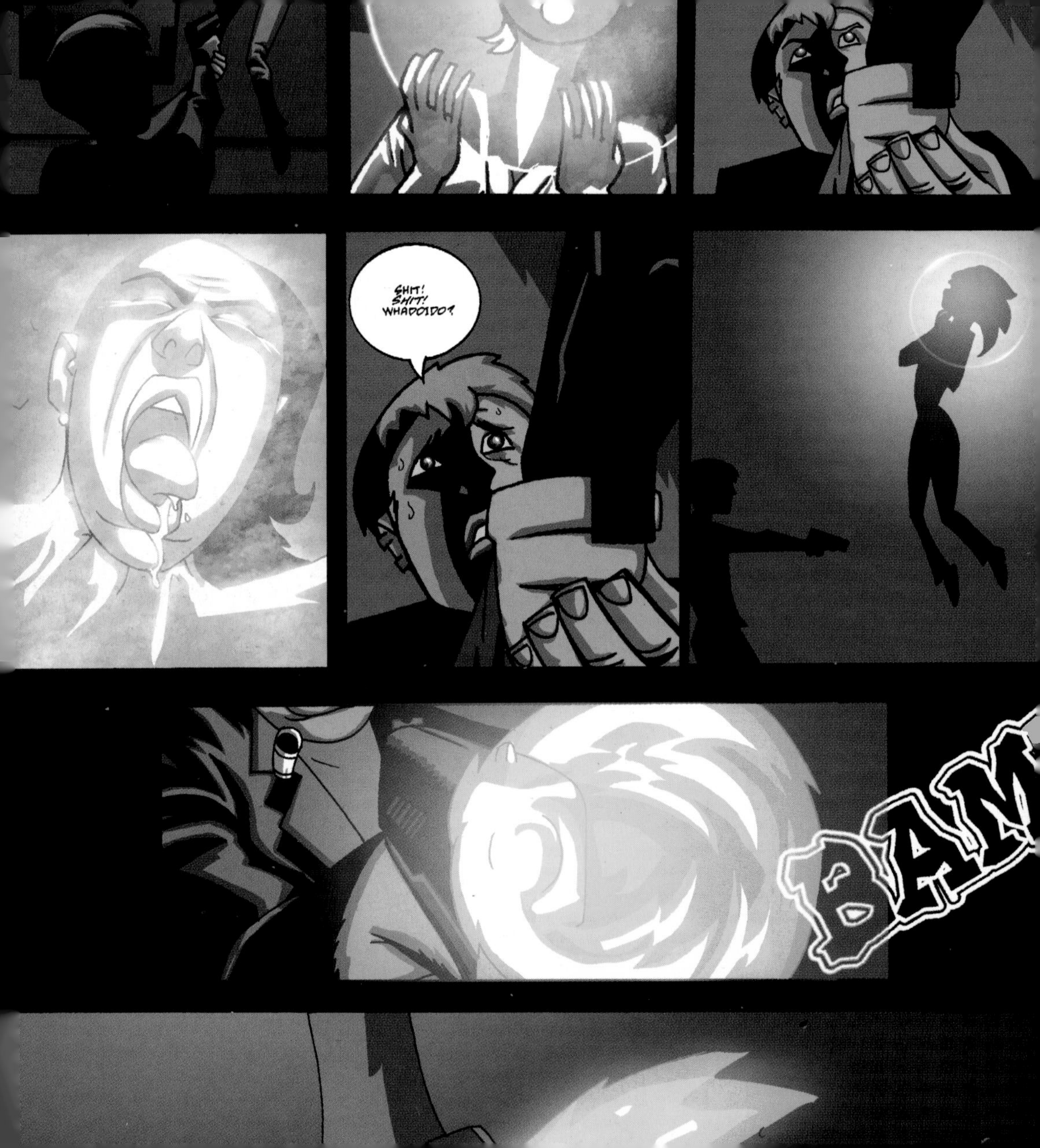
SHIT! SHIT! WHADOIDO?
BAM

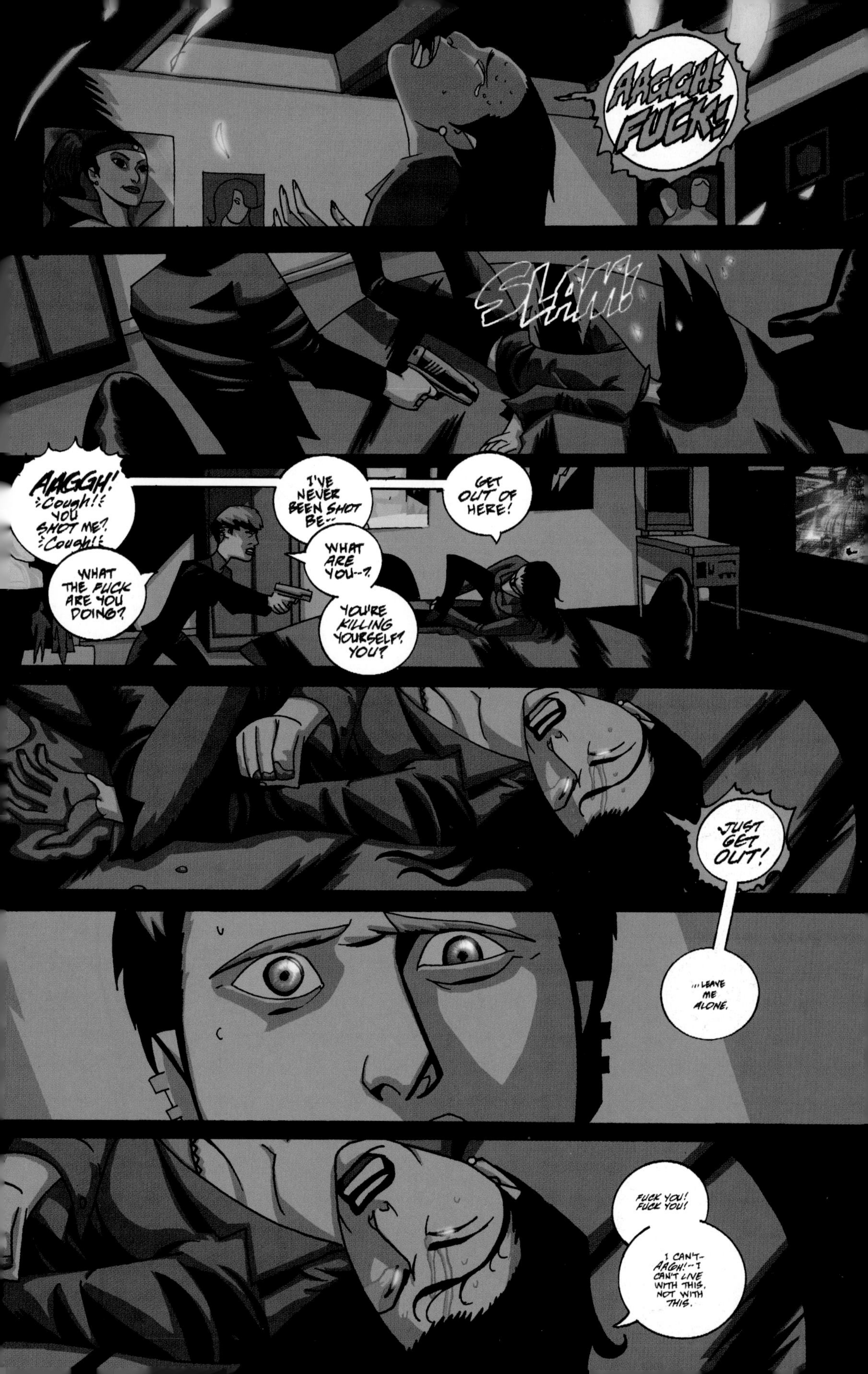
AAGGH! FUCK!
SLAM!
AAGGH! :Cough!: YOU SHOT ME? :Cough!:
WHAT THE FUCK ARE YOU DOING?
I'VE NEVER BEEN SHOT BE--
WHAT ARE YOU--?
YOU'RE KILLING YOURSELF? YOU?
GET OUT OF HERE!
JUST GET OUT!
...LEAVE ME ALONE.
FUCK YOU! FUCK YOU!
I CAN'T-- AAGH!-- I CAN'T LIVE WITH THIS. NOT WITH THIS.

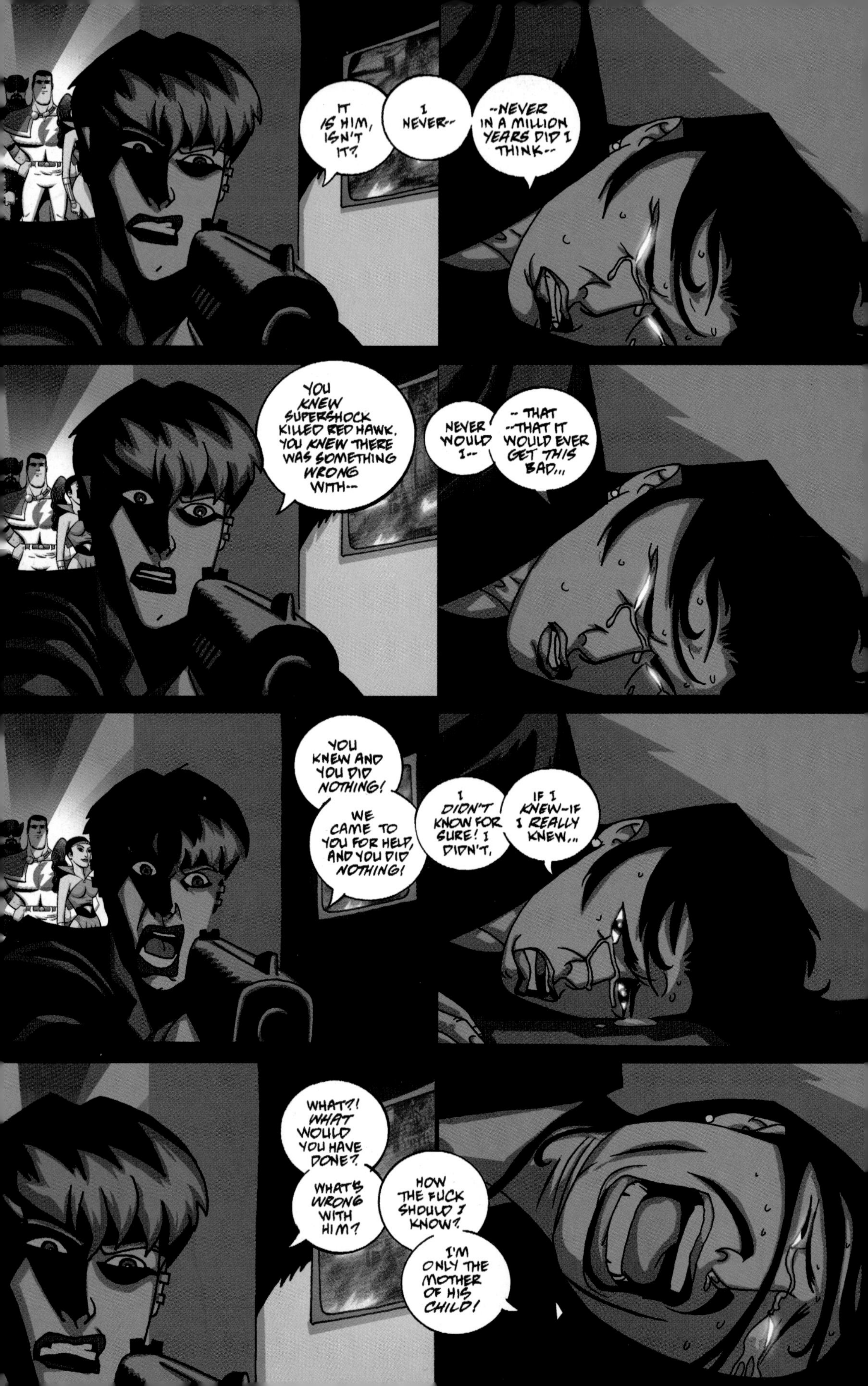
IT IS HIM, ISN'T IT?
I NEVER--
--NEVER IN A MILLION YEARS DID I THINK--
YOU KNEW SUPERSHOCK KILLED RED HAWK. YOU KNEW THERE WAS SOMETHING WRONG WITH--
NEVER WOULD I--
--THAT --THAT IT WOULD EVER GET THIS BAD...
YOU KNEW AND YOU DID NOTHING!
WE CAME TO YOU FOR HELP, AND YOU DID NOTHING!
I DIDN'T KNOW FOR SURE! I DIDN'T.
IF I KNEW--IF I REALLY KNEW...
WHAT?! WHAT WOULD YOU HAVE DONE?
WHAT'S WRONG WITH HIM?
HOW THE FUCK SHOULD I KNOW?
I'M ONLY THE MOTHER OF HIS CHILD!

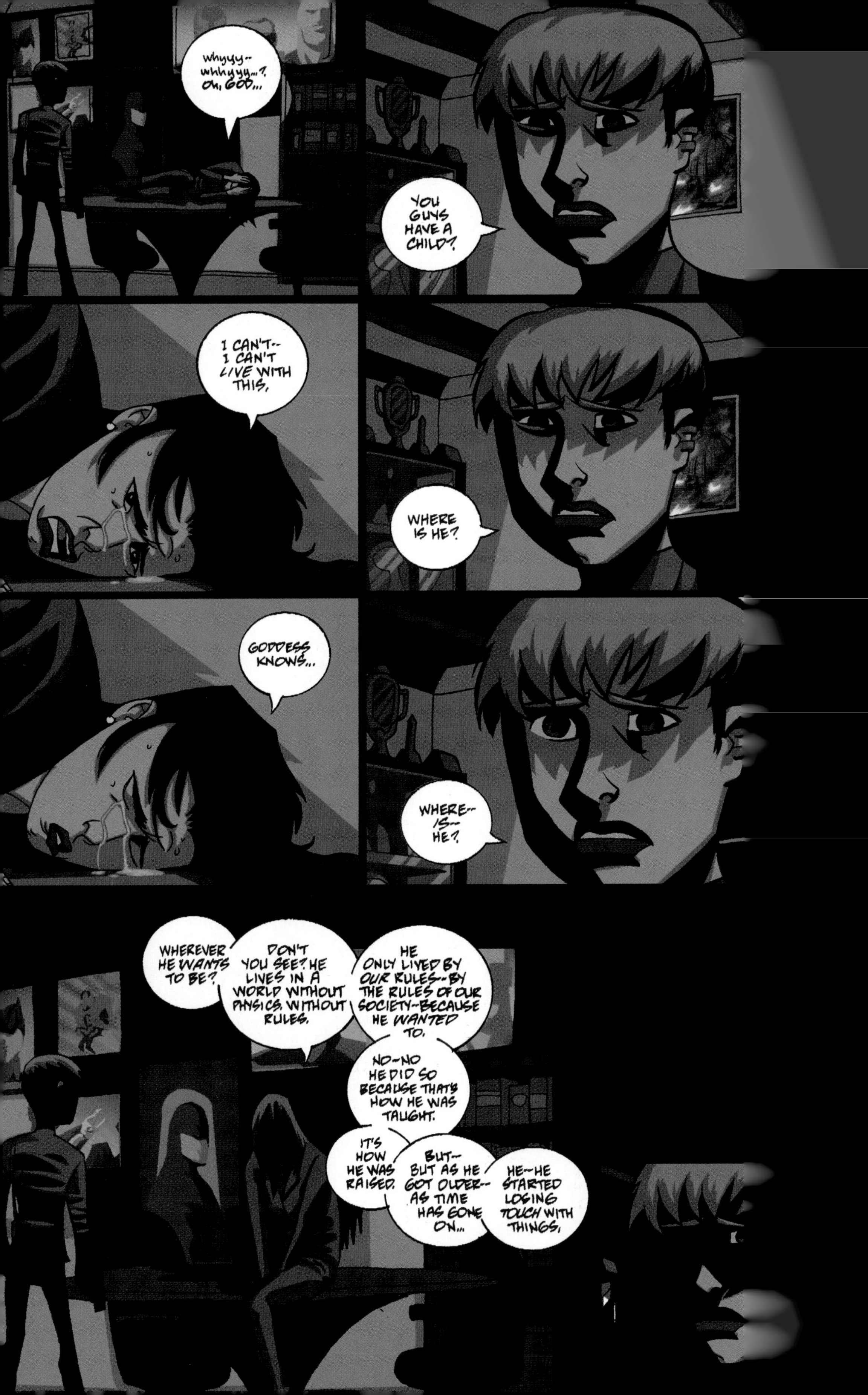
whyyy--
whhyyy...? Oh, GOD...
YOU GUYS HAVE A CHILD?
I CAN'T-- I CAN'T LIVE WITH THIS.
WHERE IS HE?
GODDESS KNOWS...
WHERE-- IS-- HE?
WHEREVER HE WANTS TO BE?
DON'T YOU SEE? HE LIVES IN A WORLD WITHOUT PHYSICS. WITHOUT RULES.
HE ONLY LIVED BY OUR RULES--BY THE RULES OF OUR SOCIETY--BECAUSE HE WANTED TO.
NO--NO HE DID SO BECAUSE THAT'S HOW HE WAS TAUGHT.
IT'S HOW HE WAS RAISED.
BUT-- BUT AS HE GOT OLDER-- AS TIME HAS GONE ON...
HE--HE STARTED LOSING TOUCH WITH THINGS.

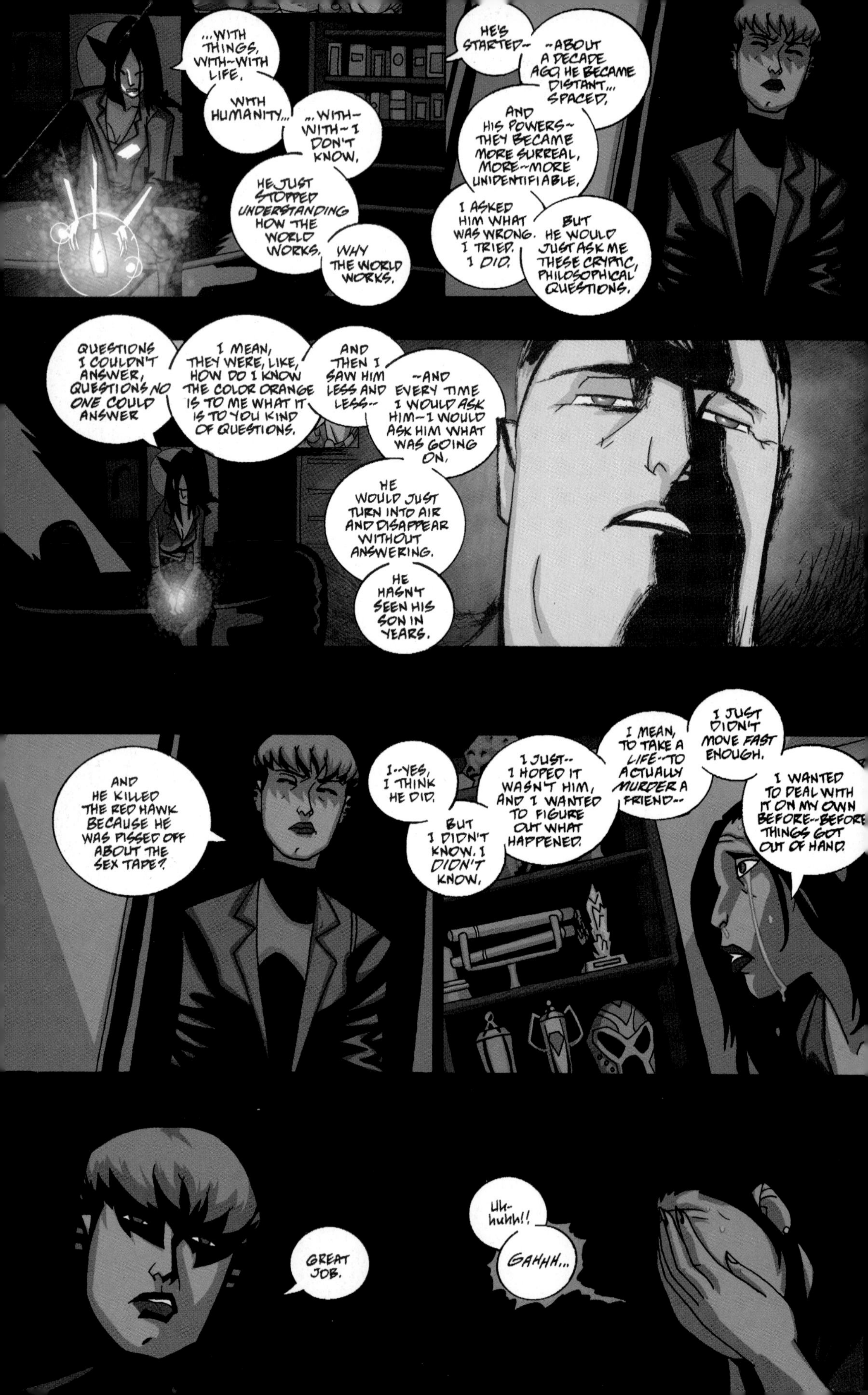
...WITH THINGS, WITH--WITH LIFE.
WITH HUMANITY...
...WITH--WITH--I DON'T KNOW.
HE JUST STOPPED UNDERSTANDING HOW THE WORLD WORKS.
WHY THE WORLD WORKS.
HE'S STARTED--
--ABOUT A DECADE AGO, HE BECAME DISTANT... SPACED.
AND HIS POWERS--THEY BECAME MORE SURREAL, MORE--MORE UNIDENTIFIABLE.
I ASKED HIM WHAT WAS WRONG. I TRIED. I DID.
BUT HE WOULD JUST ASK ME THESE CRYPTIC, PHILOSOPHICAL QUESTIONS.
QUESTIONS I COULDN'T ANSWER, QUESTIONS NO ONE COULD ANSWER
I MEAN, THEY WERE, LIKE, HOW DO I KNOW THE COLOR ORANGE IS TO ME WHAT IT IS TO YOU KIND OF QUESTIONS.
AND THEN I SAW HIM LESS AND LESS--
--AND EVERY TIME I WOULD ASK HIM--I WOULD ASK HIM WHAT WAS GOING ON,
HE WOULD JUST TURN INTO AIR AND DISAPPEAR WITHOUT ANSWERING.
HE HASN'T SEEN HIS SON IN YEARS.
AND HE KILLED THE RED HAWK BECAUSE HE WAS PISSED OFF ABOUT THE SEX TAPE?
I--YES, I THINK HE DID.
BUT I DIDN'T KNOW. I DIDN'T KNOW.
I JUST--I HOPED IT WASN'T HIM, AND I WANTED TO FIGURE OUT WHAT HAPPENED.
I MEAN, TO TAKE A LIFE--TO ACTUALLY MURDER A FRIEND--
I JUST DIDN'T MOVE FAST ENOUGH.
I WANTED TO DEAL WITH IT ON MY OWN BEFORE--BEFORE THINGS GOT OUT OF HAND.
GREAT JOB.
Uh-huhh!!
GAHHH...

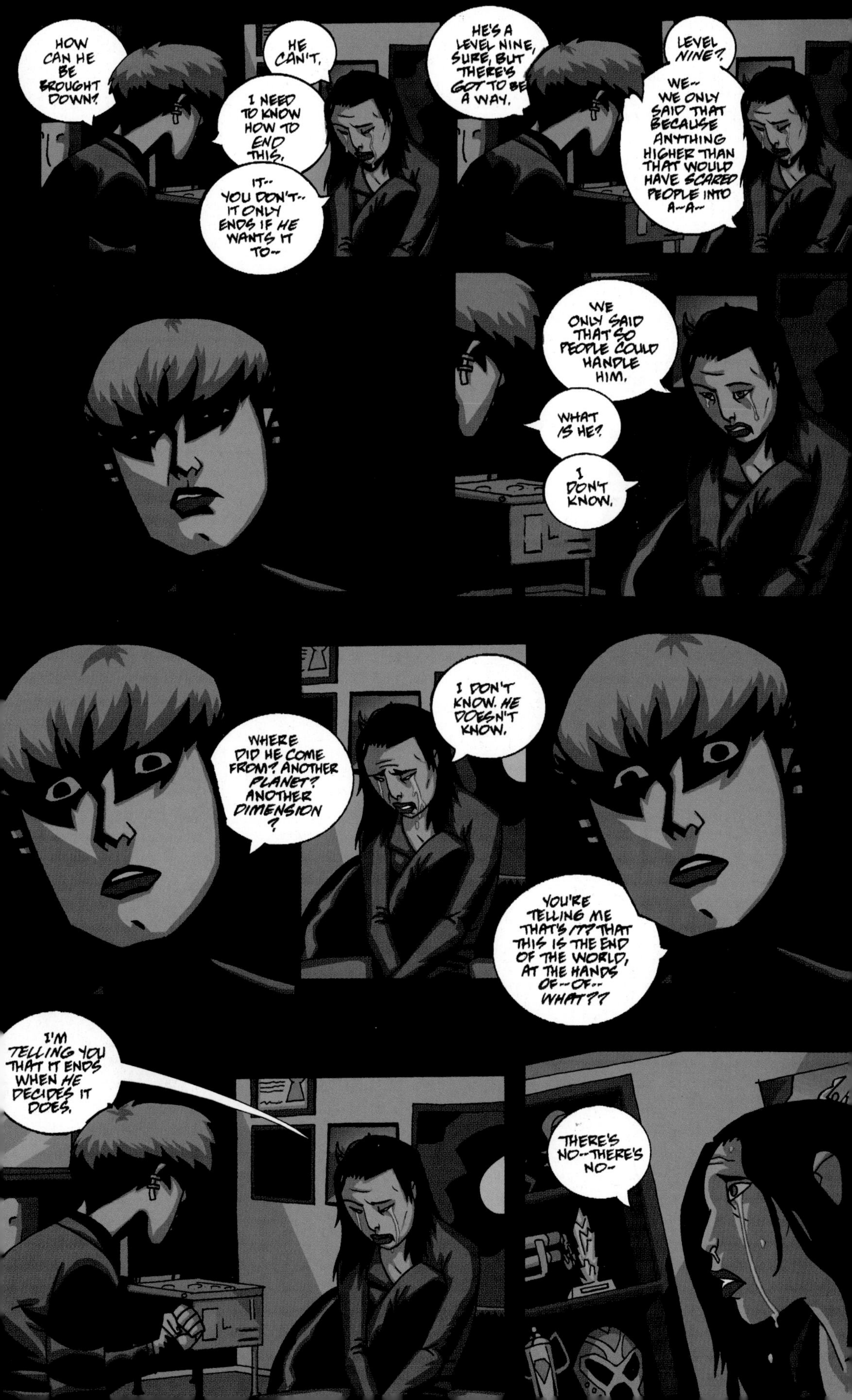
HOW CAN HE BE BROUGHT DOWN?
HE CAN'T.
I NEED TO KNOW HOW TO END THIS.
IT-- YOU DON'T-- IT ONLY ENDS IF HE WANTS IT TO--
HE'S A LEVEL NINE, SURE, BUT THERE'S GOT TO BE A WAY.
LEVEL NINE?
WE-- WE ONLY SAID THAT BECAUSE ANYTHING HIGHER THAN THAT WOULD HAVE SCARED PEOPLE INTO A--A--
WE ONLY SAID THAT SO PEOPLE COULD HANDLE HIM.
WHAT IS HE?
I DON'T KNOW.
WHERE DID HE COME FROM? ANOTHER PLANET? ANOTHER DIMENSION?
I DON'T KNOW. HE DOESN'T KNOW.
YOU'RE TELLING ME THAT'S IT? THAT THIS IS THE END OF THE WORLD, AT THE HANDS OF--OF-- WHAT??
I'M TELLING YOU THAT IT ENDS WHEN HE DECIDES IT DOES.
THERE'S NO--THERE'S NO--

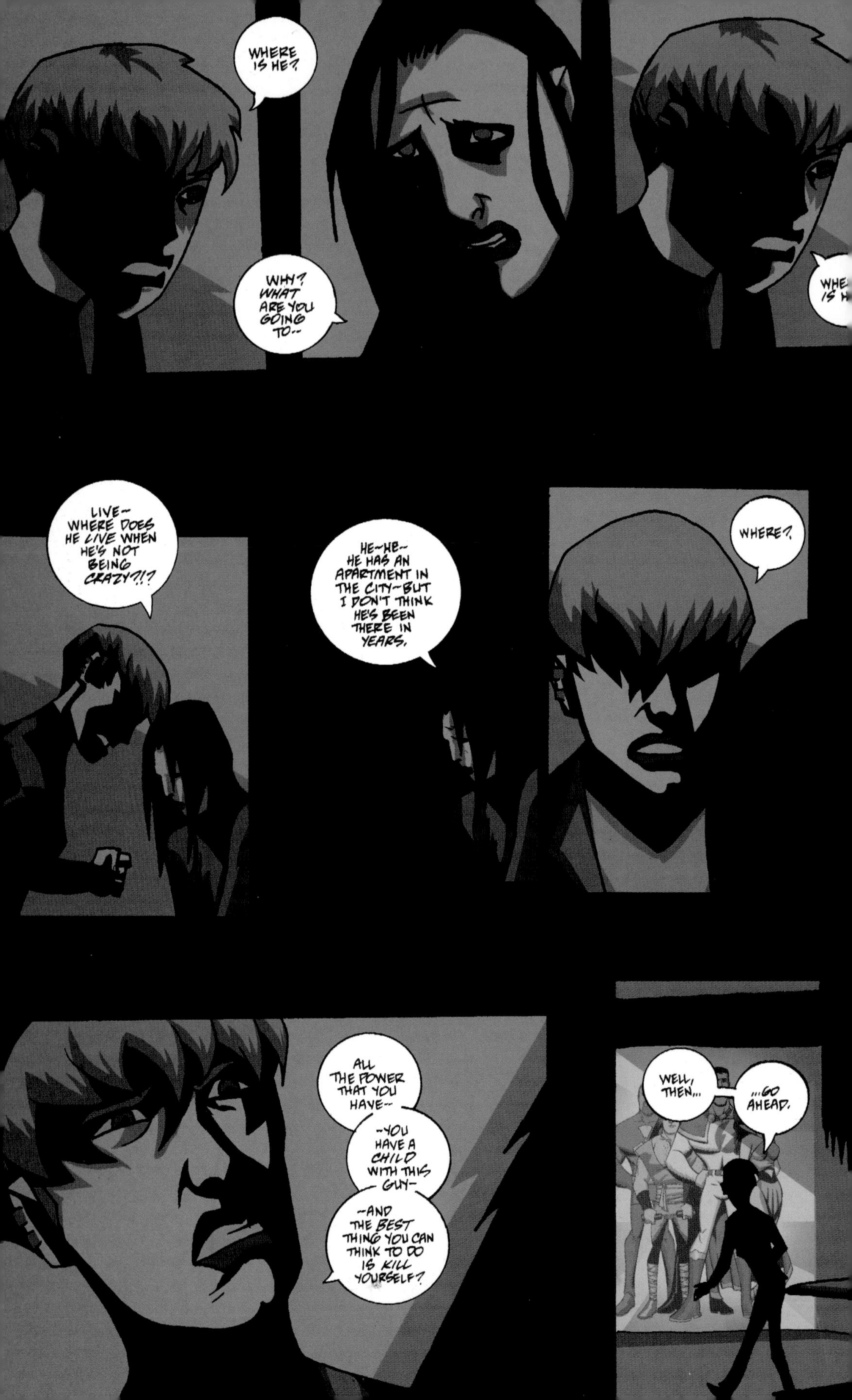
WHERE IS HE?
WHY? WHAT ARE YOU GOING TO--
WHE IS H
LIVE-- WHERE DOES HE LIVE WHEN HE'S NOT BEING CRAZY?!?
HE--HE-- HE HAS AN APARTMENT IN THE CITY--BUT I DON'T THINK HE'S BEEN THERE IN YEARS.
WHERE?
ALL THE POWER THAT YOU HAVE--
--YOU HAVE A CHILD WITH THIS GUY--
--AND THE BEST THING YOU CAN THINK TO DO IS KILL YOURSELF?
WELL, THEN...
...GO AHEAD.

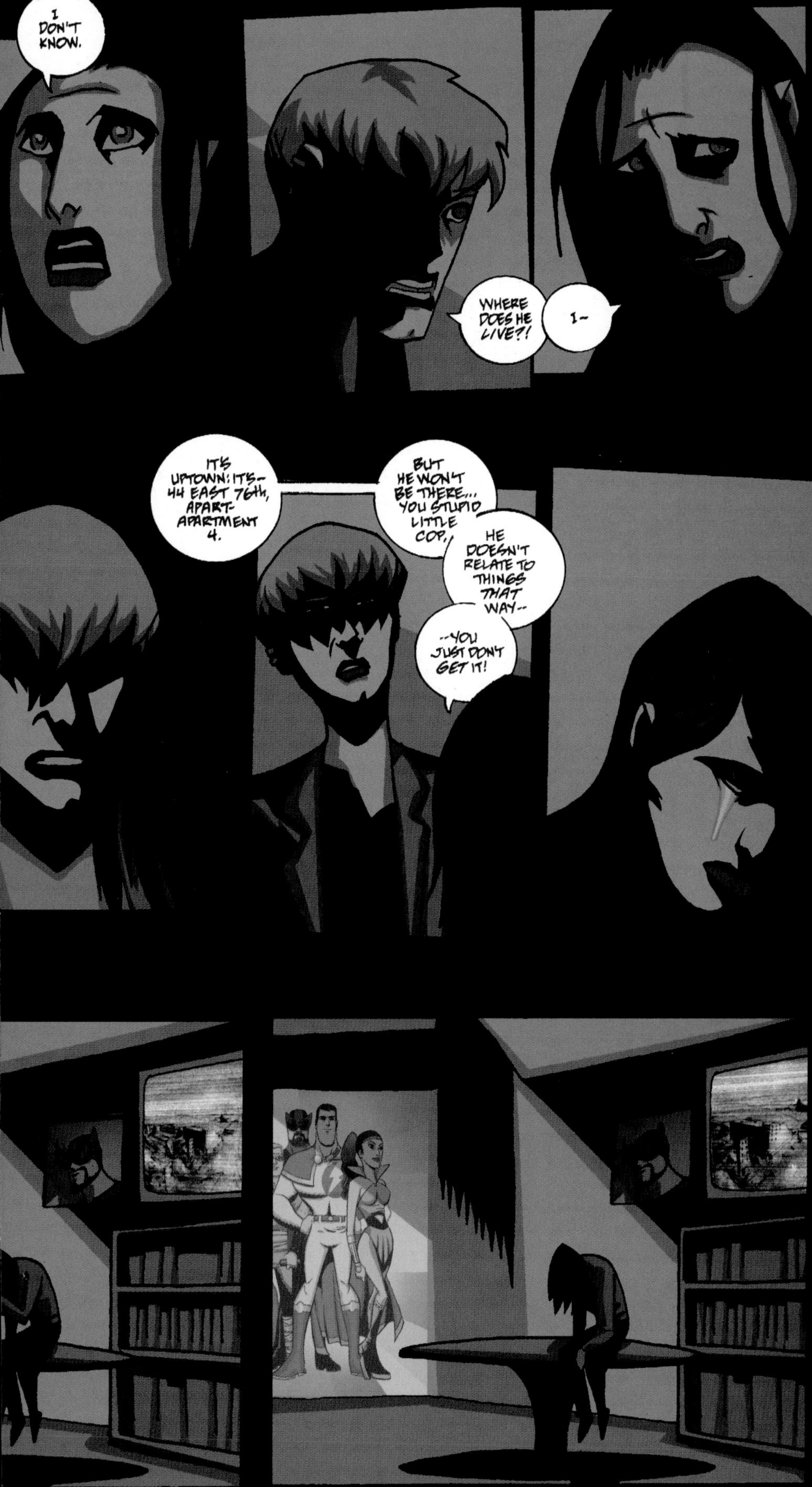
I DON'T KNOW.
WHERE DOES HE LIVE?!
I--
IT'S UPTOWN; IT'S-- 44 EAST 76th, APART- APARTMENT 4.
BUT HE WON'T BE THERE... YOU STUPID LITTLE COP,
HE DOESN'T RELATE TO THINGS THAT WAY--
--YOU JUST DON'T GET IT!

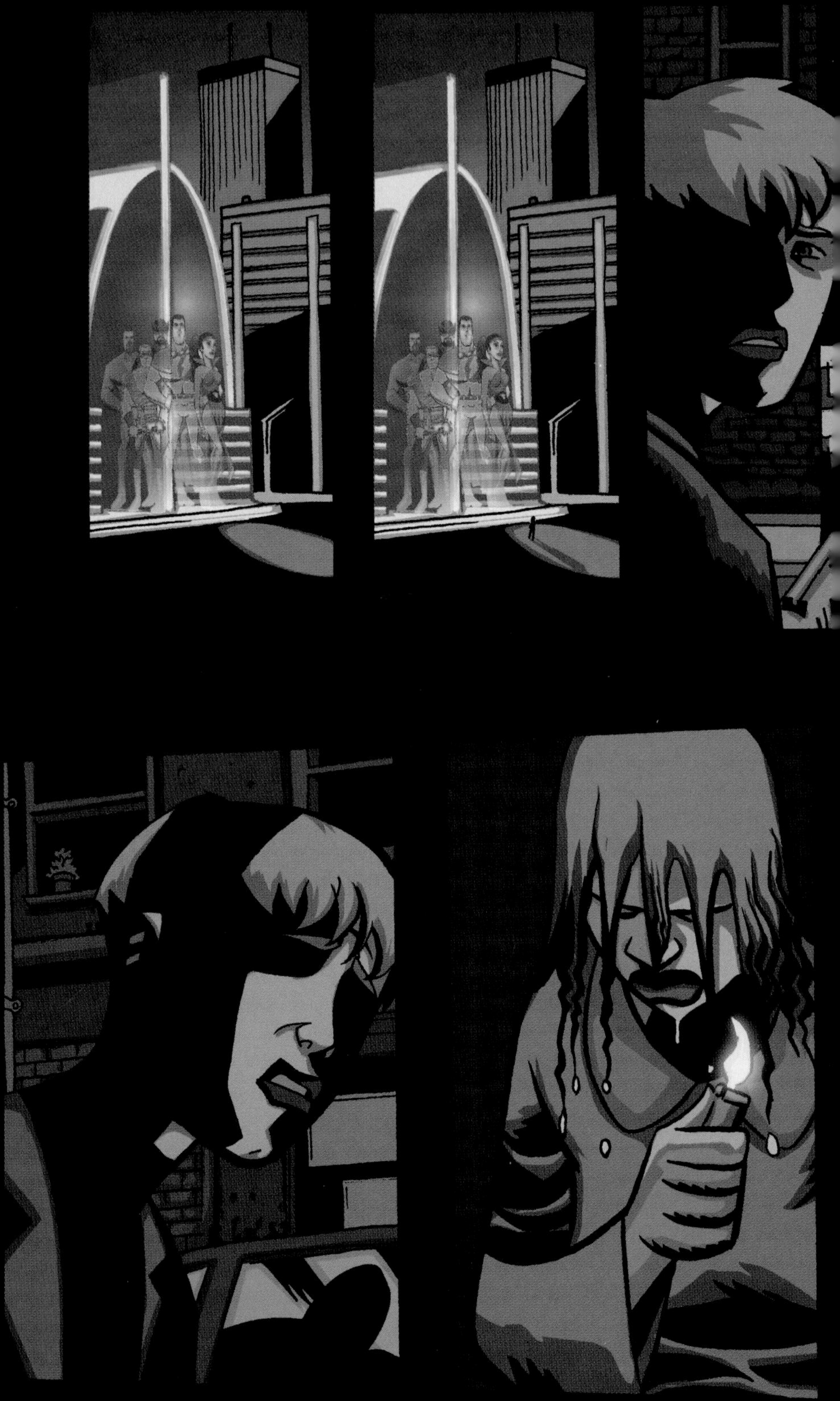

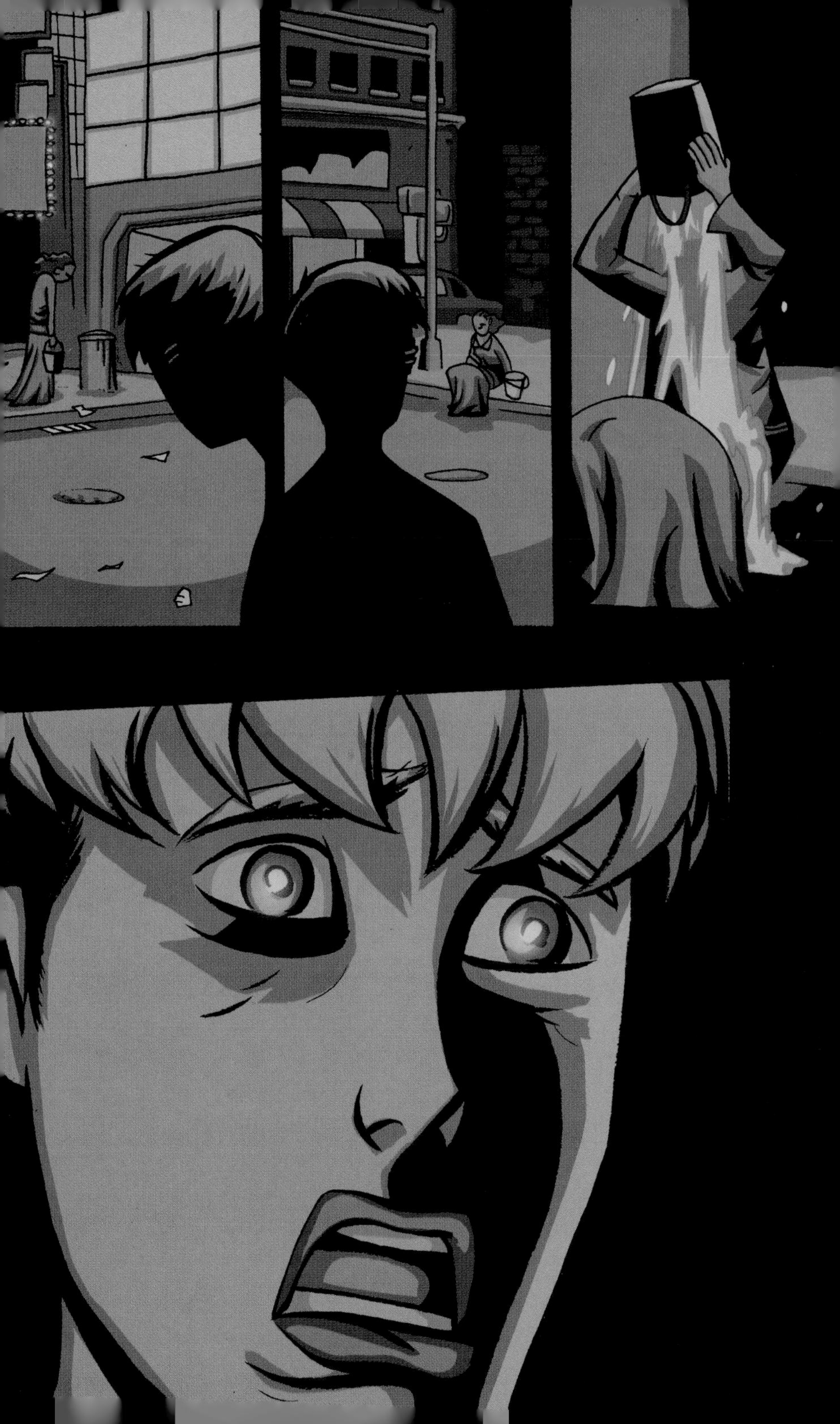

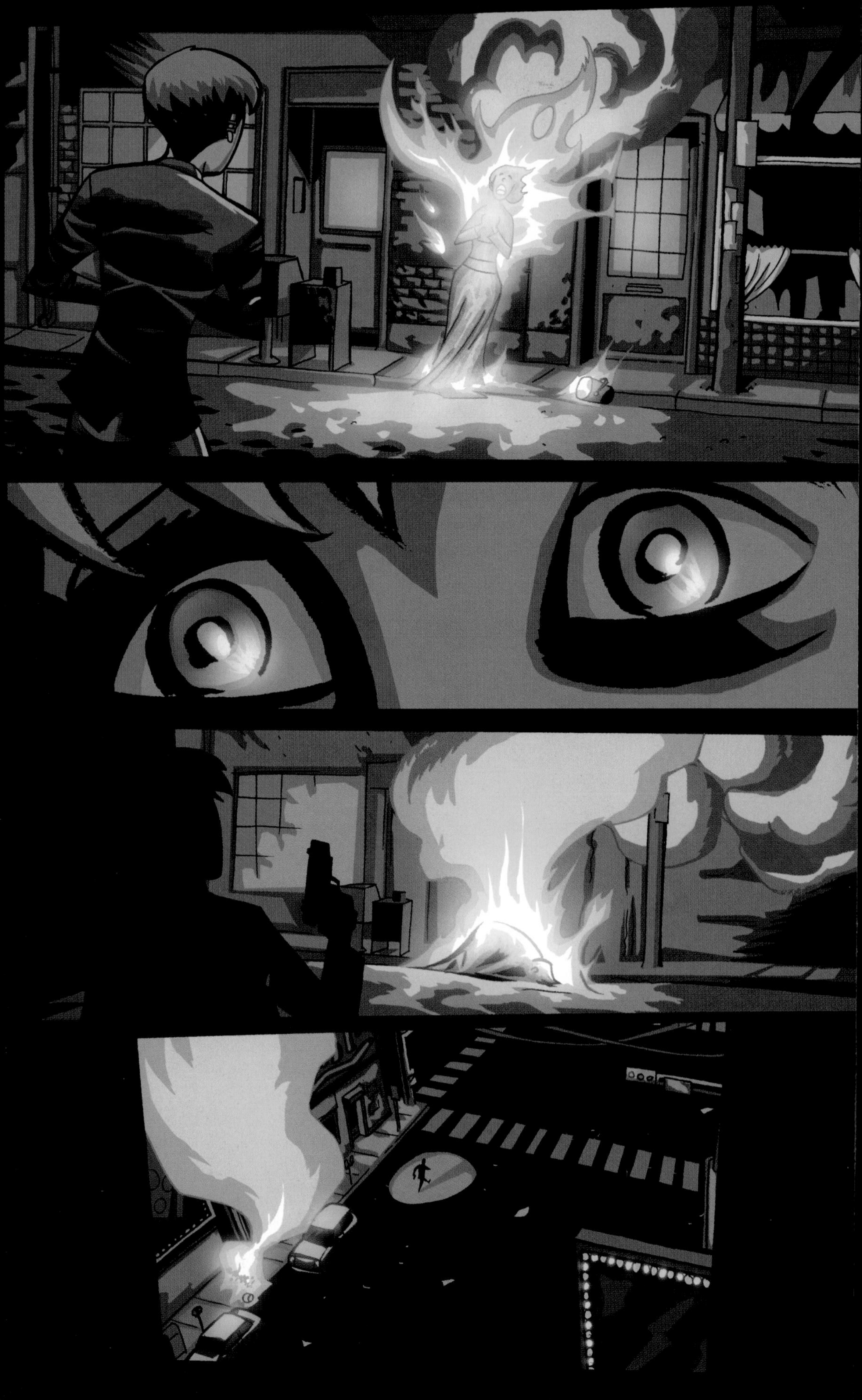

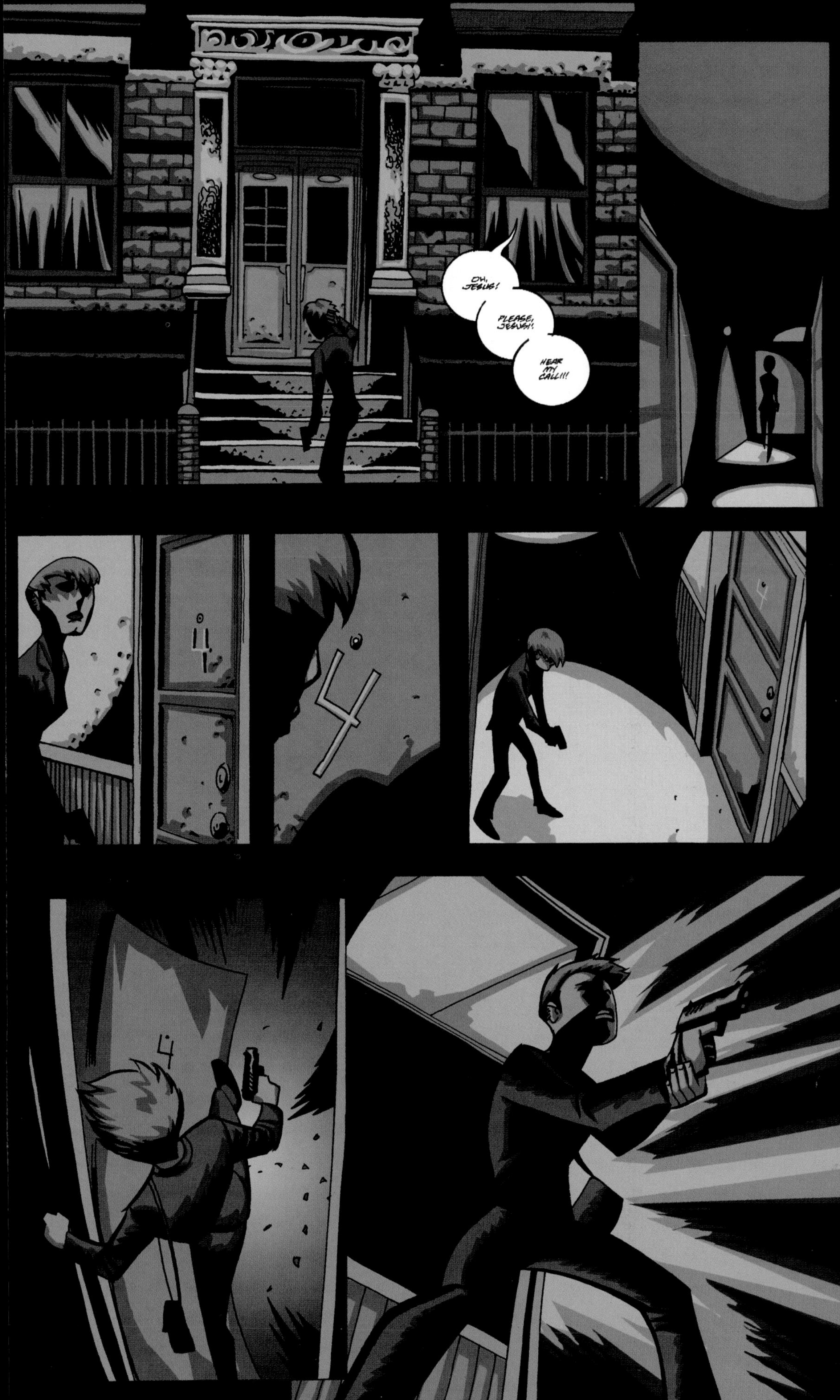
OH, JESUS!
PLEASE, JESUS!
HEAR MY CALL!!!

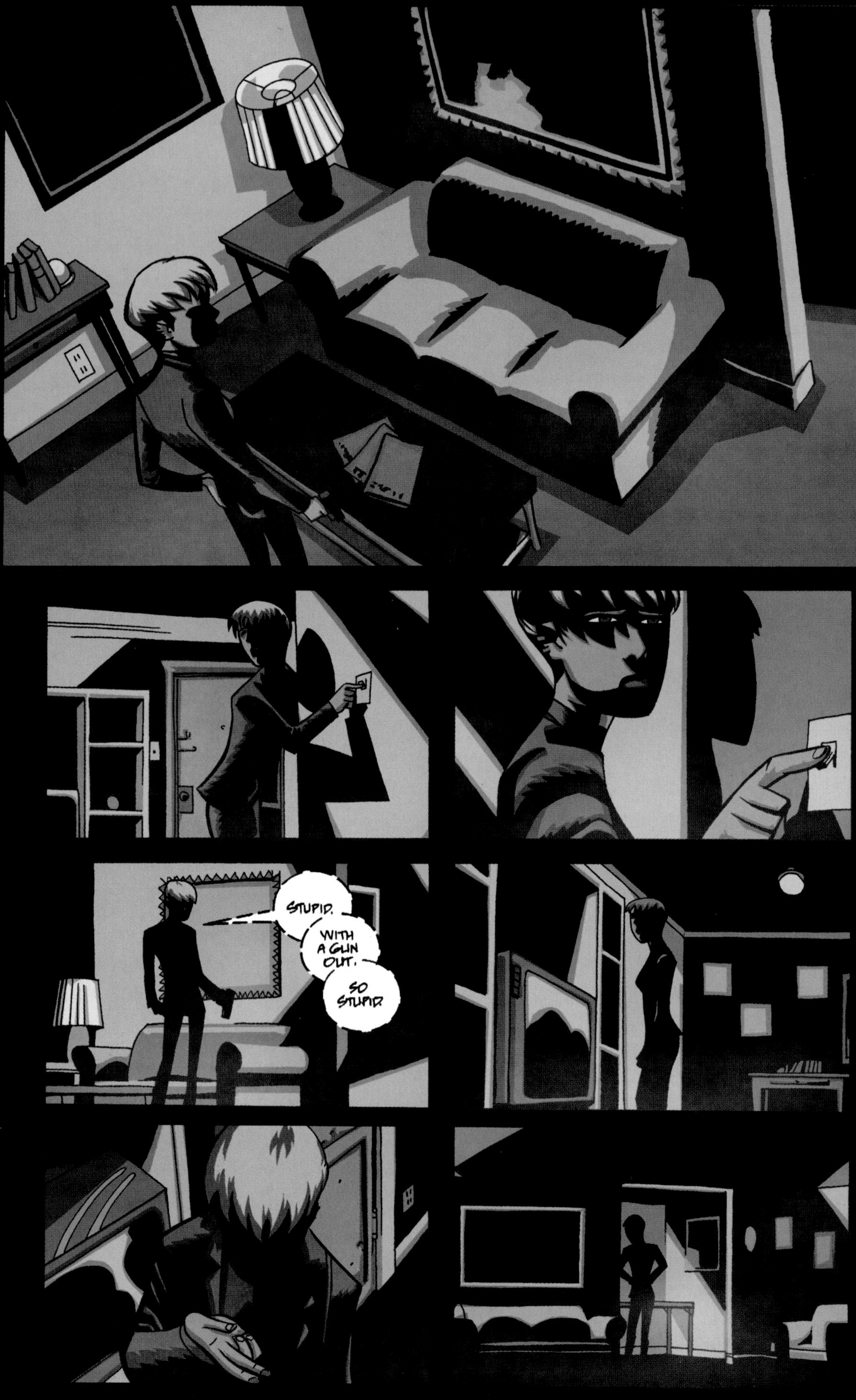
STUPID.
WITH A GUN OUT.
SO STUPID.

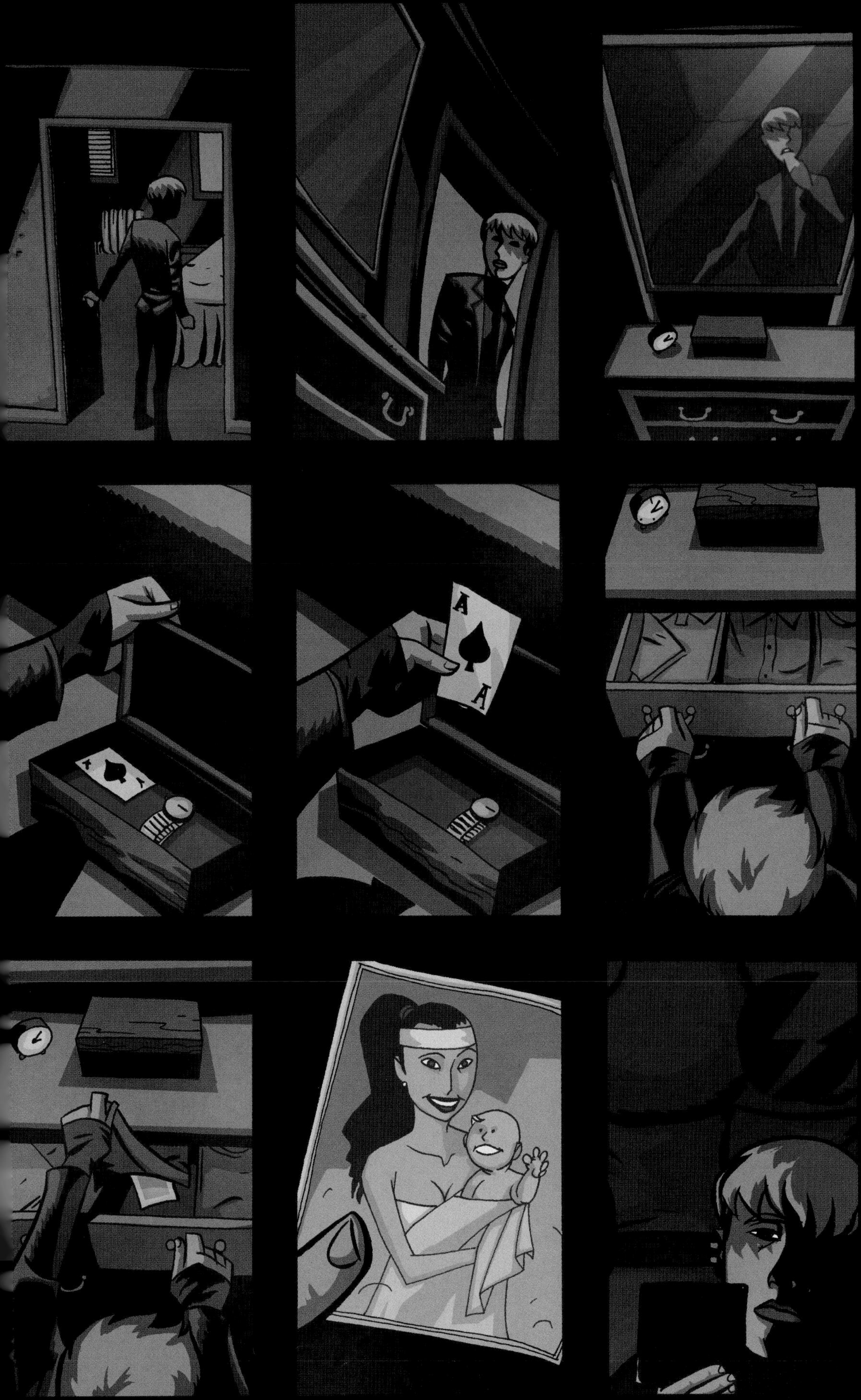

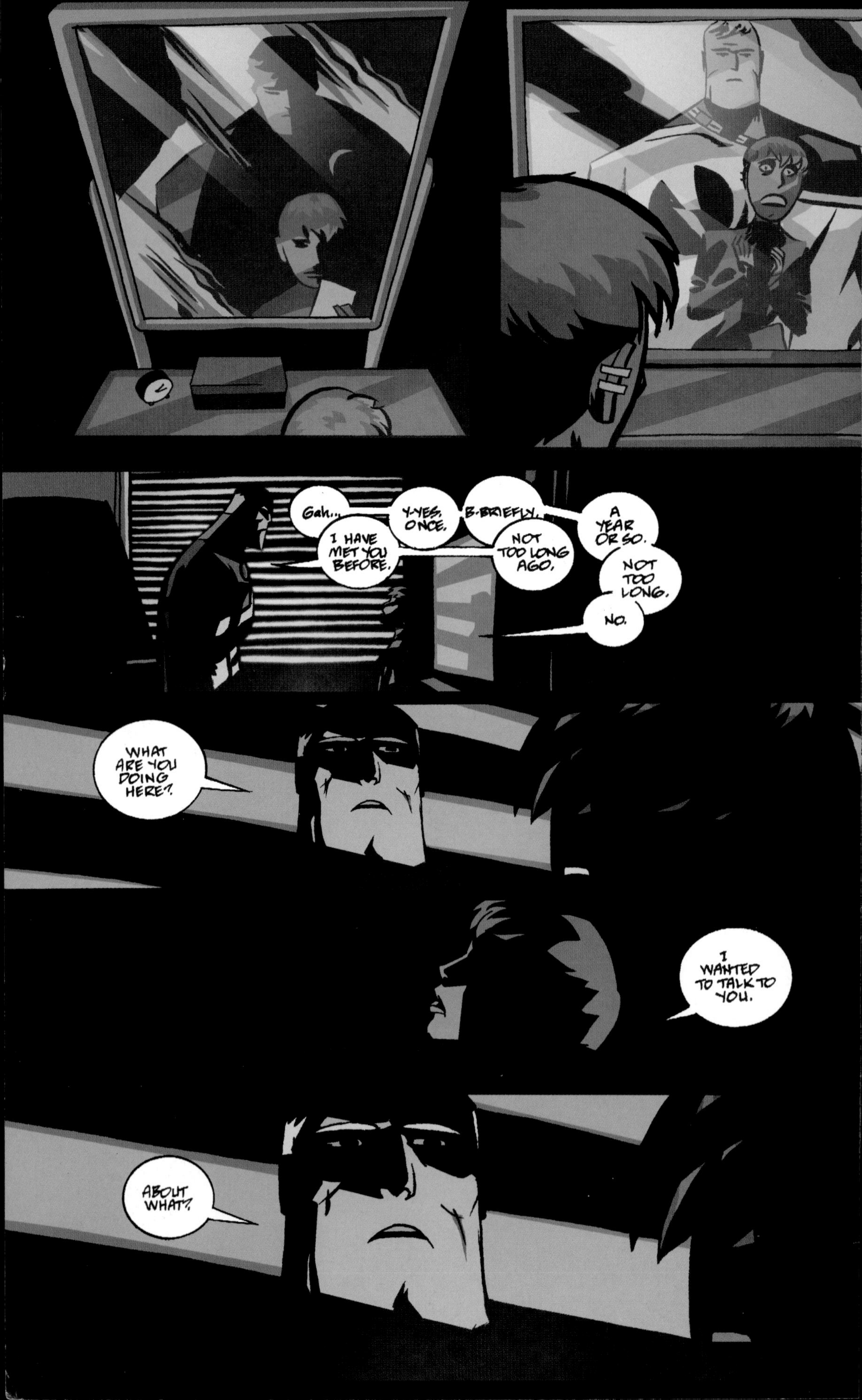
Gah...
I HAVE MET YOU BEFORE.
Y-YES. ONCE.
B-BRIEFLY.
NOT TOO LONG AGO.
A YEAR OR SO.
NOT TOO LONG.
NO.
WHAT ARE YOU DOING HERE?
I WANTED TO TALK TO YOU.
ABOUT WHAT?

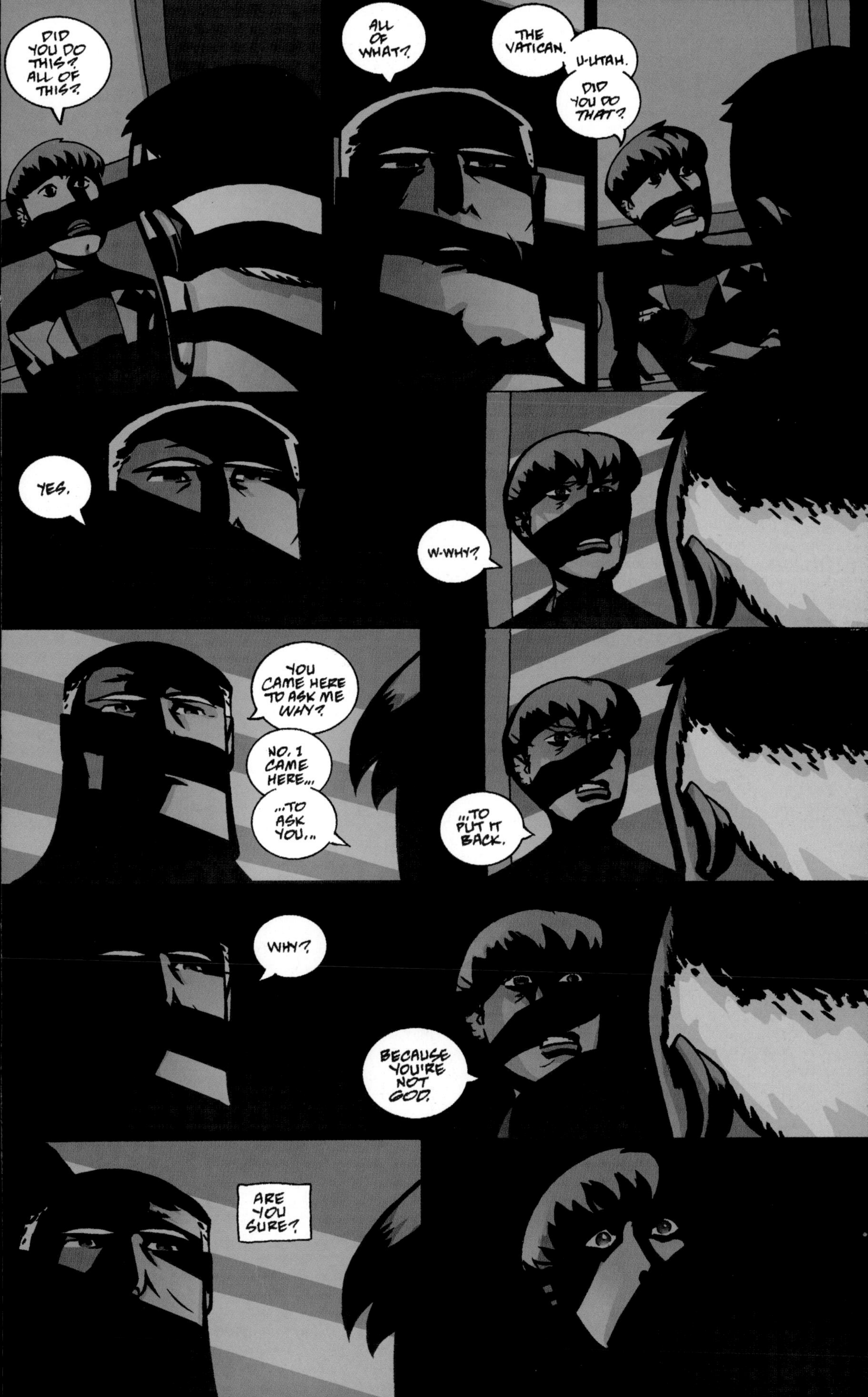
DID YOU DO THIS? ALL OF THIS?
ALL OF WHAT?
THE VATICAN.
U-UTAH.
DID YOU DO THAT?
YES.
W-WHY?
YOU CAME HERE TO ASK ME WHY?
NO, I CAME HERE...
...TO ASK YOU...
...TO PUT IT BACK.
WHY?
BECAUSE YOU'RE NOT GOD.
ARE YOU SURE?

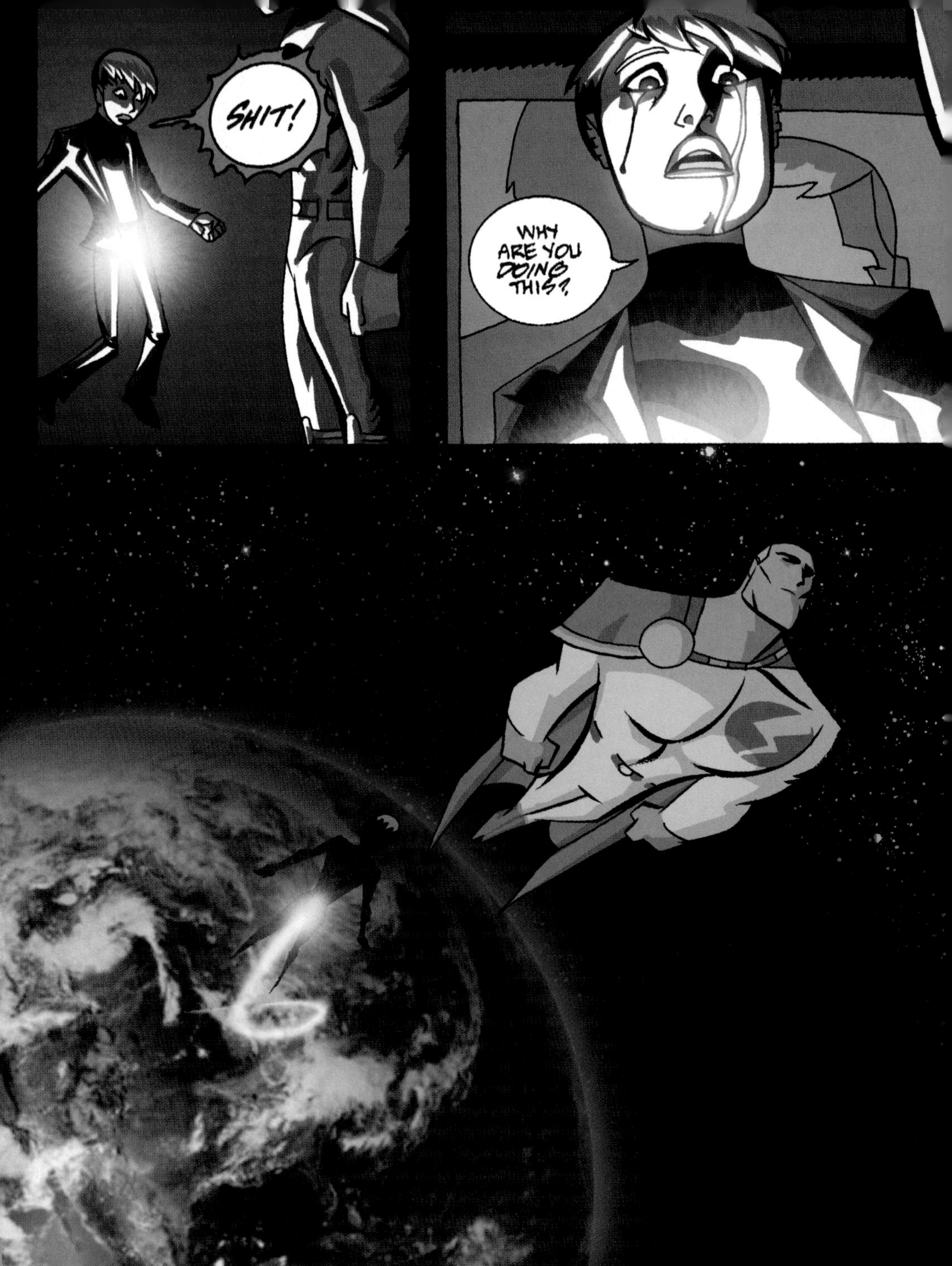
SHIT!
WHY ARE YOU DOING THIS?

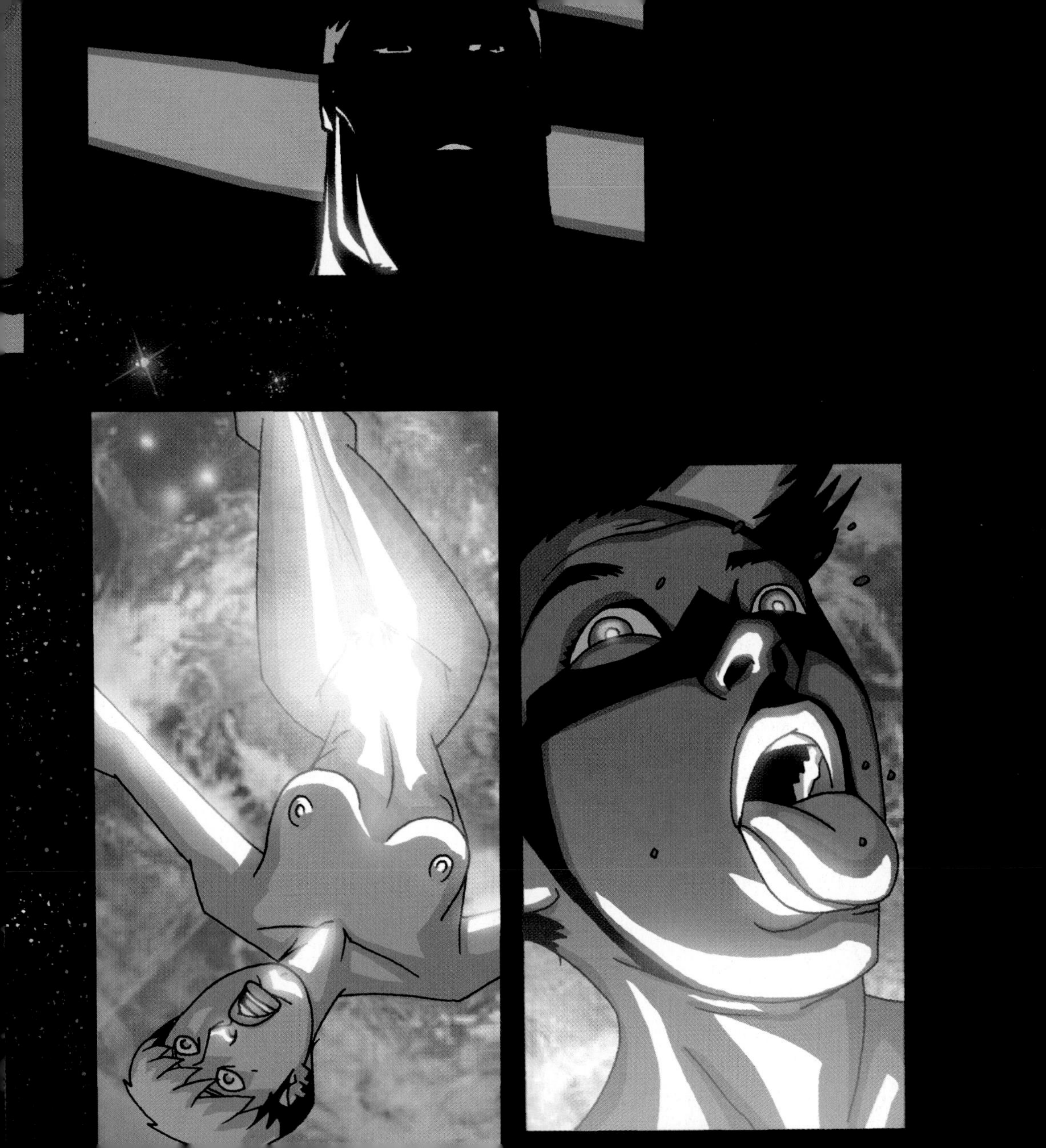

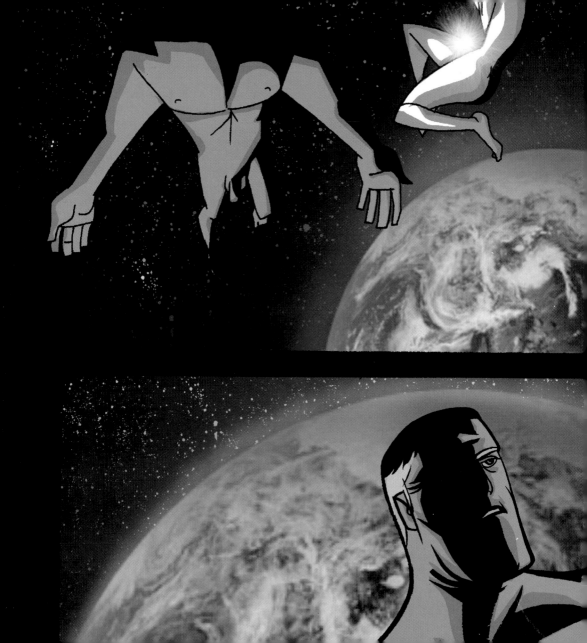

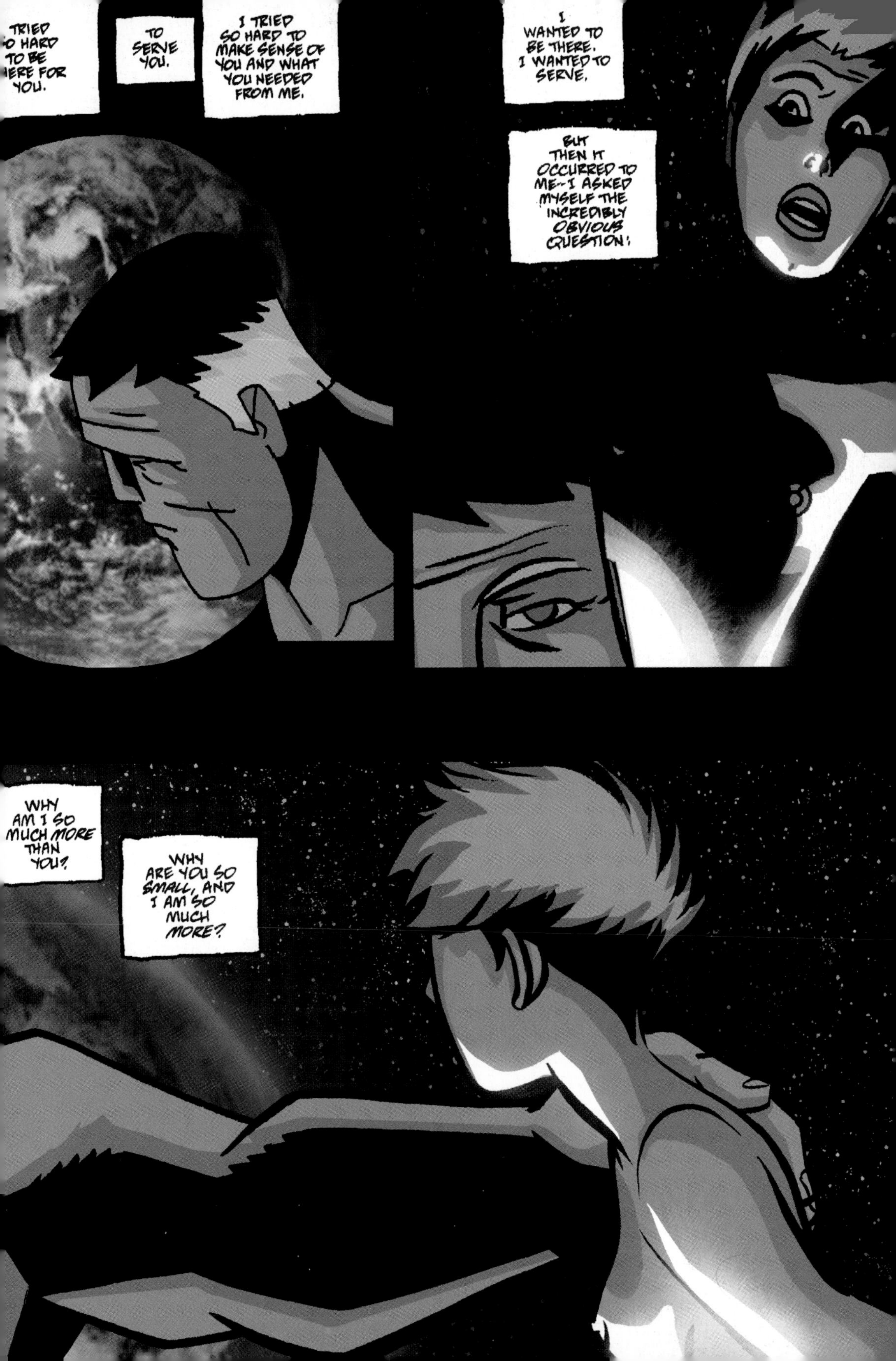
TRIED
O HARD
TO BE
IERE FOR
YOU.
TO SERVE YOU.
I TRIED SO HARD TO MAKE SENSE OF YOU AND WHAT YOU NEEDED FROM ME.
I WANTED TO BE THERE. I WANTED TO SERVE.
BUT THEN IT OCCURRED TO ME-- I ASKED MYSELF THE INCREDIBLY *OBVIOUS* QUESTION:
WHY AM I SO MUCH *MORE* THAN YOU?
WHY ARE YOU SO *SMALL*, AND I AM SO MUCH *MORE*?

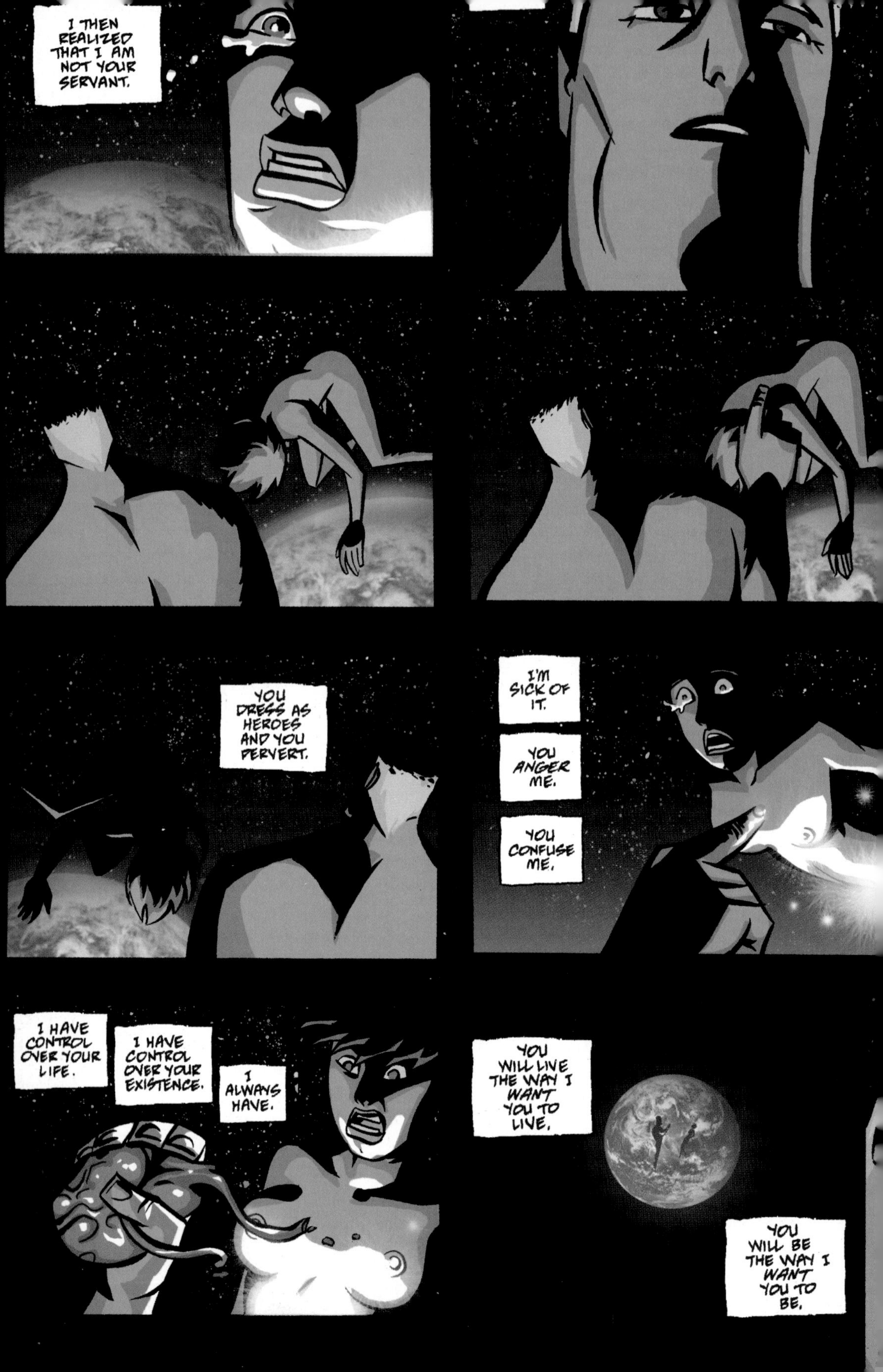
I THEN REALIZED THAT I AM NOT YOUR SERVANT.
YOU DRESS AS HEROES AND YOU PERVERT.
I'M SICK OF IT.
YOU ANGER ME.
YOU CONFUSE ME.
I HAVE CONTROL OVER YOUR LIFE.
I HAVE CONTROL OVER YOUR EXISTENCE.
I ALWAYS HAVE.
YOU WILL LIVE THE WAY I WANT YOU TO LIVE.
YOU WILL BE THE WAY I WANT YOU TO BE.

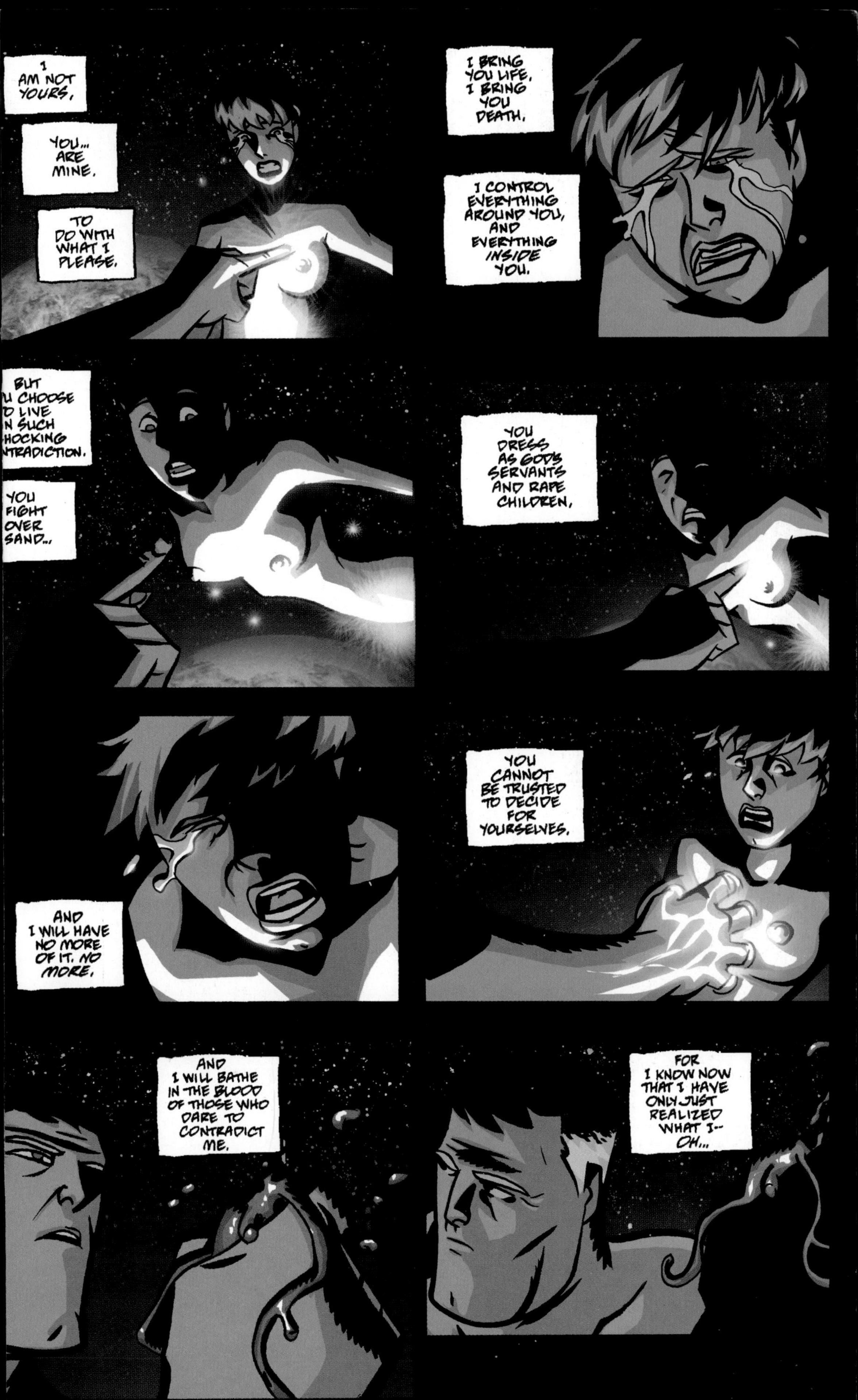

I AM NOT YOURS,
YOU... ARE MINE.
TO DO WITH WHAT I PLEASE.
I BRING YOU LIFE, I BRING YOU DEATH.
I CONTROL EVERYTHING AROUND YOU, AND EVERYTHING INSIDE YOU.
BUT U CHOOSE O LIVE N SUCH HOCKING NTRADICTION.
YOU FIGHT OVER SAND...
YOU DRESS AS GOD'S SERVANTS AND RAPE CHILDREN,
AND I WILL HAVE NO MORE OF IT. NO MORE.
YOU CANNOT BE TRUSTED TO DECIDE FOR YOURSELVES.
AND I WILL BATHE IN THE BLOOD OF THOSE WHO DARE TO CONTRADICT ME.
FOR I KNOW NOW THAT I HAVE ONLY JUST REALIZED WHAT I-- OH...

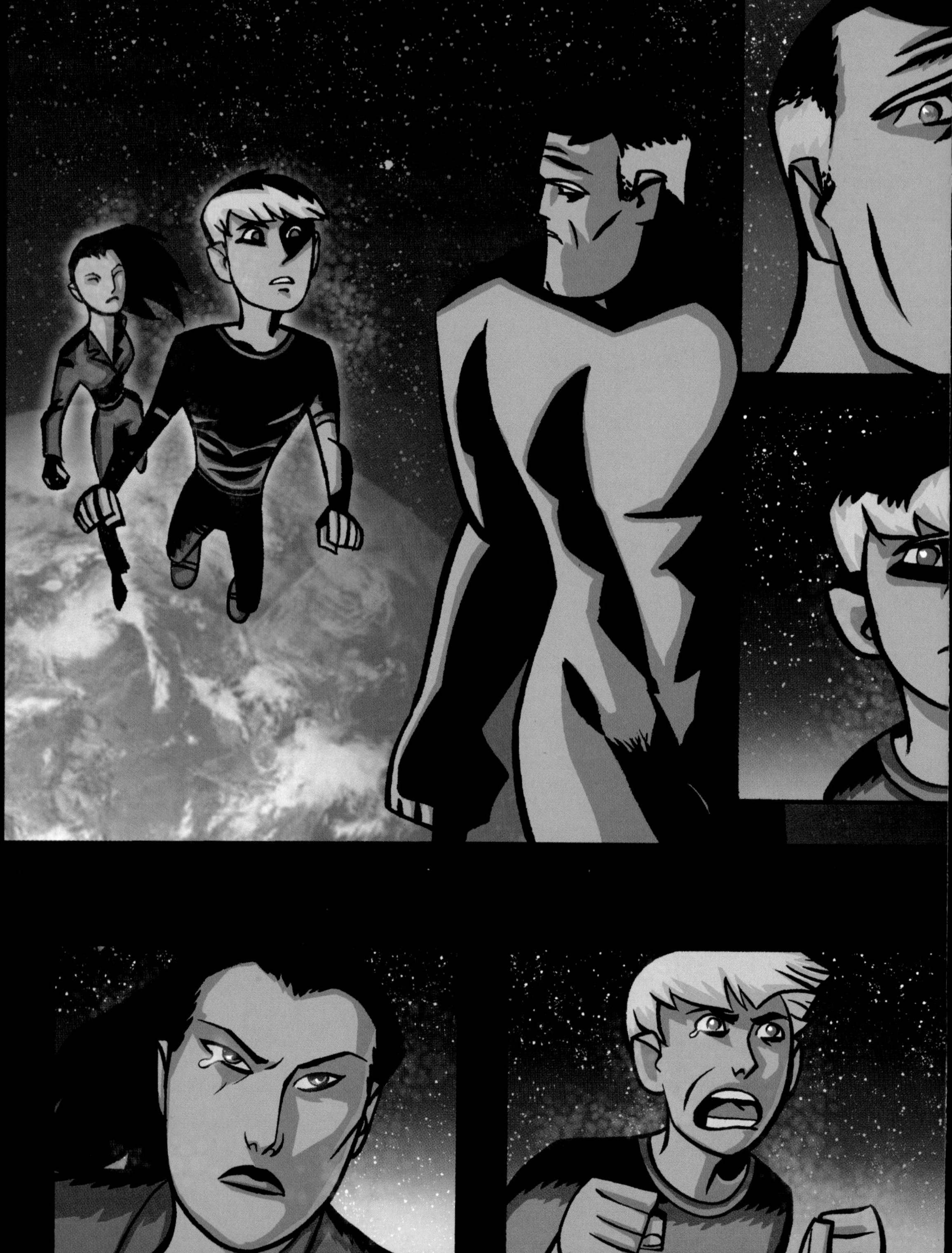

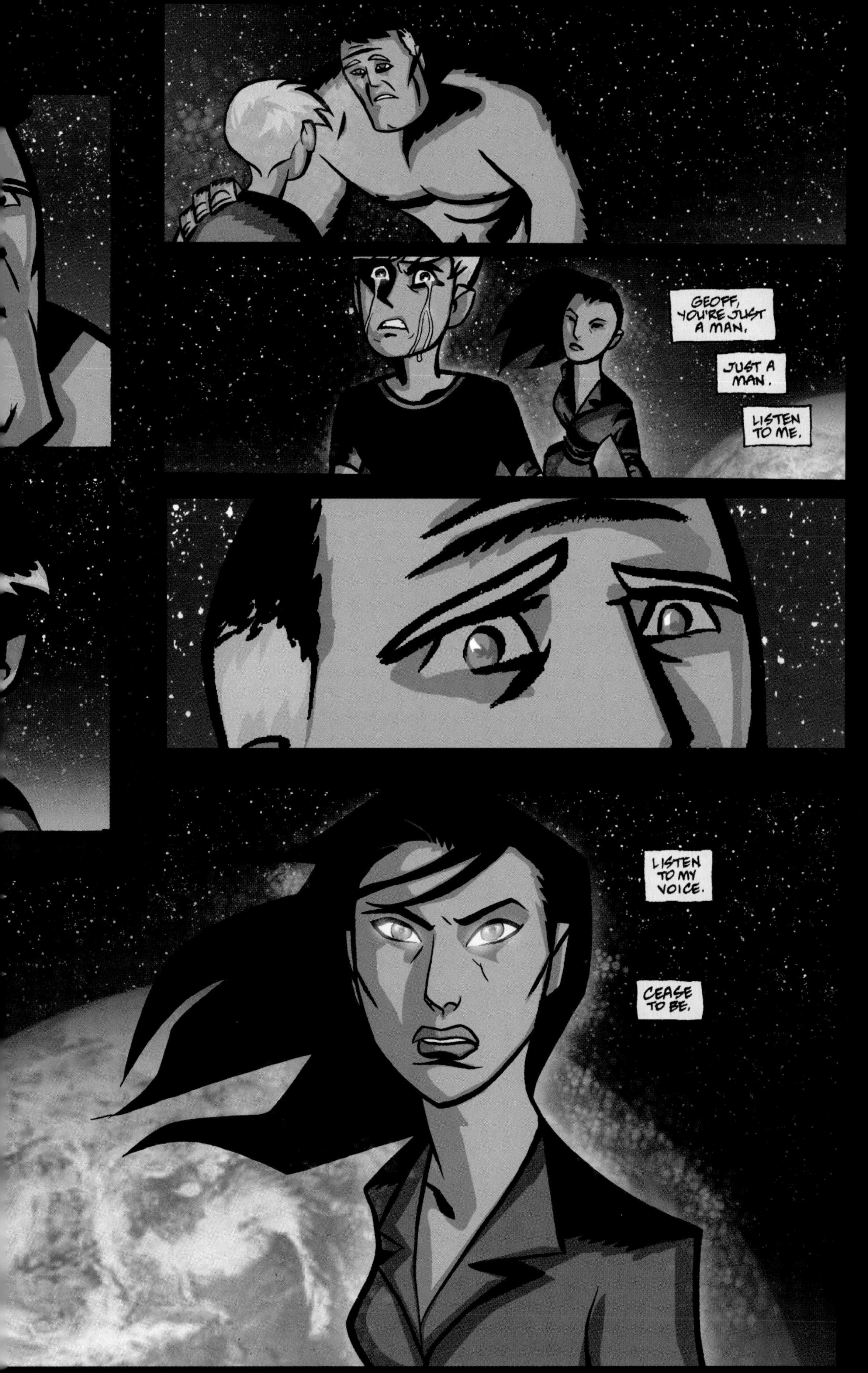
GEOFF, YOU'RE JUST A MAN.
JUST A MAN.
LISTEN TO ME.
LISTEN TO MY VOICE.
CEASE TO BE.

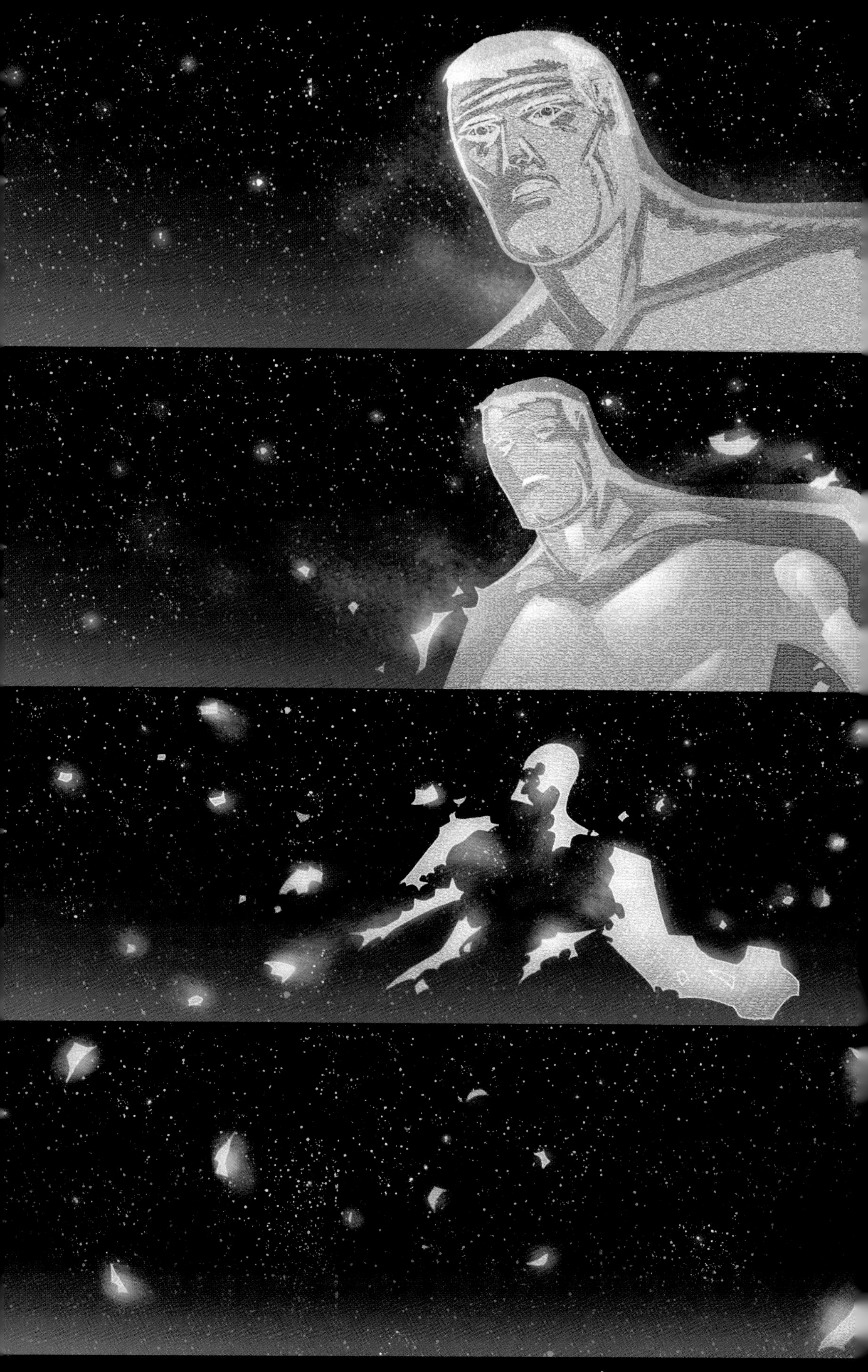

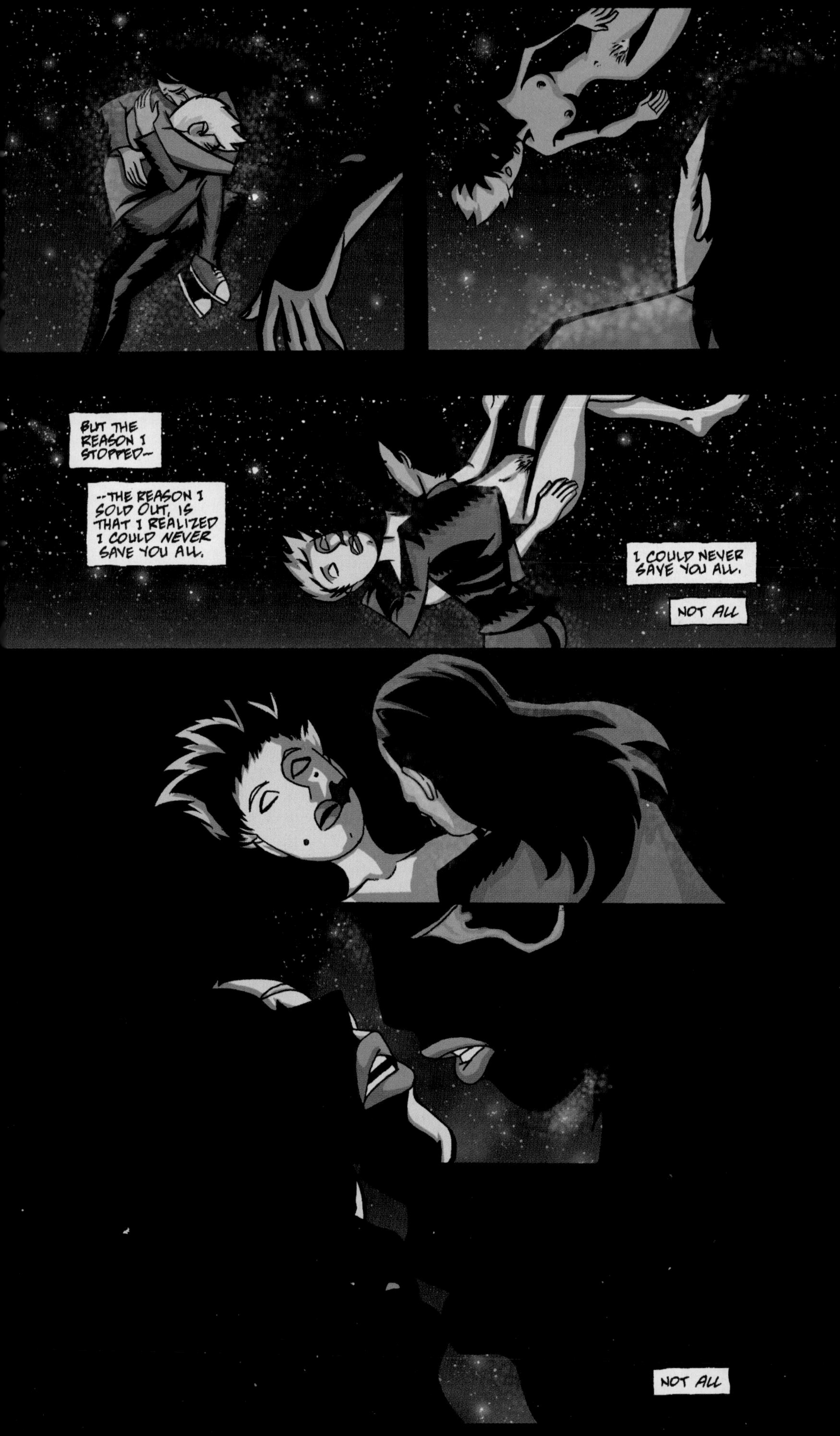
BUT THE REASON I STOPPED--
--THE REASON I SOLD OUT, IS THAT I REALIZED I COULD NEVER SAVE YOU ALL.
I COULD NEVER SAVE YOU ALL.
NOT ALL
NOT ALL

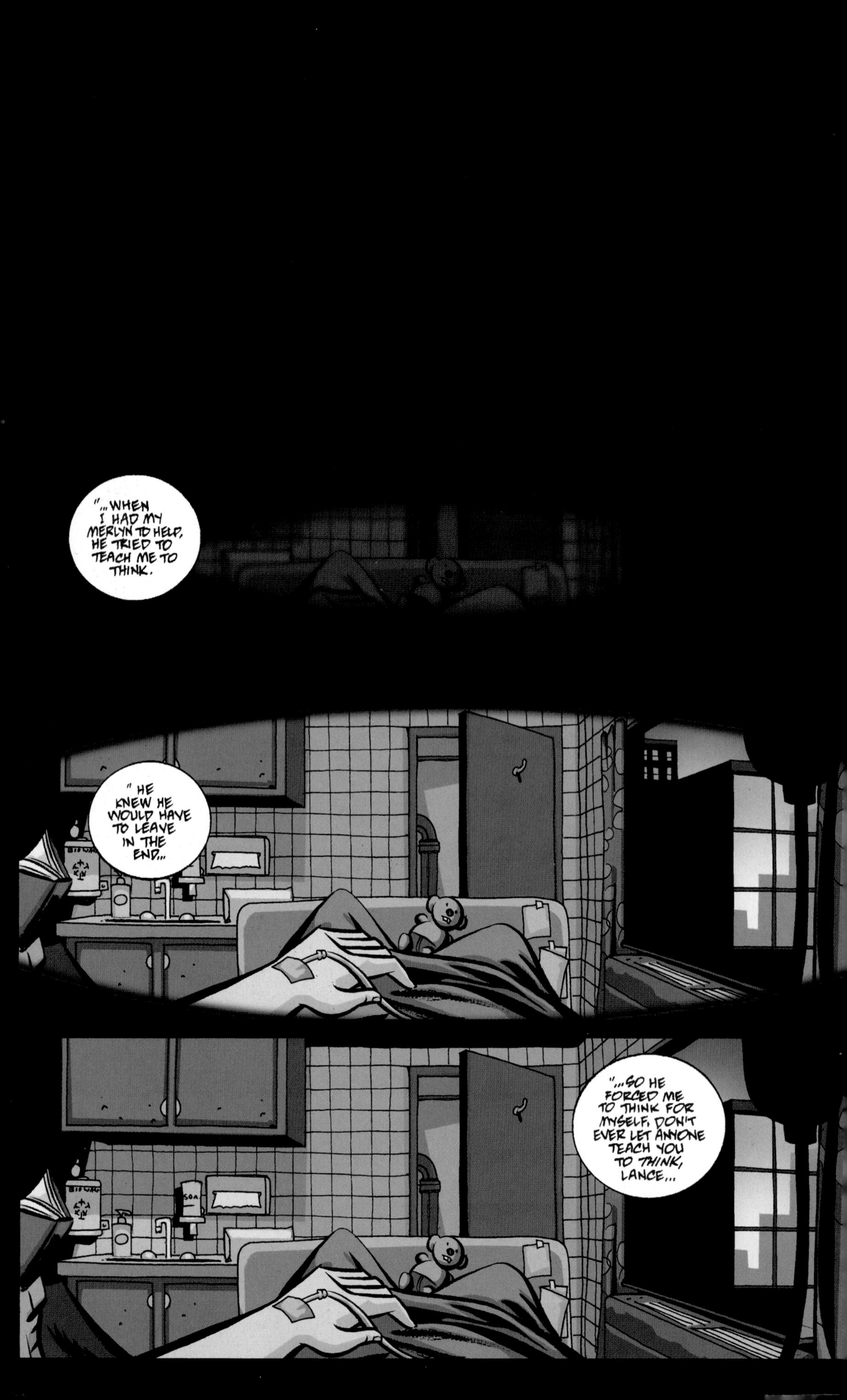
"...WHEN I HAD MY MERLYN TO HELP, HE TRIED TO TEACH ME TO THINK.
" HE KNEW HE WOULD HAVE TO LEAVE IN THE END...
"...SO HE FORCED ME TO THINK FOR MYSELF. DON'T EVER LET ANYONE TEACH YOU TO THINK, LANCE...

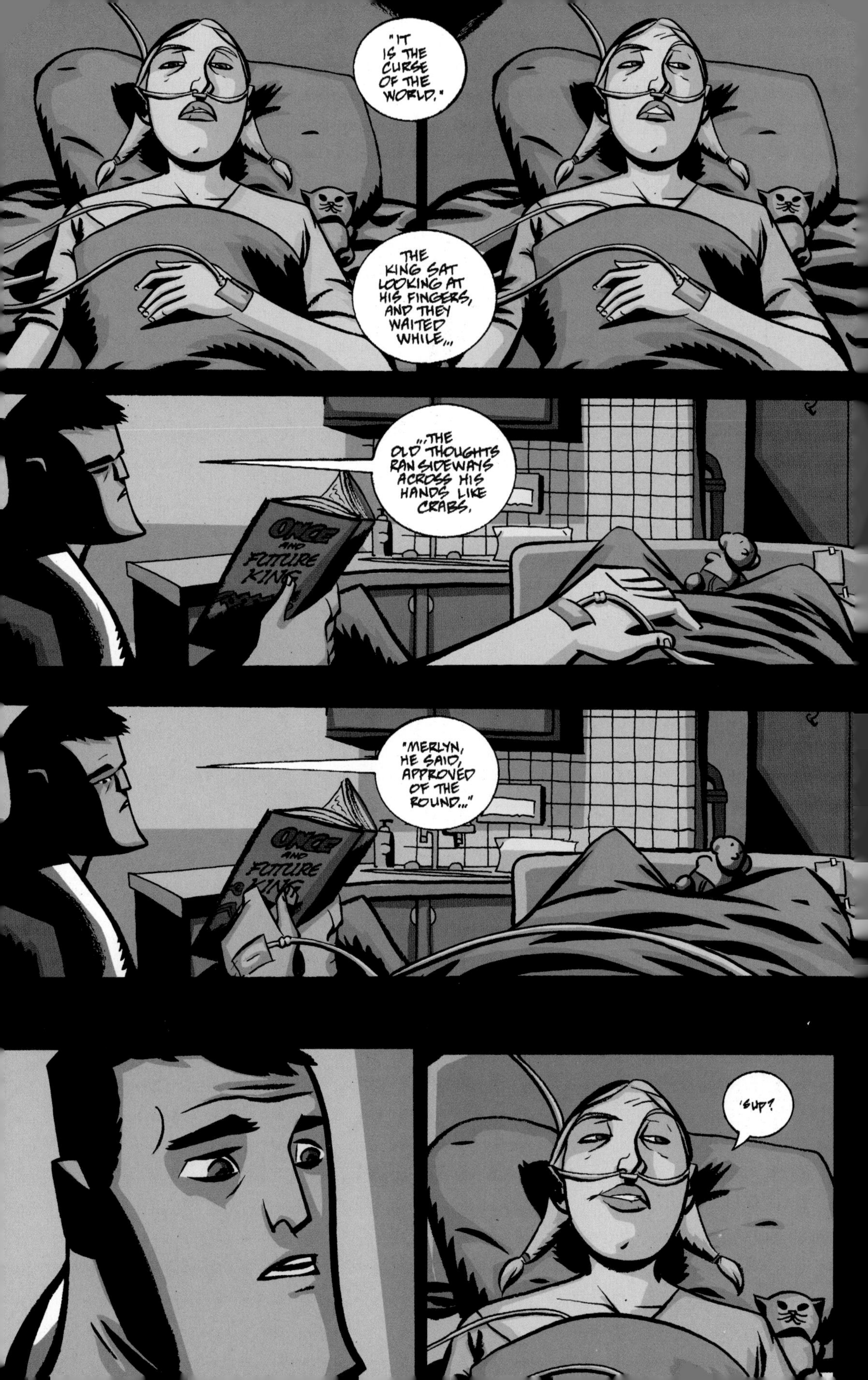
"IT IS THE CURSE OF THE WORLD."
THE KING SAT LOOKING AT HIS FINGERS, AND THEY WAITED WHILE...
"...THE OLD THOUGHTS RAN SIDEWAYS ACROSS HIS HANDS LIKE CRABS.
ONCE AND FUTURE KING
"MERLYN, HE SAID, APPROVED OF THE ROUND..."
ONCE AND FUTURE KING
'SUP?

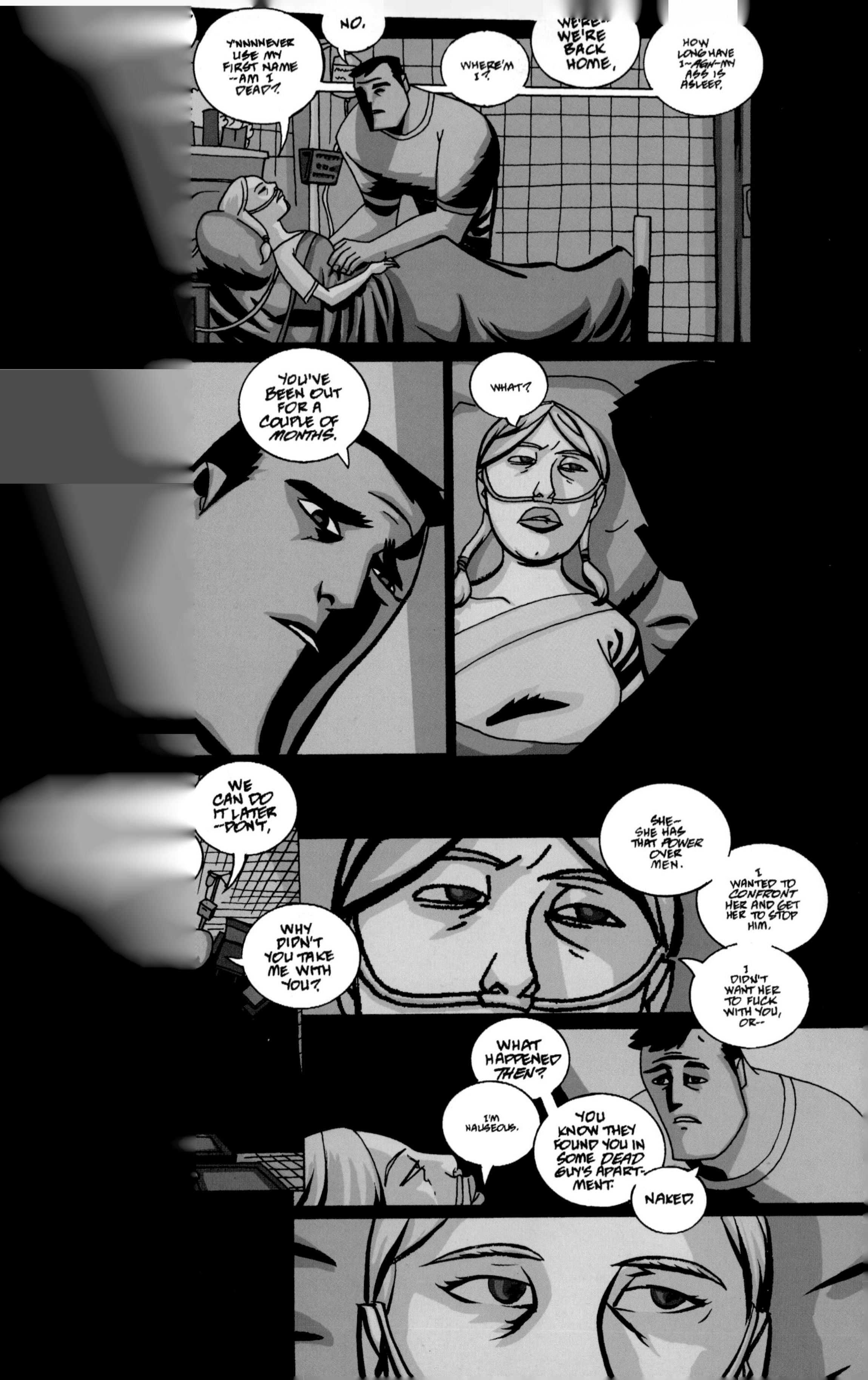
Y'NNNNEVER USE MY FIRST NAME --AM I DEAD?
NO.
WHERE'M I?
WE'RE-- WE'RE BACK HOME.
HOW LONG HAVE I--AGH--MY ASS IS ASLEEP.
YOU'VE BEEN OUT FOR A COUPLE OF MONTHS.
WHAT?
WE CAN DO IT LATER --DON'T.
SHE-- SHE HAS THAT POWER OVER MEN.
I WANTED TO CONFRONT HER AND GET HER TO STOP HIM.
WHY DIDN'T YOU TAKE ME WITH YOU?
I DIDN'T WANT HER TO FUCK WITH YOU, OR--
WHAT HAPPENED THEN?
I'M NAUSEOUS.
YOU KNOW THEY FOUND YOU IN SOME DEAD GUY'S APARTMENT.
NAKED.

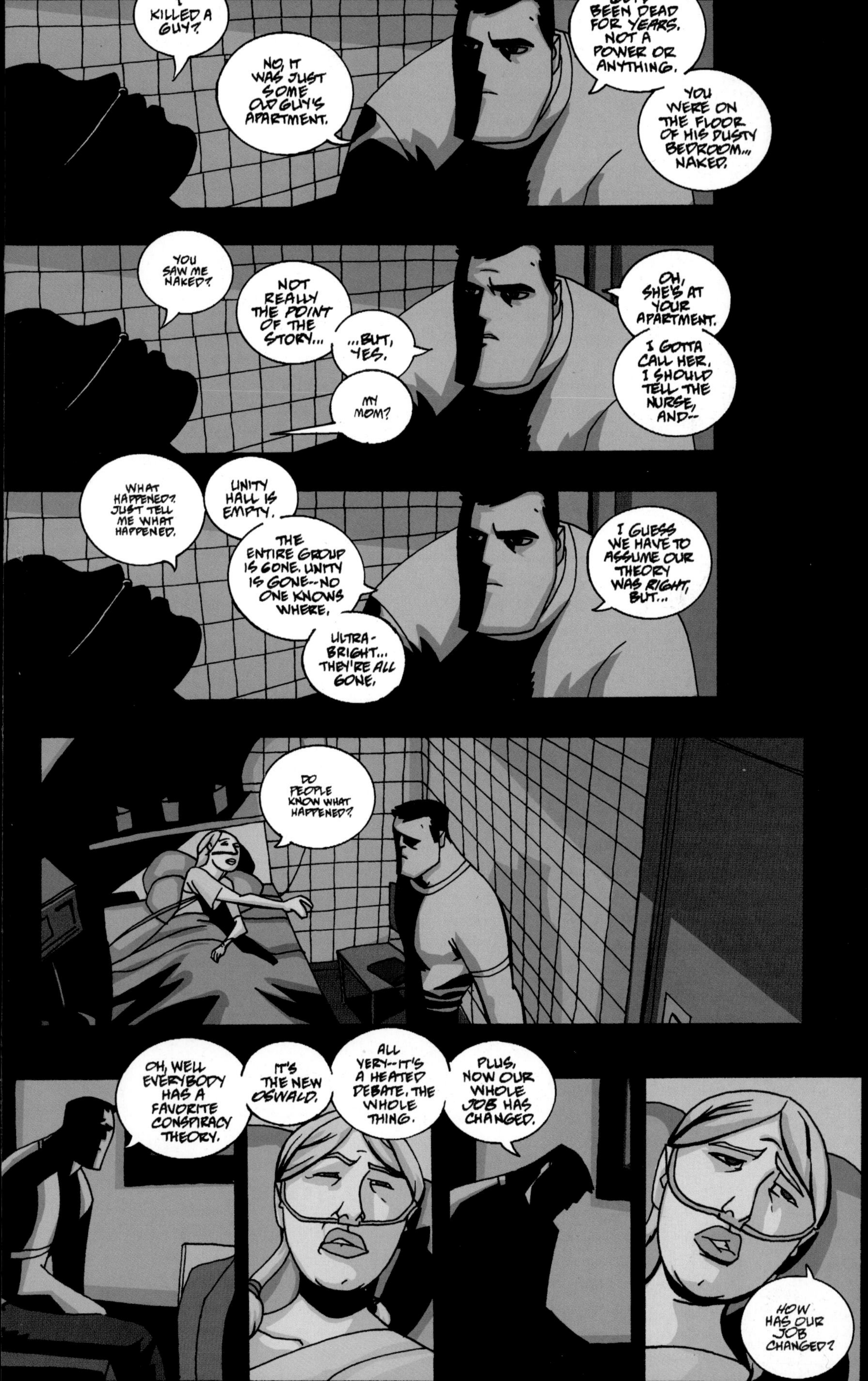
KILLED A GUY?
NO, IT WAS JUST SOME OLD GUY'S APARTMENT.
BEEN DEAD FOR YEARS. NOT A POWER OR ANYTHING.
YOU WERE ON THE FLOOR OF HIS DUSTY BEDROOM... NAKED.
YOU SAW ME NAKED?
NOT REALLY THE POINT OF THE STORY...
...BUT, YES.
MY MOM?
OH, SHE'S AT YOUR APARTMENT.
I GOTTA CALL HER. I SHOULD TELL THE NURSE, AND--
WHAT HAPPENED? JUST TELL ME WHAT HAPPENED.
UNITY HALL IS EMPTY.
THE ENTIRE GROUP IS GONE. UNITY IS GONE--NO ONE KNOWS WHERE.
ULTRA-BRIGHT... THEY'RE ALL GONE.
I GUESS WE HAVE TO ASSUME OUR THEORY WAS RIGHT, BUT...
DO PEOPLE KNOW WHAT HAPPENED?
OH, WELL EVERYBODY HAS A FAVORITE CONSPIRACY THEORY.
IT'S THE NEW OSWALD.
ALL VERY--IT'S A HEATED DEBATE. THE WHOLE THING.
PLUS, NOW OUR WHOLE JOB HAS CHANGED.
HOW HAS OUR JOB CHANGED?

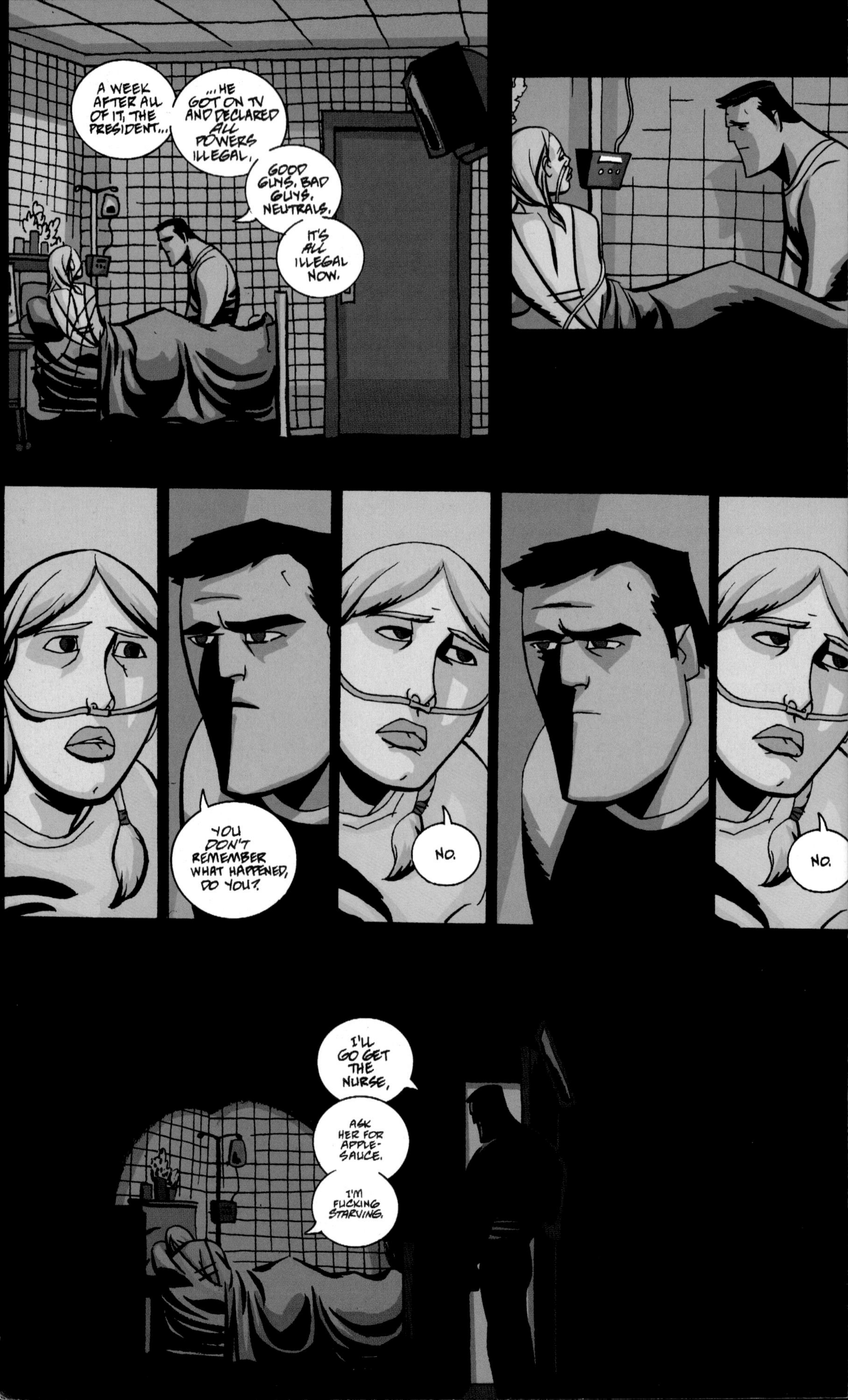
A WEEK AFTER ALL OF IT, THE PRESIDENT...
...HE GOT ON TV AND DECLARED ALL POWERS ILLEGAL.
GOOD GUYS, BAD GUYS, NEUTRALS.
IT'S ALL ILLEGAL NOW.
YOU DON'T REMEMBER WHAT HAPPENED, DO YOU?
NO.
NO.
I'LL GO GET THE NURSE.
ASK HER FOR APPLE-SAUCE.
I'M FUCKING STARVING.

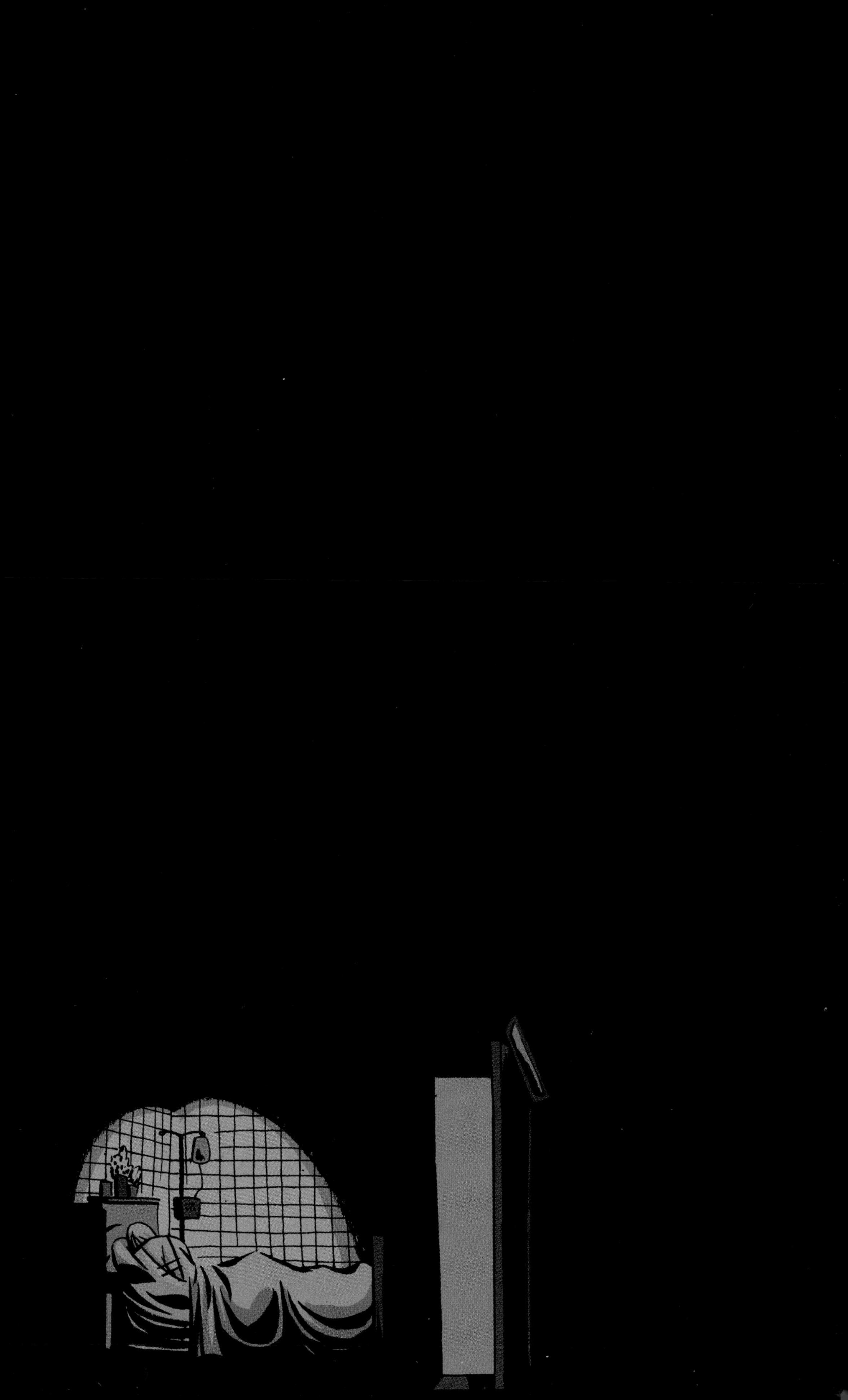

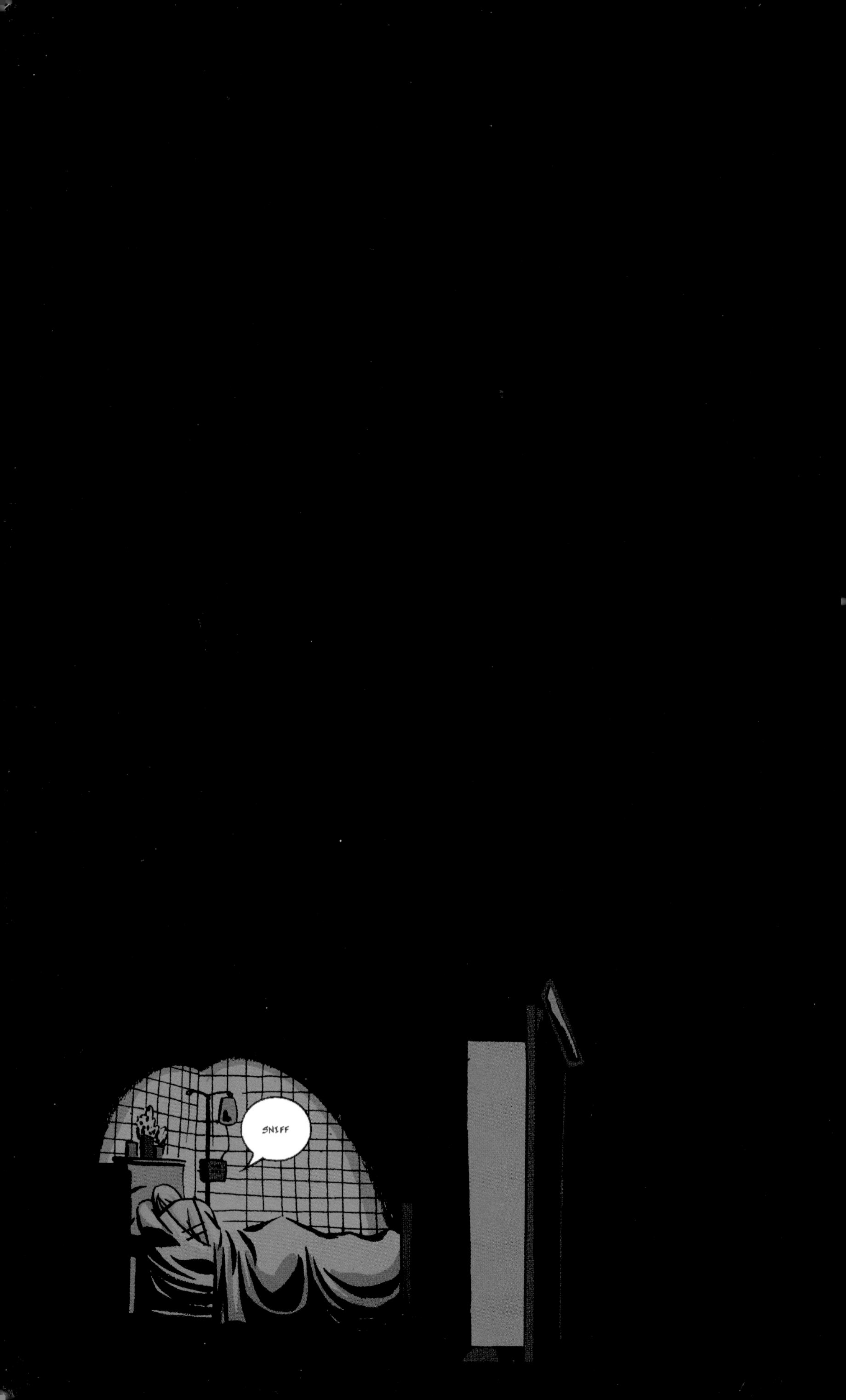
SNIFF

FORBIDDEN ACTS
P online! POWERS
YOU CAN'T FORGET
SECRET DESIRES
P.NET

Dateline: Capital of the World

Get Our Free Newsletter > search go

▪HOME ▪NEWS ▪GOSSIP ▪REVIEWS ▪CELEBS ▪CHAT

GOSSIP CONTENTS

- Under The Cape
- Costume Closet
- Ask Alisa
- Two Mikes Talkin'

POWERS NEWS

A shattered world mourns as one

How did we let it get this far?

Responsibility and Power--the real truth

Trusting the mask again--can we?

FRESH FACES

New Book Reviews: Golden Showers, *dirty little secrets no one would talk about--until NOW!*

Senate debate: *When is a power really a Super Power, and what to look out for*

An Ounce of Prevention: *Hospital administrators face tough choices in the maternity ward*

Hidden Powers: *Can you trust your neighbor--your boss--your spouse? Where DID the Powers go?*

THE HIT LIST

Today's Best Bets

- ***Cops:*** *L.A. Powers*
- *Steve Buscemi in Powers redux of **M***
- *Montel bitch slaps Surge--LIVE!*

Ted Robinson's Under The Cape

This is where the Dirty Dish gets dumped

Catch Ted Robinson on *P! News Live*
Tuesdays at 4:30 p.m. PT and
Sundays at 2:30 a.m and 7 p.m. PT

Effective Pretty Much Immediately, This Column is Finished

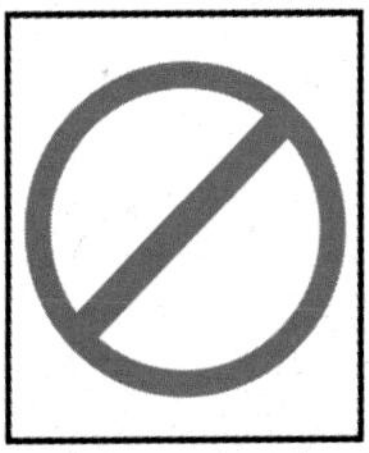

The reasons why are both personal and professional, but basically, I feel that with the recent world events that have changed all of our lives so completely, I can no longer build enthusiasm to write this frivolous column.

I just want to say thank you to everyone who made the last six years possible for me. It sounds cliche, but you people are amazing. I have made many friends from this column.

It is a time on which I will always look back fondly.

--30--

no more Ted >

tonight on P

Senator Oz: Building the case for finding and finishing Powers once and for all. P! Special; 8 p.m.

next week:
Powerless? Coping with a *brave new world without Powers! Can we do it all alone? Are we willing to? And who will provide the scandals for the press now?*

▪help ▪about P! Online ▪site map ▪membership ▪newsletter

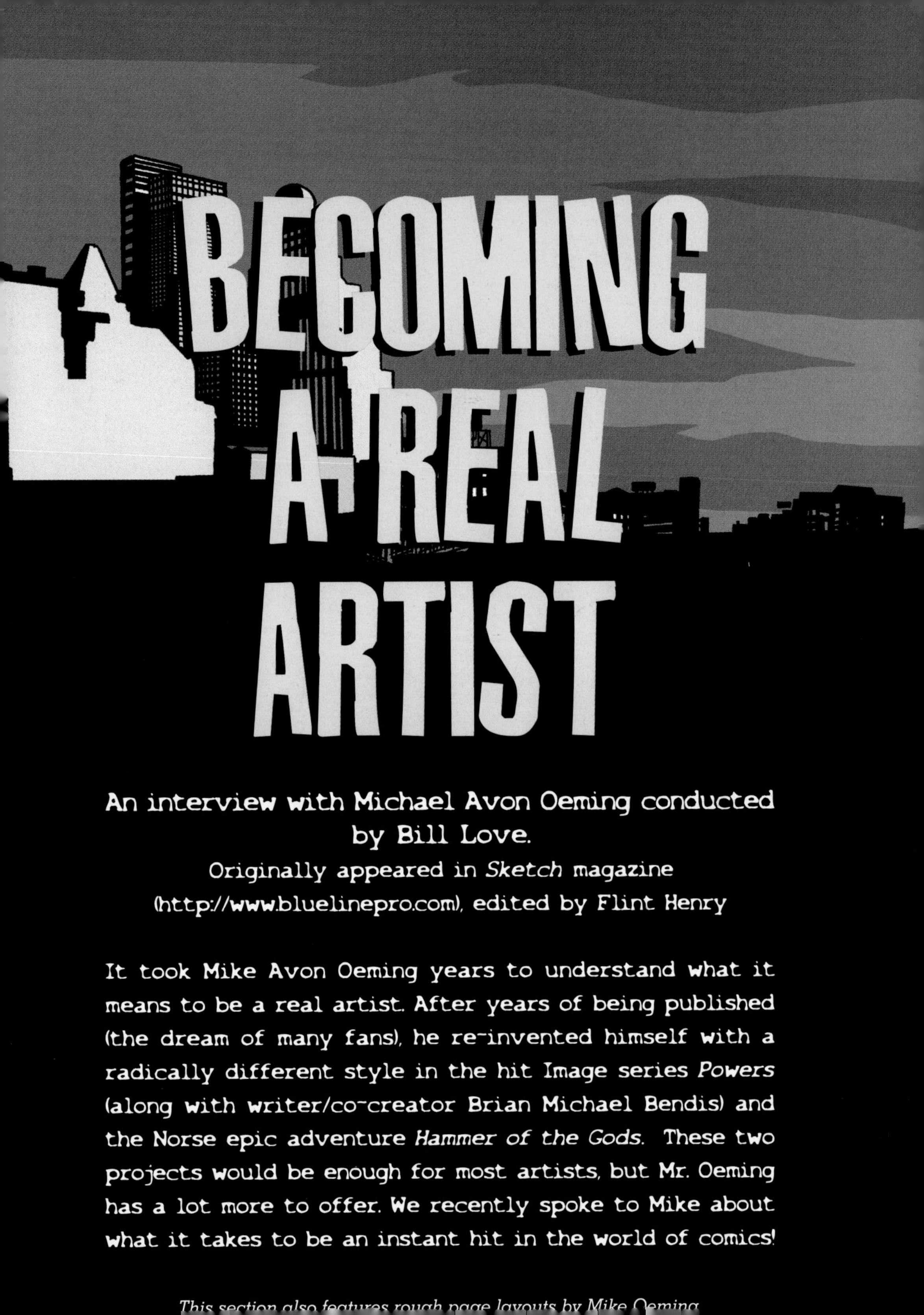

BECOMING A REAL ARTIST

An interview with Michael Avon Oeming conducted by Bill Love.

Originally appeared in *Sketch* magazine (http://www.bluelinepro.com), edited by Flint Henry

It took Mike Avon Oeming years to understand what it means to be a real artist. After years of being published (the dream of many fans), he re-invented himself with a radically different style in the hit Image series *Powers* (along with writer/co-creator Brian Michael Bendis) and the Norse epic adventure *Hammer of the Gods*. These two projects would be enough for most artists, but Mr. Oeming has a lot more to offer. We recently spoke to Mike about what it takes to be an instant hit in the world of comics!

This section also features rough page layouts by Mike Oeming

Sketch: *How many years of lonely struggle did it take for you to become an overnight success?*

Mike: Man, it took a long time. I left high school when I was 16 or 17. I was passing with Cs and Ds, but I had skipped so many days of school, they wanted me to repeat my junior year. I already hated school enough, the thought of repeating drove me insane, especially since I was "passing"... barely, but I was. So I went to get my GED, but the requirements for that were higher than the requirements for the basic classes I was taking. I decided I would give myself the summer. If I couldn't break in as an inker by the time summer ended, I'd suck it up and repeat.

I washed some dishes and delivered pizza for the spring and summer. Anyway, summer time came and I got a gig from Innovation inking *Child's Play*, so I never went back to school. From there I worked for Innovation for about a year or so, inking various titles. "I'm in, right?" Well, no, eventually they went under and I moved on. I did small press stuff, not really making any money. I struggled there for another two years until my first big break inking at Marvel. DC, too, about the same time. Pat Garrahy (who later colored *Powers*) and Andrew Helfer gave me my first big breaks. For Pat I was inking *Daredevil* issues, and Andy got me a Paradox book and then *Judge Dredd*. So I did a huge DC book, *Judge Dredd*, but I frankly wasn't ready for it. I did *Foot Soldiers* for Dark Horse... but then after that things dried up. The only real paying work was inking *Ninjack* over Neil Vokes. But from *Foot Soldiers* up till *Powers* happened– that's like three long years of a dry spell. So, even after being "in" it was still a struggle. It was about eight years worth of "overnight" success.

Sketch: *How old were you when you got your first paying work in comics?*

Mike: 14 or 15. Innovation again. It was *Newstralia* #2. I was so young and stupid, when I sent my samples in, I didn't give a phone number, so they wrote me a letter saying they had work for me. This was long before e-mail... I also didn't think to follow it up, because I didn't do a great job on it. I could have gotten more work, but it just didn't occur to me to try. I was still a sophomore in high school. I think that early success (like the *Judge Dredd* thing) was actually bad for me, though. It made me think I had what it takes to be pro, but I didn't yet. I was still an unpolished diamond. I should have stayed an inker until *Foot Soldiers*. That's the first pencil work I'm still proud of on some level.

I tell all the young guys I meet to have patience. Too many people hear stories of young guys making it big when, in fact, most people don't really break into comics until they are in their mid-twenties, and don't really start making a living until they are in their thirties.

In other words, go get a real job, hone your skills, and your day will come. You can drive yourself insane looking for work before you're ready.

Sketch: *When you started out were you interested in writing and storytelling, or did you just want to draw comics?*

Mike: I just wanted to draw comics. I wanted to do *The New Mutants* or *Batman*. I got into creator owned work as a way in. I've always written stories for myself, but only became serious about it over the past few years. Bendis has really helped me with writing and storytelling. I owe him a lot.

Sketch: *Who were your early influences and mentors? How did they affect your art style?*

Mike: My earliest influence was absolutely almost solely Art Adams. I so wanted to be him. Then I got into Steve Rude, and that opened up a whole new world. I went through different stages, like a Rick Leonardi stage, later I got into Mignola (still can't shake him) and Jamie Hewlett, Kevin Nowlan, and Mike Golden. All those directions really confused me, but after a while, things started to take shape. I think you have to go through that artistic blender before you can find yourself.

As far as mentors: Adam Hughes, a close friend whom I've known since before he was getting rejected for *Justice Machine*. He taught me lots: storytelling, composition, and especially body language.

Neil Vokes showed me lots of different artists and taught me tons, especially work ethic. Mike Baron. I almost owe my career to Mike. When I was a kid living in my own self-made early-teen hell, I would write Mike in care of Dark Horse. I was in love with *Nexus*. Steve [Rude] and Mike were my idols. Mike would write back. I'd ask tons of stupid questions and he'd not only write back, but encouraged me. He took time to stay in touch almost every letter. It meant so much to me, especially growing up in my own little world.

Sketch: *As an artist looking to break into the field, should you take any work you can get? Can it be a problem to take on a book before you are ready artistically?*

Mike: Take it if it pays. If you're not ready, you will be fired. There is a risk; if an editor hires you, over estimating your ability, when you fall flat they will remember you for that work for years to come. I think my poor work on *Judge Dredd* really hurt my chances for further work at DC for many years. They couldn't shake the memory of those pages. Not to mention I burned out and fell behind schedule. I think they've forgiven me though, better stop bringing that up or they will remember.

Sketch: *You left comics for about a year, and in that time essentially re-invented yourself as an artist. How did this come about and why did you decide to simplify your style?*

Mike: Well, not having work and having the wife pay

he bills for years... my meager earnings helping from time to time, was pretty bad on my self worth and ego... but I endured, knowing what a good living I could make in comics. Then we had our child, Ethan. After that, I had to suck it up and be a man and get a job. I had to bring something in. It was only part time, but it was a guaranteed paycheck. Also, things had *completely* dried up then. *Ship of Fools* had finished at Image, no one bought it, no one was hiring me. I was burnt from trying to please editors or read their minds or forcing styles I thought would get me work. I just needed to back off for a bit. It was hard. I hadn't had a real job since delivering pizza in '89-'90. It was hard to get work because I had no references, no prior work experience, no high school diploma or anything. I got a job as security guard for a car company. I think it was the fact I was a legal gun owner that got me the job!

Anyway, while I was there, I knew I still wanted to do

comics. I had tried out the "animated" style, trying to get on the *Adventures* books at DC, but it didn't work out. Still, I liked the style and people reacted to it well. Then I got into Toth big time. The combination of Bruce Timm and Alex Toth really changed me. In that security booth I started *Hammer of the Gods* and soon after, *Powers*.

Getting the job was great for me. I learned that I didn't need to be published to be a real artist. Art is for the self. I am an artist, published or not. I had a real job, and I was actually happy. I found a new style I loved and was comfortable in. Not only did things come together, but I learned that if need be I can always return to security work, drawing for myself, and still be happy.

With the new success of *Powers*, I also took those lessons from the past and have used them to help

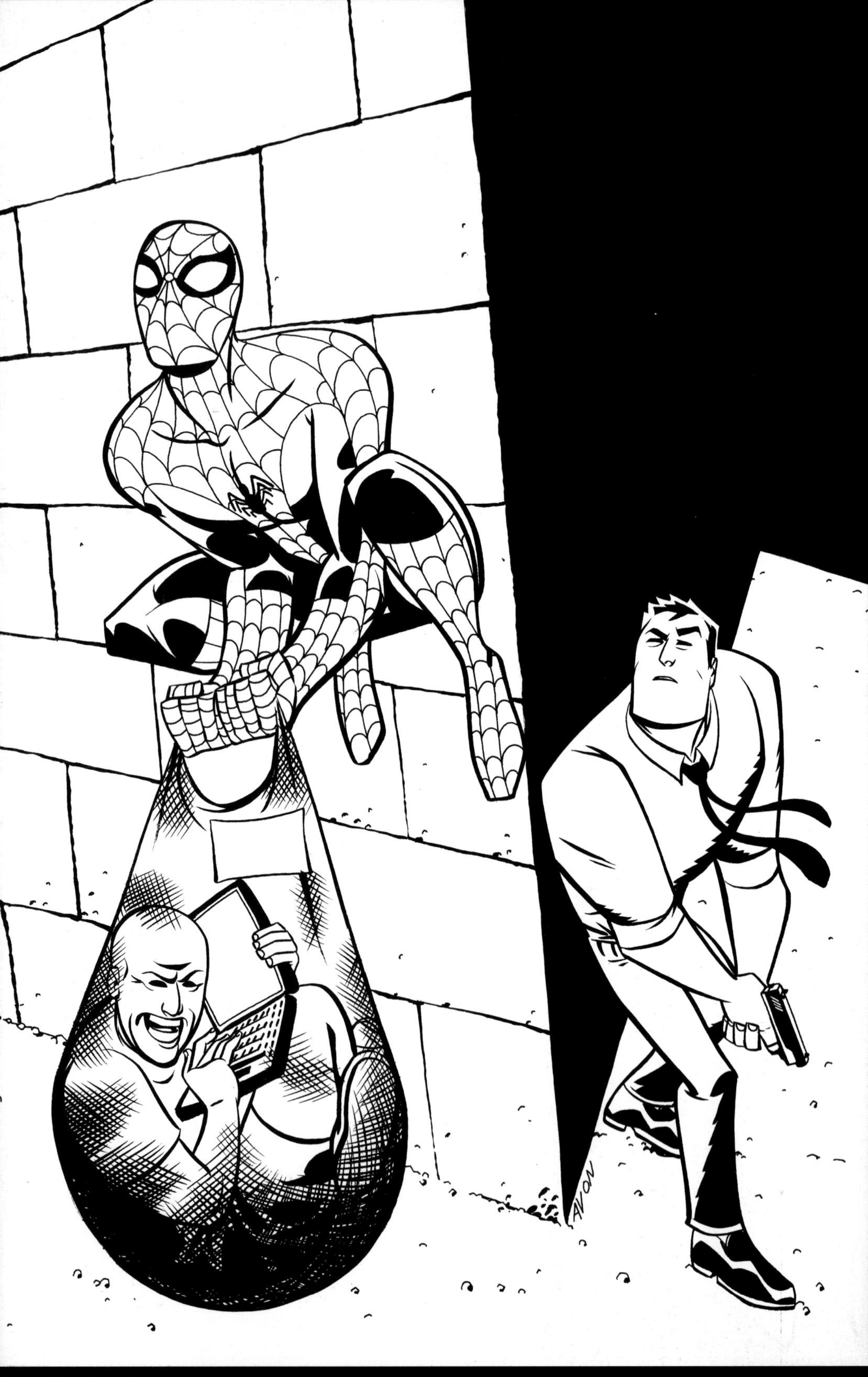

sustain a new career. I know how to communicate with editors now; I can say, "no, I can't make the deadline." I know now how valuable my career is. Too many young guys don't learn that until they have wasted it, and most of them never get a second chance.

Sketch: *Many people think a simple looking or cartoon-like style must be easy to draw. How would you respond to that attitude? Is the quality of comics art dependent on the amount of rendering in the drawing?*

Mike: It is and it isn't. There is less to *render*, but the same to draw. Less details, but the quality has to be the same, or better, because I don't have lines to hide behind. It's very difficult to keep things simple. I look at guys like Toth and Paul Grist, Jaime Hernandez, and I marvel at how stripped down they've become.

Also, this is art; it's comics, it's totally subjective, so those who think there's nothing to it – well, that's fine with me, to each their own.

Sketch: *One of the strongest aspects of your work is your ability to tell a story through your artwork. How and when do you feel you learned the importance of storytelling in comics?*

Mike: Most of it developed during *Ship of Fools*. That's where I think I learned the most out of all my books. But it didn't come together until I started working with Bendis on *Powers*. His ideas, mixed with my experience, really came together and focused everything I had learned into a laser. It would have happened anyway, but it was really Brian that helped me turn the corner. I have to say my storytelling is the best part of my work, the only thing I won't be shy about. My drawing still has lots of room to grow, but I'm very proud of the storytelling... which also still has room to grow and change.

Sketch: *How important is pacing and dialogue to comics? What challenges does it present to you as an artist to work with a writer like Bendis, who is known for his heavy use of dialogue?*

Mike: Pacing is so way overlooked in comics. People come down on Brian because sometimes his pacing *is* too slow. But 90% of the writers out there wouldn't know pacing if you were to beat them in 4/4 timing, so I'd rather see Brian take his time than do what most writers do... fake it. I'm really frustrated with the level of writing out there. I'm not a great writer at all. I can tell a story and I can get by on my writing, but I just can't stand most of the writing out there. It's just bad.

Again, I'm not saying I'm someone who should be criticizing other writers, but even a bad writer knows bad writing when he sees it.

There really isn't a challenge to me anymore when it comes to illustrating scripts with heavy dialogue. I'm very used to it and love it. One thing I do, and recommend this to others – I use huge gutters when I know there is a lot of words. The words go there and don't cover the art.

Sketch: *You recently wrote the extremely powerful* Parliament of Justice *with Neil Vokes as artist. How does it feel to see another artist interpret your story? Why not just draw your own stories? What do you get out of a collaboration like this?*

Mike: Thanks. After my last statement, I can see all the writers going over *Parliament* and tearing it apart. I wanted Neil to draw it because we wanted to work together again. Also, I knew that Neil could actually draw this particular story better than I could. I have lots of stories I want to do. I just don't have time to draw them all, so I hire others to do them sometimes. I have two more one-shots in the works

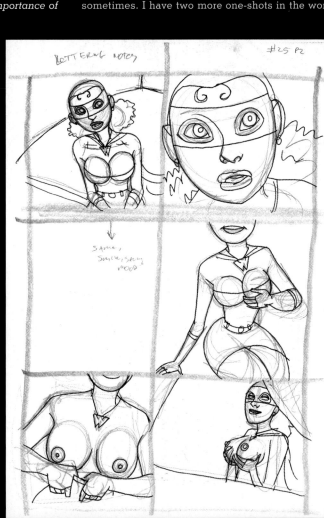

with other artists.

Sketch: *When writing your own stories, what comes first? Character, plot, structure...or does there need to be a meaning behind the story?*

Mike: For me, once I have a basic idea, one of two things happens next: I either start working on the structure, a step-by-step outline, and then I find the "meaning" as I build the structure; or I have the "meaning" first, then structure. I can write much without knowing what I'm trying to say about it. For *Parliament* I had these images in my head, and the meaning came before plot – "If you judge others and place yourself in a moral high ground, you will reap what you sow." After that came structure. With a step outline, you can really play with the story without feeling like you're tossing out tons of work. There was a whole eight-page sequence with another hero I tossed out. It was Neil's idea to take it out, and he reminds me of that any time he gets the chance.

Sketch: *How much input do you have (or do you want) in possible film versions of your work?*

Mike: It depends. In the end, my motto is "these are my comics, this is their movie," and that keeps me sane. Luckily, my manager – David Engle – is also the producer on my projects. On *Powers* we don't have a ton of input, but on *Hammer* I do. *Hammer* has a different direction, but Dave is keeping Mark Wheatley and I on board, and we are allowed feedback, which is much more than most people get. I'm also thinking on *Hammer*, I may get heavily involved in the visuals, along with Mark Wheatley as well.

Our next big pitch is *Bastard Samurai*. If that goes, I'll be very involved, especially in the martial arts aspect.

Sketch: Powers *contains many adult themes but uses a cartoony art style. Does this attract kids to the book? What are your views on ratings labels for comics and comics censorship?*

Sketch: *Would you do work-for-hire at this point in your career? Are there Marvel or DC characters that you would love to get a chance to draw?*

Mike: Sure, I'll do more work-for-hire. Mostly, it's *Powers*, *Hammer*, and other creator owned stuff. I have a two to three year plan. When I'm done with all the creator owned stuff I feel I *need* to do, then I want to hit Marvel and DC pretty hard. I hope to do some one-shots for Marvel and DC before then, between my other side gigs. Marvel has Daredevil, Spidey, Thor, Captain America, and some others I'd love to work on. DC has Batman and pretty much any of the Kirby stuff I'd love to do. Jim Krueger and I are talking about pitching something to DC with the Kirby stuff, that would be fun. You hear me, editors? But *Powers* is on my front

Mike: In general kids don't like the art in *Powers*, so they don't pick it up. I think in the three years *Powers* has been out, I'd say I've signed a total of twenty *Powers* comics to underage kids. Only one or two of them I thought was too young to have the book, but I'm not their parents, so...well, we just don't get kids reading *Powers*.

As far as censorship, I think it's simple. We don't have it in books, so we don't need it in comics. The only ones doing the censorship should be the editors and publishers, as they are responsible for the books they finance. Bookstores have the right to cover logos or covers they find offensive and that sort of thing. As far as ratings for comics, no. The day they rate novelists such as Stephen King and books like the Bible then

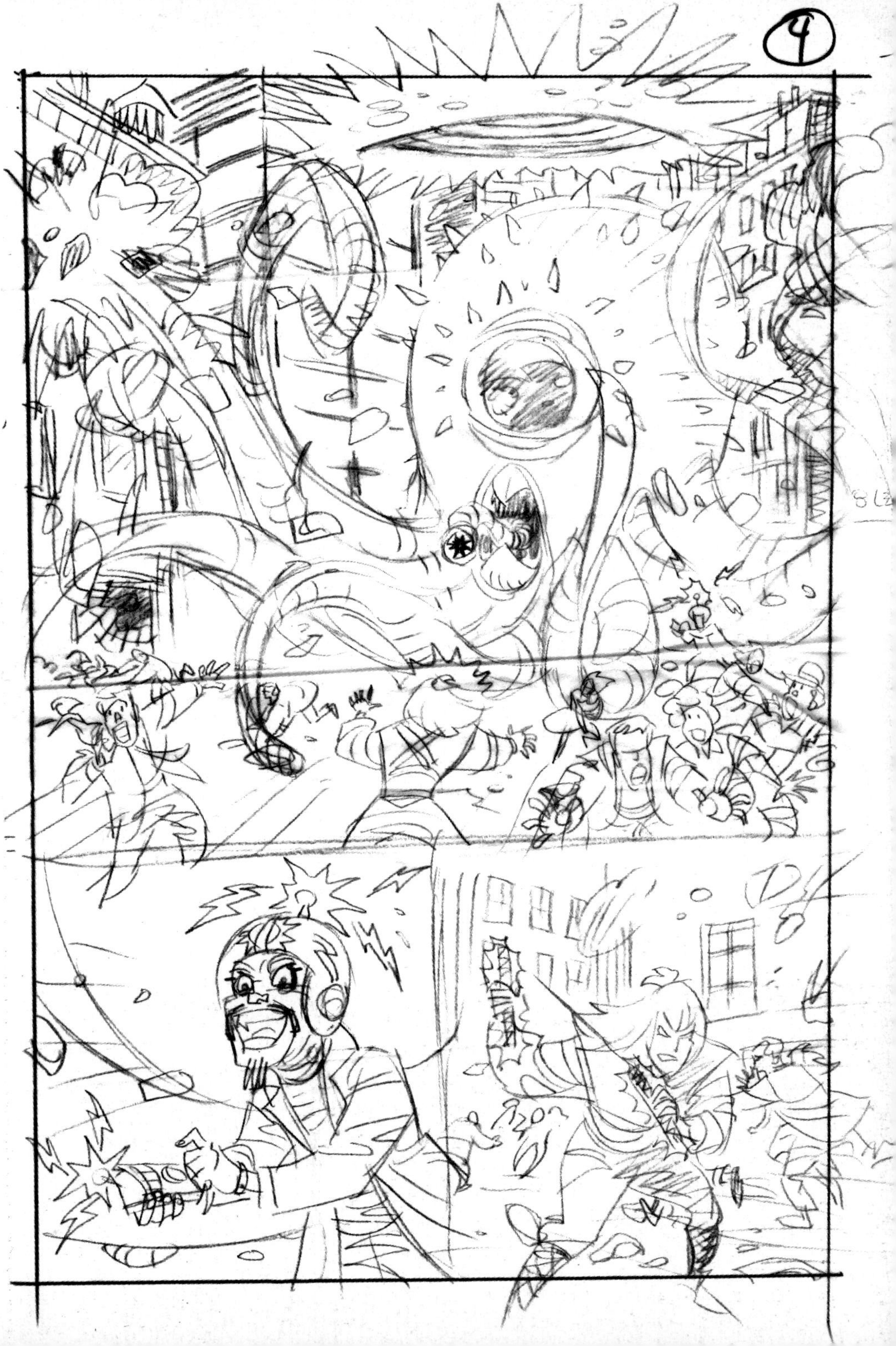

P2 PAGE 7

P6 PAGE 3
(CHECK WHERE
USED AGAIN)

X PAGE 6 -P6

Sketch: *Have you ever considered doing a book that is more all-ages friendly?*

Mike: I have at least two. *Nevermore* is my next creator owned title. I'll start on that this fall or late summer. Chris Golden (*Hellboy* and *Buffy*) is writing it. There's a sneak preview in *Hammer of the Gods: Hammer Hits China* #3. (Actually, *Hammer* is almost all ages. I'd say it's PG if you needed to label it.)

Nevermore is a Saturday morning cartoon, basically. A traveling rock band that has "Poe Powers" – solves mysteries and fights evil as they rock on. Each one has an Edgar Allen Poe inspired power such as turning into a cat or a raven, controlling ravens, and such. It was very inspired by the Beatles cartoon and Scooby-Doo and the music of Refused.

The other thing is called *Mice Templar*. You'll see a sneak of that in *More Fund Summer Special* from Skydog Comics, raising money for the Comic Book Legal Defense Fund.

Sketch: *How did* Powers *come about? I understand you wanted to do a black-and-white crime noir book with a new style, and Bendis decided to throw in super heroes and put it out in color? What was he thinking?*

superheroes in it. He promised me it was noir still. Then I figured cool; between he and I we can sell like 4,000 copies and make a little living off it in black-and-white. When he told me he wanted color, I was like "awww, shit!" Then we got the numbers in and I remember being very depressed. But as we know, those numbers quickly grew...

Sketch: *How important is your family to your work and your career? How do they influence your work?*

Mike: Well, obviously they are very important. Although I struggle with the amount of time I spend with each, the family will always win when it comes down to it. Without Melissa's support or Ethan being born, I couldn't do what I'm doing now. Ethan made me change up my whole style so that I could get a real job and do my part. Without his being born, I'd still be drowning in linework trying to be Mike Golden!

Sketch: *What projects do you have in the works? What types of challenges do you want to set for yourself in the future?*

Mike: I have a two or three-year plan on creator owned stuff, with one or two Marvel one-shots tossed in. Also *Powers*, and a two-page comic I do for *Inside Kung Fu*

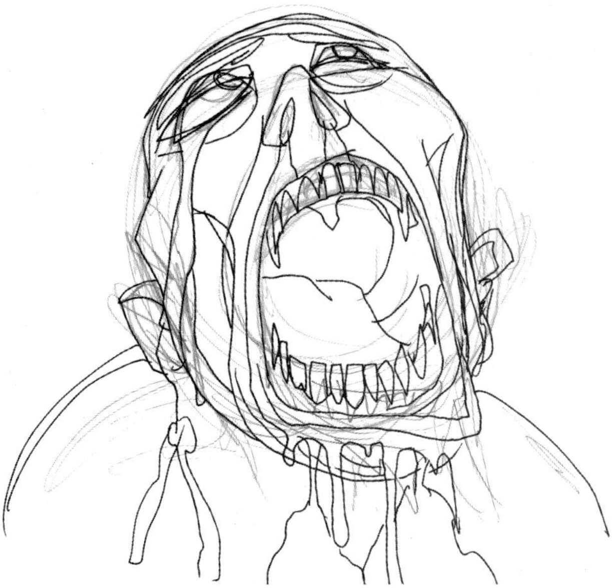

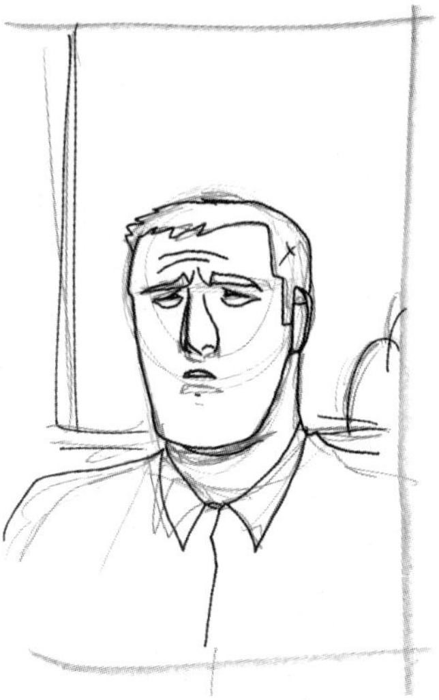

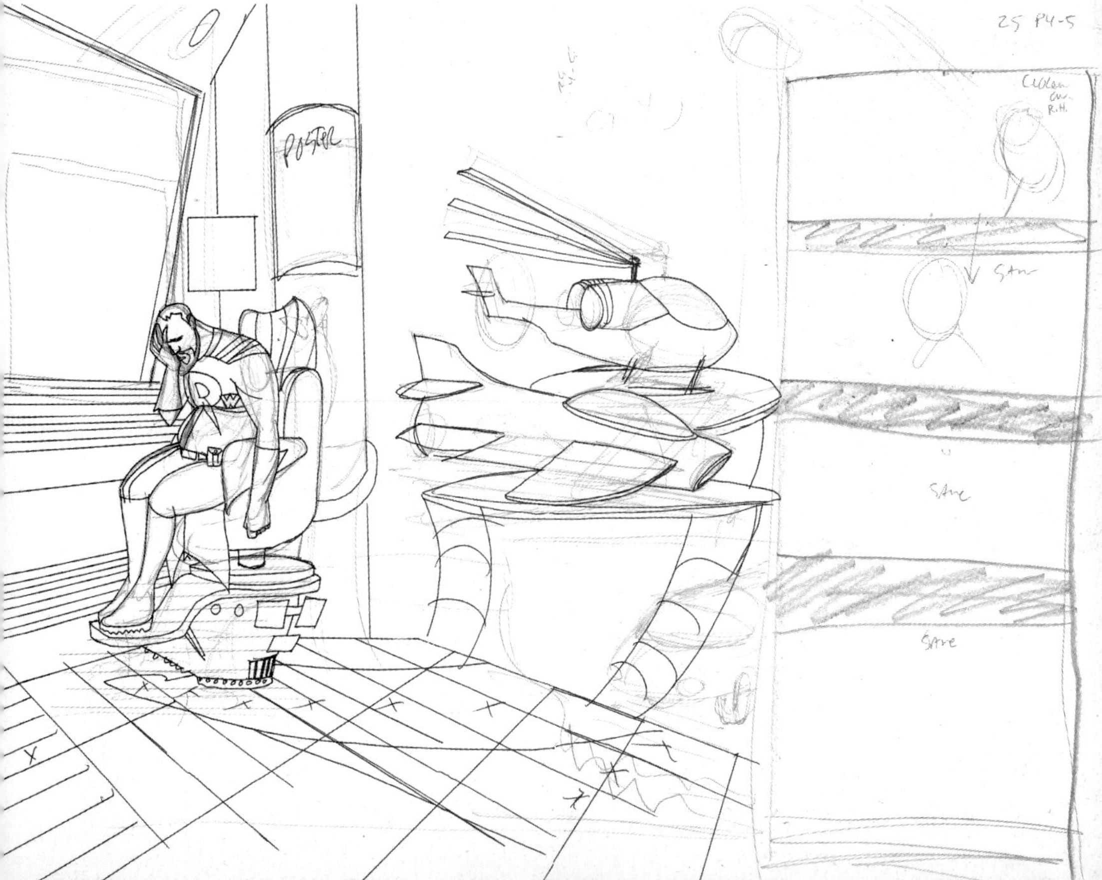
25 P4-5
POSTER
Same
Same
Same

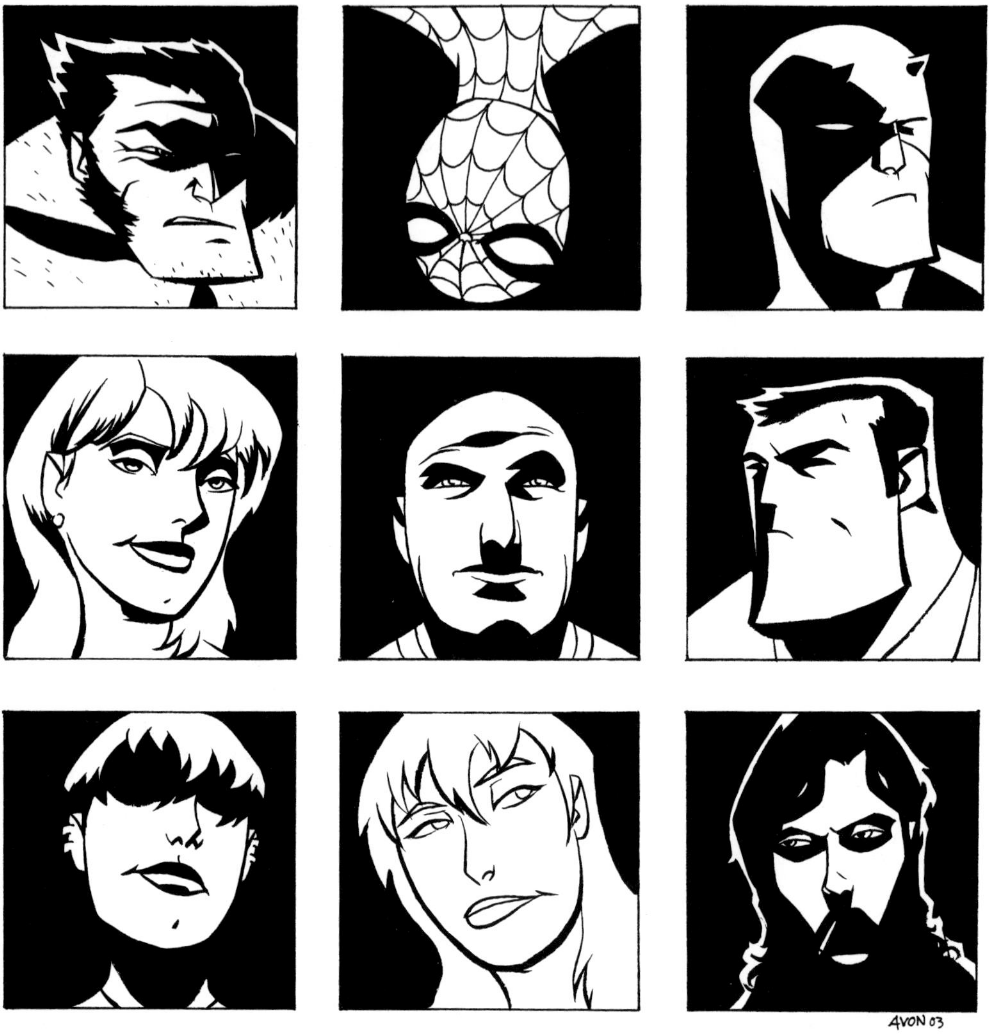
AVON 03

llos for that between now and the winter. It will be a paperback with tons of illos. I'll be working on that in bits and pieces until it's done while I'm doing these other things.

Next is *Nevermore*, then a three issue noir book I wrote with Ivan Brandon (*T3*) called *Cross Bronx*, a ghost story with cops. I may do a Marvel or DC thing between hose or just after *Cross Bronx*.

Then I'll be doing a *huge* martial arts epic I'm very psyched about, but I don't want to get into it too much. I'll be co-plotting with writer Miles Gunter (*Bastard Samurai* and *BPRD*). Then I'll probably do another Marvel or DC one-shot. That's my "two-year plan." I will get ready for *Mice Templar* as a big mini. There may be a *Mice Templar* one-shot before I get to it, just

During all that time I have a few things I've alread written for other artists to draw. After that I'll do lots more Marvel and DC stuff, maybe even a series... hopefully! Once I get these basic stories out of my head I'd like to do more mainstream work. I feel like I have a window now where people want to see my ideas. I have a savvy manager who is keen to shop my work around, so I want to make sure I take advantage of that while I can. Then I'm all about Marvel and DC, especially once we finish *Powers*... but I see *Powers* going anothe three years at least.

While not many fans will be happy to see the eventua conclusion of Powers, *it certainly will not signal the end of Mike Avon Oeming in the comics business. Whether as artist, writer, or both, Mike will continue to re-invent himself as a creator and push his talents into new*

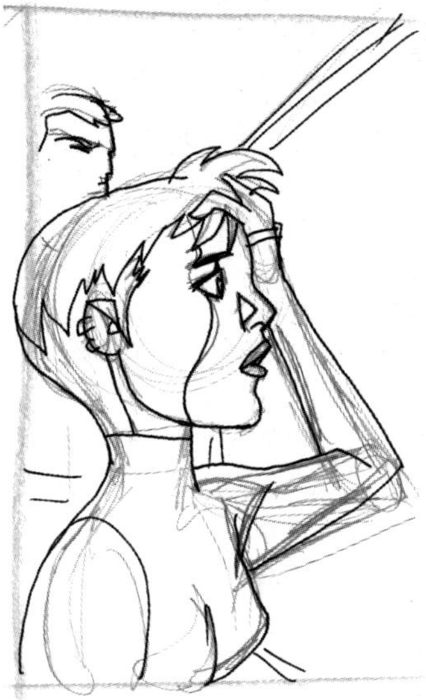

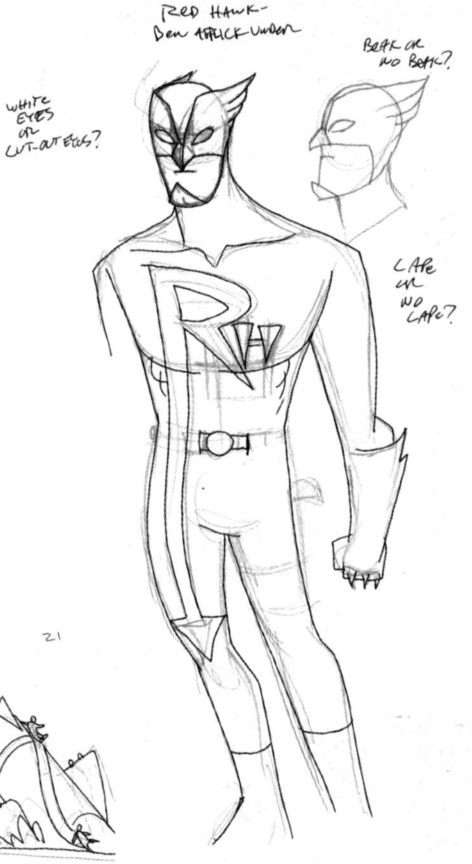
RED HAWK -
BEN AFFLICK UNDER
WHITE EYES OR CUT-OUT EYES?
BEAK OR NO BEAK?
CAPE OR NO CAPE?

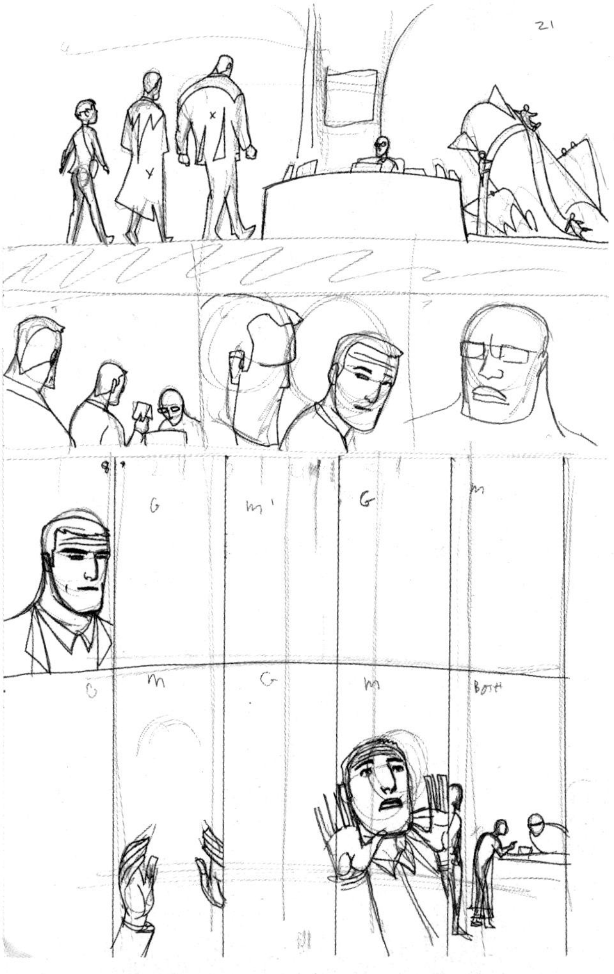
21
G
M
G
M
G
M
G
M
BOTH

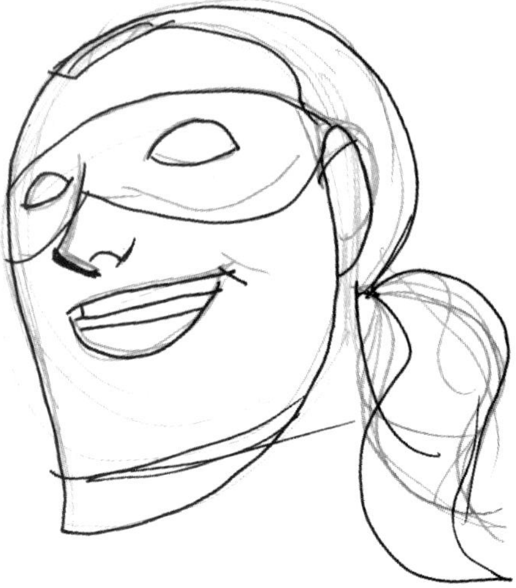

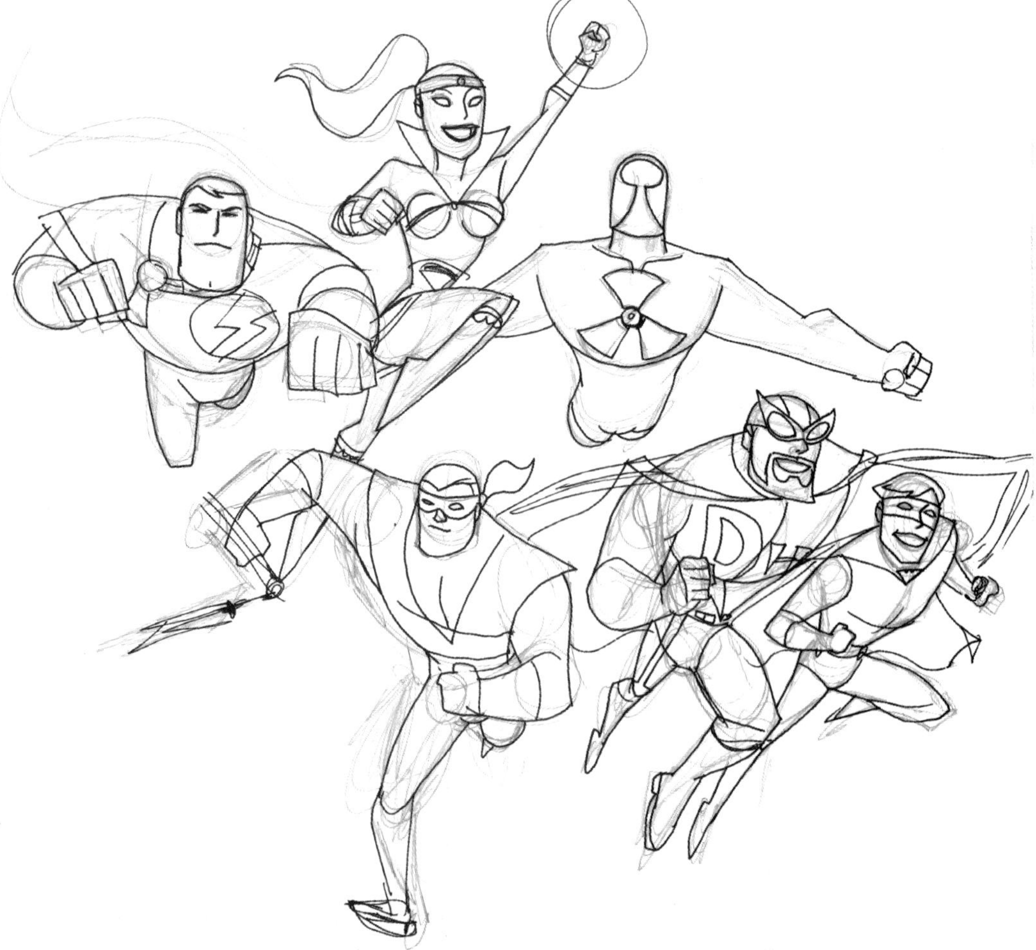

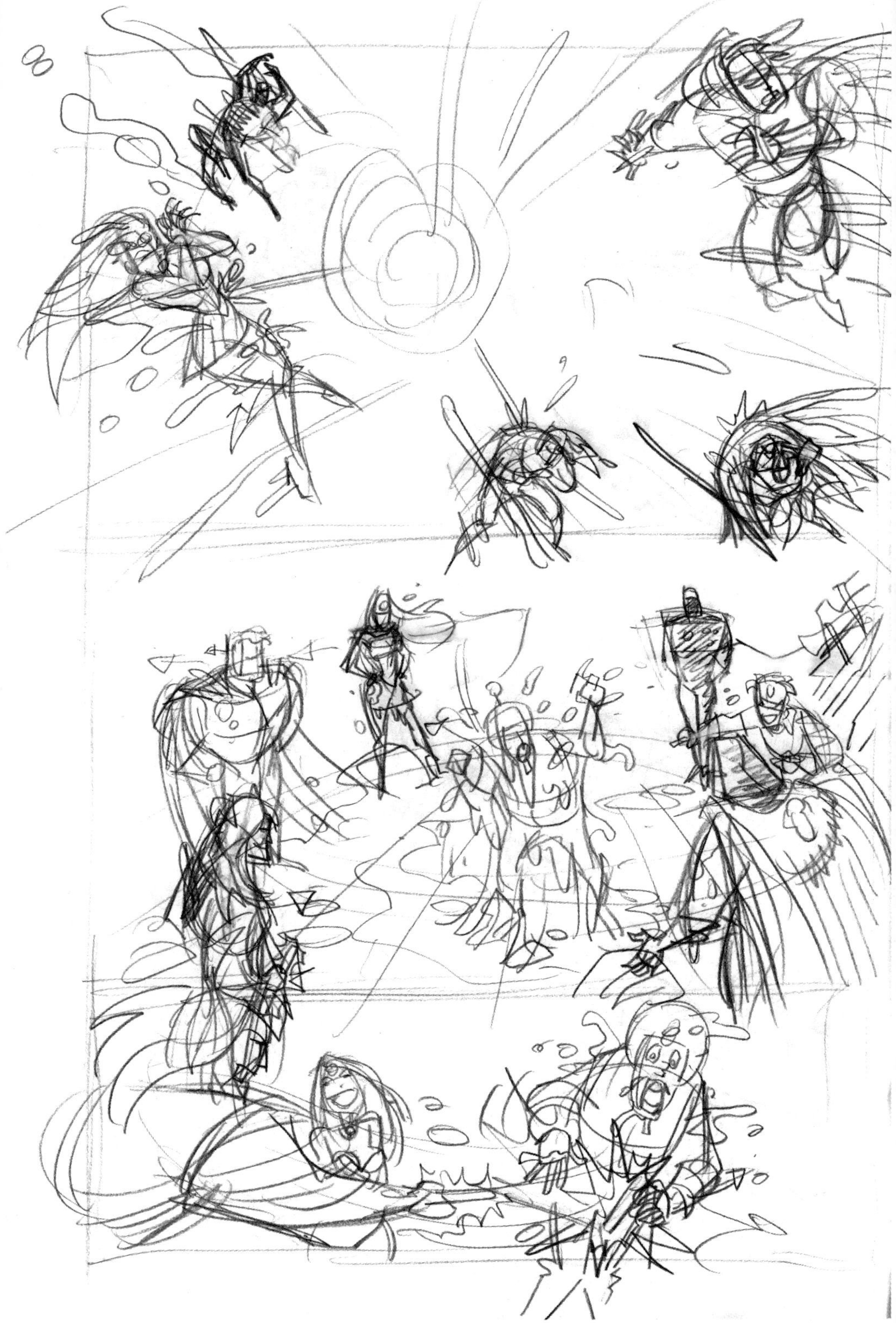

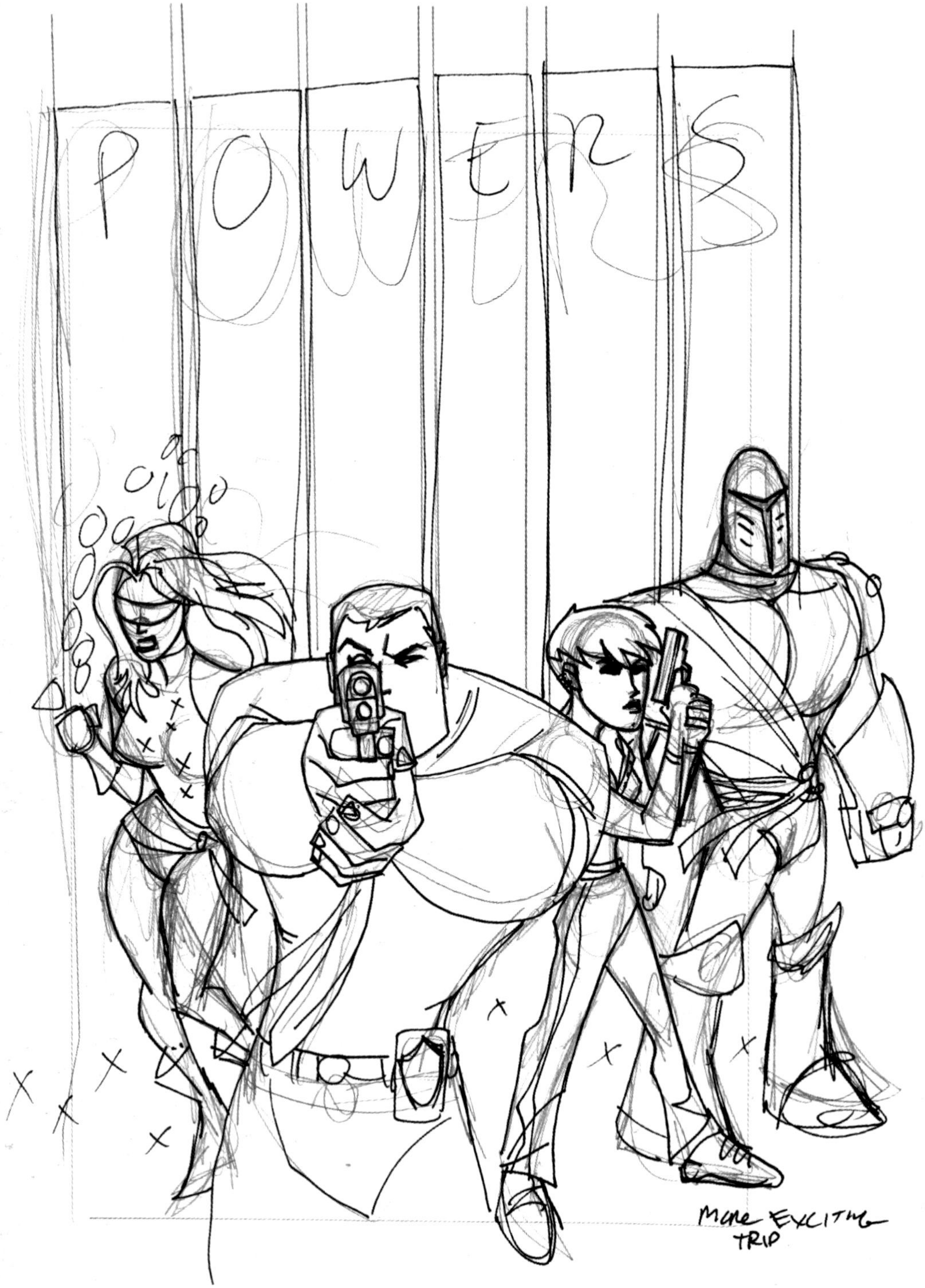
POWERS
MORE EXCITING
TRIP

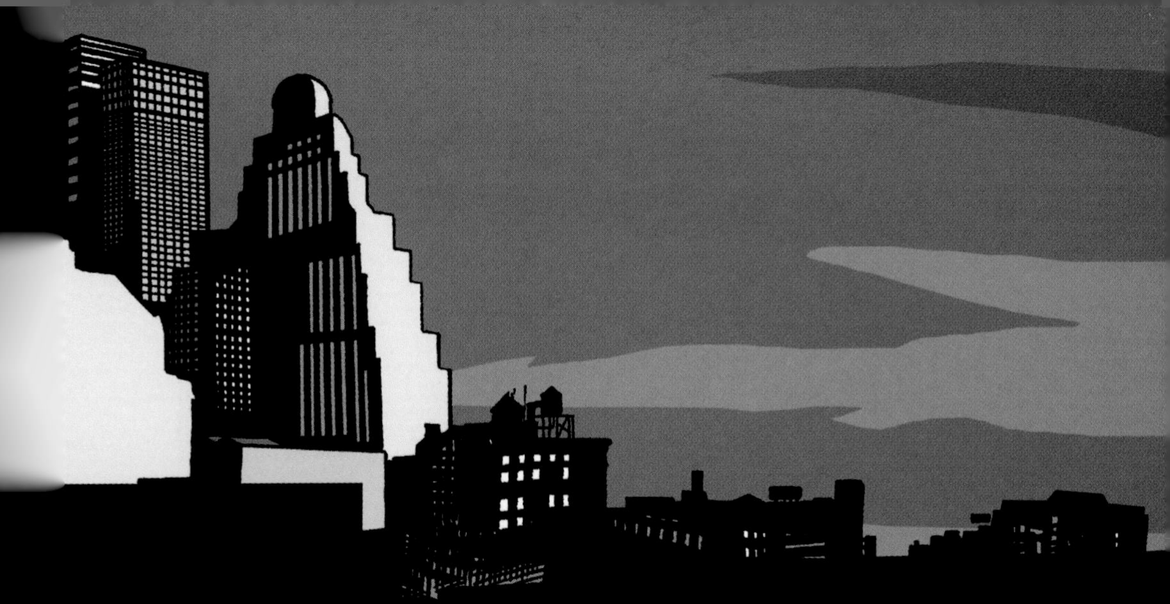

POWERS

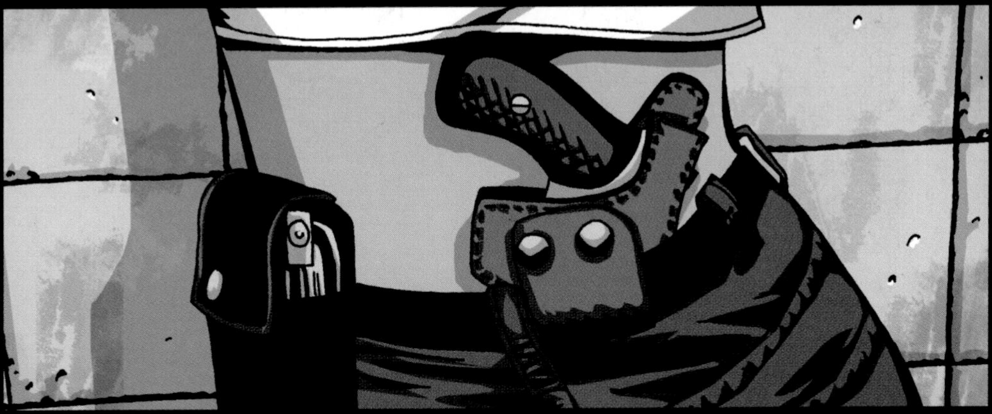

COVER GALLERY

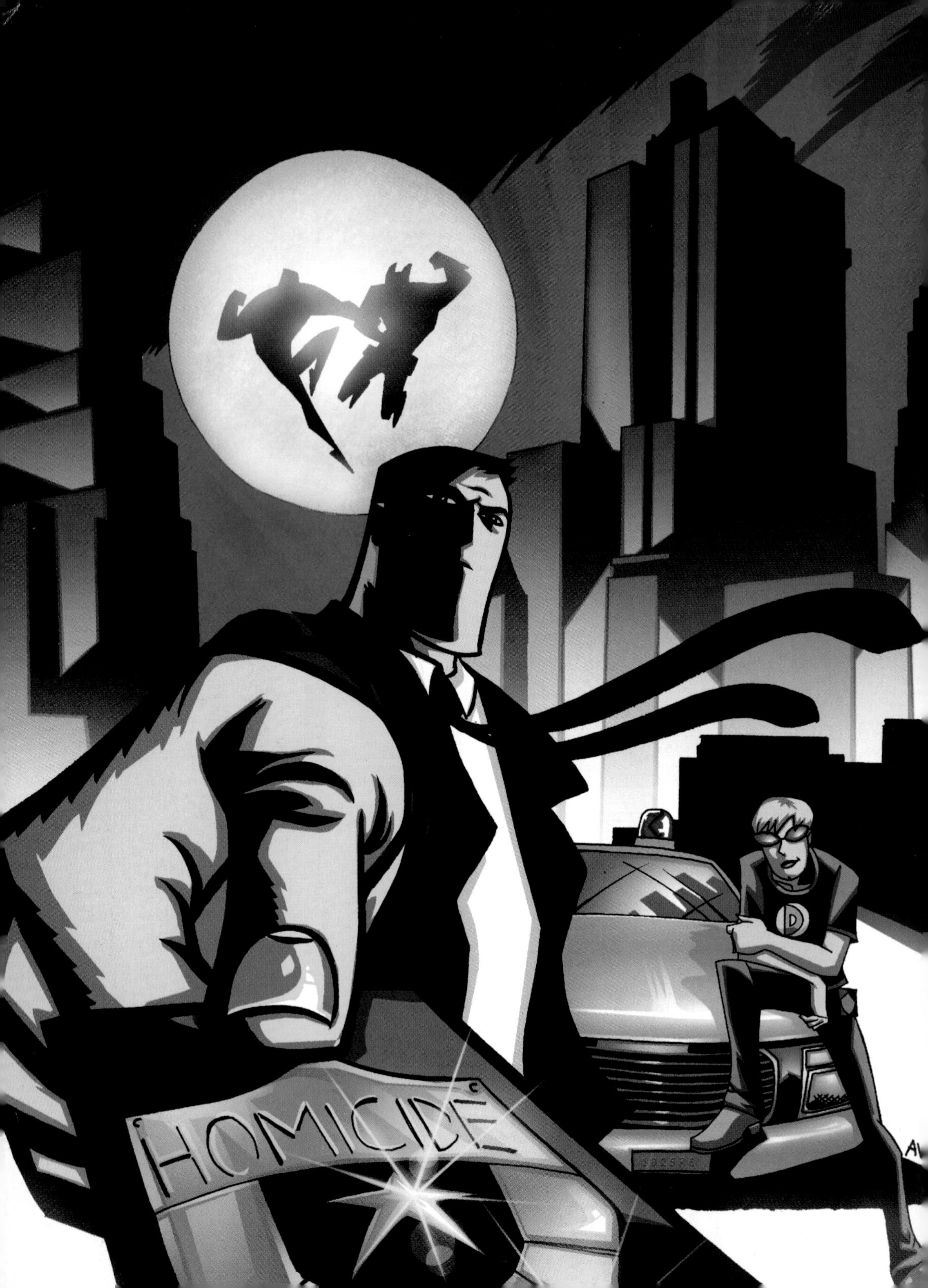
HOMICIDE

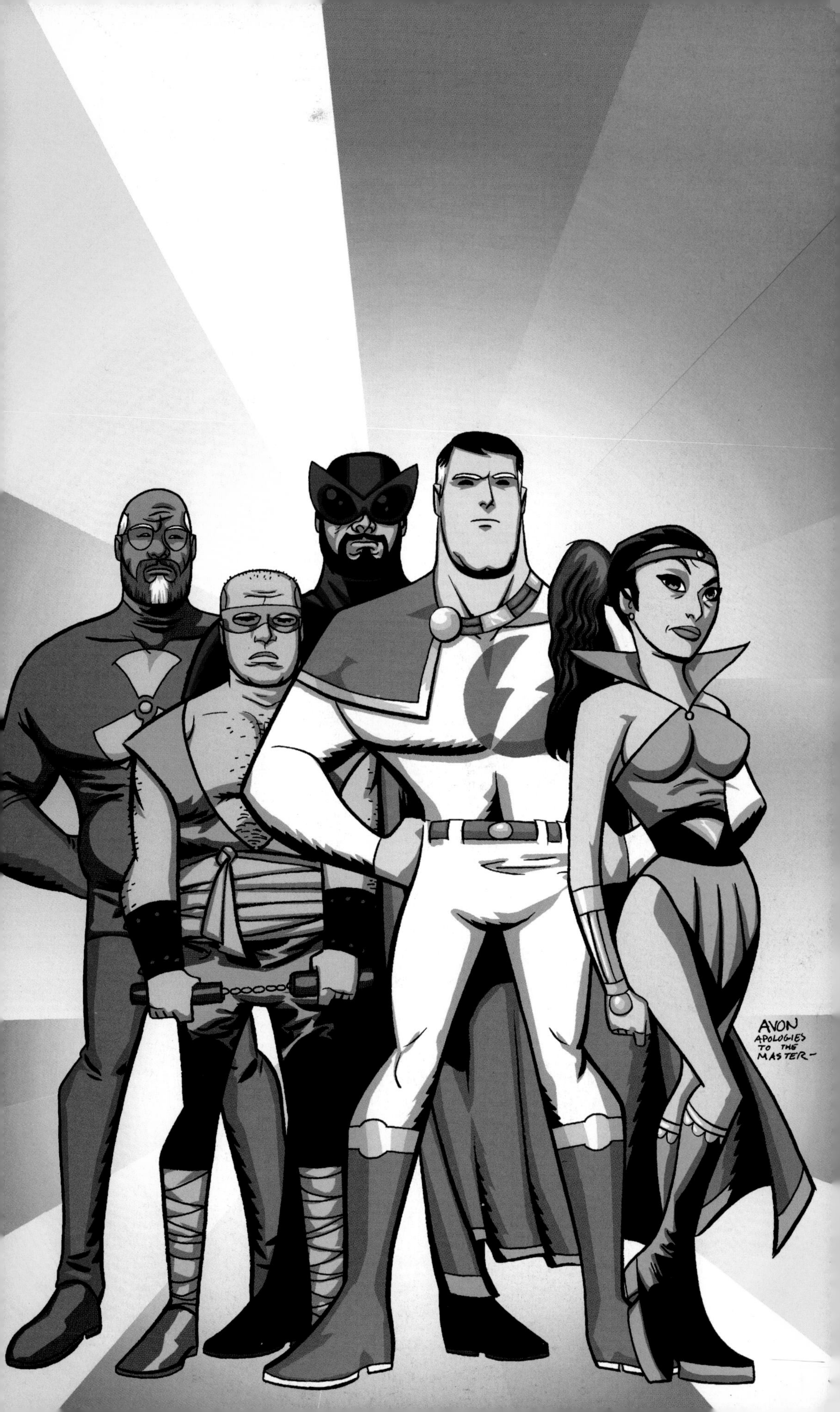
AVON
APOLOGIES TO THE MASTER-

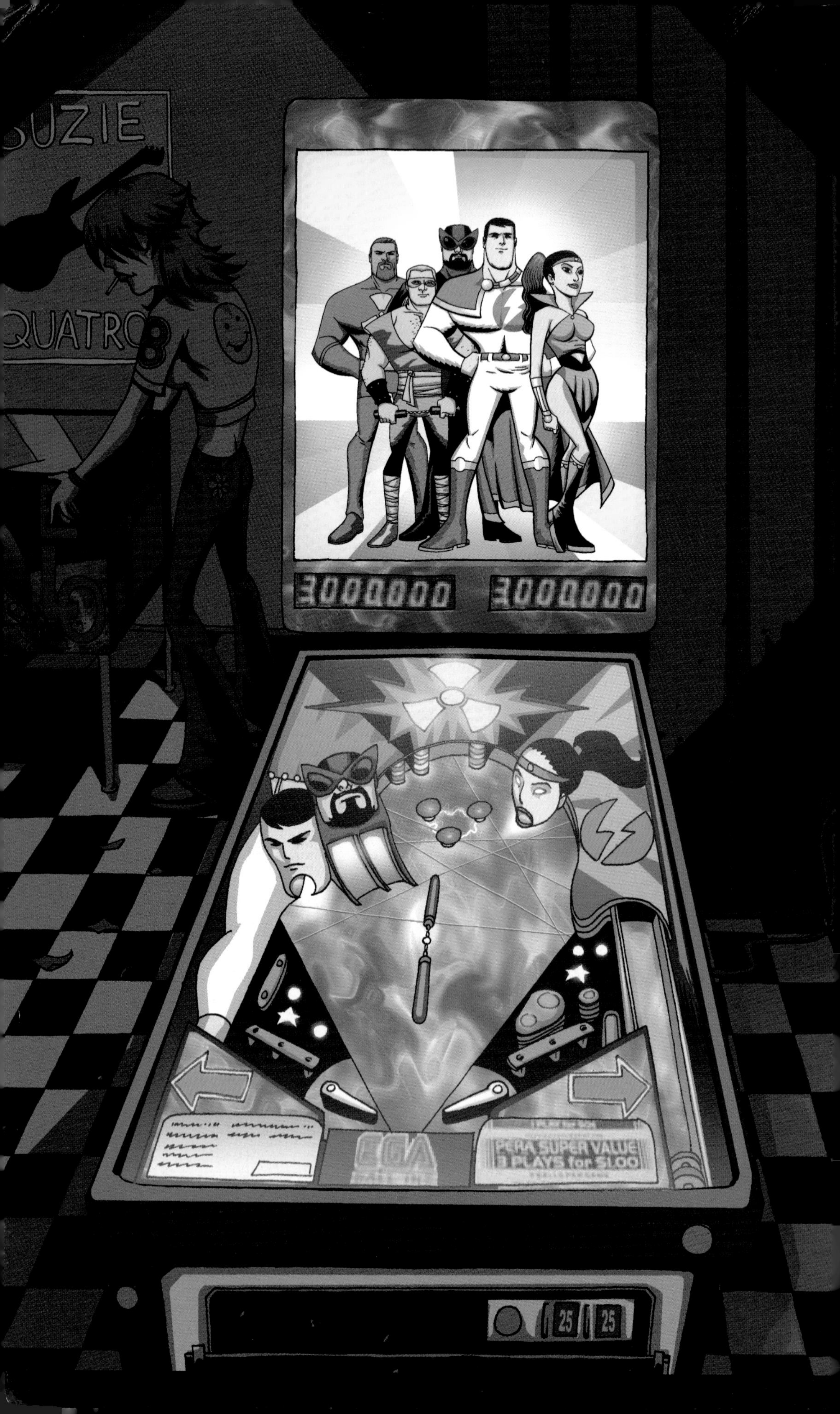
SUZIE
QUATRO
3000000
3000000
PEPA SUPER VALUE
3 PLAYS for $1.00
25
25

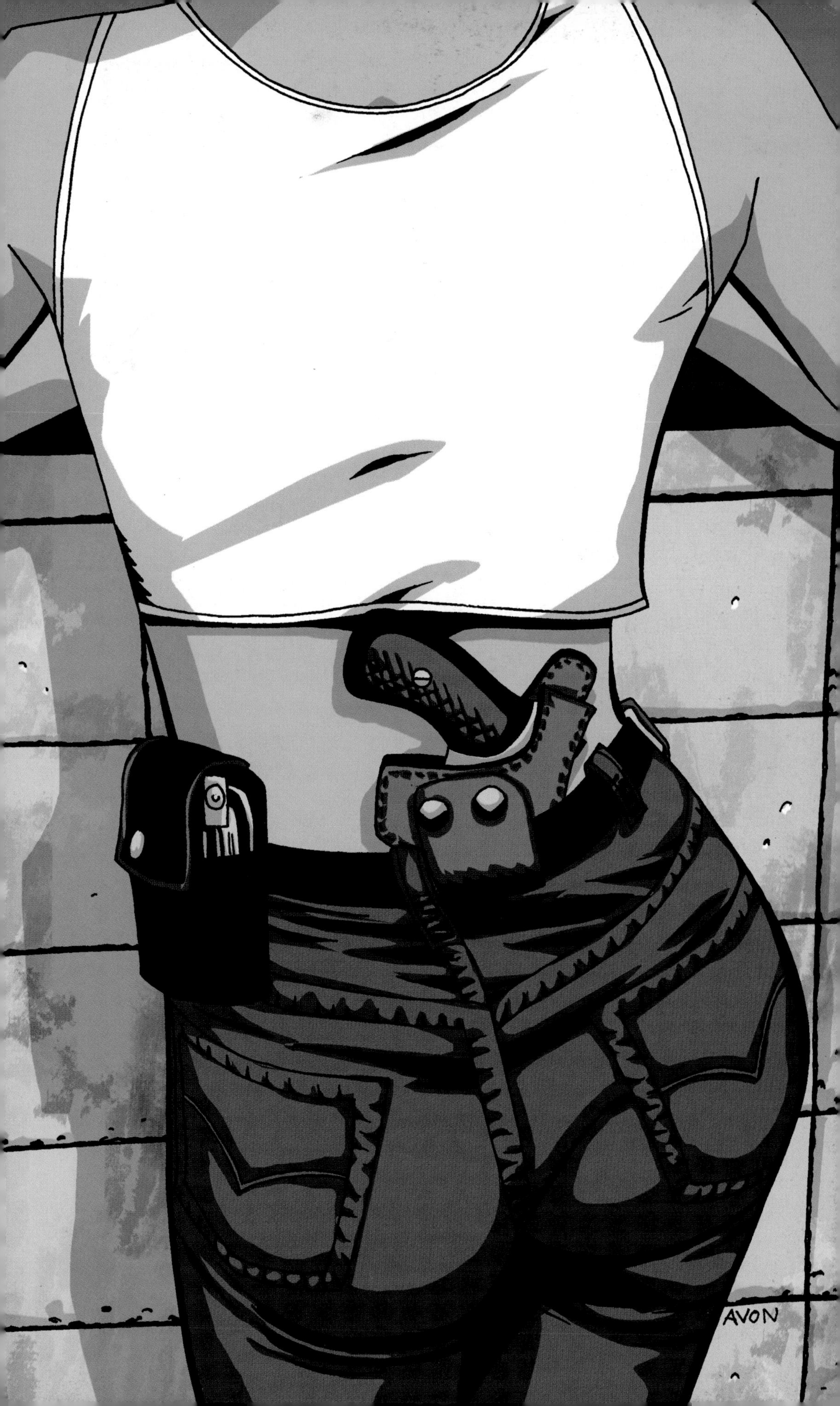
AVON

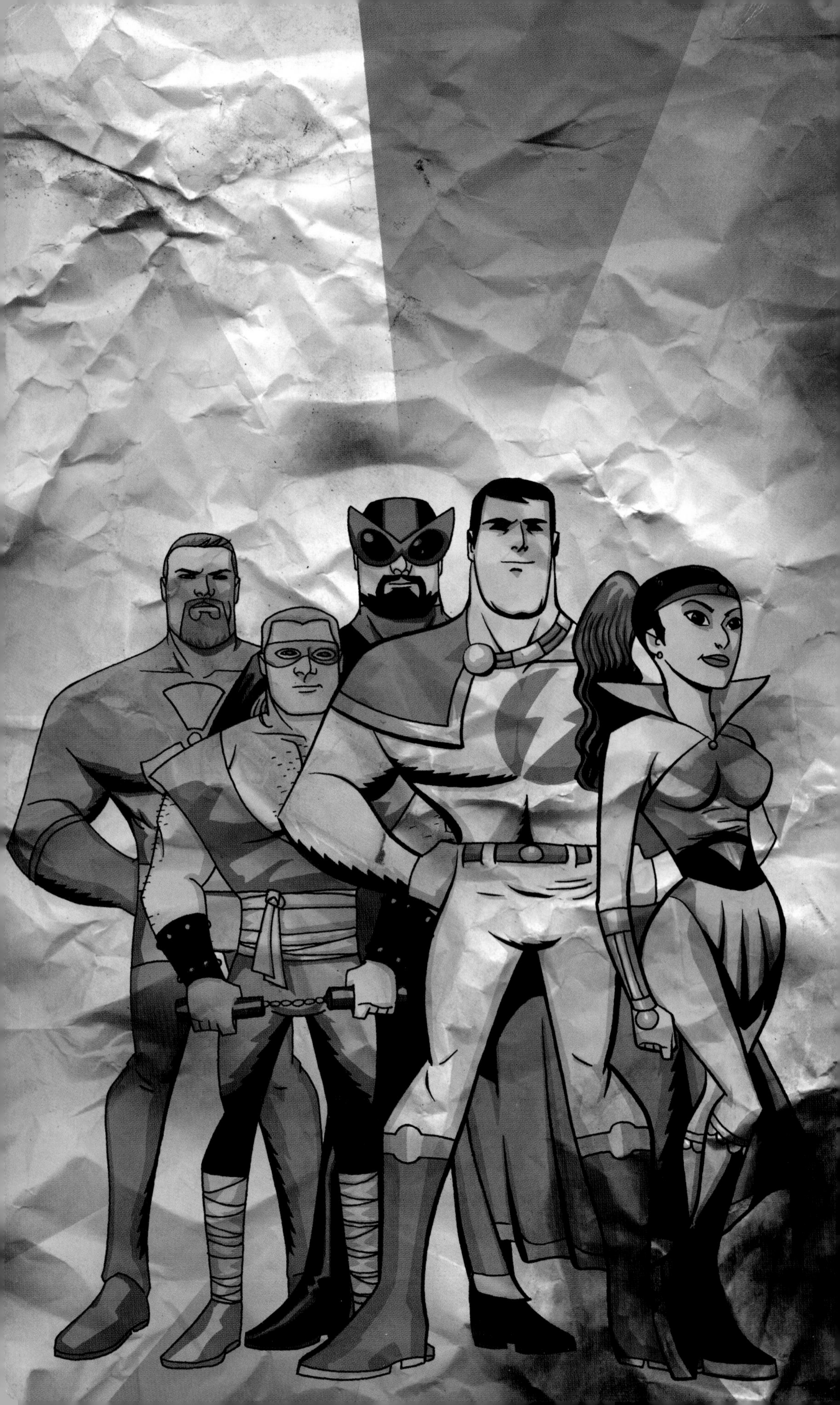